MARSHALL'S MISSION TO CHINA

MARSHALL'S MISSION TO CHINA

December 1945-January 1947:
The Report and Appended Documents

Volume I

The Report

Introduction by
Lyman P. Van Slyke
Professor of History
Stanford University

University Publications of America, Inc.
1976

Table of Contents

Introduction xiii

Chapter   Page

I   The Basis of My Mission to China 1

II   Arrival in China; Preliminary Discussions....... 6

III   Political Consultation Conference.................. 8

IV   The Committee of Three............................ 10

V   Cessation of Hostilities Order....................... 11

VI   Discussions Leading to the Agreement
         Upon the Cessation of Hostilities Order.......... 13

         (a) Manchuria 14
         (b) Jehol 16
         (c) Removal of Obstructions to Lines
             of Communications 17
         (d) Disarmament and Repatriation
             of Japanese Troops 18

VII   The Executive Headquarters 19

VIII   Resolutions Adopted by the Political
         Consultation Conference 23

IX   Issues Involved in the Political Consul-
         tation Conference Resolutions..................... 30

X   Restoration of Communications 32

XI   Military Sub-Committee............................ 36

XII   Basis for Military Reorganization and
for the Integration of the Communist
Forces into the National Army 37

XIII   Discussions Leading to Agreement on
Basis for Military Reorganization and
for the Integration of the Communist
Forces into the National Army 40

       (a) Title of the Agreement 41
       (b) Gendarmerie and Railway Guards 42
       (c) Reorganization and Integration 44

XIV   Directive to the Executive Headquarters
Implementing the Basis for Military Reorganization and for the Integration of
the Communist Forces into the
National Army 46

XV   Application of the Cessation of Hostilities
Order to Manchuria; Entry of Executive
Headquarters Field Teams into Manchuria...... 49

XVI   Background of the Failure to Implement
the Resolutions of the Political
Consultation Conference 63

XVII   Organization and Functions of the
Executive Headquarters 69

XVIII   Repatriation of Japanese Military and
Civilian Personnel from China 80

XIX   Entry of the Executive Headquarters
Field Teams into Manchuria; The
Situation in Manchuria.............................. 95

XX   The Deterioration in the Situation at the
Time of My Return to China; Events
Leading to Agreement for a Temporary
Truce in Manchuria 101

XXI   Announcement of Temporary Truce Period
in Manchuria; Establishment of Advance

Section of the Executive Headquarters
at Changchun... 132

XXII   Negotiations During the 15 Day Truce
        Period in Manchuria 136

        (a) Restoration of Communications 139
        (b) Termination of Hostilities in Manchuria... 143
        (c) Authority for Decision by U.S.
            Representatives 145
        (d) Revision of the Basic Plan for Military
            Reorganization of February 25 149

XXIII   Extension of the Truce Period in
        Manchuria until June 30;
        Negotiations during this Period 158

XXIV   Convening of the Five Man Conference
        for Discussion of the Local Government
        Problem; Spread of Hostilities and
        Deterioration of the Situation...................... 177

XXV   Negotiations during August: Unsuccessful
        Efforts to Convene the Five Man Committee
        under Dr. Stuart's Chairmanship; Exchange
        of Messages between President Truman and
        the Generalissimo; Continued Deterioration
        of the Military and Economic Situation 192

XXVI   Continued Unsuccessful Efforts to Convene
        the Five Man Committee under the Chair-
        manship of Dr. Stuart; Departure of
        General Chou En-lai for Shanghai 229

XXVII   The Possibility of a National Break as a
        Result of the Government Offensive against
        Kalgan and the Question of the Termination
        of the U.S. Mediation Effort; Communist
        Rejection of the Kalgan Truce Proposal 260

XXVIII Government Occupation of Kalgan and
        Issuance of a Mandate for the Convocation
        of the National Assembly on November 12;
        Third Party Group Participation in the

Mediation Effort; and Return of General
Chou En-lai to Nanking 310

XXIX   Continued Third Party Group Mediation;
Issuance of a Cease-fire Order by the
Generalissimo 325

XXX   Informal Meeting of the Committee of
Three; Convening of the National Assembly
on November 15; and the Return of General
Chou En-lai to Yenan 359

XXXI   Role of the United States Marines in China
and Factors Involved in Their Withdrawal 380

XXXII   Programs of Military Assistance to China
and Stoppages of Such Assistance................. 394

XXXIII   The National Assembly and the New
Constitution; President Truman's Statement of American Policy toward China........... 403

XXXIV   Termination of My Mission and of American
Participation in the Executive
Headquarters... 424

Attitude of the Chinese Communist Party
Toward the United States 440

Index 459

LIST OF ILLUSTRATIONS

(Plates between pages 216 and 217)

Unless otherwise noted, the captions originally accompanying the photographs have been retained. Romanization and spelling have been standardized [ed.].

1. Yenan, March 5, 1946: A final discussion between General George C. Marshall and Chairman Mao Tse-tung prior to Marshall's departure [for the U.S. for consultation (March 11-April 18) ed.]. (*Courtesy of U.S. National Archives*)

2. Yenan, March 5, 1946: General George C. Marshall and Madame Mao Tse-tung (Chang-Ching). (*Courtesy of U.S. National Archives*)

3. General Chou En-lai, General Marshall, General Chu Teh, General Chang Chih-chung (Nationalist Army), and Chairman Mao Tse-tung review Communist troops at Yenan airfield. (*Courtesy of U.S. National Archives*)

4. Yenan, March 4, 1946: Chairman Mao Tse-tung asking General Marshall to have tea. (Taken in the reception room of the Communist Military Headquarters). (*Courtesy of U.S. National Archives*)

5. Tangshan, North China, November 1945: U.S. Marine sergeant examines the papers of three Japanese soldiers leaving Tangshan to be repatriated. (*Courtesy of U.S. Marine Corps Photo Archives*)

6. Chinwangtao, October 24, 1946: Two Chinese Nationalist Army sentries prepare to relieve the last two Marines
   on Bridge 105 of the Peiping-Mukden Railway (note fortifications in background). (*Courtesy of U.S. Marine
   Corps Photo Archives*)

7. China, March 1947: Nationalist Chinese train with armored car, which is the protection afforded every train
   that must pass through territory possibly infiltrated by
   Communists. (*Courtesy of U.S. Marine Corps Photo
   Archives*)

8. Tientsin, 1946: Fortification on Tientsin-Peiping Highway. The Chinese Nationalist Army maintains a string
   of similar fortifications all along the highway. (*Courtesy
   of U.S. Marine Corps Photo Archives*)

9. Mukden, Manchuria, April 8, 1946: The Russian Army
   of Occupation erected this monument to the Red Army
   dead, during a six-day war with Japan, in front of the
   Mukden railroad station. (*Courtesy of U.S. Marine Corps
   Photo Archives*)

10. Mukden, Manchuria, April 6, 1946: Chinese accused
    Russian occupation forces of the damage to this formerly
    large textile mill in Mukden industrial region. (*Courtesy
    of U.S. Marine Corps Photo Archives*)

11. Chihfeng, Manchuria, April 8, 1946: Marine Colonel
    Pressley with Nationalist Lieutenant Colonel Kwang (left)
    and Communist Major Gen. Twang Shu Chuan (right)
    toast to the success of the cease-fire program. (*Courtesy
    of U.S. Marine Corps Photo Archives*)

12. Sian, 1946: Chinese Communist Party Propaganda Pos-
    ter. (Translation) After 8 bitter years in the War of Resis-
    tance, the Chinese people finally defeated the fascist ban-
    dits of Japan. Now, to get the help of American reaction-
    aries in fighting a civil war, Chiang Kai-shek turns around
    and asks American imperialists to come to China. He lets
    the American army be stationed indefinitely in China; he
    lets American warships sail freely on China's territorial
    waters and rivers. Even though China at last defeated
    Japan, it is about to be turned into an American colony!

We demand the independence of the nation and her people!

We oppose America's helping Chiang Kai-shek butcher our countrymen!

Brethren in the Central Government armies, come to your senses! Don't go along with Chiang Kai-shek's sell-out of the nation and the interests of her people [Ed. tr.] (*Courtesy of U.S. National Archives*)

13. Nan Tuan, Shansi Province, May 1946: Sino-American cease-fire team returning from a ride into Communist held territory. (*Courtesy of U.S. Marine Corps Photo Archives*)

14. China, 1946: U.S. Marine-manned Peace Team in China prepares for trip into interior. (*Courtesy of U.S. Marine Corps Photo Archives*)

15. Hsuchow, 1946: General Chang and General Marshall inspect troops. (*Courtesy of U.S. National Archives*)

16. Yenan, March 1946: The Big Three of the Chinese Communist Party; left to right: General Chou En-lai, Chairman Mao Tse-tung, and General Chu Teh. (*Courtesy of U.S. National Archives*)

INTRODUCTION*

I. THE REPORT AND APPENDICES; DOCUMENTATION OF THE MARSHALL MISSION

With the present publication, the record of the Marshall Mission to China may be considered complete, thereby greatly facilitating our understanding of this crucial episode in U.S.-China relations. If one compares the materials now available with those of just a few years ago, the great value of archival declassification and publication becomes immediately apparent. For example, in his admirable study, *America's Failure in China, 1941-1950* (published in 1963), Tang Tsou had to piece together his account of the Marshall Mission from scattered sources, most of them indirect and incomplete. The only documentary collection then available was *The China White Paper*, and its coverage of the Mission comprises but 44 documents in 90 pages of text, plus 123 pages of narrative. Although Tang Tsou's treatment is factually accurate in its main outlines, it lacks the richness and solidity which newly available materials can provide. In addition, these materials provide much fresh information on the early development of the Cold War in Asia; on policy formation in Washington; on the political, military, and economic situation in China during this period; and on the attitudes of both the Chinese Nationalists and the Chinese Communists toward the United States.

The only previously published reference to the Report is found in *Foreign Relations of the United States*, 1946, Vol. X (p. 705), which appeared in 1972. As this reference indicates, on October 1, 1946, Marshall wrote to the Secretary of State that a detailed report was being prepared for him, and that it "seemed advisable to transmit the report section by section as completed 'as they contain many details which could not be incorporated in my radios which may be of interest to the Department.'" By the end of the year, six such installments

*In preparing this Introduction, the author wishes to acknowledge the research assistance of Ms. Emily Honig.

totalling 31 chapters had been submitted. The last three chapters and the Supplement on the attitude of the Chinese Communist Party toward the United States were completed after Marshall's return to Washington, probably in February 1947: the latest reference to past events occurs near the end of January, while plans scheduled for March had not yet been carried out.

In form, the Report is a straightforward, mainly chronological narrative of the Mission, from its inception in December 1945 through its recall in January 1947. From time to time, the Report departs from a strict chronological sequence in order to present a connected account of some particular subject, as for example in the section on repatriation of Japanese personnel from China (Chapter XVIII) and the account of the role of the U.S. Marines in China (Chapter XXXI).

The Report is written primarily in the first person, from the standpoint of General Marshall himself. Many chapters end with general summaries of the situation then obtaining in China, particularly as it affected Marshall's efforts to mediate between the Nationalists and the Communists. Although the Report reflects Marshall's own position, it is written in a highly objective and detached style. Only occasionally, in the text of the Report and in a few of the appended documents, do Marshall's personality and feelings come through. The prevailing tone is one of patience, ingenuity, and dogged optimism.

Appended to the Report is the Supplement, referred to above, and a total of 115 documents. The general practice of the Report is to append documents mentioned specifically in the text, where a paraphrase or summary also often appears. In light of the way in which the Report was assembled, these appendices were obviously not intended to provide a full documentary record of the Marshall Mission. This documentation can be said, without hyperbole, to be enormous. With the publication of FRUS 1945 and FRUS 1946 (in 1969 and 1972, respectively), something on the order of 2,300 pages deal with the Marshall Mission itself, and about six hundred more are devoted to issues peripheral but relevant to the Mission, such as lend-lease, disposition of U.S. Marines, field reports, etc.

Of the 115 appended documents, all but twenty-four have

been previously published, either in the *China White Paper,*
FRUS 1945, VII, or in *FRUS* 1946, IX-X. In order to assist
the reader in using these volumes, a checklist has been prepared, indicating which documents have been previously published, and where they can be found.

II. PERSPECTIVES ON THE MARSHALL MISSION

A. Background

When General Patrick J. Hurley resigned, in frustration
and pique, as Ambassador to China on November 27, 1945,
the situation in China was extremely grave. Despite sporadic
negotiations between the Chinese Nationalists (KMT) and the
Chinese Communist Party (CCP)—which included face-to-
face meetings between Chiang Kai-shek and Mao Tse-tung—
no real agreements had been reached, and China seemed headed once again over the brink of civil war.

This prospect was no surprise to anyone familiar with
events in China during the previous twenty years. For most
of this period, the KMT and the CCP had been engaged in
bloody conflict, with no quarter asked or given. On occasion—
during the 1927 terror and on the eve of the Long March in
1934—the CCP was nearly destroyed, only to survive and
grow again. It was the brute fact of Japanese aggression
which forced the two erstwhile enemies to compose their differences, realizing that if they did not do so there would be
no China for either of them to control.

But this united front, established in 1937, soon showed
signs of breaking down. After a honeymoon of about two
years, friction began anew. Clashes became increasingly frequent, climaxed by the pitched battle known as the "New
Fourth Army Incident" in January 1941. Because of the war
against Japan, however, neither side was willing to bear the
onus of initiating and prosecuting a full-scale civil war, and
both parties subsequently backed off a little. By the early
1940's, nearly 400,000 of the best remaining Nationalist forces were blockading those Communist-held areas not surrounded by the Japanese. KMT-CCP relations, as one observer put it, were characterized by chilly politeness at the

top, mistrust and hostility at middle echelons, and a no-holds-barred contest on the local level.

Although Japanese pressure held civil war in abeyance, the struggle powerfully affected the relative strengths of the two parties. The Nationalists, driven out of their strongholds in the lower Yangtze valley into the secure but backward regions of west China centered on Chungking, were seriously weakened. After an initial period of selfless determination, war weariness began to set in among the Nationalists, and one began to hear, with increasing frequency, the discouraging litany of corruption, misgovernment, repression, inflation, and low morale.

The Communist response to the Japanese challenge led in the opposite direction, to much greater strength than they had had before the war. The Japanese controlled the cities and communication lines in North China, where the Communists had their main strength, but the CCP scarcely missed what it had never possessed. Meanwhile, relying on a combination of nationalist appeals, solid social reform, and disciplined enthusiasm, the CCP expanded behind Japanese lines into the countryside which the invader could not possibly garrison. The Japanese brought terrible pressure against these base areas from 1940 to 1943, but they were unable to destroy them. From this time onward, Japan had to spend most of its resources in a vain effort to stem the inexorable advance of the United States; the last two years of the war saw the resurgence once again of CCP power.

The entry of the U.S. into the war against Japan added a new dimension to the situation in China. In terms of aid and support, China was low man on the World War II totem pole: Europe took top priority, China was all but isolated from avenues of outside supply, and the growing success of the island-hopping strategy made China an even less significant theatre of operations. Nevertheless, it was important to the U.S. to keep China in the struggle to tie up as much Japanese manpower and materiel as possible. Furthermore, as the U.S. looked forward to the postwar era, it envisioned a strong and unified China replacing Japan as the major power in Asia.

In the United States, there was a nagging sense of guilt that we had done so little, were doing so little even now, to assist a nation that had fought alone, heroically and at awful cost, for over four years before Pearl Harbor. Chiang Kai-shek and his Wellesley-educated wife were successful in projecting an image of personal dedication and national popularity—the very embodiment, in the eyes of the American public, of China and Chinese resistance. The Cairo Conference (1943) saw the international recognition of Chiang as one of the Big Four—at the insistence of Franklin D. Roosevelt over the misgivings of Winston Churchill. For us, Chiang had become synonomous with China—as he already was to himself.

Chiang was able to play from weakness with shrewd success. He engaged in subtle threats of reluctant surrender to Japan in order to obtain more material and financial aid on better terms. He could plead his very weakness as reason for being unable to prosecute the war with greater vigor, while at the same time implying criticism of the U.S. for its niggardliness. In fact, Chiang realized quite early that Japan would eventually be defeated by the United States, and he saw little reason to expend his power—power which would be needed after the war—in unnecessary and unappreciated campaigns. Moreover, in an army where personal loyalty took precedence over competence, combat effectiveness was frequently lacking.

This attitude infuriated General Joseph W. (Vinegar Joe) Stilwell, U.S. commander in the China-Burma-India theatre (CBI). An acerbic infantry general with long and intimate service in China, Stilwell was determined to do the job he had been assigned: to prosecute the war against Japan, and to improve the efficiency of the Chinese army. Checked and undermined by Chinese leaders with concerns other than his, and who realized perhaps more clearly than he the relative unimportance of operations in China, Stilwell came into repeated and bitter collision with Chiang and his colleagues. In September 1944, matters came to a head, and Washington was faced with the choice of either backing Stilwell, which implied a major shift in our relations with Chiang, or of backing Chiang, which meant Stilwell's removal. Stilwell was recalled in October, replaced by the more tactful General Albert C. Wedemeyer. At the same time, General Patrick J. Hurley was sent to China as Roosevelt's personal representative and, later, ambassador.

Hurley, a man with perhaps as much confidence as FDR

in the force of his own personality, was charged with keeping China in the war, with trying to bring the Nationalists and the Communists together, and with seeking a basis for the political and military unification of China under the leadership of Chiang Kai-shek. Hurley knew almost nothing of China, but he was convinced that the Communists would come to terms once they were sure the Soviet Union would not support them, and if both parties would subscribe to the principles of "government of the people, by the people, and for the people," which he insisted on writing into most of his draft proposals. In Hurley's imperfect vision, the Communists resembled an opposition party in America—like "Oklahoma Republicans," he once said, although he realized that they had guns. It was only later that Hurley swung around, in condemnatory terms, to see CCP leaders as dedicated Stalinists and as intractable revolutionaries.

The wonder is not that Hurley failed in his mission, but that initially promising negotiations were begun at all. It is easy to criticize Hurley for his ignorance and his egotism, but his failure was not simply a personal one. It was rooted deep in Chinese realities and in the contradictory nature of U.S. policy. This was where matters stood when the explosions over Hiroshima and Nagasaki precipitated Russia's hasty occupation of Manchuria, and then led to the unexpectedly early surrender of Japan.

Japan's surrender caught all parties somewhat unprepared. In August and September 1945, the Nationalists reoccupied much of Central China and the lower Yangtze area, and insisted upon their right to accept Japanese surrender everywhere. Meanwhile, the CCP expanded considerably in North China. In late September and October, the U.S. landed Marines at several northern ports to assist in the surrender arrangements, and the process of transporting Nationalist forces began. Clashes were already taking place between KMT and CCP units, not only in North China, but in Central China as well. It was during this chaotic period that the conversations between Chiang and Mao took place, with the encouragement of General Hurley. But Hurley, already feeling himself compromised, returned to Washington in September, where he sulked until issuing his bitter statement of resignation on November 27, blaming his failure on disloyal subordinates—unfair charges which later returned to haunt these men.

Thus, in these crucial months just following the end of World War II, events were left largely to drift in China. The Soviet Union was in full occupation of Manchuria, and civil war, which only Japanese aggression had held in check, now threatened to break into the open. At this critical juncture, President Truman asked General George C. Marshall to go to China as his special representative with the personal rank of ambassador.

In sending so eminent a figure to China, President Truman made a very large commitment of American prestige to the Mission, and indicated the importance which the U.S. attached to its purposes. General Marshall was not an old China hand, but he knew far more about that country than his predecessor. He had served there for three years (1923-26) with the 15th Infantry, based at Tientsin. During these years, he came to know Joseph W. Stilwell, who was assigned to the same unit. They became friends, a friendship which lasted until Stilwell's death in 1946; during Vinegar Joe's difficult days in CBI, Marshall was his superior and sometime confidant. Finally, Marshall had a sense of global politics deriving from his unparalleled wartime experience.

B. Marshall, the Mission, and U.S. Policy

General Marshall's position was difficult and contradictory. It was the same contradiction which had done so much to compromise Hurley's mission, despite the vast differences in temperament and ability which separated the two men. The contradiction lay in the fact that Marshall was expected to mediate between the Nationalists and the Communists as a neutral, while at the same time the United States recognized one side, the Nationalist regime, as the sole legal government in China. The consequences of this contradiction were both symbolic and substantive.

It encouraged the Nationalists in their belief—which previous events had done little to weaken—that the U.S. would not, or could not, abandon them, no matter how much it might grumble, criticize, or impede. By the same token, the suspicion of the Communists that the U.S. was not truly neutral was thereby increased. On a more practical level, there were the many wartime and immediate post-war agreements to provide aid and support to China—and this meant the Nationalists exclusively. These involved such matters as training and equipment for the Chinese army, lend-lease supplies, surplus materiel sales, ship and air lift for Chinese forces to Manchuria and North China. Marshall was determined that the U.S. not intervene in China's civil strife, but he insisted on fulfilling these agreements, even though they might have some irreducible "incidental effects" upon the two contenders.

But General Marshall was not simply the victim of this contradiction; in part, he was its author. The Report is quite summary in its treatment of the origin of the Mission, presenting only public statements of China policy and Truman's formal letter of instruction. Documents now available in the *Foreign Relations of the United States* (*FRUS*) series present a fuller picture. In a memorandum to Admiral William D. Leahy, Chief of Staff of the U.S. armed forces, Marshall wrote on November 30, 1945, "I assume that the Communist group will block all progress in negotiations as far as they can, as the delay is to their advantage. . . . Also the longer the delay the less probability of the Generalissimo's being able to establish a decent semblance of control over Manchuria, with the consequent certainty that the Russians will definitely build up such a control." (*FRUS* 1945, VII, p. 748) At other points, also, Marshall and his colleagues indicated that the creation of a strong and peaceful China, while desirable in itself on humanitarian grounds, was strategically important to them as being the best way to deny or to check Russian influence in the Far East.

Related to this consideration was the question of U.S. policy toward the Nationalist Government of Chiang Kai-shek. On December 11, 1945, shortly before his departure, Marshall met with Secretary of State James F. Byrnes and President Truman. After agreeing that transportation of Nationalist troops to Manchuria should be public policy, it was further agreed that preparations should be made to ship and air lift Nationalist forces to North China, but that these preparations should be kept secret so as to enable Marshall to use uncertainty as a lever against both the Nationalists and the Communists. If the Communists proved intransigent and obstructive, the lift was to go ahead.

Finally, General Marshall stated, that if the

Generalissimo, in his (General Marshall's) opinion, failed to make reasonable concessions, and this resulted in the breakdown of the efforts to secure a political unification, and the U.S. abandoned continued support of the Generalissimo, there would follow the tragic consequences of a divided China and of a probable Russian reassumption of power in Manchuria, the combined effect of this resulting in the defeat or loss of the major purpose of our war in the Pacific. Under these circumstances, General Marshall inquired whether or not it was intended for him, in that unfortunate eventuality, to go ahead and assist the Generalissimo in the movement of troops into North China. This would mean that this Government would have to swallow its pride and much of its policy in doing so.

The President and Mr. Byrnes concurred in this view of the matter. . .

(*FRUS* 1945, VII, p. 768)

Three days later, General Marshall spelled out in broader terms the implications of this decision:

I stated that my understanding of one phase of my directive was not in writing but I thought I had a clear understanding of his [Truman's] desires in the matter, which was that in the event that I was unable to secure the necessary action by the Generalissimo, which I thought reasonable and desirable, it would still be necessary for the U.S. government, through me, to continue to back the National Government of the Republic of China—through the Generalissimo within the terms of the announced policy of the U.S. Government.

(*FRUS* 1945, VII, p.770)

Both President Truman and Under Secretary of State Dean Acheson explicitly confirmed this understanding. One aspect of Marshall's mission was therefore inseparable from the Cold War considerations which were already gripping policy makers in Washington.

It is only at first glance curious that none of these understandings were referred to in the Report (secrecy in preparing for troop transport is ordered in the Report, but the reasons for it are not spelled out). Most of the Report was prepared in China, prior to the end of the mission, by the Embassy staff, as amplification of radio dispatches to the Department of State. To have included these enormously sensitive understandings in the Report was clearly inconceivable.

While Marshall had a vision of the strategic need to limit Russian influence in the Far East, these same understandings reflect more than a trace of suspicion concerning Chiang Kaishek's willingness to cooperate in a peaceful resolution of China's internal difficulties. During the course of his year in China, this suspicion grew until it became an inescapable conviction—though he usually sought to blame "reactionaries" around Chiang, rather than the Generalissimo himself.

In the Report, one rarely sees this larger strategic vision, although occasionally it can be felt lurking between the lines. Instead, we are plunged into the tactical arena of day-to-day negotiations, of proposals and counter-proposals, new demands from both sides, and charges of bad faith enough for all. In this arena, General Marshall was impressively even-handed and fair. Furthermore, he maintained a staggering schedule of briefings, meetings, and conferences—nearly all of which involved matters of great complexity and most of which required the strenuous exercise of alertness, judgment, and tactful candor. Whereas the mission of his predecessor had been an unalloyed ego trip, Marshall was self-effacing, although there could be no mistaking his strength and centrality. On this level, there is no sign of manipulation or duplicity, and Marshall might well have defended his impartiality against charges to the contrary by both sides.

Indeed, the Report is, on balance, more critical of the Nationalists than it is of the Communists. This is particularly true of the first months of the Mission, when hopes for peace were brightest. These hopes were contained in three sets of agreements, the first of which was indirectly attributable to Marshall's efforts, the other two directly so. First were the deliberations of the Political Consultative Conference (PCC), involving representatives of all parties and groups, which met from January 10 to 31, 1946. Convening of the PCC had long been discussed, but its actual convocation was clearly the result of Marshall's assignment to China. The PCC adopted a number of ground rules and procedures for the political broadening and reorganization of the government which was to follow. Second was the work of the Committee of Three, which first met on January 7, 1946, leading to the cease-fire order of January 13 and to the creation of the Executive Headquarters in Peiping as the mechanism for implementing cessation of hostilities. Third was the agreement on the basic plan for military reorganization and the integration of Communist forces into the National Army, concluded after long and tortuous discussions on February 25.

All participants and observers recognized, of course, that these were not final solutions but only promissory notes for the future whose value would depend upon the good faith with which they were carried out. Nevertheless, in the fearful mood of the moment, they were understandably hailed as major accomplishments. It was during these various deliberations and particularly in the efforts to take the next steps beyond them that the Nationalists appeared to Marshall the more guilty of bad faith, even (he said on occasion) of "stupidity," while the Communists seemed to exhibit greater flexibility and reasonableness. Marshall was blunt in his criticism of the Communists on occasion, as at the time of their occupation of Changchun in April, and for their anti-American propaganda, but his most frequent and pointed remarks were aimed at the Nationalists. He was particularly galled by their persistent and largely successful efforts to exclude Manchuria from the terms of the cease fire and from inspection by truce teams of the Executive Headquarters. Manchuria, he knew, was the torch which could set all China aflame, and he realized that the Nationalists' confidence in their ability to settle the issue there by force was a dangerous illusion.

It was only after June 1946, when steady deterioration of the situation in North China and particularly in Manchuria had dimmed all but the staunchest hopes for the three agreements (and Marshall's were among the staunchest) that the pendulum of Marshall's criticism swung back in the direction of the Communists. This followed the breakdown of a last-ditch truce in Manchuria (June 7-30), a breather obtained to try to get negotiations going again. But no negotiations took place; misplaced Nationalist confidence was still waxing, and now the Communists, feeling cornered, were increasingly stubborn, evasive, and tough. Demands which neither side could be expected to accept became the currency of the day. Even then, Marshall hardly criticized the Nationalists less, but he blamed the Communists more.

Reading the Report from the events of early July to the recall of the Mission (formally announced on January 6, 1947, but decided upon in December), one has the feeling that Marshall was simply playing out his hand, valiantly but without avail. By late September, Marshall was giving serious thought to terminating the mission, and in October he actually drafted orders for his recall and transmitted them to Washington to be issued when he gave the word. It was only a last minute appeal from the Generalissimo that persuaded Marshall, reluctantly, to stay on. Meanwhile Chou En-lai had absented himself to Shanghai, and Chiang Kai-shek was also frequently away from Nanking.

Where January and February had witnessed substantive negotiations, summer and fall saw only abortive attempts to find some basis—any basis—on which to begin to talk: the Five-man Conference, the Committee of Three, Third Party mediation. All failed. Thus, in January 1947, Marshall left China pronouncing a pox on both houses, blaming "reactionaries" among the Nationalists and "irreconcilables" among the Communists for the failure of his mission and for the civil war in which the issue was now being decided.

Interestingly, the Report sheds new light on one section of Marshall's parting shot. Marshall wrote,

> The salvation of the situation, as I see it, would be the assumption of leadership by the liberals in the Government and in the minority parties, a splendid group of men, but who as yet lack the political power to exercise a controlling influence. Successful action on their part under the leadership of Generalissimo Chiang Kai-shek would, I believe, lead to unity through good government.

(Appended Documents, Doc. S-1)

This passage has often been interpreted as reflecting Marshall's naivete in thinking that this miscellaneous and powerless group had even the remotest chance for leadership. But it is clear that Marshall was simply trying to do what he could to strengthen their hand, a gesture in their direction, without imagining that it would do very much good.

Perhaps it was the tenor of the Report, as we have tried to describe it here, that led to the Supplement, "Attitude of the Chinese Communist Party Toward the United States," prepared after Marshall's return. Speculatively, it was as though the Report itself had not been sufficiently critical of the Communists, and that to right the balance it was now necessary to reiterate and amplify their transgressions, as Marshall saw them. He focussed, in particular, upon anti-American propaganda emanating from the Communists, including repeated personal attacks upon himself—even while noting that privately stated attitudes of Communist leaders such as Chou En-lai were usually sympathetic and supportive of his efforts. Also described at length were incidents involving U.S. Marines and Communist forces, especially the Anping skirmish of July 29, in which three Marines were killed and twelve wounded. The Supplement concludes where the Marshall Mission itself began, with the Cold War: "At the end, however, the Chinese aspects of their [CCP] behavior seemed to have been more or less submerged in the utilization of techniques common to Communist movements elsewhere in the world and their reactions and attitudes to be of a pattern with other such movements, particularly in relation to the United States."

C. Nationalists and Communists

In retrospect, civil war between the Nationalists and the Communists seems to have been almost inevitable. Certainly neither party had any confidence—or perhaps any understanding—of a multi-party, parliamentary democracy resting on the periodic mandate of the electorate. Neither party was prepared to put itself at the mercy of the other, nor to accept conditions inimical to its chances for eventual supremacy. Nor did the two parties view themselves in comparable terms. To the Nationalists, the Communists were rebels against the constituted, legal, recognized government of all China; they had a degree of power, but no rights from which to base legitimate demands. On the other hand, the Communists saw themselves as a fully sovereign regime, governing a large territory and population, legitimated by their war record and by the support of the people in the areas they ruled. Both reposed ultimate confidence in their military power.

Through all the tangled events described in the Report and the documentation of the Marshall Mission, the fundamental impasse was clear enough. The Nationalists insisted on the integration of Communist armed forces and territory *prior* to the reorganization of the political and military instruments of government (which they expected to dominate). The Communists refused to compromise control of their armies and political leadership in their base areas until *after* reorganization satisfactory to them had taken place (and maybe not even then). Marshall sought some formula for the *concurrent*, or closely sequential, solution of these problems, meanwhile trying to prevent or minimize ongoing hostilities and jockeying for position by both sides through cease fire arrangements and the Executive Headquarters.

Yet each party had weaknesses as well as strengths, and each felt the force of certain constraints. It was at least conceivable that some sort of coalition, a shift from the battlefield to the political arena, might compensate for weaknesses without unduly compromising strengths. It was on this shaky and ambiguous ground that hope for peace in China flickered briefly before guttering out.

There were two principal, inter-related constraints. The first involved that uncertain quantity known as Chinese public opinion. However different the workings of public opinion in China from its American counterpart, there could be no doubt that the Chinese people desired peace and stability. This was variously true of educated Chinese in the cities and of peasants in the countryside. Neither side could afford the loss of legitimacy and support attendant upon an openly avowed policy of civil war.

The second constraint had to do with the attitude of the United States, symbolized in China by General Marshall. For the Nationalists, the goal was to press every advantage against the Communists short of action so blatant that it might cause the United States to withdraw its recognition and support. Despite the private understandings described above, President Truman had implied the possibility of such a withdrawal in his public statement when he called for peace in China and stated that "a China disunited and torn by civil strife could not be considered realistically as a proper place for American assistance . . ." (*Report*, Doc. A-1a)

Chiang Kai-shek may have sensed, particularly after the Stilwell affair in 1944, that U.S. policy options in China were few and unappealing; nevertheless, it was important to placate the U.S., and to derive from it as much moral and material aid as possible. This involved the continual testing of General Marshall, pushing him nearly to the limit, then appearing temporarily more conciliatory. These partial concessions, usually vague and conditional, were then used as basis for the next push along the lines the Nationalists wished to follow.

Marshall was, of course, entirely aware of this gambit; it disgusted him and he sought to check it as much as possible within the limited means afforded by overall U.S. policy. His major effort in this area, apart from blunt talk to Nationalist leaders and support of Communist positions when he felt them justified, was to order an embargo on arms shipments to China on July 29, 1946. The effect of such action was largely vitiated, however, in the eyes of both the Nationalists and the Communists by the several other forms of aid which continued during the same period. One example, which angered the Communists, was the conclusion of the Sino-American surplus property sale agreement, on August 30, 1946. Although Marshall stoutly insisted that this was non-military equipment (*i.e.*, that it did not include weapons and munitions), he acknowledged with discomfiture to Chou En-lai his awareness that the Nationalists were selling much of this equipment on the open market and using the money for military purposes. In the Report, Marshall concluded with shrewd pessimism; the Nationalists, he wrote, felt

> . . . that in spite of the statement of American policy toward China announced by President Truman in December 1945 and in spite of the continued American mediation effort, the United States must in the long run support the National Government against the Chinese Communists. The Kuomintang, therefore, felt, I believe, that if it could reduce the Communist forces to a relatively weak position militarily

during this period, when, according to their intelligence reports, the Soviet Union would be in no position to interfere openly by aiding the Chinese Communists, then it could afford to forego for the moment desired American military, financial and economic aid. That would come, they apparently thought, after they had succeeded in strengthening their hold on the country in opposition to the Communists and had introduced constitutional government through adoption of a constitution and participation in the government of all minority groups except the Communists.

(*Report*, p. 379)

For the Communists, as well, the U.S. posed both problems and opportunities. They seem to have envisioned a range of possibilities which led them, as the Nationalists, to present a favorable image to Marshall, without however compromising themselves vis-a-vis Nationalist power. The maximum possibility, in which the CCP probably placed only modest hopes after the debacle of the Hurley mission, was that the U.S. might recognize the Communists as a legitimate political contender in China, thus breaking the monopoly of the Nationalists as sole claimants of U.S. support. This probably lay behind their quick acceptance of the proposal (never carried out) that U.S. training and supply detachments work with both Communist and Nationalist military units in preparation for eventual integration into a national army. They may also have been encouraged in this hope by Marshall's even-handed conduct during the early negotiations.

Even if this goal could not be achieved, it was still important to try to detach Marshall and the U.S. from the Nationalist cause so far as possible, to induce neutrality if it could not gain support, and to discourage the U.S. from full-scale support and intervention on behalf of the Nationalists. In the Report, Marshall refers often and with evident anger to anti-American statements, including personal attacks, coming from Communist sources. Often intemperate and distorted, these statements nevertheless underlined the conflict of interest inherent in Marshall's dual role as honest broker and as representative of a government continuing to support the other side. This propaganda, as already noted, was usually in marked contrast to the attitudes expressed privately to him by Chou En-lai and others that they had confidence in his integrity and appreciated his efforts. The Communists, no less than Marshall himself, were operating on both the strategic and tactical levels, acknowledging Marshall's fairness on the latter, while condemning U.S. policy on the former.

If these were the constraints—public opinion in China and the role of the United States—which acted upon both parties, each party also had a balance sheet of strengths and weaknesses which negotiations—or the time purchased by negotiation—might help to improve.

Superficially, the balance sheet seemed clearly to favor the Nationalists, and this undoubtedly contributed to their unwillingness to make real concessions and binding commitments. The Nationalists enjoyed a monopoly of international recognition; their armed forces, partially U.S. trained and equipped, were roughly three times the size of that of their adversaries and had a nearly total advantage in larger and more sophisticated equipment, including aviation; their economic situation showed some bright spots, including nearly $1 billion in unspent credits in the U.S. On the other hand, the size of the military could not conceal the deplorable conditions, inadequate leadership, and low morale which characterized large segments of it. Runaway inflation had already begun, and corruption was eating away Nationalist support. Reconstruction, after years of war, was a huge task.

Finally, the Nationalists were poorly positioned to follow a policy of immediate reintegration of North China and Manchuria, where their influence had always been weak and in recent years totally absent. But these weaknesses were not in all cases immediately apparent, nor were their implications fully realized—least of all by Chiang Kai-shek.

Marshall saw them, however, and predicted in August what they might mean: "I differed from the Generalissimo and his immediate advisers in that I thought their present procedure [of seeking a military solution] would probably lead to Communist control in China, and that the chaotic condition now developing would not only weaken the Kuomintang but would also afford the Communists an excellent opportunity to undermine the Government." (*Report*, pp. 194-195)

The balance sheet for the Communists was the mirror image of that of the Nationalists. They had no international recognition, and received no outside help, with the important exception of Japanese arms which the USSR permitted them to take over in Manchuria (it should be noted, however, that the Nationalists received much more of this surrendered equipment in Central and North China than did the Communists in Manchuria). The CCP was treated as an illegal party save in its own domains. Their armed forces were smaller and more scantily equipped, but they had superb leadership, morale, and tactics. They occupied relatively poor parts of the country, but their economy was on a soundly spartan basis. Like the Nationalist weaknesses, the full import of Communist strengths was frequently underestimated. But their weaknesses, coupled with the greater political acumen of Communist leaders, resulted in the initially more pragmatic course which Marshall noted in his Report.

Indeed, as early as April 1945, at the Seventh Congress of the CCP, Mao Tse-tung had assessed both strengths and weaknesses in his major report, "On Coalition Government," and indicated the terms under which the Communists might be prepared to participate in such a government. A few months later, shortly after V-J Day, Mao was even more specific in an inner-Party directive. After noting that the USSR, the U.S., and Great Britain all opposed civil war in China, Mao observed that the Nationalists had strengthened themselves by returning to their former base of power in the Nanking-Shanghai area. He then went on:

> Nevertheless, it [the KMT] is riddled with a thousand gaping wounds, torn by innumerable inner contradictions and beset with great difficulties. It is possible that after the negotiations the Kuomintang, under domestic and foreign pressure, may conditionally recognize our Party's status. Our Party too may conditionally recognize the status of the Kuomintang. This would bring about a new stage of cooperation between the two parties (plus the Democratic League, etc.) and of peaceful development. . . . We on our side are prepared to make such concessions as are necessary and as do not damage

the fundamental interests of the people. Without such concessions, we cannot explode the Kuomintang's civil war plot, cannot gain the political initiative, cannot win the sympathy of world public opinion and the middle-of-the-roaders within the country and cannot obtain in exchange legal status for our Party and a state of peace. But there are limits to such concessions; the principle is that they must not damage the fundamental interests of the people.

If the Kuomintang still wants to launch civil war after our Party has taken the above steps, it will put itself in the wrong in the eyes of the whole nation and the whole world, and our Party will be justified in waging a war of self-defense to crush its attacks.

(Selected Works, IV, pp. 48-49)

It was at about the end of June 1946, with the expiration of the temporary truce in Manchuria, that the CCP apparently concluded the time for concessions had passed. They still sought to "win the sympathy" of public opinion at home and abroad, but they had written off the possibility of a negotiated settlement. Mobilization orders were issued during July.

Nationalist armies were on the advance everywhere, taking cities, as Marshall noted, but not engaging and defeating Communist forces. With every victory—in reality, with each further overextension of their lines—the Nationalists grew more cocksure of their ability to crush the Communists by force, and less amenable to compromise. The grounds for peace, like the loess soil of North China, thus eroded, crumbled, and gave way.

D. Epilogue

At the time General Marshall returned from China in January 1947 to become Secretary of State, he was already convinced that the U.S. could do no more to influence the outcome in China. He was prepared to continue to recognize Chiang and the Nationalist government—there was little alternative to that—but he was determined not to involve the U.S. any more deeply than absolutely necessary in that unhappy land. Yet the momentum of events, in this case political pressures at home, forced him to hedge this determination. Under strong pressure from Chiang's many supporters in Congress and in the country at large, the arms embargo was finally lifted in May 1947. Economic aid continued under a variety of agreements and acts.

By early 1948, the Cold War was far more bitter and intense than it had been two years earlier, when Marshall had just arrived in China. Furthermore, lobbying on behalf of the Nationalists was correspondingly stepped up, not only because of the Cold War but because of the serious reverses suffered by the Nationalists during the previous six or eight months. Now the initiative was with the Communists, and the balance sheets were changing rapidly. Moved by these twin pressures, Marshall stated in March 1948 that "the Communists were now in open rebellion against the Government and that this matter (the determination of whether the Communists should be included in the Chinese government) was for the Chinese government to decide, not for the United States Government to dictate." (*WP*, p. 272) In August, Marshall outlined U.S. policy in even stronger terms:

> 1. The United States Government must not directly or indirectly give any implication of support, encouragement or acceptability of coalition government in China with Communist participation.
> 2. The United States Government has no intention of again offering its good offices as mediator in China.
>
> (*WP*, p. 279)

The final allocation of substantial U.S. support to Chiang and the Nationalists prior to their defeat and flight to Taiwan was the controversial China Aid Act, finally passed in April 1948, which led ultimately to the appropriation of $275 million in economic aid and $125 million to be used "at the discretion of the Chinese Government" (*i.e.*, for military purchases). Marshall had grave misgivings about this bill, but he supported it for two reasons. First, it was part of the price of wide, bipartisan support for the Marshall Plan in Europe: the bill was part of the omnibus Foreign Assistance Act, which also included the European Recovery Program. Second, it was a limited measure designed to spike the guns of those calling for all-out intervention to save the Generalissimo and his regime. A portion of Marshall's testimony in executive session is worth quoting at some length:

> There is a tendency to feel that wherever the Communist influence is brought to bear, we should immediately meet it, head on as it were. I think this would be a most unwise procedure for the reason that we would be, in effect, handing over the initiative to the Communists. They could, therefore, spread our influence out so thin that it could be of no particular effectiveness at any one point.
>
> We must be prepared to face the possibility that the present Chinese Government may not be successful in maintaining itself against the Communist forces or other opposition that may arise in China. Yet, from the foregoing, it can only be concluded that the present Government cannot reduce the Chinese Communists to a completely negligible factor in China. To achieve that objective in the immediate future it would be necessary for the United States to underwrite the Chinese Government's military effort, on a wide and probably constantly increasing scale, as well as the Chinese economy. The U.S. would have to be prepared virtually to take over the Chinese Government and administer its economic, military and governmental affairs. . . . It would be impossible to estimate the final cost of a course of action of this magnitude. It certainly would be a continuing operation for a long time to come. It would involve this Government in a continuing commitment from which it would be practically impossible to withdraw, and it would very probably involve grave consequences to this nation by making of China an arena of international conflict. An attempt to underwrite the Chinese economy and the Chinese Government's military effort represents a burden on the U.S. economy and a military responsibility which I cannot recommend as a course of action for this Government.

(*WP*, p. 382)

Lost in the confusion and furor of all these events was a report sent by George F. Kennan, U.S. Ambassador in Moscow, to the Secretary of State over two years before the passage of the China Aid Act, and just a few days after Marshall's arrival in China. Although carefully qualifying his conclusions, Kennan wrote, "We would not be surprised for example to learn that Yenan [*i.e.*, the Chinese Communists] enjoyed what might seem to be a surprising degree of independence of Moscow. Our reasons are:

> 1. Chinese Communists have little reason to be grateful to USSR. They have survived and grown not because of but despite relations with Moscow. Adherence to early Comintern directives resulted in near disaster for CCP. And in Sino-Jap conflict USSR supplied only Chungking which used some of those arms in blockading Yenan. Current Soviet stripping of Manchuria is plucking plums on which Chinese Communists have long had their eye.
> 2. Chinese Communist Party is most mature of all Communist Parties and has developed its own brand of Marxism and indigenous traditions.
> 3. Chinese Communists are no fugitive band of conspirators. For 10 years they have had an established *de facto* regime, their own army and civil administration. Consequently they have developed substantial vested interests.
> 4. Chinese Communists have taken on nationalist coloration. From 1936 to Jap surrender they were confronted with and their propaganda concentrated against an external foe. Rapid expansion of their armed forces and civilian following was largely on basis of nationalism.
>
> (*FRUS* 1946, IX, p. 119; Jan. 10, 1946)

There is no evidence that Marshall ever saw this dispatch, nor any indication of how he might have reacted to it if he had. Meanwhile, it was to be fourteen years before the Sino-Soviet split fully confirmed Kennan's tentative analysis, and more than a decade beyond that before a genuine dialogue between the leaders of the United States and the Chinese Communist Party was once again resumed.

Lyman P. Van Slyke
July 4, 1976

CHECKLIST OF APPENDED DOCUMENTS

Documents previously published are identified by source and page number. "WP" is the abbreviation for *The China White Paper*, i.e., *United States Relation with China, with Special Reference to the Period 1944-1949* (Washington, 1949). "FRUS" designates the series *Foreign Relations of the United States*. Absence of a notation indicates that the document has not been previously published.

A-1a WP, 605-06; FRUS, 1945, VII, 773 (slightly abridged)
A-1b WP, 606-07; FRUS 1945, VII, 760-61
A-1c WP, 607-09; FRUS 1945, VII, 770-73
A-1d FRUS 1945, VII, 754-57 (slight editorial differences)
A-2
A-3
B-1   FRUS 1946, IX, 125-26
B-2   FRUS 1946, IX, 125-26
B-3   WP, 609-10
B-4a FRUS 1946, IX, 43-59
B-4b FRUS 1946, IX, 59-75
B-4c FRUS 1946, IX, 98
B-4d FRUS 1946, IX, 76-98
B-4e FRUS 1946, IX, 98-104
B-4f FRUS 1946, IX, 104-116
B-4g FRUS 1946, IX, 119-125
B-5   WP, 627-28
B-6   FRUS 1946, IX, 127-28
B-7   FRUS 1946, IX, 127-28
B-8   FRUS 1946, IX, 128-29
C-1a WP, 610-11
C-1b WP, 612-17
C-1c WP, 617-19
C-1d
C-1e WP, 619
D-1   FRUS 1946, IX, 398-423
D-2a FRUS 1946, IX, 422-23

D-2b	FRUS 1946, IX, 423-24
D-2c	FRUS 1946, IX, 424-25
E-1	FRUS 1946, IX, 188-89
E-2	FRUS 1946, IX, 188-89
E-3	WP, 622
E-4	FRUS 1946, IX, 295-300
E-5a	FRUS 1946, IX, 220-22
E-5b	FRUS 1946, IX, 224-35
E-5c	FRUS 1946, IX, 235-47
E-5d	FRUS 1946, IX, 248-58
E-5e	FRUS 1946, IX, 278-89
E-5f	FRUS 1946, IX, 265-77
E-5g	FRUS 1946, IX, 291-95
E-5h	FRUS 1946, IX, 302-17 (slightly abridged)
E-6	WP, 577-81
E-7	
F-1	WP, 639; FRUS 1946, IX, 375-76
F-2	FRUS 1946, IX, 603
G-1	FRUS 1946, IX, 603
G-2a	
G-2b	
G-3a	
G-3b	
G-3c	
G-4	
H-1	FRUS 1946, IX, 435-37
H-2	
H-3	
H-4	
H-5	FRUS 1946, IX, 906
I-1	WP, 640-41; FRUS 1946, IX, 848-49
I-2	FRUS 1946, IX, 865
J-1	
J-2	FRUS 1946, IX, 1058-59
K-1	WP, 642-43; FRUS, IX, 1187-88
K-2	FRUS 1946, IX, 1186-87
K-3	
K-4	WP, 644; FRUS 1946, IX, 1189
K-5	FRUS 1946, IX, 1075-76
K-6	WP, 646-47; FRUS 1946, IX, 1076
K-7	
K-8a	
K-8b	
K-9	WP, 644-45; FRUS 1946, IX, 1196-98

```
K-10a  WP, 645-46; FRUS 1946, IX, 1240-42
K-10b  WP, 646; FRUS 1946, IX, 1248
K-11   WP, 647
K-12   WP, 648
L-1    WP, 648-49; FRUS 1946, X, 1
L-2    WP, 652
L-3    WP, 649-51
L-4
L-5
L-6    WP, 653
M-1    WP, 654
M-2    FRUS 1946, X, 192-93
M-3    WP, 654-56; FRUS 1946, X, 189-92
M-4    WP, 656-57; FRUS 1946, X, 194
N-1    WP, 657; FRUS 1946, X, 208-09
N-2    WP, 657-59; FRUS 1946, X, 212-14
N-3    FRUS 1946, X, 224
N-4    WP, 659-60; FRUS 1946, X, 237
N-5    WP, 660-61; FRUS 1946, X, 238-39
N-6    WP, 661-62; FRUS 1946, X, 258-59
N-7    WP, 662-63; FRUS 1946, X, 267-68
N-8    WP, 663-64; FRUS 1946, X, 270-71
N-9    WP, 664; FRUS 1946, X, 299-300
N-10   WP, 665; FRUS 1946, X, 310-11
N-11   WP, 665-67; FRUS 1946, X, 312-13
N-12   WP, 667-69; FRUS 1946, X, 345-48
O-1    WP, 669-672
O-2    WP, 673-74; FRUS 1946, X, 367-69
O-3    WP, 674-75; FRUS 1946, X, 373-75
O-4    FRUS 1946, X, 380
P-1    WP, 675; FRUS 1946, X, 445
P-2    WP, 676-77; FRUS 1946, X, 484
P-3    WP, 678-79; FRUS 1946, X, 495
P-4    WP, 677-78; FRUS 1946, X, 493-94
Q-1    WP, 679-83
Q-2    WP, 683-85
Q-3a
Q-3b
Q-3c
R-1    WP, 685-86; FRUS 1946, X, 590-91
R-2    WP, 689-94
R-3
S-1    WP, 686-89
S-2    WP, 685; FRUS 1946, X, 710
```

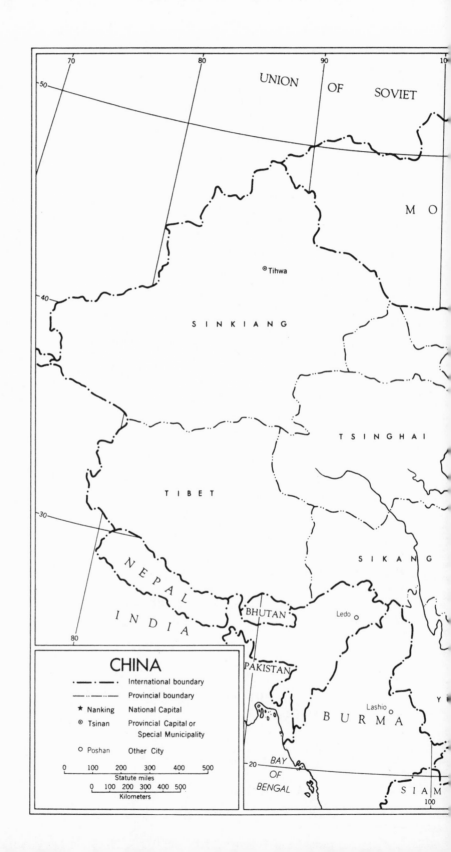

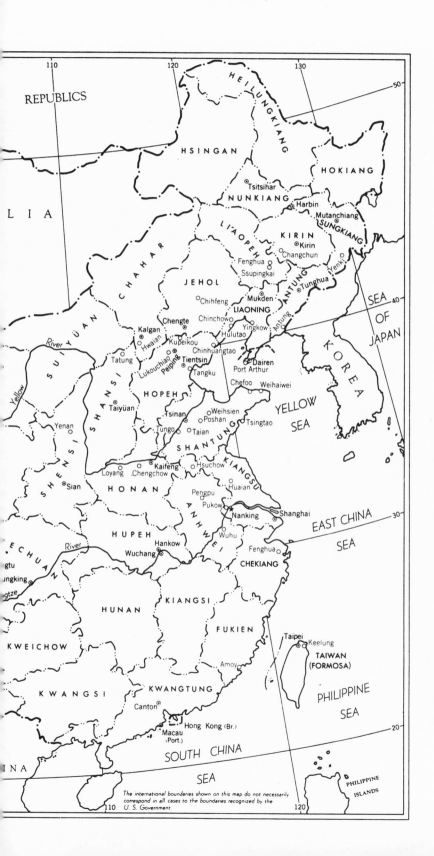

I.

THE BASIS OF MY MISSION TO CHINA

The President of the United States, in his letter to me of December 15, 1945,[1] established the basis for my mission to China as his Representative with the personal rank of Ambassador. In this letter, the President expressed his very real concern with regard to the situation in China and stated:

> "Specifically, I desire that you endeavor to persuade the Chinese Government to call a national conference of representatives of the major political elements to bring about the unification of China and, concurrently, to effect a cessation of hostilities, particularly in north China."

The President suggested that the convening at Chungking of the Political Consultation Conference, composed of representatives of the various political groups in China, including the Chinese Communists, should afford me an opportunity for discussions with the various political leaders. He referred to the plans of the U.S. Government for the evacuation of Japanese troops from China and for the subsequent withdrawal of U.S. armed forces from that country and pointed out that the success of such plans would depend largely upon the success of my efforts to achieve the objectives described above. The President authorized me to speak with the utmost frankness to Generalissimo Chiang Kai-shek and other Chinese leaders and to indicate that a China disunited and torn by civil strife could not be considered realistically as a proper place for American assistance in the form of credits, technical aid in the economic field and military aid—the latter with particular reference to the proposed U.S. military advisory

[1]See Volume Two, Appendix A, Document 1, for the full text.

group. He concluded with the request that I keep the President and Secretary Byrnes currently informed of the progress of my negotiations and of the obstacles encountered.

Attached to the President's letter as enclosures were the following documents initialled by him:

(1) A memorandum,[2] under date of December 9, 1945, to the War Department from Secretary of State Byrnes, in which were set forth the objectives of the U.S. Government in China and an outline of the directives which Mr. Byrnes wished the War Department to issue to Lieutenant General A.C. Wedemeyer, Commanding General, United States Forces, China Theater. These directives provided for arrangements to assist the National Government in transporting Chinese troops to Manchurian ports, including the logistical support of such troops; for stepped-up arrangements for the evacuation of Japanese troops from the China Theater; for the holding in abeyance of further transportation of Chinese troops to north China, except as north China ports might be necessary for the movement of troops and supplies into Manchuria, pending the outcome of my discussions at Chungking for the purpose of arranging a national conference of representatives of the major political elements and for a cessation of hostilities; and for the completion of arrangements for the transportation of Chinese troops into north China, without communicating information of such arrangements to the Chinese Government— the arrangements to be executed when I should determine either that (1) such troop movements would be consistent with my negotiations or (2) the negotiations between the Chinese groups had failed or showed no signs of success and that the situation was such as to make the movement of Chinese troops into north China necessary to effectuate the surrender terms and to secure the long-term interests of the United States in the maintenance of international peace.

(2) A statement[3] of U.S. policy toward China, which was to be released by the White House upon my departure for China.

(3) A statement[4] of U.S. policy toward China, drafted by the State and War Departments, which was to serve as the basis for the statement to be released by the White House.

[2]See Volume Two, Appendix A, Document 1, for the full text.

[3]See Volume Two, Appendix A, Document 1, for the full text.

[4]See Volume Two, Appendix A, Document 1, for the full text.

The statement issued by the White House at the time of my departure for China set forth the basic principles of U.S. policy toward China. It expressed the belief of the United States Government that "a strong, united and democratic China is of the utmost importance" to the success of the United Nations organization and for world peace and pointed out that the United States Government believed it essential:

"(1) That a cessation of hostilities be arranged between the armies of the National Government and the Chinese Communists and other dissident Chinese armed forces for the purpose of completing the return of all China to effective Chinese control, including the immediate evacuation of the Japanese forces.

"(2) That a national conference of representatives of major political elements be arranged to develop an early solution to the present internal strife which will bring about the unification of China."

It was explained in the statement that the present National Government of China, recognized by the United States and the other United Nations as the only legal government in China, was the proper instrument to achieve the objective of a unified China. It was further stated that the United States and the United Kingdom by the Cairo Declaration in 1943 and the U.S.S.R. by adhering to the Potsdam Declaration of July 1945 and by the Sino-Soviet Treaty and Agreements of August 1945, were all committed to the liberation of China, including the return of Manchuria to Chinese control, these agreements having been made with the National Government of the Republic of China. The statement explained that "in continuation of the constant and close collaboration with the National Government of the Republic of China in the prosecution of this war, in consonance with the Potsdam Declaration, and to remove possibility of Japanese influence remaining in China, the United States has assumed a definite obligation in the disarmament and evacuation of the Japanese troops" and that the United States was assisting and would continue to assist the National Government to that end, the United States Marines being in north China for that purpose. The statement added that United States support would not extend to United States military intervention to influence the course of any Chinese internal strife.

3

More specifically, in furtherance of the aim of bringing about a unified, democratic and peaceful China, it was asserted:

"The United States is cognizant that the present National Government of China is a 'one-party government' and believes that peace, unity and democratic reform in China will be furthered if the basis of this Government is broadened to include other political elements in the country. Hence, the United States strongly advocates that the national conference of representatives of major political elements in the country agree upon arrangements which would give those elements a fair and effective representation in the Chinese National Government. It is recognized that this would require modification of the one-party 'political tutelage' established as an interim arrangement in the progress of the nation towards democracy by the father of the Chinese Republic, Doctor Sun Yat-sen.

"The existence of autonomous armies such as that of the Communist army is inconsistent with, and actually makes impossible, political unity in China. With the institution of a broadly representative government, autonomous armies should be eliminated as such and all armed forces in China integrated effectively into the Chinese National Army."

The statement concluded:

"As China moves toward peace and unity along the lines described above, the United States would be prepared to assist the National Government in every reasonable way to rehabilitate the country, improve the agrarian and industrial economy, and establish a military organization capable of discharging China's national and international responsibilities for the maintenance of peace and order. In furtherance of such assistance, it would be prepared to give favorable consideration to Chinese requests for credits and loans under reasonable conditions for projects which would contribute towards the development of a healthy economy throughout China and healthy trade relations between China and the United States."

Additional documents, which are supplementary to the President's letter of December 15, 1945, and which have served as a guide in my mission within the framework of the Presidents's letter and of the statement of U.S. policy toward China, are as follows:

(1) A message[5] of December 13, 1945, from the Joint Chiefs of Staff to General Wedemeyer, General MacArthur and Admiral Spruance, quoting pertinent portions of Secretary Byrnes' memorandum of December 9, 1945, to the War Department and a letter of December 11, 1945, from the President to the Secretaries of War and Navy and Administrator, War Shipping Administration. To this letter is attached a plan for the use of shipping in the transport of Chinese armies into north China and Manchuria, in the movement of maintenance supplies to those armies and in the repatriation of Japanese from China. The message concludes with a statement that the implementation of this plan is to be guided by the State Department policy as set forth in Secretary Byrnes' memorandum of December 9, 1945, to the War Department.

(2) A directive[6] for operations in the China Theater issued by the Joint Chiefs of Staff on December 14, 1945, to the Commanding General, United States Forces, China Theater. This directive embodies the suggestions made by Secretary Byrnes in his memorandum of December 9, 1945, to the War Department.

Both the instructions and objectives outlined above have remained unchanged throughout the duration of my mission to China, and it is in the light of these instructions and of the statement of policy that I have endeavored to achieve the objectives sought by the United States Government in China.

[5]See Volume Two, Appendix A, Document 2, for a paraphrase of this message.

[6]See Volume Two, Appendix A, Document 3, for the full text.

II.

ARRIVAL IN CHINA; PRELIMINARY DISCUSSIONS

After a brief stop-over at Shanghai upon my arrival in China, I proceeded to Nanking on December 21, where I was received by Generalissimo and Madame Chiang Kai-shek. During my first conversation with the Generalissimo, on the night of my arrival, I endeavored to point out to him very frankly the position of my Government in relation to the situation in China and its desire to see an early realization of unity and peace. I indicated clearly to him that the American people would strongly disapprove any action on the part of their government which would involve them in the internal disputes of another nation, that the primary interest of the American people was in a peaceful world, and that in spite of their great friendship for the Chinese people they would not permit the President to maintain military aid in China and to extend economic assistance to China unless they saw positive evidence of success in the efforts being made to reach a peaceful solution of Chinese internal disputes.

Generalissimo Chiang in turn expressed his appreciation of my remarks and his approval of President Truman's statement of U.S. policy toward China. He emphasized the determination of the National Government to seek a solution of China's internal problems by peaceful means and pointed out as the most important portion of the President's statement that which referred to the necessity of eliminating autonomous armies in China, such as those of the Chinese Communists. The Generalissimo then asserted that there was a definite connection between Soviet Russia and the Chinese Communists, that the latter relied upon Soviet Russia in matters of broad policy, that Soviet Russia had extended aid to the Communists in Manchuria in the form of arms and equipment and that the Chinese Communists were guilty of insincere and dilatory tactics. He described as unfriendly and uncooperative the attitude of Soviet Russia in regard to the question of the landing of Chinese National Government troops at Dairen, Hulutao and Yingkou and in regard to the establishment of the National Government's Staff Headquarters at Changchun. He charged that the Soviet aim was to establish a puppet regime in Manchuria under the Chinese Communists and

6

that the Soviet military commander in Manchuria had purposely delayed the withdrawal of Soviet troops from Manchuria as a means of aiding the Chinese Communists and not at the request of the Chinese Government as that commander had publicly stated.

I have described this conversation in some detail because it serves in many ways to point up the entire situation in China. On the one hand, the National Government fears and distrusts Soviet Russia and is convinced that the Chinese Communists are Soviet puppets. The National Government does not believe in the good faith and sincerity of the Chinese Communists. On the other hand, the Chinese Communists are equally distrustful of the National Government. They do not believe in the good faith and sincerity of the National Government when the latter expresses its willingness to give up its one-party rule and establish a coalition government. They fear the Government's secret police organizations and are unwilling to surrender their armies until they receive a voice in the government sufficient to ensure their continued existence as a party and freedom for their party activities. Bolstering this attitude of fear and distrust is the conviction of each party that the other is intent solely upon complete control of the government. This barrier of fear, distrust and suspicion between the rival parties has been the greatest obstacle to the realization of peace and unity in China, a barrier which has grown through years of strife between the Kuomintang and the Chinese Communist Party.

During the initial period of my residence at Chungking, where I arrived on December 22, 1945, I endeavored to receive all visitors who wished to discuss with me the situation in China and who, I felt, had appropriate reasons for so doing or were representatives of legitimate organizations. Included among these visitors were representatives of the Democratic League, the China Youth Party and many other Chinese organizations. Coincidental with my arrival in China and complementary to a steady stream of visitors at my residence in Chungking, I received a tremendous volume of letters from Chinese throughout the country. The vast majority of these constituted evidence of the awareness of the Chinese people of the critical condition of their country and many of them were pathetic in their assumption that the fate of China rested solely on the success of my mission. This attitude is indicative of the state of mind of many Chinese at present, who see little hope for their country except through the influence of the United States. I believe that the majority of the Chinese people have welcomed American assistance in seeking a solution for the peaceful settlement of China's internal problems and that the fund of Chinese good-will toward the United States is a tangible asset to our credit in this country and a factor which exists outside the realm of ideologies and political parties.

My first meeting with Chinese Communist Party representatives took place at Chungking on December 23, 1945, when General Chou En-lai, Communist Party representative at Chungking, General Yeh Chien-ying, Chief of Staff of the Communist 18th Group Army, and Mr. Tung Pi-wu, member of the Communist Party Central Committee, called at my residence to welcome me to China and to express the appreciation and approval of the Communist Party in regard to my mission. In their conversation, the Communist representatives emphasized their desire for a cessation of hostilities and for the establishment of a coalition government, the basis for which they felt should be laid at the forthcoming meeting of the Political Consultation Conference. They pointed out that under such a government both political and military administration would be unified.

Attention is drawn to this conversation because it points to another fundamental cleavage between the viewpoints of the Kuomintang and the Communist Party. The former contends that the integration of the Communist forces into a national army should precede the establishment of a coalition government, while the Communists are equally insistent that the formation of a coalition government in which they have a substantial voice is a prerequisite to the integration of their armies into a national army. Each side found in the President's statement of U.S. policy toward China justification for its attitude.

III.
POLITICAL CONSULTATION CONFERENCE*

Inasmuch as the convening of a national conference of representatives of the major political elements in China to bring about the unification of China was stated as one of the

*Also called Political Consultative Council.

8

major objectives of my mission in the President's letter of December 15, 1945, it appears desirable to explain something of the background of the Political Consultation Conference.

The establishment of the Political Consultation Conference was provided for during the conversations held at Chungking between the National Government and the Chinese Communist Party in September 1945. The exact formula therefor is contained in Section 2 of the Text of the Summary of National Government-Communist Conversations issued on October 11, 1945, as follows:

(2) On political democratization.

It was agreed that the period of political tutelage should be brought to an early conclusion, that constitutional government should be inaugurated and that necessary preliminary measures should be immediately adopted, such as the convocation by the National Government of a Political Consultative Council, to which all parties and non-partisan leaders will be invited, to exchange views on national affairs and discuss questions relating to peaceful national reconstruction and the convocation of the National Assembly. Both parties are now conferring with various interested quarters on the membership, organization, and functions of the proposed Council. It was agreed that, as soon as such consultations are completed, the proposed Council shall be convened.

In other sections of the Text of the Summary of National Government-Communist Conversations provision is made for referring to the "Political Consultative Council" questions which were not settled during those conversations: (1) On the National Assembly—"Both parties agreed that the points concerned shall be brought before the proposed Political Consultative Council for settlement." (2) On local governments in the liberated areas—"Finally, the Communist representatives suggested that this particular problem be submitted to the Political Consultative Council for discussion and settlement. The Government, desirous of the early establishment of administrative integrity so that peaceful reconstruction might not be delayed, hoped that an agreement could soon be worked out on this matter. The Communist representatives concurred. Discussions will continue."

9

Subsequent to the end of these conversations, in which Mr. Mao Tze-tung, Chairman of the Chinese Communist Party, had participated, negotiations went on between representatives of the two parties for the nomination of delegates to the Political Consultation Conference. Lack of agreement on the non-party delegates to the Council and perhaps a general deterioration of the relations between the two parties served to cause an apparently indefinite postponement of the convocation of the Conference. In December, however, with the statement of U.S. policy toward China and the announcement of my mission, increased attention was devoted to the convening of the Conference in the Chinese Press and among Chinese in general and on December 31 the National Government announced that the Generalissimo had decided upon January 10, 1946, as the opening date of the Conference and that sessions would continue from that date through January 23.

The scope of the authority of the Conference and the binding power of its decisions were not clearly defined prior to its meeting but it was assumed that legally the Executive Committees of the various parties participating therein would be required to approve its decisions and that morally all of the parties represented in the Conference would be bound by decisions to which their delegates had agreed. Prior to the convening of the Conference, representatives of the Kuomintang and the Communist Party held preliminary discussions of questions related to the work of the Conference. The results of the Conference's sessions will be dealt with in a subsequent section of this report.

IV.

THE COMMITTEE OF THREE

In keeping with the President's instructions that I endeavor to persuade the Chinese Government to call a national conference of representatives of the major political elements to bring about the unification of China and, concurrently, to effect a cessation of hostilities and as a result of conversations I had with Generalissimo Chiang Kai-shek along these lines after my arrival at Chungking, the National Government agreed to the formation of a committee to be composed of one representative of the National Government, one representative of the Chinese Communist Party and myself, as Chairman, to discuss measures for the cessation of hostilities and related problems. This arrangement was subsequently put in concrete form when the National Government presented to the Communist Party a three point proposal for the cessation of hostilities, in which it was suggested that the National Government and the Chinese Communist Party each appoint a representative to discuss and formulate with me measures for the settlement of the problem of cessation of hostilities and related matters. The Communist Party on January 3, 1946, presented a counter-proposal to the National Government on this subject, in which agreement was given to the appointment of a representative of each party to confer, together with me, on the subject of the cessation of hostilities and certain matters related thereto.

Under these arrangements, there was formed the Committee of Three, consisting of General Chang Chun, Chairman of the Szechuan Provincial Government, as the National Government representative, General Chou En-lai as the Communist party representative and myself, as Chairman of the Committee. Following preliminary conversations between the two Chinese representatives and separate exploratory discussions held by me with each of the two Chinese members, the first formal meeting of the Committee of Three was held on January 7, 1946, at my residence in Chungking. Our primary objective was to arrive at an agreement for the cessation of hostilities, as a condition essential to any solution of China's internal problems and as a prelude, highly desirable psychologically, to the opening of the Political Consultation Conference, scheduled to convene in Chungking on January 10.

V.

CESSATION OF HOSTILITIES ORDER

On January 10, 1946, after four days of formal meetings of the Committee of Three, an agreement was reached by the Committee for the issuance of an order for the cessation of hostilities, the order to be issued by Generalissimo Chiang Kai-shek to all units, regular, militia, irregular and guerrilla, of the National Armies of the Republic of China, and by Chairman Mao Tze-tung of the Chinese Communist Party to similar units of the Communist-led troops of the Republic of China. The Order was set forth in separate, similar memoranda,[7] signed by each member of the Committee of Three on January 10 and forwarded on that day through their respective representatives on the Committee to Generalissimo Chiang Kai-shek and Chairman Mao Tze-tung for their approval and necessary action.

The Order provided for the immediate cessation of hostilities. In view of the difficulties of communicating the Order to troops in wide-spread areas, however, the Committee of Three agreed in formal meeting that there would be a period of three days, terminating on January 13, inclusive, during which both the National Government and the Communist Party would issue orders for the cessation of hostilities so that by midnight of January 13 all hostilities would be expected to have ended.

The Order prohibited, except in certain specific cases, all troop movements in China but made provision for movements necessary for demobilization, redisposition, supply, administration and local security. These specific cases, referred to in the Order, were enumerated in Stipulations regarding the Order, which were agreed upon and made a matter of record in the minutes of the meetings of the Committee of Three and which were made public on January 10 in a press release,[8] signed by General Chang Chun and Chou En-lai. In the press release, it was stated that General Chang Chun, Representative of the National Government, and General Chou En-lai, Representative of the Chinese Communist Party, had recommended to Generalissimo Chiang Kai-shek and Chairman Mao Tze-tung the issuance of an order for the cessation of hostilities and had been authorized by them to announce that this Order, as described in the release, had been issued. Under the above-mentioned Stipulations, movements of National Government troops were to be permitted south of the Yangtze River for continued execution of the National Government's military reorganization plan and movements of National Government troops were to be permitted into and within Manchuria for the purpose of restoring Chinese sovereignty. It was provided that National Government troop movements under

[7]See Volume Two, Appendix B, Documents 1 and 2, for the full texts.

[8]See Volume Two, Appendix B, Document 3, for the full text.

these Stipulations should be reported daily to the Executive Headquarters, which was to be established under the Cessation of Hostilities Order for the purpose of carrying out the agreements reached.

The Order further provided for the cessation of destruction of and interference with all lines of communications and for the removal of obstructions placed against or interfering with such lines of communications. In the Stipulations, it was stated that lines of communications included post communications.

The final paragraph of the Order provided for the immediate establishment of an Executive Headquarters* at Peiping for the purpose of carrying out the agreements for the cessation of hostilities. The Headquarters was to consist of three Commissioners, one representing the Chinese National Government, one representing the Chinese Communist Party and one representing the United States. The necessary instructions and orders agreed upon unanimously by the three Commissioners would be issued in the name of the President of the Republic of China, through the Executive Headquarters.

In the press release announcing the Cessation of Hostilities Order, it was made clear that the agreements, recommendations and directives of the Executive Headquarters would deal only with the immediate problems raised by the cessation of hostilities and that American participation therein would be solely for the purpose of assisting the Chinese members in implementing the Order.

VI.

DISCUSSIONS LEADING TO THE AGREEMENT UPON THE CESSATION OF HOSTILITIES ORDER

A study of the meetings[9] of the Committee of Three and of the preliminary discussions held by me with Chinese representatives is of value in that it reveals the attitude of the National Government and of the Chinese Communist Party toward certain important questions, which subsequently had

---

*The organization of the Executive Headquarters will be discussed in a separate section of this report.

[9]See Volume Two, Appendix B, Document 4, for the full text of the minutes.

considerable bearing on the functioning of Executive Headquarters and on the general problem of the relations between
the two rival parties.

(a) *Manchuria*

Foremost among these questions is that of Manchuria
and the control of that area. This problem was high-lighted
by Generalissimo Chiang Kai-shek and other Chinese officials
with whom I talked upon my arrival in China. It was their
firm conviction that the Soviet Union had obstructed the efforts of the Chinese Government to assume control over Manchuria by (1) refusing to permit the landing of National Government troops at Dairen; (2) by facilitating Chinese Communist control of Yingkou and Hulutao and thus preventing the
landing of National Government troops at those two ports;
(3) by tacitly permitting Chinese Communist forces to sur-
round the airfield at Changchun, thus making impossible the
transportation by air of sufficient National Government troops
to Changchun; (4) by delaying the withdrawal of Soviet troops
from Manchuria and thus paving the way for Chinese Communist infiltration into that area; and (5) by extending material aid to the Chinese Communist forces in the form of arms
and equipment.

In the light of (1) the statement of U.S. policy toward
China, which points out that the United States, the United
Kingdom and the U.S.S.R. are by various agreements reached
by them with the Chinese National Government committed to
the return of all China, including Manchuria, to Chinese control, and (2) of the directives issued to the Commanding General, United States Forces, China Theater, providing for assistance to the National Government in transporting Chinese
troops to Manchurian ports and for the logistical support of
such troops, I have endeavored to approach the Manchurian
problem with a view to a solution which would be in accord
with the above-described agreements and which would result
in bringing this area under the control of a unified China.

With that end in view, in a discussion with General Chou
En-lai on January 4 of the problem of the cessation of hostilities and of troop movements related to that problem, I informed him that the United States Government was committed to the movement of National Government troops in Manchuria. General Chou, in this conversation and in subsequent
discussions of the question, agreed that there should be an

14

exception in the cessation of hostilities agreement to permit the movement of National Government troops into Manchuria and stated that the Chinese Communist Party recognized the right of the National Government to take over in Manchuria. He added that the movement of such troops conformed to U.S. policy and to the Sino-Soviet Treaty and that the Chinese Communists did not wish to interfere with Chinese obligations to the United States and the U.S.S.R. He expressed a desire that the exception made for the movement of National Government troops into Manchuria not be made a part of the Cessation of Hostilities Order, explaining that the public might mistakenly think that the Chinese Communists opposed such movement.

At the first meeting of the Committee of Three on January 7, General Chou formally expressed his agreement that an exception be made in regard to troop movements to permit the movement of National Government troops into Manchuria, but again voiced his desire that this be recorded in the minutes of the meetings rather than inserted in the Cessation of Hostilities Order. General Chang Chun insisted that this exception be made a part of the Order. General Chou thereupon suggested that, if it were included in the Order, provision should be made for consultation between the two parties in connection with such movements. General Chang then pointed out that Communist representatives in previous negotiations had agreed to the exception providing for troop movements into Manchuria and that the only point for debate was whether National Government troops should be transported to Manchuria by rail. General Chou referred also to previous negotiations on this subject and said that the Communist authorities had suggested the desirability of consultation prior to troop movements by rail, inasmuch as the rail line from Shanhaikuan to Chinchou in southern Manchuria ran through a section which had been a base for Communist guerrilla operations prior to the Japanese surrender. Agreement was finally reached on this question at a meeting of the Committee of Three on January 10. It was agreed that the movement of National Government troops into and within Manchuria for the purpose of restoring Chinese sovereignty would be an exception to the prohibition against troop movements and that it would not be inserted in the Order but would be made a matter of record in the minutes and published in the Stipulations regarding the Order, which were contained in a press release on January 10.

(b) *Jehol*

Closely connected with the problem of the movement of National Government troops into Manchuria during the discussions was the question of the National Government's right to occupy Chihfeng, a town in north Jehol, and Tolun, a town in Chahar on the Chahar-Jehol border. (It should be explained that the Japanese had incorporated the province of Jehol into their puppet kingdom of "Manchukuo" and that Soviet troops had apparently at some time during their campaign against the Japanese occupied the towns of Chihfeng and Tolun and certain regions in Jehol south of these points.)

During the meetings of the Committee of Three, the National Government representative had strongly insisted that, in accordance with the terms of an agreement with the Soviet Union, the National Government forces should take over the towns of Chihfeng and Tolun, as well as other points outside Manchuria then occupied by Soviet troops. General Chou replied that insofar as he knew Outer Mongolian troops may have occupied these two towns at one time after the Japanese surrender but that they had subsequently withdrawn, and that Communist Eighth Route Army troops had occupied the towns and still held them. General Chou added that the agreement mentioned by General Chang was not a part of the Sino-Soviet Treaty and that he had no knowledge of such an agreement. He referred to reports he had received of the continued advance of National Government troops toward these towns and pointed to the danger inherent in the situation. General Chang then explained that General Hsiung Shih-hui, Director of the Generalissimo's Field Headquarters in Manchuria, had reached an agreement with the Soviet Chief of Staff in Manchuria in regard to the National Government's taking over of Manchuria and of other places occupied by Soviet forces; that it was agreed that there would be five stages for the completion of the Soviet withdrawal and Chinese occupation, during the fourth of which the Chinese were to have taken over Chihfeng and Tolun on November 20; that the delay had been caused by the postponement of the Soviet withdrawal; that the date of Chinese occupation was now set for February 1; and that the Soviet military authorities had agreed to leave small forces for the maintenance of peace and order until the Chinese troops arrived to occupy the points being evacuated. General Chang stated that a small force of Soviet and Mongol troops still remained in occupation of Chihfeng and Tolun in accordance with this agreement.

General Chou replied that it was not now a question of taking over as the Communist forces had already occupied the towns; that the immediate problem was that of cessation of hostilities and not that of taking over places within China proper; and that after a study of General Hsiung's telegram reporting the agreement (the text of which had been handed him by General Chang), he did not yet know whether the agreement was verbal or written as the telegram only described the stages of Soviet withdrawal.

Further discussion along similar lines continued in the meetings of the Committee of Three until it became apparent that neither side would yield on this particular question. With the reaching of agreement on all other questions relating to the cessation of hostilities, it was clear that the only solution to the problem lay in an approach to Generalissimo Chiang Kai-shek. On the evening of January 9, therefore, I discussed the matter with the Generalissimo and obtained his approval for the issuance of the Cessation of Hostilities Order without reference to Chihfeng and Tolun. At the meeting of the Committee of Three on January 10, it was proposed and approved that the Executive Headquarters to be established in accordance with the Cessation of Hostilities Order be instructed to send a committee, composed of a representative from each of the three branches of the Headquarters, to Chihfeng and Tolun to report on conditions in those two towns. Reports from Executive Headquarters of the findings of the team sent to Chihfeng indicated that Soviet troops were at that time still in occupation of Chihfeng but that Chinese Communist authorities were in control of civil adminstration and had organized local peace preservation corps for the purpose of controlling the town. A U.S. observer sent by the Executive Headquarters to Tolun on February 12 reported Chinese Communist forces in occupation of the town, earlier air reconnaissance having indicated no unusual activity in this area.

(c) *Removal of Obstructions to Lines of Communications*

The removal of obstructions to lines of communications was provided for in paragraph c of the Cessation of Hostilities Order of January 10 as follows:

> "Destuction of and interference with all lines of communications will cease and you will clear at once obstuctions placed against or interfering with such lines of communications."

17

In the first meeting of the Committee of Three on January 7, General Chou En-lai proposed that the section of the Cessation of Hostilities Order relating to the removal of obstructions to lines of communications should imply the restoration of everything that had been destroyed and the removal of all barriers and fortifications. He insisted that the Order should require the removal of "blocks and fortifications," explaining that the Japanese had built many fortifications for the purpose of blocking the travel and movement of civilians. He added that both "blocks and fortifications" were necessary in the Order and that it be "left to the Executive Headquarters to decide." It was then agreed that the section regarding the lines of communications should be adopted, as shown in its final form, and that the minutes of the meeting should contain the understanding that "everything that obstructs the railway operations be removed, but those structures which are for the defense of the railway should be left intact."

As part of this general problem and closely connected with the question of cessation of hostilities, provision was made in the agreement for the establishment of an Executive Headquarters for the submission by that Headquarters of recommendations for measures for the restoration of lines of communications. It was envisaged that such measures would eventually be implemented under the supervision of Executive Headquarters.

This question of the removal of obstructions to lines of communicatons is of some importance, as the Communist branch of Executive Headquarters subsequently entered strong protests against the National Government for its failure to remove fortifications along railway lines. The Communist representatives charged that these fortifications interfered with the lines of communications, that the National Government was thereby enabled to prevent the travel of civilians across the railway lines and that the fortifications were not, therefore, used or intended solely for the protection of these lines. Much of the delay in the restoration of railway lines can be attributed to lack of agreement on the interpretation of this section of the Cessation of Hostilities Order.

(d) *Disarmament and Repatriation of Japanese Troops*

Of vital interest to the United States and closely related to the problem of the cessation of hostilities was the question of the disarmament and repatriation of Japanese troops in

18

China. Many Japanese troops were at this time still under arms and were being used by the National Government to garrison various points along the railways in north China where National Government troops had not yet been able to proceed. Also bearing upon this subject was the contention of the Chinese Communists that they should be permitted to accept the surrender of Japanese troops in China. This had been one of the factors leading to the state of semi-civil war which had gone on intermittently since the Japanese surrender in August 1945. The chief prize consisted of Japanese arms and equipment. It was felt necessary, therefore, to arrive at some statement in connection with the agreement for the cessation of hostilities which would ensure future action leading toward the disarmament and repatriation of Japanese troops and the elimination of Japanese influence in China.

There was no difficulty in reaching an agreement on this general question. Provision was made in the agreement for the establishment of Executive Headquarters that one of the functions of that Headquarters would be to make recommendations for measures for the disarmament of Japanese forces and the coordination of the movement of Japanese forces to the coast for repatriation.*

VII.

THE EXECUTIVE HEADQUARTERS

The authorization for the establishment of the Executive Headquarters is contained in an agreement[10] entitled "The Executive Headquarters," signed on January 10, 1946, by General Chang Chun as the authorized representative of the National Government, and by General Chou En-lai as the authorized representative of the Chinese Communist Party. In the Preamble of the agreement it is stated that the two duly authorized representatives "do hereby establish, with the approval of the National Government of China, an Executive Headquarters empowered to implement the agreements for the cessation of hostilities." In the final paragraph of the agreement it is stated that the Executive Headquarters will remain

---

*The repatriation of the Japanese from China is discussed in a separate section of this report.

[10]See Volume Two, Appendix B, Document 5, for the full text.

in existence and operate until the agreement is rescinded by the President of the Republic of China or the Chairman of the Central Committee of the Chinese Communist Party after due notification to the other party.

The various sections of this agreement deal with the functions, organization, housing and supply, location, procedure and the duration of authority of the Executive Headquarters. The agreement provides for the submission by the Headquarters of recommendations covering necessary subsidiary agreements to ensure more effective implementation of the Cessation of Hostilities Order and for the issuance, in the name of the President of the Republic of China, of formal instructions unanimously agreed upon by the three Commissioners. The organization of the Headquarters provides for three Commissioners, with authority to vote and negotiate among themselves, one representing the National Government, one the Chinese Communist Party and one the United States, with the latter acting as chairman. The implementing agency of the Executive Headquarters is the Operations Section, with a United States Army Officer as Director, to be composed of officers and men required to supervise in the field the various agreements and render the required reports, with an equal number of National Government and Chinese Communist Party personnel. According to the agreement, the National Government is to furnish adequate living and office accomodations and subsistence for the Headquarters. Over all security is to be provided by the local authorities at the location of Executive Headquarters, which is to be established initially at Peiping under the agreement, while small units of each army (National Government and Chinese Communist Party) are to provide immediate security for offices, quarters and installations as required and agreed upon. The agreement provides for unanimous agreement by the three Commissioners for all action by the Executive Headquarters and for the submission of daily reports, prepared by the Operations Section, by the three Commissioners to their respective chiefs. Provision is also made for the establishment by the Operations Section of sub-stations and for the sending of supervisory and reporting teams to the field as required to implement the policies and agreements. It is provided in the agreement that each branch of the Executive Headquarters should maintain its independent signal communications at the location of the Headquarters.

Similar memoranda,[11] *mutatis mutandis*, signed by each member of the Committee of Three on January 10, were forwarded on that day to Generalissimo Chiang Kai-shek and Chairman Mao Tze-tung. These memoranda described the organization of the Executive Headquarters and announced the nomination of Mr. Walter S. Robertson as the United States Commissioner of the Headquarters and Colonel Henry A. Byroade, U.S. Army, as the Director of the Operations Section. Attached to each memorandum was a proposed list of United States personnel for the Operations Section and it was requested that a similar group from the respective Chinese branches of the Executive Headquarters be provided in order to ensure the early functioning of the Headquarters. The desirability was indicated of having, as a beginning, 40 officers and 90 enlisted men for each branch of the Executive Headquarters.

It was vitally necessary, in my opinion, that the Executive Headquarters be established and begin functioning immediately upon the reaching of an agreement for the cessation of hostilities and that adequate personnel be available to permit the sending of Executive Headquarters teams into the field to investigate possible reported conflicts, troop movements or other violations of the Cessation of Hostilities Order. I expected initial delay in getting this Order to all military units in the field and felt that the Executive Headquarters must act quickly and effectively in order to prevent possible misunderstanding arising from the failure of one side or the other to receive the Order or from the desire of one side or the other to gain last minute advantages.

It was with the foregoing circumstances in mind that I instructed Colonel Byroade, Director of the Operations Section of the Executive Headquarters, to proceed to Peiping on January 11, the day after the signing of the Cessation of Hostilities Order, to make all necessary preliminary arrangements for the arrival of the three Commissioners and their staffs. On January 10, in a memorandum[12] forwarded to Generalissimo Chiang Kai-shek, under the signatures of the members of the Committee of Three, it was pointed out that the successful functioning of the Executive Headquarters was dependent

[11]See Volume Two, Appendix B, Documents 6 and 7, for the full texts.

[12]See Volume Two, Appendix B, Document 8, for the full text.

21

upon the securing of adequate living and office accomodations and subsistence for the personnel involved. The Generalissimo was requested to designate appropriate officials to arrange for the necessary accommodations and subsistence based upon an initial estimate of Executive Headquarters personnel to include 125 officers, enlisted men and civilians for the United States branch and 170 officers, enlisted men and civilians for each of the Chinese branches.

The National Government nominated Lieutenant General Cheng Kai-min, Member of the Board of Operations of the Ministry of War, as its Commissioner in the Executive Headquarters and the Communist Party named Lieutenant General Yeh Chien-ying as its Commissioner. The three Commissioners and their staffs arrived at Peiping on January 13 and on the following day held their initial meeting.

The belief in the need of adequate personnel for the initial operations of the Executive Headquarters was amply justified in the days following the establishment of this organization. The first team, composed of a representative of each of the three branches of the Executive Headquarters and accompanied by the necessary interpreting and communications personnel, was sent to Chihfeng, Jehol Province, the town which had been the cause of a near-breakdown in the negotiations for the cessation of hostilities. The second team was despatched to Chining, Suiyuan Province, as a result of a complaint from the National Government of Communist Party violation of the Cessation of Hostilities Order in besieging this town held by National Government forces. The Communist Party charged that National Government forces had attacked the town after the receipt of the Order and that the Government had never gained full control of Chining. Additional teams were sent into the field for investigations and subsequent report to the Executive Headquarters as further reports of violations were received by the Executive Headquarters from the two Chinese branches.

Initial difficulties in the functioning of the Executive Headquarters arose from (1) the lack of sufficient Communist personnel to enable the Executive Headquarters to send out the desired number of teams to the field for the investigation of reported violations of the Order, a situation which is believed to have been caused largely by communications difficulties as there was no ready access to Peiping from Communist-held areas; (2) lack of sufficient signal equipment in the initial stages to ensure adequate communications between the Executive Headquarters and a large number of field teams;

and (3) the obvious feeling of distrust between the two Chinese factions. Evidence of opposition to this effort to bring together the two factions in a unified China was seen in the publication in a Chinese newspaper at Peiping, closely connected with a powerful reactionary clique in the Kuomintang, of a distorted version of a statement made by the Communist Commissioner to the press at the time of his arrival at Peiping. This incident, which served to create some feeling, led to the reaching of an agreement by the three Commissioners forbidding the holding of individual press conferences regarding the activities of the Executive Headquarters by the personnel of that Headquarters and providing for the issuance, from time to time, of unanimously agreed upon press releases concerning the activities of the Headquarters.

The operations and functions of the Executive Headquarters increased as the scope of its activities was enlarged. (Subsequent operations of the Executive Headquarters will be described in other sections of this report.) It is pertinent to emphasize, however, that the auspicious beginning of the Executive Headquarters, which, after the initial difficulties, began to function most effectively in implementing the Cessation of Hostilities Order, reflected the improvement in the overall situation in China and was itself an indicaton of the spirit of compromise then felt to exist, rather than the cause itself. I do not mean that Executive Headquarters as an instrument for the carrying out of the Cessation of Hostilities Order was not vitally necessary to the implementation of that Order, but it cannot be over-emphasized that if the spirit of cooperation between the National Government and the Chinese Communist Party, which had permitted the reaching of the agreement for the cessation of hostilities, ceased to exist on the higher levels the Executive Headquarters was powerless to prevent a deterioration of the situation.

VIII.
RESOLUTIONS ADOPTED BY THE POLITICAL CONSULTATION CONFERENCE

The Political Consultation Conference (hereafter called the PCC), which was in session at Chunking from January 10 to 31, was composed of representatives of the Kuomintang, the Chinese Communist Party, the Democratic League, the Youth

Party and non-party delegates. The PCC met as a consultative body without any legal authority to enforce its decisions. Morally, all groups represented were obligated to accept the decisions, but legally the PCC resolutions were subject to approval by the central committees of the various parties represented in the PCC.

In his opening address to the PCC, Generalissimo Chiang Kai-shek stated that the Government was prepared "to accept all decisions of the Conference if they are beneficial to national reconstruction, tend to promote popular welfare and can help in the democratization of the country." In his address to the closing session of the PCC on January 31, the Generalissimo made the following statements* regarding the resolutions adopted by the PCC: "I have followed and studied closely the various resolutions adopted by the Conference. . . . I wish to declare first on behalf of the Government that they will be fully respected and carried out as soon as the prescribed procedures have been completed. . . . I pledge at the same time that I will uphold this program faithfully and will also see to it that all the military and civil subordinates follow it strictly. . . . From now on, I will, whether in the Government or out of it, faithfully and resolutely observe, as a citizen should, all the decisions of this Conference."

In contrast to Generalissimo Chiang Kai-shek's pronouncements on the subject of the PCC resolutions were indications of strong opposition to the PCC among powerful reactionary groups in the Kuomintang. Minority party reaction to the decisions of the PCC was shown in the issuance of categorical statements by the Communist Party, the Democratic League and the Youth Party of their intention to carry out the PCC resolutions.

At the opening session of the Political Consultation Conference, Generalissimo Chiang Kai-shek announced the Government's decision to grant immediately certain fundamental democratic rights. They were:

> (1) Freedom of person, creed, speech, publication, assembly and association—no authorities other than the judiciary and police shall cause any person to be arrested or punished.

*As reported by the International Department of the Kuomintang Ministry of Information under date of January 31, 1946.

(2) All political parties shall have equal legal status and may operate openly within the law.

(3) Popular elections will be held and local self-government permitted.

(4) Political prisoners, except traitors and those found to have committed definite acts injurious to the Republic, will be released.

In the public sessions, which followed the opening of the PCC, the chief topics of discussion were: (1) reorganization of the government, (2) reorganization of the armies, (3) administrative policy, (4) the National Assembly and (5) the draft constitution. At the conclusion of discussion upon each of these subjects in the public sessions, the views and recommendations presented were referred to sub-committees for the drafting of specific proposals to be submitted to the PCC for consideration. These sub-committees, which met in closed session, were composed of representatives of each delegation, nominated by the delegation and appointed by Generalissimo Chiang Kai-shek in his capacity as Chairman.

On January 31, the PCC held its final session and released to the press the text of the resolution[13] agreed upon by that organization. These resolutions were divided into five main headings as follows: (1) Government Organization, (2) Program for Peaceful National Reconstruction, (3) Military Problems, (4) Agreement on the National Assembly and (5) The 1936 Draft Constitution.

(1) Government Organization

(a) *The State Council*

Pending the convocation of the National Assembly, scheduled according to agreement reached in the PCC for May 5, the Kuomintang is to revise the organic law of the National Government to make the State Council the supreme organ of the Government in charge of national affairs. The Council is to decide on legislative principles, administrative policy, important military measures, financial plans and the budget, the appointment and dismissal of Ministers of State, the appointment of members of the Legislative and Control Yuan, mat-

[13]See Volume Two, Appendix C, Document 1, for the full text.

ters submitted by the President of the National Government and proposals submitted by one-third or more of the State Councillors. The President may veto any decision of the State Council but a three-fifths vote in the Council is sufficient to override the veto. General resolutions must be approved by a majority of the Councillors present, but resolutions involving changes in administrative policy must obtain a two-thirds vote of members present for approval. A majority vote of members present is sufficient to decide whether a resolution involves a change in administrative policy. The Council is to meet once every two weeks, but the President may call emergency sessions. The Councillors are to be nominated by the President upon their selection by the respective parties. The Council is to be composed of 40 members, who are to be chosen by the President from Kuomintang and non-Kuomintang personnel, and is to include the Presidents of the five Yuan as ex-officio members. Half the Councillors will be members of the Kuomintang and half members of other parties and non-party personnel. Non-party Councillors are to be appointed by the President, but if the nomination is opposed by one-third of the other Councillors, the President shall reconsider the nomination. The specific allotment of non-Kuomintang Councillors shall be the subject of separate discussion.

(b) *The Executive Yuan*

All Ministers of the Executive Yuan are *ipso facto* Ministers of State. There may be three to five Ministers of State without portfolio. Of the existing Ministers in the Executive Yuan and the proposed Ministers without portfolio, seven or eight will be non-Kuomintang personnel. Members of all political parties as well as non-party personnel may become Ministers of State with or without portfolio.

(2) Program for Peaceful National Reconstruction

Under this program all parties recognize the *San Min Chu I** as the principles for national reconstruction and the national leadership of President Chiang Kai-shek. The program

---

*The *San Min Chu I* are the "Three People's Principles" advanced by Dr. Sun Yat-sen as the basis for China's development as a modern state and consist of the principles of (1) nationalism, (2) democracy (or people's rights) and (3) the people's livelihood.

provides for a guarantee of civil liberties, organization of a civil service system, local self-government, popular elections, a national army divorced from political control and civil administration, revision of the taxation system, economic planning with the field open to private enterprise, reduction of farm rents and interest rates, increase of farm loans and the maintenance of the *status quo* in liberated areas where the government is under dispute until a settlement is made by the National Government after its reorganization.

(3) Military Problems

Fundamental principles for the creation of a national army: The army shall be a national army belonging to the State and no political parties shall be allowed to carry on political activities within the army. The army shall not interfere in political affairs and army personnel on active duty shall not serve as civil officials. A Ministry of National Defense shall be organized under the Executive Yuan and all troops are to be under the unified control of this Ministry. The Executive Yuan shall decide upon the number of troops and military expenditures, with the approval of the Legislative Yuan. The Three-Man Military Commission* should proceed according to schedule and agree upon practical methods for the reorganization of the Communist troops at an early date. The Government troops should be reorganized according to the plan laid down by the Ministry of War into 90 divisions and this reorganization should be completed within 6 months. When the reorganization of troops as above-mentioned has been completed, all troops of the country should be again reorganized into 50 or 60 divisions. A commission for the supervision of the reorganization plan shall be established within the National Military Council, members of this commission to be drawn from "various circles."

(4) Agreement on the National Assembly

The National Assembly shall be convened on May 5 for the purpose of adopting the constitution, which shall be ratified by a vote of three-fourths of the delegates present. The

---

*This Commission is the Military Sub-Committee on which I was serving as advisor.

1200 geographical and vocational delegates who have already or are going to be elected shall be retained. Delegates from the Northeast and Taiwan (Formosa) shall be increased by 150 and an extra 700 seats in the Assembly shall be apportioned among the various parties and social leaders according to a ratio to be decided upon later. The total number of delegates will thus be 2050. An organ to enforce the constitution will be elected six months after the adoption of the constitution.

(5) The 1936 Draft Constitution

A committee for reviewing the May 5, 1936, Draft Constitution shall be established to draw up a detailed plan for revision of the Draft Constitution, based on the principles agreed upon by the PCC as well as recommendations of various associations connected with the promotion of constitutionalism.* "This plan will be submitted to the National Assembly for adoption." The principles for revision are as follows:

(a) *The National Assembly.* The entire electorate, when it exercises the rights of election, recall, initiative and referendum, shall be called the National Assembly. Pending the extension of universal suffrage, the President shall be elected by the district, provincial and national representative assemblies.

(b) *The Legislative Yuan.* This Yuan is to be the supreme law-making body of the State and is to correspond to the parliament in a democratic country. It will be elected by the electorate.

(c) *The Control Yuan.* This Yuan, to be elected by the provincial assemblies and the assemblies of the self-governing areas of minority peoples, will exercise the functions of consent, impeachment and control.

(d) *The Judicial Yuan.* This Yuan shall be the Supreme Court of the State but shall not be responsible for judicial administration. The justices shall be without party affiliations and shall be appointed on the nomination of the President with the consent of the Control Yuan.

(e) *The Examination Yuan.* This Yuan, whose members

*These associations were organized throughout free China toward the end of 1943 in accordance with a resolution approved by the Supreme National Defense Council.

shall be appointed on the nomination of the President with the consent of the Control Yuan, shall examine candidates for civil service. The members shall be without party affiliations.

(f) *The Executive Yuan.* This Yuan shall be the supreme executive organ of the State. The President of the Executive Yuan shall be appointed on the nomination of the President of the National Government and with the consent of the Legislative Yuan. The Executive Yuan is to be responsible to the Legislative Yuan, and if the latter expresses non-confidence in the Executive Yuan, the Executive Yuan may either resign or may ask the President of the National Government for the dissolution of the Legislative Yuan for a second time.

(g) *Presidency of the National Government.* The President may promulgate emergency decrees according to law when the Executive Yuan has so decided, but the action must be reported to the Legislative Yuan within one month. The right of the President to call the President of the five Yuan into conference need not be written into the Constitution.

(h) *The System of Local Government.* The province is to be regarded as the highest unit of local government, the division of powers between it and the National Government to be decided according to a "fair distribution of power." The provincial chairmen will be elected by the people and the provinces may have provincial constitutions, which must not, however, contravene the provisions of the National Constitution.

(i) *The Rights and Duties of the People.* All those freedoms and rights generally enjoyed by people in democratic countries should be protected by the constitution. The right of self-government must be guaranteed to minority peoples who live together in one particular locality.

(j) *Elections.* A separate chapter on elections shall be written into the constitution.

(k) *Fundamental National Policies.* A separate chapter in the constitution should be devoted to fundamental national policies, including items on national defense, foreign relations, national economy, culture and education.

(l) *Amendments to the Constitution.* The right to amend the constitution shall be vested in a joint conference of the Legislative and Control Yuan, the proposed amendment then being subject to approval by the same body which has the right to elect the President of the National Government.

IX.
ISSUES INVOLVED IN THE POLITICAL
CONSULTATION CONFERENCE RESOLUTIONS

In connection with the question of the reorganization of the government, the Kuomintang had originally proposed that its Central Executive Committee retain the power of nomination, that the President of the National Government retain his emergency powers and that a two-thirds vote be required in the State Council for over-riding a presidential veto. The final resolution, which gave most of the powers of nomination to the State Council, took the emergency powers out of the hands of the President and lowered to three-fifths the vote necessary to override a presidential veto, represents a concession by the Kuomintang. By the agreement on the reorganization of the government, the Communists were assured that the State Council would be a real governing body, but they were not, however, guaranteed a strong voice in the government. That would depend upon the number of non-Kuomintang seats in the Council they were able to obtain in the discussions after the adjournment of the PCC. If the Communist Party and the Democratic League, which had throughout the PCC session closely aligned itself with the Communists, could obtain between them 14 of the 20 non-Kuomintang seats in the Council, they would thus have the minimum one-third necessary to make proposals and to veto any government nomination of the non-party personnel to the Council which they considered undesirable. Subsequent discussions on this subject among the non-Kuomintang groups did not result in the reaching of any agreement on this point, the Youth Party (which supported the Kuomintang during the PCC sessions) strongly opposing the efforts of the Communists and the Democratic League to obtain 14 seats in the Council and indicating that it would not participate in the Government if the Communists were given 10 seats or if the Democratic League were given more seats than the Youth Party.

The agreement on the National Assembly represents a concession on the part of the Communist Party since it most closely approaches the original Kuomintang demand to retain the previously elected delegates and to enlarge the membership of the Assembly, as opposed to the Communist demand that an entirely new election be held for delegates to the assembly. In return for this concession, the Kuomintang made a certain number of concessions regarding the Draft Constitution.

The clearest divergence of views between the Kuomintang and the opposition parties was revealed in the question of revision of the Draft Constitution. This divergence is of particular importance as subsequent developments indicated that the strongest opposition in the Kuomintang to the implementation of the PCC resolutions was directed at revision of the constitutional principles approved by the PCC. The Kuomintang wanted the "four powers"—election, recall, initiative and referendum—exercised by a centralized body of some 2000 persons; a strong semi-independent President; a separation of powers of the various branches of government; a strong central government; and the "five Yuan" system. The Communists and the Democratic League wanted the "four powers" to be exercised by the people, leaving the National Assembly as a synonym for "the electorate"; a President with as great a limit as possible on his powers; a system of checks and balances similar to that of the United States; and a decentralized federal government and a "tri-power" government, again similar to that of the United States. In the final decision, the Kuomintang yielded on all of these points in return for Communist acquiescence on the question of the National Assembly. In that the resolution provides for a "cabinet system" in which the executive branch is responsible to the legislative branch of the govenment, the decision most closely approaches the French system. However, the "tri-power" government and the system of checks and balances use for their models the governments of the United States and Great Britain.

Indications of Kuomintang reaction to the revision of the constitution were seen in a statement issued on February 13 by the previously elected delegates* to the National Assembly, in which the delegates asserted that, although the National Assembly would respect public opinion and give careful consideration to the PCC recommendations, the National Assembly itself was the only legal organ for making the constitution and would uphold the inviolability of its right to make all decisions in this connection. Prior to the opening of the Kuomintang Central Executive Committee's session at Chungking on March 1 for the purpose of passing upon the PCC resolutions, those elements in the Kuomintang who had previ-

*These delegates were elected in 1936 and 1937.

ously been critical of the PCC resolutions indicated that they would definitely oppose the resolution on the revision of the constitution. Indications of displeasure with the PCC agreements on this subject had been apparent when Generalissimo Chiang Kai-shek, in his closing speech to the PCC, had stated that there might be some difficulty encountered in obtaining acceptance of the revisions by the National Assembly, which was legally the constitution-making body. Further indication of the Kuomintang reaction in this regard is contained in the report of Generalissimo Chiang Kai-shek's speech to the People's Political Council, as published by the *Hsin Min Pao* of April 2: "President Chiang said that the Government is determined to implement the resolutions of the PCC with the exception of the principles governing the amendment of the Draft Constitution."

X.

RESTORATION OF COMMUNICATIONS

Closely related to the question of the cessation of hostilities was that of the restoration of communicatons and with that end in view provision had been made in the agreement for the establishment of the Executive Headquarters for submission by that Headquarters of recommendations for measures for the restoration of lines of communications.

On January 19, 1946, therefore, General Henry A. Byroade,* Director of the Operations Division** of the Executive Headquarters, in a meeting of the Executive Headquarters Commissioners, issued a directive to the Combined Chiefs of Staff of the Operations Division for the immediate preparation of a preliminary plan for the restoration of communications. It was felt that sufficient progress had been made in effecting cessation of hostilities to permit the institution of measures to restore communications, as a means both of aiding in the urgently needed resumption of normal economic life in China and in the repatriation of Japanese troops. The Communist Commissioner indicated a desire to include the problems of

*General Byroade's promotion from Colonel to Brigadier General was confirmed by the United States Senate on February 1.

**Originally called Operations Section, but subsequently changed to Operations Division because of the number of control sections established under its authority.

disarmament and repatriation of the Japanese with the question of restoration of communications and subsequently insisted upon full discussion of railway guards and operational management of railway lines along with reconstruction problems. Bitter argument developed over these points, with the National Government Chief of Staff, in meetings of the Combined Chiefs of Staff, refusing to discuss the question of neutral railways. The National Government branch of the Executive Headquarters also contended that discussion of joint operation and control of the railways should be limited to the areas in which construction work would be carried out and should not include areas where no destruction had occurred. This meant that the areas affected would be almost entirely within communist-held territory, as most of the railway lines destroyed lay within such areas. After continued discussion of these questions, without the reaching of an agreement in the Executive Headquarters, General Byroade proceeded to Chungking with the drafts of the documents prepared in Peiping, on which he had been unable to obtain agreement.

After several conferences with the individual members of the Military Sub-Committee,* General Byroade met with the Committee[14] on February 9 in order to obtain the Committee's approval of an agreement for the restoration of communications. Agreement was obtained, after some discussion and revision, and the documents[15] embodying the agreement were signed on February 9 by General Chang Chih-chung, General Chou En-lai and myself as members of the Committee, with indication that the documents had been approved by the Committee. This procedure was adopted in order to allow for signing of the documents by the three Commissioners of the Executive Headquarters as an agreement reached by the three Commissioners, it being so indicated in the documents.

---

*Formed for the purpose of developing a plan for the reorganization of the armies of China and related matters. The establishment of this Committee and its functions are discussed in subsequent sections of this report.

[14]See Volume Two, Appendix D, Document 1, for the text of the minutes of this meeting.

[15]See Volume Two, Appendix D, Document 2, for the full text.

The agreement for the Restoration of Communications consists of three documents as follows: (1) Document "A"— a directive to all National Government and Communist Party military commanders in north and central China; (2) Document "B"— a memorandum to Generalissimo Chiang Kai-shek quoting Document "A" and requesting the National Government to furnish the necessary technical staff for carrying out railway reconstruction; and (3) Document "C"—the general principles for the restoration of communications.

Document "A," entitled "To: All National Government and Communist Party Military Commanders in North and Central China," directs all commanders to assist in the reconstruction of lines of communications and enumerates the various communications facilities included within the scope of the order. The commanders are directed to remove or destroy at once all "mines, blockades, fortifications or other military works on and along lines of communications which interfere with the operation of such lines." (It should be noted that this sentence added nothing to the previous agreement reached on the question of removal of obstructions to the lines of communications, as set forth in paragraph c of the Cessation of Hostilities Order, and still left open to debate the question of whether fortifications for the defense of the railway lines could be considered as constituting interference with lines of communications. This loophole was admittedly small as the minutes of the Committee of Three meetings contained the understanding that "everything that obstructs the railway operations should be removed, but those structures which are for the defense of the railway should be left intact." The Communist representatives in Executive Headquarters, however, subsequently insisted that fortifications along railway lines enabled the National Government to prevent the travel of civilians across these lines. It is of some interest that neither of the two Chinese representatives of the Military Sub-Committee, during the discussion of this sentence on February 9, raised any question regarding its interpretation.) In Document "A" the commanders are further directed not to interfere with civilian travel and passage of goods, to be responsible for the protection of repair units on the lines of communications and to permit no troop movements for this purpose without the prior approval of the Executive Headquarters. The directive provides for reconstruction work by representatives of the Ministry of Communications under the general supervision of the Executive Headquarters and for the sending of field teams by that Headquarters to major areas of re-construction. The directive prohibits the movement of troops or armament over the reopened transportation lines unless authorized by the Executive Headquarters.

Document "B" is addressed to Generalissimo Chiang Kai-shek and informs him that agreement has been reached by the three Commissioners of the Executive Headquarters on the immediate institution of measures for the restoration of lines of communications. The document then quotes the directive issued to all National Government and Communist Party commanders and requests the National Government to furnish the necessary technical staff to carry out the railway reconstruction. It is also requested that the headquarters of the representatives of the Ministry of Communications selected for this task be located at Peiping and that liaison be established by them as soon as possible with the Operations Division of the Executive Headquarters.

Document "C" sets forth the general principles under which railway reconstruction is to be effected. It is explained that the term "interim period," during which the agreement is to apply, will be that period prior to the formation of, and assumption of authority by, an agreed form of national government. This was intended to allow for the formation of a co-alition government, as envisaged in the decisions of the Political Consultation Conference, and its eventual assumpton of authority. Provision is made in the document for (1) supervision by the Executive Headquarters over the representatives of the Ministry of Communications in matters of railway reconstruction and operation in north and central China; (2) the establishment of a railway control section under the Operations Division of the Executive Headquarters, consisting of representatives of the National Government, the Chinese Communist Party and the United States, which would devote itself not to technical matters of reconstruction and operation but to matters of policy with a view to accelerating reconstruction; (3) the organization and despatch to the field of railway control teams, similar to other field teams of the Executive Headquarters, for each of the eight railway lines in north and central China; (4) the protection of repair units and prevention of further destruction to lines of communication, responsibility for which is placed upon the National Government and Communist Party commanders within their respective areas; (5) the placing of train guards, administrative control and operating personnel under the direct control of the representatives of the Ministry of Communications, under the general supervision of the Executive Headquarters; and (6) the determination of priority of reconstruction of the various railway lines in accordance with their relation to economic recovery, with full consideration being given, however, to the railway requirements for facilitating the disarmament and repatriation of the Japanese.

XI.

MILITARY SUB-COMMITTEE

On January 5, Generalissimo Chiang Kai-shek broached to me the question of the reorganization of the Chinese armies. I pointed out that this matter was not within the scope of my conversations at that time, feeling that the problem of cessation of hostilities was of primary importance at the moment and that the introduction of other important issues might complicate the situation. On the following day General Chang Chun informed me that the formation of a three man military committee had been discussed by National Government and Communist Party representatives in the past and that agreement had been reached for the establishment of such a committee to formulate measures for the reorganization and redisposition of the Chinese armies. General Chang explained that the committee had never met because of the failure of the Communist Party to send its representative.

On January 10, during the fifth meeting of the Committee of Three, General Chang suggested the desirability of the formation of this committee and my participation therein and proposed that the Committee of Three submit an urgent recommendation for the immediate establishment of such a committee to proceed with the development of an acceptable plan for the reorganization of the Armies of China. General Chou En-lai expressed approval of the proposal. In accordance with this proposal, similar memoranda,[16] under date of January 14, 1946, signed by the members of the Committee of Three, were forwarded to Generalissimo Chiang Kai-shek and Chairman Mao Tze-tung, urgently recommending that the Military Sub-

[16]See Volume Two, Appendix E, Documents 1 and 2, for the full texts.

Committee, agreed to by the National Government and the Chinese Communist Party during the negotiations in September 1945 and set forth in the Text of the Summary of National Government-Communist Conversations of October 11, 1945, be convened immediately to develop a plan for the reorganization of the Armies of China at the earliest possible date. Under date of January 22, 1946, General Chang, in his capacity as representative of the National Government, addressed a letter to me expressing approval of my participation in the Military Sub-Committee in an advisory capacity. In a letter of January 23, 1946, General Chou informed me of the approval of Chairman Mao Tze-tung of the establishment of the Military Sub-Committee and of my participation therein as advisor.

Prior to a formal meeting of the Military Sub-Committee, to which General Chang Chih-chung, Director of the Political Training Board of the National Military Council, was named as the National Government representative, and General Chou En-lai as the Communist Party representative, separate discussions on the subject of the reorganization of the Armies of China and related problems were held by the two Chinese members of the Committee and by me with each of the Chinese representatives. The first formal meeting of the Military Sub-Committee was held on February 14, 1946.

XII.

BASIS FOR MILITARY REORGANIZATION AND FOR THE INTEGRATION OF THE COMMUNIST FORCES INTO THE NATIONAL ARMY

Following the first formal meeting of the Military Sub-Committee on February 14, 1946, almost daily meetings of the Committee continued until agreement was reached and the formal document embodying this agreement, entitled "Basis for Military Reorganization and for the Integration of the Communist Forces into the National Army,"[17] was signed on February 25, 1946, by General Chang Chih-chung as representative of the National Government, by General Chou En-lai as representative of the Chinese Communist Party and by me as Advisor to the Committee. Public announcement of

[17]See Volume Two, Appendix E, Document 3, for the full text.

the articles of this agreement was made on the same day in a press release,[18] in which it was stated:

> "We, General Chang Chih-chung, representative of the Government, and General Chou En-lai, representative of the Chinese Communist Party, constituting the Military Sub-Committee of which General Marshall is advisor have been authorized to announce that an agreement has been reached on the basis for military reorganization and for the integration of the Communist forces into the National Army."

In the press release, it was explained that the object of the agreement was to facilitate the economic rehabilitation of China and at the same time to furnish a basis for the development of an effective military force capable of safeguarding the security of the nation, including provisions to safeguard the rights of the people from military interference. It was also pointed out in the press release that the Military Sub-Committee was in the process of preparing the detailed measures for the execution of the terms of the agreement and that the Executive Headquarters at Peiping would be the agency charged with the responsibility of transmitting the orders to the troops in the field and the supervision of the execution of such orders. The press release further stated that these measures would be carried out over a period of 18 months under the agreement.

The document embodying the agreement is divided into eight articles under the headings of command, functions and restrictions, organization, demobilization, integration and deployment, Peace Preservation Corps, special provisions and general. The terms of the agreement, which represent the general principles for military reorganization and the integration of Communist forces into the National Army, envisage the reduction of the National Government armies to 90 divisions at the end of 12 months and the reduction of the Communist forces to 18 divisions during that same period. A further reduction at the end of the following 6 months provides for 50 National Government divisions and 10 Communist Divisions, the total of 60 divisions of not more than 14,000 men each to be formed into 20 armies. The process of integration

[18]See Volume Two, Appendix E, Document 4, for the full text.

is provided for initially during the seventh month through the formation of an army group composed of one National Government and one Communist army of three divisions each. This process is to continue until four such army groups have been formed during the first 12 month period. The staffs of these army groups under the agreement are to be composed of approximately equal numbers of National Government and Communist staff officers. In order to prevent hardship and lawlessness arising from the demobilization, the National Government and the Communist Party is each required under the agreement to make provisions for the supply, movement and employment of their respective demobilized personnel, with the National Government to assume this responsibility for all demobilized personnel as soon as practicable. The agreement also provides for the establishment of 8 service areas under directors responsible to the Minister of National Defense (or National Military Council) for various functions within their respective areas relating to supply, quartering, pay, storage and reconditioning of equipment, issue of weapons, processing of demobilized personnel and recruits and elementary training of recruits. It is specifically provided, however, that service area directors are to have no military command and are to be prohibited from interfering with or influencing civil administration or affairs. A check on these directors is provided through the stationing of representatives of the various armies within each service area at the service area headquarters and for bi-monthly meetings presided over by the director and attended by the representatives of each army within the area and a representative of the Minister of National Defense (or the National Military Council) at which the instructions of the Minister are to be presented and the state of supply and similar matters are to be discussed. For purposes of integration and deployment, China is divided under the agreement into five general areas as follows: Northeast, Northwest, North China, Central China and South China (including Formosa). A specific number of armies is provided for each area at the end of the 12 month period and again at the end of the full 18 month period. For purposes of quelling civil disorders with which the civil police of any province has been unable to cope, each province is permitted under the agreement to maintain a Peace Preservation Corps of not more than 15,000 men, this Corps to be equipped only with light weapons. The agreement further provides that neither the Government nor any political party, group or association is to be permitted to maintain, or in any way support, any secret or independent armed force after the effective date of the agreement. Provision is also made for the disarming and disbanding of all puppet and irregular troops as soon as possible, the detailed plans for the implementation of the agreement to establish a definite time limit for the execution of this measure. The agreement concludes that demobilization shall begin at the earliest practical date, that the establishment of the service areas shall be effected gradually and that both the National Government and the Communist Party shall be responsible for the good order and supply of their respective troops during the initial transitional period.

XIII.
DISCUSSIONS LEADING TO AGREEMENT ON BASIS FOR MILITARY REORGANIZATION AND FOR THE INTEGRATION OF THE COMMUNIST FORCES INTO THE NATIONAL ARMY

In the separate discussions held by me with each of the Chinese members of the Military Sub-Committee and in the formal meetings of that Committee, I endeavored to emphasize as strongly as possible the necessity of creating in China a national, non-political military force along the lines of western military tradition, to be used as a democratic army and not as an authoritative weapon. The agreement reached is based upon the general principle of separating the army from politics and, although this idea is not expressly stated in the agreement, the various articles adhere to this general plan. This principle is of the greatest importance in China, where political power in the final analysis is now dependent upon the possession of military force, where the military constantly interfere with civil administration or are themselves legally in control of civil administration and where there are still a few relics in the outlying provinces of the days of warlordism.

Application of this principle in the agreement is seen in the following provisions: (1) the separation of the directors of the service areas from troop command, the prohibition against interference by the directors with civil affairs and the check on the directors through bi-monthly meetings with representatives of the armies and of the Ministry of National Defense (or National Military Council); (2) the prohibition against the possession or support by the Government or by any organization or group of secret or independent armies; (3) the formation of Peace Preservation Corps in the provinces to be used for quelling civil disorder only when the civil police are unable to cope with the situation; (4) the prohibition against the use of the National Army in quelling domestic disorder in any province except when the chairman of the provincial government of that province shall have certified that the civil police and Peace Preservation Corps have been unable to deal with such disorder and when the President, in his capacity as Commander-in-Chief, shall have received the approval of the Council of State therefor; and (5) in the establishment of an adequate personnel system in which political prejudice shall have no part.

Proposals to include in the agreement a ban on membership in a political party or on positions in the Central committee of such a party by officers on active military duty were said by the two Chinese members of the Committee to be unnecessary. They stated that the decisions of the Political Consultation Conference provided that officers on active duty should not participate in party activities or in any party or similar organization. The National Government representatives said that during the meetings of the Political Consultation Conference it was agreed by both the Kuomintang and the Communist Party that they would not dismiss from their respective parties those officers on active duty in their armies; the two parties also agreed that officers serving as members of the central committees of the two parties would not be dismissed as they had been elected by the party congresses and new elections would have to await the convening of the congresses. In view of the foregoing, the proposed article banning political activity or membership in a political party was not included in the final agreement.

A study of the minutes[19] of the meetings of the Military Sub-Committee and of the various separate discussions held by me with the two Chinese members of the Committee indicates the viewpoints of the Kuomintang and the Communist Party toward certain fundamental points at issue.

(a) *Title of the Agreement*

The question of the title for the agreement led to consid-

[19]See Volume Two, Appendix E, Document 5, for the full text.

41

erable discussion between the Chinese representatives. General Chang Chih-chung pointed to Article 9[20] of the Text of the Summary of National Government-Communist Conversations of October 11, 1945, as the basis for the establishment of the Military Sub-Committee and stated that this Article provided for the formation of the Committee to develop a plan for the reorganization of the Communist forces into 20 divisions. General Chang informed me privately that he was, however, willing to permit the discussions of the Committee to extend to and include the question of the reorganization of all armies of China. General Chou En-lai, in the discussion of this subject during the meetings of the Committee, said that the Military Sub-Committee had been established for the discussion of the reorganization of the armies of China and that this purpose had been clearly stated in the recommendation, subsequently approved, made by the Committee of Three to Generalissimo Chiang Kai-shek and Chairman Mao Tze-tung and that this interpretation of the Military Sub-Committee's functions had also been set forth in the decisions of the Political Consultation Conference. General Chou suggested a title which would reflect the broad terms of the Committee's discussions and the actual content of the agreement. During the discussions the National Government representative was always careful to avoid any wording of the title which would jeopardize the legal status of the National Government armies, desiring to emphasize that the agreement was for the purpose of reorganization and integration of the Communist forces. The Communist representative was desirous of giving clear indication that the reorganization and integration were equally applicable to both the National Government and Communist forces. The title adopted, "Basis for Military Reorganization and for the Integration of the Communist Forces into the National Army," represents a compromise between the two views.

(b) *Gendarmerie and Railway Guards*

The point of difference between the National Government and Communist Party most difficult of settlement in these discussions was that of the gendarmerie and railway police. (It should be explained that the gendarmerie in China is or-

---

[20]See Volume Two, Appendix E, Document 6, for the text.

42

ganized along Japanese lines and is under the control of the Board of Operations of the Ministry of War. Its functions, however, have not been limited to those of a military nature, such as is true in western countries, but have included the inspection of civilian travellers and their baggage, the arrest of civilians and the search of civilian homes.) Underlying much of the Communist Party's distrust of the Kuomintang is fear of the gendarmerie and secret police organizations. General Chou En-lai made repeated references during the discussions to the necessity of providing in the agreement for safeguards against interference by the gendarmerie with civil administration. In private talks with me, he expressed his concern over the reported organization of 18 regiments of railway guards under General Tai Li, head of the National Government's secret police. In formal meeting, General Chou referred to the plan for the organization of 18 regiments of railway guards under the Ministry of Communications and expressed strong opposition to the creation of independent armies under separate agencies of the Government. General Chou wished to limit the number of gendarmes in the agreement and to restrict their function to that of military, as opposed to civil affairs, pointing out that the gendarmerie was particularly active in the large cities. General Chang Chih-chung was obviously reluctant to permit the inclusion of the question of the status or strength of the gendarmerie in the agreement and suggested that, inasmuch as the Communist Party would have representation in the Executive Yuan under the government reorganization plan provided for in the decisions of the Political Consultation Conference, the Communist Party would be able to take up this question on a high governmental level. After lengthy discussion of this question with no apparent indications that either side was willing to recede from its position, it was finally agreed that General Chang would recommend to the Executive Yuan that he be authorized to discuss with General Chou the matter of railway guards and that prior to a settlement of the problem of the gendarmerie and the railway guards, the agreement for the restoration of communications, under which the commanders of the National and Communist armies were responsible for the protection of the railway lines in their respective areas, should continue to apply. This agreement was made a matter of record in the minutes of the meetings.

(c) *Reorganization and Integration*

In connection with the general question of reorganization and integration, I was informed by General Chang Chun, a member of the National Government delegation on the Political Consultation Conference, that the Government had proposed in the PCC's Military Sub-Committee meetings that plans be developed in one month for reorganization and integration and that such plans, including the integration of the Communist forces, be carried out in the following two months by an organ to be established under the National Military Council for necessary supervision and planning. The plans also envisaged the reorganization of the National Government armies into 90 divisions within six months. General Chou En-lai, serving as a member of this Sub-Committee of the PCC, was said to have opposed any program of this kind unless the National Military Council was reorganized to provide for Communist Party representation therein.

It was my opinion that demobilization and reduction of the National Government armies from 250 divisions to 90 divisions within 6 months was too rapid and might be carried out without proper provisions to prevent banditry and to arrange for the disposal of arms and equipment. I felt that demobilization and integration should proceed progressively and simultaneously and that final reorganization of all armies into a total of 60 divisions should be carried out in a period beyond the first stage of 12 months. Pertinent to these problems was the statement of General Chou En-lai that the reduction of their forces would present less of a problem to the Communist Party than to the National Government as a large number of Communist troops were already participating in agricultural activities.

Discussion of the problem of integration of the Communist forces into the National Army revealed Communist fears of too rapid integration and National Government desires to achieve complete integration as quickly as possible. In keeping with these attitudes, the National Government argued for integration in the first stages of 12 months while the Communist Party desired to postpone integration of their armies until the second stage of the final 6 months of the plan. The National Government representative pointed out that the Government wished to avoid the existence of separate National and Communist divisions at the end of the 18 months envisaged in the plan and proposed that there be no separation of the 50 National Government and 10 Communist divisions, provided for in the agreement at the end of 18 months. He desired that these divisions be put together into a National Army. The Communist Party representative said that the PCC had agreed upon integration of the armies and not fusion. He explained that the Communist Party preferred to postpone integraton until the second stage of the plan. I stressed that it was not advisable to permit military integration to lag too far behind political unification and suggested that the possibility of beginning integration within 6 months be given consideration.

Later discussions indicated that the Communist Party wished to postpone integration of their armies until the beginning of the 13th month and that the Yenan authorities were opposed to an earlier integration of their armies and to fusion, rather than integration. I then proposed as a means of initial integration the formation, beginning with the 7th month, of army groups, each to consist of one National Government and one Communist army, with integration during the second stage to be achieved through the integration of divisions into armies and the dissolving of the army groups. It was felt that integration into army groups presented less difficulty in that the size of such groups and their separation on the ground made it more feasible in the initial stages. It was also felt that in this way concentration could be placed upon the training and equipment of the divisions to be retained.

In this connection, it was believed that Communist reluctance to agree to an early integration of their armies, inviting inevitable comparisons, arose largely from the lack of formal organization of their troops and that this reluctance might be overcome through an offer of assistance to provide elementary basic training and instruction in organization of 3 months to representatives of the ten divisions which they designated to be retained. Accordingly, with the approval of the National Government representative on the Military Sub-Committee, I communicated to General Chou En-lai an offer to provide such instruction by U.S. Army officers to selected personnel of the Communist forces prior to their integration. General Chou welcomed this offer and subsequently informed me of the enthusiastic acceptance by Chairman Mao Tze-tung of the program of integration in two stages as proposed by me and of the establishment of a transitional training school for Communist officers and men. General Chou explained that the delay in the Communist Party's acceptance of my proposal had been due to certain difficulties the Communists foresaw with respect to the preparation of the Communist forces for integration. In this connection, and of interest in the light of subsequent Yenan radio broadcasts calling for the withdrawal of American troops and the U.S. military advisory group from China, General Chou informed me at this time that the Communist Party desired that the training school to be established for the Communist forces continue in existence for two or three years and that the Communist Party would welcome training units assigned by the proposed U.S. military advisory group to Communist divisions.

XIV.
DIRECTIVE TO THE EXECUTIVE HEADQUARTERS IMPLEMENTING THE BASIS FOR MILITARY REORGANIZATION AND FOR THE INTEGRATION OF THE COMMUNIST FORCES INTO THE NATIONAL ARMY

Agreement was reached by the Military Sub-Committee on February 27, 1946, on a directive[21] to the Executive Headquarters implementing the Basic Plan for military reorganization and integration of the Communist armies into the National Army and the English and Chinese texts of the directive were signed on March 17 by General Chang Chih-chung, representing the National Government, General Chou En-lai, representing the Chinese Communist Party, and General A.C. Gillem, Jr., acting as my representative during my absence in the United States.

The salient points of the directive are as follows: The Executive Headquarters will be the agency for the execution of the Basic Plan and will establish a control group for planning and supervising in matters relating to the execution of the plan, the group to be composed of National Government, Communist Party and U.S. personnel. Executive Headquarters field teams will supervise on the ground the demobilization, deployment and integration of the National Government and Communist Party troops. Demobilization will require the gradual elimination of military commands on levels higher than Army headquarters. Complete disbandment of puppet units will be effected by D-Day plus 3 months. Military equip-

[21]See Volume Two, Appendix E, Document 7, for the full text.

ment and munitions in the hands of these units are to be turned over to the local Service Area, if established, or as directed by the Executive Headquarters. A 12 week's basic training program is to be established for the National Government and Communist Party divisions designated to be retained. A school of elementary instruction is also to be established, under the Interim Military Advisory Group of the U.S. Army, for the 10 Communist divisions designated for integration in the final 6 months of the plan and this school is to provide a series of basic courses of three months in organization, training procedure and administration. Planning for the schools is to be coordinated with the Executive Headquarters. Troop movements necessary for redeployment and integration will be ordered by the Executive Headquarters in accordance with the general directive of the Ministry of National Defense (or National Military Council); logistic requirements for demobilization, redeployment and integration will be coordinated with that Ministry (or National Military Council). The Executive Headquarters will prepare the detailed logistic and administrative plans for personnel to be demobilized.

In the discussions leading to the agreement upon this directive, attention was given particularly to the questions of the disposition of Japanese equipment and of the establishment of a Demobilized Manpower Commission. In the case of Japanese equipment it was agreed to enter in the minutes as a matter of record the understanding that the issue or employment of this equipment might be directed by the Executive Headquarters, if found necessary as a temporary measure, to units of the 60 divisions to be retained in the National Army, but that when this was done complete battalions would be so equipped. It was realized that the dearth of military equipment in China, in addition to the unlikelihood of Chinese agreement to any other procedure, would prevent the carrying out of measures for the destruction of Japanese military equipment.

It was revealed by National Government representatives in the Military Sub-Committee meetings that the Government had worked out a plan for the employment of deactivated military personnel. I felt it desirable to include in the directive a recommendation for the establishment of a Demobilized Manpower Commission, which should coordinate its efforts with those of the National Government, the Communist Party, civilian agencies, relief organizations and the Executive

Headquarters, and believed it advisable that the Commission begin functioning within two months, at the time when the flow of deactivated personnel might be expected to begin. I also thought it appropriate that the Executive Headquarters should be kept clear, in its planning related to this subject, from matters pertaining directly to government ministries or agencies. It was generally agreed that the Executive Headquarters would not be responsible for the execution of these matters and that the Military Sub-Committee would give further consideration to the question of a Demobilized Manpower Commission. Subsequent developments, which delayed the implementation of the Basic Plan for military reorganization, prevented final action on a draft proposal for the establishment of such a commission. Similar results were reached with regard to proposals for the establishment of service areas and the Peace Preservation Corps, drafts of which were prepared for eventual study.

Of considerable importance was the formation of the control group under the Executive Headquarters to effect actual implementation of the Basic Plan. It was my opinion that consideration should be given to proper integration with the methods and procedures of the various National Government and Communist Party organizations concerned so that matters decided upon would be in accordance with Chinese traditional procedure but would not lose their effectiveness thereby. There was the danger that in too hasty acceptance of American suggestions there might be lack of understanding and inappropriate procedures. Careful and proper integration and preparation were needed to prevent such conditions. The control group was, therefore, set up in Chungking on a combined basis and after thorough planning and preparing was removed to the Executive Headquarters at Peiping for actual implementation of the plan, liaison with the Executive Headquarters being maintained in the interim period.

Article IV, Section 1, of the agreement signed on February 25, 1946, for military reorganization and for the integration of the Communist forces into the National Army required the National Government to prepare and submit to the Military Sub-Committee, within 3 weeks of the promulgation of the agreement, a list of the 90 divisions to be retained and the order of demobilization of units during the first 2 months. The agreement similarly provided for the preparation and submission to the Committee by the Communist Party, within 3 weeks of the promulgation of the agreement, of a complete list of all its military units, together with a list of the 18 divisions to be retained and the order of demobilization of units during the first 2 months. It was further provided that within 6 weeks after the promulgation of this agreement both the National Government and the Communist Party should furnish to the Committee lists of the units to be demobilized. On March 26, 1946, General Chen Cheng, Chief of Staff of the Chinese Armed Forces, forwarded to the Military Sub-Committee a list of the 90 divisions to be retained by the National Government and the order of demobilization of units during the first 2 months. The Communist Party, however, refused to submit the required lists, maintaining that, because of the failure of the Kuomintang to implement the PCC resolutions agreed upon, they would not submit a list of their nominees to the State Council or the required lists of military units until the reaching of full and public agreement upon the implementation of the PCC resolutions. Under these circumstances, the carrying out of the military reorganization plan was necessarily postponed indefinitely.

XV.
APPLICATION OF THE CESSATION OF HOSTILITIES ORDER TO MANCHURIA; ENTRY OF EXECUTIVE HEADQUARTERS FIELD TEAMS INTO MANCHURIA

The Cessation of Hostilities Order issued on January 10 made no mention of any exemption of any part of China from its provisions, except in regard to the movement of troops. Those exceptions were contained in the Stipulations to the Cessation of Hostilities Order, which were agreed upon and made a matter of record in the minutes of the Committee of Three and which were made public in the press release of January 10 announcing the Order. They are as follows:

"1. Paragraph b*, Cessation of Hostilities Order, does not prejudice military move-

---

*Paragraph b, Cessation of Hostilities Order, reads: Except in certain specific cases, all movements of forces in China will cease. There also may be the movements necessary for demobilization, redisposition, supply, administration and local security.

ments south of the Yangtze River for the continued execution of the plan of military reorganization of the National Government.

"2. Paragraph b, Cessation of Hostilities Order, does not prejudice military movements of forces of the National Army into or within Manchuria which are for the purpose of restoring Chinese sovereignty."

In discussions with me and in meetings of the Committee of Three, General Chou En-lai, Communist Party representative on the Committee, clearly recognized the right of the National Government to move troops into Manchuria for the purpose of restoring Chinese sovereignty. He also indicated his understanding that such movements were consistent with the Sino-Soviet Treaty of August 1945 and that American assistance in transporting National Government troops to this area was in accordance with commitments made by the U.S. Government to the Government of the Republic of China. There was no indication, or implication, in the meetings of the Committee of Three that Manchuria was not included within the scope of the Cessation of Hostilities Order.

At a press conference held on January 18 by the three Commissioners of the Executive Headquarters at Peiping, however, the Commissioners, in reply to questions from newspaper correspondents, stated that the Executive Headquarters had no jurisdiction in Manchuria. It was generally recognized that it would be preferable not to send field teams to points in Manchuria then occupied by Soviet troops, but I felt very strongly that the authority of the Executive Headquarters in Manchuria must be asserted in order to avoid possible future clashes and difficulties between the two opposing Chinese forces as the Soviet troops should withdraw from Manchuria. The matter was complicated, of course, by the continued delay in the withdrawal of Soviet troops, resulting in increased suspicion on the part of the National Government of Soviet intentions and aims in Manchuria and in the consequent inability of the National Government to assume control in that area.

With these circumstances in mind and as a result of reports of serious conflict in the vicinity of Yingkou, a port in south Manchuria, I addressed similar memoranda[22] on Janu-

---

[22]See Volume Two, Appendix F, Document 1, for the full text.

ary 24, 1946, to the two Chinese representatives on the Committee of Three, proposing that the Committee direct the Executive Headquarters to despatch a field team immediately to Yingkou. I also proposed that, in the event of future action of this kind in Manchuria under the terms of the Cessation of Hostilities Order, directives be issued by the Committee of Three to the Executive Headquarters for action in each case. General Chang Chun, National Government representative on the Committee, informed my Headquarters on January 28 that Generalissimo Chiang Kai-shek did not wish to send a team to Yingkou for fear of possible complications arising with the Soviet authorities because of the presence of an American on the team. The Communist Party, however, approved the proposal to send an Executive Headquarters team to Yingkou and on February 14 General Chou En-lai again raised the question, as a result of further reports of conflict in the Yingkou area.

Some indication of possible Soviet attitude in regard to the activities of the Executive Headquarters field teams in areas under Soviet control had been seen in the case of the situation at Chihfeng, Jehol Province. The crew of a U.S. Army plane, which had been sent to Chihfeng shortly after the establishment of the Executive Headquarters at Peiping for the purpose of reconnaissance of the airfield prior to the intended despatch of a team, had misinterpreted its orders and had landed at the field. The crew and plane were immediately detained by the Soviet garrison at Chihfeng. When, however, the mission of the plane had been explained in leaflets dropped at Chihfeng the following day by another Executive Headquarters plane, and apparently following the receipt of instructions from the ranking Soviet authorities in Manchuria, the crew and plane were released and the Executive Headquarters team proceeded to Chihfeng, where it functioned without hindrance from the Soviet forces there.

The Generalissimo gave as the reason for his opposition to the sending of field teams to Manchuria the possibility of a Soviet demand for participation in the work of the field teams. Subsequently I came to the conclusion that one reason for his refusal to approve such action lay in his desire to avoid recognition of the Communist Party forces in Manchuria. Also it appeared to me that his commander in that region desired to avoid any interference by Executive Headquarters teams directed toward halting the sporadic fighting then in progress. Evidences of the reluctance to acknowledge the presence of

Communist troops in Manchuria were seen later in editorial comment and placards appearing in Manchurian cities occupied by the National Government. These editorials and placards referred to the Communist forces as "bandits" and consistently withheld any recognition of the existence of the Chinese Communist forces as such with whom the National Government might have to deal under the terms of agreements reached at Chungking.

The Communist Party representative on the Committee of Three, perhaps partially for the converse reason, continued to urge the sending of Executive Headquarters teams to Manchuria. On February 18, General Chou En-lai informed me that the Communist Party was desirous of sending teams into Manchuria to settle questions at issue in order to facilitate the taking over of sovereignty by the National Government. General Chou pointed out that as the reorganization of the armies included both National Government and Communist Party troops he did not believe that the Soviet Union would object to the entry of Executive Headquarters teams into Manchuria. It was my opinion that General Chou's continued insistence on the sending of a team to Yingkou lay partially in his desire to have aid in handling some of his own military commanders. On February 20, I again, but without success, raised the question of sending Executive Headquarters teams into Manchuria with General Chang Chih-chung, National Government representative on the Military Sub-Committee, pointing out the need of such teams both in stopping possible conflicts and in establishing a basis for the demobilization of the armies under the plan for military reorganization and integration. On February 21, upon his return from a visit to Yenan, General Chou informed me that he had discussed the question of Manchuria with Chairman Mao Tze-tung and that they had reached the following conclusions: (1) The Committee of Three should visit Manchuria; (2) the Cessation of Hostilities Order was applicable to Manchuria; and (3) the military reorganization plan included Manchuria. On February 25, in further discussion of this subject with me, General Chou reiterated that the Cessation of Hostilities Order and the military reorganization plan both provided for jurisdiction by appropriate agencies in Manchuria and said that he had communicated his views in this regard to General Chang Chih-chung. The latter, said General Chou, was attentive but noncommital. General Chou stressed that it was important to establish a policy on Manchuria now in order to avoid later misunderstanding. I agreed with this view and pointed out that it was important to reach a peaceful solution rather than create additional trouble. On February 27, prior to the departure of the Committee of Three on an inspection tour to Peiping and other points in north China, the subject of Manchuria was again discussed in the light of the replies to be given to possible inquiries by correspondents or other persons. Both General Chou and I agreed that we should say that the basic agreements applied to Manchuria and that, with regard to questions on the cease fire agreement as it related to Manchuria, we should merely say that the matter was being considered. In this discussion, the National Government representative volunteered no opinion.

During the trip of the Committee of Three, at the time of our visit to Yenan on March 4, I had occasion during a talk with Chairman Mao Tze-tung to bring up the question of Manchuria. Mr. Mao stated that he hoped the Cessation of Hostilities Order would apply to Manchuria and that Executive Headquarters teams would be sent there. During this period, and in spite of a deterioration in the situation in Manchuria, the National Government remained adamant on the question of sending teams into Manchuria. In view of my plans for a brief trip to the United States in connection with certain matters related to my mission and of the obvious urgent need for sending teams into Manchuria at the earliest possible date, I felt it necessary to obtain action on the question of sending teams into Manchuria prior to my departure and again approached the Generalissimo on the subject. I finally obtained his approval in principle for such action, but limited by a series of stipulations which I drafted into a proposed directive for such teams. This was presented to the Chinese members of the Committee of Three for consideration.

On March 11, the Committee of Three discussed this draft, without, however, reaching an agreement. This draft reads as follows:

> "Draft of Instructions for Executive Headquarters Regarding the Entry of Field Teams into Manchuria:

> "Field Teams, with carefully selected personnel, will be sent into Manchuria immediately under the following conditions:

> "1. The mission of the teams will pertain solely to military matters.

"2. The teams should accompany Government troops, keeping clear of places still under Russian occupation.

"3. Teams should proceed to points of conflict or close contact between the Government and Communist troops to bring about a cessation of fighting and to make the necessary readjustments in order to avoid future trouble. They should visit Communist commanders and headquarters.

"4. The Government troops are authorized to reestablish the sovereignty of China in Manchuria. Specifically, they are to exercise exclusive control of a strip 30 kilometers to either side of the two railroads mentioned in the Sino-Soviet Treaty.

"5. Communist troops will be required to evacuate such places as are necessary for the occupation by Government troops in reestablishing the sovereignty, including coal mines. Communist troops will not be permitted to move in and occupy places evacuated by Russian troops."

In discussion of the draft, General Chou En-lai referred to paragraph No. 1 and asked that political matters be dealt with at the same time by the Committee of Three, which should issue instructions to Executive Headquarters teams on political matters in Manchuria. He pointed out that there was no question regarding sovereignty in Manchuria, as the Cessation of Hostilities Order provided for entry of National Government troops into Manchuria to restore sovereignty and the Basic Plan for military reorganization provided for overwhelming National Government military superiority in numbers. He explained that the Communist Party, however, in making concessions on these points had looked to the establishment of democratic institutions in Manchuria as well as in other parts of China and that it desired the reorganization of the Northeast Political Council and the establishment of local self-government. He feared that if these political and military questions were not settled simultaneously trouble would result from the administrative confusion arising from the various political systems in different areas. General Chou further stated that the National Government did not at that time have sufficient troops to take over all places in Manchuria and that he felt that the number of Government troops to be sent to Manchuria and the places they would take over should be determined according to a fixed plan and schedule. He pointed out that the military reorganization plan was to become effective in two weeks, under which garrison points for armies would be established, and suggested that the taking over of sovereignty by the National Government and the reorganization of the armies, therefore, be coordinated. General Chou said that this draft directive was only an interim measure and that the important thing was to stop fighting. He felt, therefore, that the Committee of Three should go to Manchuria, where he could explain the situation on the spot to Communist field commanders.

General Chang Chih-chung expressed doubt that the Committee of Three had authority to discuss political matters in Manchuria and added that it would be preferable to send teams to Manchuria to clarify the situation and political problems could thus be easily solved. He pointed out that the Cessation of Hostilities Order applied to all China and pertained to military and not political matters and that General Chou would have other opportunities to discuss political matters, the subject now under consideration being that of the cessation of conflict in Manchuria.

General Chou En-lai, in turn, pointed out that the situation in Manchuria differed from that in other parts of China as, while troop movements were frozen elsewhere, troops were on the move in Manchuria and that political settlements could not, therefore, be delayed. General Chou continued that there was no question of the Government's taking over sovereignty in places then being evacuated by Soviet troops and of the Government's taking over the two railway lines named in the Sino-Soviet Treaty, but pointed out that the draft directive contained an all inclusive clause, providing for the taking over by the National Government of such places as are necessary for restoring sovereignty in Manchuria, which might cause trouble and misunderstanding should National Government troops move into Communist-held areas.

The discussions above-described are reported in some detail as they serve to highlight the opposing views of the two Chinese sides on the vital question of Manchuria. It was apparent from the discussion that General Chou En-lai expected difficulty in obtaining compliance by his military commanders in Manchuria with his instructions or with the decisions reached by the Committee of Three unless he was able to discuss the matter with them on the spot. He was obviously concerned over the possibility of the movement of National Government troops into areas then held by the Communists or into areas into which he thought the Communist troops would move as the Soviet forces withdrew. He was also concerned over the question of the local governments which the Communist Party was establishing in its areas of occupation. General Chang Chih-chung reflected the determination of the National Government to restore Chinese sovereignty in Manchuria through the movement of its own troops and was not willing to restrict in any way the right of the National Government, as provided for in the Cessation of Hostilities Order, to move troops to any point in Manchuria for the restoration of Chinese sovereignty. Each Chinese representative was willing to concur in the first three paragraphs of the draft proposal and each recognized the desirability of sending teams into Manchuria, but was unwilling to yield on the points at issue. The National Government refusal, since January 24, to approve the sending of Executive Headquarters teams into Manchuria was in my opinion a grave error on its part, permitting the situation subsequently to develop to a point practically beyond control. The Communist Party's position in Manchuria was becoming steadily stronger as its forces withdrew to the north and, as subsequently developed, within reach of Japanese arms and equipment, while the long lines of communication of the National Government left the latter in a dangerously over-extended position as National Government troops advanced in the wake of the Soviet withdrawal. The Government forces were not able to advance with sufficient rapidity to prevent Chinese Communist occupation of places from which the Soviets were withdrawing, and the Soviet officials were not helpful in allotting rolling stock on the railroad— quite the contrary.

This meeting of the Committee of Three on March 11 was the last meeting which I attended prior to my departure on the same evening for the United States, and at the time of my departure I thought that an understanding for a compromise agreement on a directive for the entry of teams into Manchuria had been reached. During my absence in the United States I appointed, with the approval of the National Government and the Communist Party, Lieutenant General A.C. Gillem, Jr., U.S.A., to serve as my representative on the Committee of Three.

On March 13, at the next meeting of the Committee of Three, General Chou stated that he had not yet received a reply from Yenan in response to his request for further instructions and suggested, in view of the slowness of his communications with Yenan and Manchuria, one of two alternative plans: (1) that the Committee of Three proceed to Mukden, from which the Soviet troops had withdrawn, a procedure which would enable him to explain the situation to Communist commanders in Manchuria and thus avoid future trouble and which would enable the Committee to work out a final directive on the ground there or (2) that the Committee await his receipt of further instructions from Yenan. In the general discussion which followed this statement, both Chinese representatives suggested the advisability of sending teams to Manchuria to gather data on which a directive could be based by the Committee, but General Gillem insisted that the teams should have guiding principles in a directive before proceeding to Manchuria, as otherwise there would be no basis for their operations. General Chang Chih-chung said that, since the Communists had agreed to exclusive National Government control of the railways and of the places evacuated by the Soviet troops and as the National Government did not have sufficient troops to take over every locality in Manchuria, there should be no cause for dispute. In an effort to break the deadlock General Gillem suggested the revision of the original draft to permit National Government occupation of the railways and a 30 kilometer strip on either side thereof, with a prohibition against Communist occupation of places evacuated by Soviet troops, but with the omission of the all-inclusive clause permitting Government troops to take over such places as are necessary to restore sovereignty. General Chang objected to this revision, saying it would restrict the Government's right to restore sovereignty to the railways and places occupied by the Soviet Union. General Gillem then suggested the retention of only the first three paragraphs of the draft as the directive to the teams and the early departure of the Committee to Manchuria after the arrival of the field teams. General Chang also objected to this procedure on the grounds that as the Soviet troops withdrew both Chinese armies would move in and hostilities would eventually occur. (In the light of subsequent developments and of the directive finally approved, which consisted substantially of the first three paragraphs of the draft, this proved to be an evident error in tactics on the part of the National Government and one which had serious consequences in that it delayed the departure of the teams for two weeks.) General Chang continued that the National Government would make no concessions which would restrict the places where it could restore sovereignty, as this was provided for in the Cessation of Hostilities Order, and that the directive to be issued must contain this principle.

At a meeting of the Committee of Three on March 17, it was stated that near agreement on a seven point draft directive had been reached between the two Chinese members in private discussions on March 15, but that the National Government had subsequently refused its approval of this compromise agreement because (1) of the use of the word "now" in a clause giving the Government the right to move troops into localities "now" being evacuated by Soviet troops and (2) of the desire of the Communist Party to arrange through discussion for the movement of Government troops into areas at that time occupied by Communist forces. General Chang pointed out that the first restriction would prevent Government troop movements into areas subsequently evacuated by Soviet forces and that the Government preferred to arrange through the field teams, rather than by discussion with the Communists, for movement of its troops into areas held by the Communists. General Chou emphasized that the directive was an interim measure designed to effect the entry of the teams into Manchuria and was not intended to provide an over-all solution to all problems in Manchuria.

On March 18 another meeting of the Committee of Three was held which indicated that an agreement between the two sides hinged on the retention or deletion of the word "now," as described in the preceding paragraph. General Chou pointed out that he had already exceeded the scope of his authority for negotiating and that he must await further instructions from Yenan. He urged that the first three paragraphs of the compromise draft proposal be used as a directive and that discussions continue after the despatch of the teams.

Some bitterness was displayed by General Chou at this point as he spoke of the failure of the Government to submit to the Executive Headquarters daily reports of its troop movements, as was required in the Cessation of Hostilities Order. (The repeated failure to submit these reports was a fact.) He also referred to the situation in the Canton area, where the National Government commanding general still refused to recognize the application of the Cessation of Hostilities Order, and to the situation in the Hankow area, where Communist troops were surrounded by Government troops and were allegedly having difficulty in obtaining food supplies. He revealed that he had been criticized in Yenan for his inability to obtain appropriate settlement of these questions, while at the same time he had made concessions on questions related to north China and Manchuria.

The problem in the Canton area involved the presence of a Communist force of from 2500 to 3000 men, called by the Communist Party the Anti-Japanese East River Column. An Executive Headquarters team, sent to Canton to investigate the situation in that area as it related to these troops, was informed by the National Government Commanding General at Canton that there were no Communist forces in that area, only bandits, and that the authority of Executive Headquarters did not extend south of the Yangtze River. The field team was unable to make contact with the Communist forces. During subsequent months, General Chou continued to press for the recognition of these Communist troops, but the National Government Commander at Canton remained adamant in his refusal to recognize the Communist forces in this area, in spite of repeated assurances from the Government representative on the Committee of Three that orders had been issued to him to do so. The problem was finally solved, after long and involved negotiations and discussion, by the transportation of these Communist forces on board U.S. Navy LSTs from Kwangtung to Chefoo, a port in Shantung Province, held by the Communists.

The problem in the Hankow area involved the presence of about 60,000 Communist troops in the north Hupeh-south Honan area, where they were surrounded by National Government forces. In the discussions prior to the signing of the Cessation of Hostilities Order, General Chou had unsuccessfully endeavored to obtain agreement for the movement of these forces out of this area, either to the northwest or east to the Anhui-north Kiangsu area. The problem of food for these troops, he said, made such movement necessary. He was given repeated assurances by the National Government that provision would be made to enable these troops to obtain food supplies and in a local agreement arrangement by the field team at Hankow a procedure was established to enable the Communists in this area to purchase food. In subsequent months, this question again rose on several occasions and the National Government repeated its assurance of assistance in solving the food problem for these troops. However, these promises were apparently never fulfilled. In May, as a result of charges by General Chou that the Government was preparing an offensive against these encircled Communist troops with a view to their elimination, General Chou, accompanied by a National Government and a U.S. representative, made a special tour of investigation of this area and the food problem was again discussed. In July, however, the National Government, claiming offensive action on the part of the Communists endeavoring to break out from the encirclement, did undertake an offensive against the Communist forces north of Hankow and the latter, breaking through the encirclement, fled to the northwest.

These two problems and the continued failure of General Chou to achieve any solution thereof, it is believed, subjected him to severe criticism at Yenan and eventually served to handicap him in his negotiations as a member of the Committee of Three. It was at this stage of the negotiations regarding the entry of field teams into Manchuria that General Chou was being criticized because of the Canton and Hankow situations and that he returned to Yenan for further instructions. It was feared that he might indefinitely delay his return to Chungking for a renewal of the discussions. With this possibility in view, Colonel J. Hart Caughey, member of my staff at Chungking, flew to Yenan to discuss with General Chou possible compromises in the directive for the entry of field teams into Manchuria and his return to Chungking for the resumption of the discussions by the Committee of Three. General Chou returned only after it was ascertained by radio that agreement on a directive was virtually assured.

Shortly after General Chou's return from Yenan, a compromise agreement was reached in the Committee of Three on March 27 for the issuance of a directive[23] which was substantially identical with the first three paragraphs of the draft proposed prior to my departure for the United States. An understanding was recorded in the minutes of the meetings of the Committee that the Committee would further discuss military matters and that separate discussions regarding political matters would be held. This agreement was signed by the members of the Committee and released to the press on March 27.

[23]See Volume Two, Appendix F, Document 2, for the full text.

In the meeting of the Committee of Three on March 27, General Chou said that General Chang Chun in past meetings of the Committee had stated that the number of Government troops to be sent into Manchuria would not be large and that the U.S. representative on the Committee had explained that the United States was committed to move five Government armies into Manchuria.* General Chou said that this figure had now been reached and that this was also the figure called for in the military reorganization plan. He voiced his fear of the danger of further hostilities should additional government troops be sent into the Northeast, and pointed out that the National Government should inform the Executive Headquarters, in accordance with the Cessation of Hostilities Order, of the number of National Government troops moved into Manchuria. General Chou then presented a formal proposal that the Government not move additional troops into Manchuria, that the Executive Headquarters be instructed to send field teams to Mukden to establish contact with both Chinese sides and that the Committee of Three proceed to Mukden shortly thereafter.

General Chang Chih-chung, carefully choosing his words, replied that, according to the military reorganization plan, the National Government would have five armies in the Northeast and that the Government had no intention of exceeding that number after reorganization. He added that furthermore Government troop movements would be reported to the Executive Headquarters and would not be secret. General Chang also pointed out that the Communist Party had effected troop movements into the Northeast from the Shantung Peninsula to Dairen and overland from Shansi and that, while the National Government reported its troop movements, the Communist forces were moving secretly into the Northeast. General Chou denied that such Communist troop movements had occurred after the signing of the Cessation of Hostilities Order but admitted that some individual officers might have proceeded to Manchuria.

This exchange on the subject of the number of National Government troops in Manchuria is of importance, as the

*This statement was incorrect, as the U.S. Government was committed to the movement by U.S. transport facilities of 7 Government armies into Manchuria, a commitment of which I had informed General Chou.

Communist Party subsequently stated in its propaganda that the National Government had, with United States aid in providing transportation, exceeded the number of troops which they had agreed should be stationed in Manchuria. This statement had no basis, since the limitation on the number of Government troops in the Northeast, as stated in the military reorganization plan, was to be effective at the end of 12 months, at which time the Government armies were to be reorganized into five armies of three divisions each. If the Communist Party claims were valid, its forces would have been limited to one army of three divisions, as provided for in the military reorganization plan at the end of the first 12 months' period. The Communist Party was claiming, however, at this time that its forces in Manchuria, together with the forces under Communist leadership, totalled 300,000 men. Although the National Government publicity organs from time to time attacked the Communist Party for the movement of its forces into Manchuria, this was never made a point of formal issue by the Government, presumably because to have done so would have been equivalent to the recognition of the application of the Cessation of Hostilities Order to Manchuria and of the existence of Communist forces in that area. The National Government had studiously avoided any expression of its recognition of these two points.

Following the discussion of limitation of armies in Manchuria, without any real change in the position of the two Chinese members of the Committee, General Gillem proposed, and it was agreed, that a telegram be sent to the Executive Headquarters directing teams to proceed immediately to Mukden and thence to critical areas after a preliminary survey in Mukden to enable the teams to determine the relative priority of need for team investigation. It was also proposed and agreed that the Executive Headquarters be informed of the impending visit of the Committee of Three to Mukden in order to assist in determining critical areas and in making such readjustment of the field teams as the Committee would deem necessary.

Thus, after a fatally prolonged and unnecessary delay, it finally became possible for the Executive Headquarters to extend its jurisdiction to Manchuria. The extended delay in the sending of teams to this area, caused first by the National Government's refusal to give its approval for such action and later by the inability of the two Chinese representatives to agree on a suitable directive for the teams, had already resulted in a serious situation. The directive under which the teams were sent provided an insufficient operating basis but by this time it was imperative that some groundwork for Executive Headquarters functions in Manchuria be laid, even though the directive was an incomplete and inadequate document.

XVI.
BACKGROUND OF THE FAILURE TO IMPLEMENT THE RESOLUTIONS OF THE POLITICAL CONSULTATION CONFERENCE

The immediate reaction of the Chinese public to the announcement of the PCC resolutions was one of enthusiastic approval, tempered by the realization that the implementation of the resolutions would be the acid test by which the sincerity of the two rival parties could be gauged. The indication of strong resentment against the PCC on the part of the dominant CC clique within the Kuomintang and the opposition by the powerful group of Whampoa generals in the National Government army to any reorganization of the armies which would threaten their position were seen as obstacles, on the Kuomintang side, to successful implementation of the resolutions. Disquieting incidents, such as the attack by alleged Kuomintang plain-clothes men on a mass meeting held at Chungking to celebrate the success of the PCC, police interference with minority party delegates to the PCC and the attack on the Communist Party newspaper premises at Chungking, all served to strengthen the fears of opposition to the PCC by irreconcilable elements in the Kuomintang.

With the conclusion of the PCC sessions, the chief problem was that of the reorganization of the armies and the integration of the Communist Party armed forces into a national army. Discussions in the Military Sub-Committee, which were begun shortly after the adjournment of the PCC, resulted in an agreement on these matters and the "Basis for Military Reorganization and for the Integration of the Communist Forces into the National Army" was signed at Chungking on February 25. The conclusion of this agreement marked the third major step in bringing peace to China and in establishing a basis for unification of the country. The Cessation of Hostilities Order was designed to bring to a halt actual fighting in order that negotiations for a political and military settlement could be carried on in an atmosphere of peace. The PCC resolutions provided an agreement on the vital questions of governmental reorganization and the establishment of a constitutional government. The Basis for Military Reorganization similarly provided an agreement on the vital question of integration of the Communist Party's armed forces into the National Army and the reorganization of all armies in China on a democratic base.

The next step was that of obtaining legal action by the National Government to approve the PCC resolutions. This procedure necessitated approval by the Central Executive Committee (hereafter called the CEC) of the Kuomintang, which met at Chungking from March 1 to 17 for the purpose of reviewing and passing upon the PCC resolutions. Simultaneously with the CEC sessions, there were also held at Chungking meetings of the PCC Steering Committee and the PCC Constitutional Reviewing Committee, in which discussions were held of points which the CEC reportedly wished to have revised. Although the CEC announced at the end of its sessions that it had approved the PCC resolutions *in toto,* there were indications that approval had been hedged by reservations and that irreconcilable elements within the Kuomintang were endeavoring to sabotage the PCC program. Their efforts were reportedly directed toward revision of the principles approved by the PCC as the basis for revising the Draft Constitution and toward obtaining close adherence to the May 1936 Draft Constitution, on which the Kuomintang had originally insisted in the PCC sessions.

On March 20, shortly after the conclusion of the CEC session, the PCC Steering Committee, presided over by Dr. Sun Fo, President of the Legislative Yuan, and including as its Kuomintang members Dr. Wang Shih-chieh, Minister for Foreign Affairs, and General Wu Tieh-chen, Secretary-General of the Kuomintang, was reliably said to have reached an agreement on three points as follows:

> (1) That the draft constitution now in preparation by the PCC Constitutional Reviewing Committee in accordance with the principles set forth in the PCC agreement on the constitution will be definitive and the only document presented to the National Assembly for acceptance;

(2) That all parties are under moral obligation to have their delegates to the National Assembly support the draft constitution as presented; and

(3) That the CEC of the Kuomintang will nominate only the Kuomintang members of the State Council, other members to be nominated by their respective parties and non-party members by Generalissimo Chiang Kai-shek.

Dr. Sun Fo was said to have stated that the Kuomintang members of the Steering Committee had been authorized by Generalissimo Chiang Kai-shek clearly to establish these points. It was expected that a statement then being drafted, in which these points were embodied, would be released shortly by the press. Subsequent meetings of the Steering Committee, however, indicated that the Kuomintang members of the Committee were unable to give authorization for the publication of a statement expressing unequivocal Kuomintang concurrence with these three points. It appeared that, under pressure from right-wing elements of the Kuomintang, that Party's representatives on the Steering Committee were seeking revision of the constitutional principles approved by the PCC in order to (1) change the system of executive branch responsibility to a popularly elected legislative body to a system under which the supreme authority would be vested in a president without provision for checks and balances, such as exist in the United States Government, (2) create a national assembly to meet at two to three year intervals, which would have nominal powers of election, recall, initiative and referendum and (3) limit drastically provincial autonomy.

During this period the Communist Party and Democratic League representatives maintained the general position that the PCC resolutions had been agreed upon by duly authorized representatives of all parties and indicated that they would oppose any major changes which would tend to result in continuation of one-party rule or the creation of an "authoritarian" state. The Communist Party and Democratic League, therefore, refused to nominate members to the State Council for participation in a reorganized government until the Kuomintang should publish a statement of any revisions of the PCC resolutions agreed upon and of a definite commitment by the Kuomintang to implement the PCC program as revised.

In the meantime, the Communist Party postponed its Central Committee meeting, originally scheduled for March 31 for the purpose of passing upon the PCC resolutions, and refused to submit a complete list of its military units, including a list of the 18 divisions to be retained and the order of demobilization during the first two months, although provisions had been made for the submission of such lists within three weeks of the promulgation of the agreement for military reorganization.* The PCC Constitutional Reviewing Committee was compelled, under these circumstances, to suspend its work upon preparation of a revised constitution to submit to the National Assembly, scheduled to meet on May 5.

Coincidental with this impasse in the discussions of the PCC resolutions and closely related thereto was the situation then developing in Manchuria. The Chinese Communist Party was there steadily extending the area of its control,** both in areas from which the Soviet forces were withdrawing (apparently with at least tacit Soviet approval) and in the hinterland between the lines of communications where there were no forces of occupation. The movement of National Government troops into and within Manchuria for the purpose of restoring Chinese sovereignty had been provided for in the Cessation of Hostilities Order, but the continued advance of National Government forces in Manchuria had been seriously blocked by the delay in the withdrawal of the Soviet occupation armies. Further delay and increased distrust between the National Government and the Communists had resulted from the ruthless manner employed by General Tu Li-ming, Commander of the National Government's Northeast Peace Preservation Corps,*** in seeking to establish National Government military control in the countryside areas removed from the main

*Article IV, Section 1, of the Basis for Military Reorganization and for the Integration of the Communist Forces into the National Army, signed on February 25, 1946, provided for the submission of such lists within 3 weeks of the promulgation of the agreement. The National Government had submitted to the Military Sub-Committee such a list on March 26.

**The Communist forces were apparently reenforced by the movement of hastily organized or reenforced units from Chahar and Jehol provinces. While these movements started in August and September 1945, there was evidence of the unauthorized continuation of the movement after January 10, 1946.

***The National Government armies in Manchuria were organized under the title of the Northeast Peace Preservation Corps.

lines of communication, there being no teams from Executive Headquarters to moderate or regulate the procedure where National and Communist forces were in contact. These tactics had brought him in violent conflict with Chinese Communist forces in the hinterland and had aroused Communist suspicion that his chief aim was to eliminate their forces rather than to restore Chinese sovereignty in Manchuria. When the Soviet forces did withdraw toward the north, the National Government found itself with extended lines of communications, limited railroad stock, and insufficient forces to move into areas evacuated by the Soviet armies in time to prevent Chinese Communist occupation of such territory.

This situation made a solution of the impasse in the discussion of the PCC resolutions immeasurably more difficult, as it created considerable misgivings among Chinese with regard to the relationship of the Chinese Communists vis-a-vis Soviet Russia and strengthened the position of irreconcilable elements within the Kuomintang, who would have been opposed to the PCC agreements under any circumstances. The situation in Manchuria, however, presented them with a plausible excuse for resisting any limitation of Kuomintang governmental authority under such circumstances.

In spite of the deterioration in the general situation, agreement was reached in the PCC Steering Committee on April 1 in regard to the National Assembly. By this agreement, the National Assembly to be established under the constitutional government would be an actual organ of the government meeting once in six years or as necessary to perform the following functions: election and recall of the president, initiation of amendments to the constitution and passing upon constitutional amendments initiated by the legislative body of the government. The National Assembly thus created was believed to have resulted from a compromise measure intended to satisfy the Kuomintang's desire for the inclusion of Dr. Sun Yat-sen's "four powers" of election, recall, initiative and referendum in the formal governmental structure. Following this agreement, subsequent meetings of the PCC Steering Committee ended in a virtual stalemate and with the worsening of the situation in Manchuria it became apparent that no real settlement of government and constitutional questions in China could be reached as long as the Manchurian problem remained unsolved.

During early April press recriminations regarding Manchuria were intensified by both sides and Generalissimo Chiang Kai-shek was reported to have stated in an address to the People's Political Council on April 1 that there would be no discussion of political problems in Mancuria until National Government sovereignty had been reestablished in that area. The Yenan press on April 7 published a vitriolic personal attack on Generalissimo Chiang, accusing him of fostering civil war in Manchuria for selfish reasons. The Government press replied with equal bitterness, openly charging the existence of a Chinese Communist Party-Soviet link in Manchuria. These developments made more difficult, and more remote the likelihood of, any implementation of the PCC resolutions, although each side continued to announce publicly its firm adherence to the decisions of the PCC and its willingness to carry out such decisions.

Of vital importance in any consideration of the problem of the PCC resolutions is the position of Generalissimo Chiang Kai-shek. Public statements issued by him regarding the PCC program have shown him to favor its implementation. The Generalissimo, however, has a dual position as a national leader and a party leader, and the question thus arises whether as party leader he has sufficient authority to override strong right-wing opposition in the Koumintang to the PCC resolutions. There seems to be no doubt that the only opposition to the implementation of the PCC resolutions has come from important and powerful figures in the Kuomintang. The Communist Party, however, and the Democratic League to a lesser extent, has maintained that the Generalissimo himself has been behind the movement for the adoption of an "authoritarian" constitution and that he wishes to establish the facade of a coalition government in order to impress American public opinion and thereby pave the way for U.S. financial and economic aid. In the absence of indications of any effective challenge to the Generalissimo's authority, it is believed that a satisfactory settlement of the Manchurian question would enable him, in spite of opposition within the Kuomintang, to effect the implementation of the PCC resolutions without further material revision.

XVII.
ORGANIZATION AND FUNCTIONS OF THE
EXECUTIVE HEADQUARTERS*

As described in a previous section of this report, the Executive Headquarters was established at Peiping, in accordance with an agreement signed by the Committee of Three at Chungking on January 10, 1946, as the agency for the implementation of the Cessation of Hostilities Order signed on the same day. The three Commissioners of the Executive Headquarters and their immediate staffs arrived at Peiping on January 13 and the Headquarters began its official functions on the following day. On January 18 the Executive Headquarters established its offices in the buildings of the Peiping Union Medical College, which was used as the official home of the Headquarters.

The functions of the Executive Headquarters were set forth in the document providing for its establishment as follows:

> "The Executive Headquarters will implement the agreed policies for the cessation of hostilities. The Headquarters will submit recommendations covering necessary additional subsidiary agreements to ensure more effective implementation of the cessation of hostilities orders; such recommendations to include measures for the disarmament of the Japanese forces, restoration of lines of communication and coordination of the movement of Japanese soldiers to the coast for repatriation. The formal instructions unanimously agreed upon by the three Commissioners will be issued in the name of the President of the Republic of China."

As provided for in the agreement signed at Chungking,

*The Chinese name of the Executive Headquarters was *Chun Shih T'iao Ch'u Chih Hsing Pu* or Military Adjustment Executive Headquarters. In view of the varied functions of the Headquarters and the cumbersome translation of the Chinese title, the English title used was simply "Executive Headquarters."

the Executive Headquarters was headed by three Commissioners; Lieutenant General Cheng Kai-min, representing the National Government, Lieutenant General Yeh Chien-ying, representing the Chinese Communist Party, and Mr. Walter S. Robertson, representing the United States and serving as Chairman. Decisions reached by the three Commissioners had to be unanimous, as stated in the agreement, and it was envisaged that matters on which they were unable to reach agreement would be referred to the Committee of Three for decision, a procedure which was ultimately followed.

Immediately under the three Commissioners and directly responsible to them was a Director of Operations. In accordance with the agreement for the establishment of the Executive Headquarters, in which it was stated that a U.S. Army officer would act as Director of the Operations Section (subsequently changed to the Operations Division), Brigadier General Henry A. Byroade, U.S.A., was named as the Director of Operations. The Division served as the implementing agency within the Executive Headquarters for the execution of the three Commissioners' decisions and directives. The functions of the Director of Operations were: to draw up plans and directives for the execution of the decisions reached by the three Commissioners and for the implementation of the Cessation of Hostilities Order and of other agreements reached by the Committee of Three which required action by the Executive Headquarters. The Director operated through the Combined Chiefs of Staff, on which the National Government, the Communist Party and the United States each had a representative, the last named serving as chairman. The functions of the Combined Chiefs of Staff were: to receive directives from the Director of Operations and agree upon secondary decisions necessary for the execution of such directives. The Combined Chiefs of Staff were expected to direct their respective staffs to make studies and prepare plans on any matters referred to their level and, after the receipt of these plans, to reconcile any differences therein. The agreed upon plan was then presented to the Director of Operations for its execution.

All orders and directives issued by the Executive Headquarters were signed by the three Commissioners and were issued in the name of the President of the Republic of China. Daily reports of the situation relating to the activities of the Headquarters, agreed upon by the three Commissioners, were forwarded by radio to Generalissimo Chiang Kai-shek, Chairman Mao Tze-tung and to me, these taking the form of reports by the three Commissioners to their respective chiefs.

In the initial stages of the operations of the Executive Headquarters, the following sections were established under the Operations Division: Plans and Operations Section, Logistics and Supply Section and Public Relations Section. The organization provided for parallel sections and combined functions of the three branches at each level in the Headquarters. Subsequently, additional sections were added and the designation "section" was changed to "group." As of August 30, 1946, the Executive Headquarters consisted of the following groups under the Operations Division: Conflict Control Group (originally a part of the Plans and Operations Section); Communication Group (originally Logistics and Supply Section); Army Reorganization Group; and Public Relations Group.[24] The United States branch of the Executive Headquarters[25] also included the Current Section, which had originally been a part of the Plans and Operations Section and which took over that part of the latter's functions related to intelligence and information.

The "housekeeping" tasks for the U.S. branch of the Executive Headquarters were performed by the Peiping Headquarters Group,[26] set up as a United States Army command in China with General Byroade as the Commanding General. Its mission was to provide logistical and administrative support for the U.S. branch of the Executive Headquarters.*

[24]See Volume Two, Appendix G, Document 1, for the organizational chart of the Executive Headquarters.

[25]See Volume Two, Appendix G, Document 2, for the organizational chart of the U.S. branch of the Executive Headquarters.

[26]See Volume Two, Appendix G, Document 3, for the organizational chart of the Peiping Headquarters Group and for the diagrammatical explanation of the relationship between that Group and the Executive Headquarters.

*The personnel of the U.S. branch, including the field teams, consisted almost entirely of U.S. Army commissioned and non-commissioned officers and enlisted men, supplemented by a few U.S. Marine officers and some U.S. and alien civilians, the latter being used for work not involving security considerations.

The Plans and Operations* Section's functions were: to receive and record information regarding the strength, location and movements of all troops (National Government, Communist Party and Japanese) and to present to the three Commissioners daily situation reports; to receive directives from the Director of Operations through the Combined Chiefs of Staff and, based upon these directives, to recommend necessary supplementary decisions, such decisions to be presented in the form of a plan to the Combined Chiefs of Staff; and to prepare directives to the field teams to ensure the carrying out of such plans.

The Logistics and Supply** Section's functions were: to receive and execute directives from the Director of Operations on all matters concerning supply, transportation and the condition and maintenance of the lines of communications; to plan and coordinate supply and transportation responsibility for the support of plans, directives and orders of the Executive Headquarters; to record conditions and make recommendations regarding the maintenance and repair of the lines of communications; to make recommendations for coordinating the disarming and repatriation of the Japanese;*** and to plan and recommend measures for the handling and disposition of Japanese military equipment and supplies.

The functions of the Public Relations Section were: to establish and maintain a public relations policy consistent with the objectives of the Executive Headquarters; to handle directly all matters pertaining to the press, radio and other public information agencies; and to assure a simultaneous and joint release policy of the parallel Public Relations Sections of the three branches of the Executive Headquarters.

Following the reaching of an agreement by the Military Sub-Committee on February 25 for the reorganization of the Chinese Armies and for the integration of the Communist forces into the National Army, an additional section was estab-

---

*The functions of the Plans and Operations Section were subsequently divided between the Conflict Control Group and the Current Section in the U.S. branch of the Executive Headquarters.

**The name of this section was subsequently changed to the Railway Control Section and later to the Communications Group, as its functions were enlarged.

***The subject of repatriation of the Japanese from China is dealt with in another section of this report.

lished in the Executive Headquarters called the Army Reorganization Group. This Group was first formed at Chungking and laid the groundwork for its functions prior to its actual incorporation into the Headquarters.

Of primary importance in the functioning of the Executive Headquarters was the problem of transportation of personnel and equipment from Peiping to the various points to which field teams were sent. In the absence of normal communications in China, the only possible means of transportation to the locations of practically all the field teams was by plane. The 332d Troop Carrier Squadron of the United States Army Air Force, China, was, therefore, based at Peiping to serve as the transportation agency for the movement of personnel and supplies between Peiping and the various field teams. This Squadron was assisted in the early stages of the organization of the Executive Headquarters by the United States Marine Air Force, which performed invaluable services in reconnaissance and in leaflet dropping missions for the purpose of ensuring the receipt by the various Chinese armed units of the order for the cessation of hostilities.

The key personnel in the functioning of the Executive Headquarters over widespread areas in China were the members of the field teams. Field teams were composed of one representative of each of the three branches of the Headquarters, one representing the National Government, one the Chinese Communist Party and one the United States. Each branch included in its field team membership communications and interpreting personnel. Travel in the field was chiefly by jeep, transported to the team location by plane, and this in turn necessitated repair personnel for the teams. No limitation was originally placed on the number of members on a team each branch might employ, but it was subsequently found advisable to limit to 12 the number of members each branch might have on a single team, including within that number such liaison personnel from local military units as might be appointed on the ground by the local military commanders, as provided for in the directives issued by the Executive Headquarters. This restriction was adopted because of the practice of the Communist Party in staffing its team lists with an unduly large number of persons, who, it was suspected, were being used for propaganda activities rather than as functioning members of the teams.

The functions of the field teams were: to receive and execute orders of the Executive Headquarters; to transmit orders of the Executive Headquarters to appropriate military commanders in the field; to determine whether the orders and directives were being carried out; if orders were not being carried out, to make recommendations to the forces concerned regarding the action necessary to carry out such orders and directives; and, when the team's recommendations were not adopted by the forces concerned, to fix the responsibility for failure to comply with the orders and report the facts to the Executive Headquarters.

At the outset, it was decided that the principle of unanimous vote, under which the Committee of Three and the three Commissioners of the Executive Headquarters operated, would also be applicable to the work of the various sections in the Headquarters and of the field teams. In the case of the field teams, this was specifically set forth in a "Letter of Authority for Field Teams" prepared and approved by the Combined Chiefs of Staff on January 18 and addressed to "All Unit Commanders of the National Government and Chinese Communist Forces." In this letter, it was stated *inter alia* that "any decision regarding the cease fire order jointly reached by this team may be transmitted in the names of these three members to the various commanders of the National Government and Communist forces for compliance."

Practical experience in the field subsequently revealed that the effectiveness of the field teams could be hampered and necessary investigations actually blocked in cases where one Chinese member of the team vetoed any proposal which might be disadvantageous to his side. With this situation in view, the U.S. branch of the Executive Headquarters proposed in a Commissioners meeting on March 31 a revision of this requirement of unanimity. It was proposed that, in case unanimous agreement could not be reached among team members for the movement of a team for the purpose of investigating reported violations of the Cessation of Hostilities Order, the U.S. team member as Chairman be permitted to make his decision and thus break the deadlock. It was pointed out that this right of decision would not include the results of the investigation or the action to be taken but would merely empower the U.S. team member to decide where the team should go for purposes of investigation. The National Government Commissioner approved this proposal, but the Communist Commissioner said that any action taken by the other than unanimous agreement involved the principle under which the Executive Headquarters operated and that decision

74

on such a change in operating procedure must be made by the higher authorities of the Government and the Communist Party. At the beginning of May, as the Executive Headquarters was being faced with increased instances of the blocking of team investigations by the refusal of the Communist Party team members to agree on the movement of the teams—this was particularly true in Jehol Province—the U.S. branch of the Executive Headquarters submitted a proposal to the three Commissioners providing for decision for investigation by a majority vote of the team members. The National Government Commissioner approved this proposal but the Communist Party Commissioner again refused to give assent to the suggested procedure, repeating the arguments previously advanced.

During the inspection tour of the Committee of Three in north China, it became evident that the role of unanimity required for decisions by the field teams was in some cases preventing even the submission of reports of the results of team investigations because of the refusal of one or the other of the Chinese team members to agree. The Committee of Three, therefore, agreed that in cases of this kind, where unanimous decision could not be reached by the field teams, the U.S. team member as Chairman would be authorized to submit his own report to the three Commissioners accompanied by his own recommendations for action. It was understood that the opinions of the dissenting Chinese team member could also be included in this report, if the latter so desired. In this way long delays were avoided in endless debate over the results of team investigations and the Executive Headquarters was thus enabled to obtain information of team activities which otherwise might in some cases have been delayed indefinitely. In cases of serious and prolonged disagreement among team members, the teams were frequently recalled from the field for the purpose of enabling the three Commissioners to hear at first hand the teams' reports and to resolve the differences which had prevented agreement.

Each Chinese side, in approaching problems at issue, both in the Executive Headquarters and in the field, was too often intent upon protracted debate designed to wring the last possible advantage to its cause from the argument, rather than being interested in broad principles and compromise in order to create a spirit conducive to the settlement of differences between the two sides. One side or the other would be willing to block all investigation of reported violations of the Cessation of Hostilities Order unless it received a *quid pro quo* from the rival party, even though there would be no relation between the incidents under discussion. Evidences of continued distrust between the two Chinese parties were frequently encountered, and sharp exchanges in meetings of the three Commissioners and at other levels in the Headquarters sometimes brought to light the bitterness of feeling between the two. Distrust on the Communist side was increased by the National Government's nomination as its Commissioner of General Cheng Kai-min, the second most powerful figure in General Tai Li's gestapo organization, and by the presence of other Tai Li adherents in positions of importance in the Executive Headquarters. The distrust was further heightened by incidents involving field teams. The Communists complained that their members on field teams were on several occasions arrested and beaten and that in some cases their representatives had been kidnapped and had not been heard of since their disappearance. In two cases the Communist forces fired on and killed National Government members of field teams and in another incident the U.S. member of a field team was wounded slightly by a Communist sniper's bullet. Each side apparently organized mass demonstrations in the areas under its control for the purpose of propagandizing the field teams. Such demonstrations sometimes grew out of hand and resulted in incidents leading to near attacks on members of the teams. Perhaps the most inexcusable of the mass demonstrations was that directed against the Communist branch of the Executive Headquarters by alleged refugees from Communist-held areas in Hopei Province, resulting in the storming of the Executive Headquarters itself by a mob of several hundred persons. National Government gendarmes and Peiping municipal police made no effort to stop this action although the participants in the demonstration had begun to assemble openly several hours prior to the incident. A similar incident in Communist territory involved a mob demonstration against the U.S. team member and the simultaneous and obviously planned withdrawal of the Communist guards customarily stationed for his protection at the entrance to his compound. While these incidents in themselves should not be magnified out of proportion, they were indicative of the bitterness between the two Chinese parties and show some of the difficulties under which the Executive Headquarters and its field teams functioned.

High praise can be given to the U.S. members of the field teams, who were often stationed in isolated places under primitive and difficult living conditions. The field teams were the key personnel in effecting the cessation of hostilities and it was they who supervised on the spot the carrying out of the directives issued by the Executive Headquarters. These directives, together with other tasks performed by the teams, dealt with various matters, such as: the investigation of reports of actual conflict; the determination of the position of the opposing forces at midnight on January 13, the time at which the Cessation of Hostilities Order became effective; the separation of opposing forces on the ground; reports of troop movements; the formulation of procedures under which troops in conflict could be separated and under which withdrawal from points of conflict would take place; safe passage for food and medical supplies into towns under seige; liaison with UNRRA and CNRRA representatives in effecting passage of their relief supplies; the discussion of local agreements or arrangements by which settlement could be reached of conflict between opposing forces; general supervision of reconstruction of railway lines and other communications facilities; establishment of liaison with commanders of local units within the areas of team authority; agreement upon procedures for reopening or operation of coal mines in connection with the resumption of rail traffic; repatriation of the Japanese; and demobilization and reorganization of the Chinese armies. These tasks were a part of the daily routine of the members of the field teams and covered vast areas, sometimes being performed under conditions of actual danger to the members of the teams from hostilities going on in areas under investigation. U.S. members of the teams were often under fire, travelled by jeep over near-impassable roads in performance of their duties and in many ways accomplished miracles in their efforts to bring about cooperation between the two Chinese sides.

Every effort was made to ensure the impartiality of the U.S. members of the field teams, as their usefulness would have ended if they were felt to be biased. There was inevitably feeling, from time to time, that some U.S. team members had shown partiality, the majority of such accusations coming from the Communist side. It was felt, however, that this arose chiefly through Communist Party press and radio propaganda directed against what the Communists described as U.S. aid to the Kuomintang, which, not always adhering too closely to the truth, naturally served to arouse bitter feeling among the lower echelons of the Communist forces against the United States. It was not believed that any U.S. member of a field team consciously or intentionally displayed partiality in dealing with problems handled by the teams, and that misunderstanding that arose was due chiefly to the above-described propanganda campaign and perhaps in some cases to honest and unintentional errors of judgement, which were inevitable under the circumstances and which may have been to the advantage of either side.

The immediate task of the Executive Headquarters at the time of its establishment was to despatch field teams as quickly as possible to areas of reported conflict between the National Government and the Communist forces inasmuch as the first and principal function of the Headquarters in the initial stages was to effect the cessation of hostilities. On January 17, the first field team arrived at Chihfeng, Jehol Province, and by the end of January teams had been sent to the following points: Chining, Suiyuan Province; Taiyuan, Shansi Province; Hsuchow, Kiangsu Province; Kalgan, Chahar Province; Tsinan, Shantung Province; Canton, Kwangtung Province; Hankow, Hupeh Province; Hsinhiang, Honan Province; and Chengte, Jehol Province. Six of the team locations were in National Government territory and four in Communist-held areas. It had been decided by the Executive Headquarters to station senior teams at important, centrally located points and to have secondary teams, under the general supervision of the senior teams, stationed at points nearby, thus enabling rapid action to ensure the desired investigations. Subsequently, with the organization of the Railway Control Section (later known as the Communications Group) in the Executive Headquarters, railway field teams were despatched to the major areas of railway repair, whose function was to assist in accelerating the task of railway reconstruction, the technical details of reconstruction and operation of the railway lines being the task of the Ministry of Communications representatives under the general supervision of the Executive Headquarters. Regular field teams were sometimes assigned railway matters and at times the railway teams were in turn given cease-fire authority in their areas. The Executive Headquarters also from time to time despatched special teams to the field for investigation and on a few occasions sent, with the approval of the three Commissioners, a single U.S. observer to designated points, such as Chefoo in Shantung Province and Tolun in Chahar Province, for purposes of investigation of alleged Communist troop movements. As of September 11, the total number of Executive Headquarters field teams was 36[27] and there had been established a wide network of communications facilities to link these outposts with the Executive Headquarters at Peiping.

With the reaching of an agreement by the Committee of Three on March 27 for the entry of field teams into Manchuria, the Executive Headquarters for the first time was enabled to despatch teams to the Northeast. Prior to this time field teams had been operating solely in north and central China, with the exception of one team located at Canton. The effectiveness of the teams sent to Manchuria was handicapped by the inadequacy of the directive under which they operated,* but they were able to achieve limited results and success. With the withdrawal of the Soviet troops from Manchuria at the end of April and the subsequent northward advance of the National Government forces to Changchun, an advance section of the Executive Headquarters was established in that city. Difficulties in Manchuria experienced by the field teams arose largely from the question of the applicability of the Cessation of Hostilities Order to that area, a subject which has been discussed in another section of this report. However, without the presence of the teams in Manchuria, it is believed that the situation would have grown completely out of hand, thus affecting the situation in other parts of China and leading almost inevitably to a general outbreak of hostilities throughout the country.

The chief task of the Executive Headquarters at the time of its establishment was that of effecting a cessation of hostilities. Other equally vital functions of the Headquarters, either envisaged in the original agreement for its establishment or in subsequent agreements reached by the Committee of Three (or the Military Sub-Committee), were the restoration of communications, the repatriation of the Japanese military and civilian personnel and the demobilization and reorganization of the Chinese armies. It is an interesting commentary that the only one of the above-named functions that

[27]See Volume Two, Appendix G, Document 4, for a list of field teams.

*See the section of this report entitled "Application of the Cessation of Hostilities Order to Manchuria."

the Executive Headquarters has been able to carry out successfully is that of repatriating the Japanese military and civilian personnel. The restoration of communications and the demobilization and reorganization of the Chinese armies were necessarily dependent upon the cessation of hostilities and neither of these two tasks could be carried to completion or even successfully begun so long as armed conflict continued and there was no solution of the political issues involved. The net result is that Executive Headquarters has functioned extremely successfully within the limits of its possibilities and that its success has been governed largely by the over-all political situation. A deterioration in the relations between the National Government and the Chinese Communist Party was soon reflected in the increased difficulties experienced by the Executive Headquarters and among its field teams in effectively preventing violation of the Cessation of Hostilities Order or in carrying out the directives and decisions already agreed upon.

In any event, however, the Executive Headquarters, as the agency for the implementation of the major non-political agreements reached between the two Chinese parties, has played a necessary and vital part in the efforts to bring peace and unity to China and restore the economic life of the country. If its efforts have not been completely successful, the responsibility can be charged not to Executive Headquarters, but rather to Chinese elements whose bitterness and distrust of each other defeated the peaceful purpose of the teams.

XVIII.

REPATRIATION OF THE JAPANESE MILITARY AND CIVILIAN PERSONNEL FROM CHINA

One of the objectives set forth in the statement of U.S. policy made by President Truman on December 15, 1945, was that of effecting the repatriation of Japanese troops from China with a view to the elimination of Japanese influence in that country. In this statement it was pointed out that the United States had assumed a definite obligation in the disarmament and evacuation of Japanese troops from China and that the United States was assisting and would continue to assist the Chinese Government to that end.

Although this statement of policy indicated that the elimination of Japanese influence in China was to be achieved through the evacuation of Japanese troops, it was obvious that the elimination of Japanese influence in China also called for the repatriation of Japanese civilians, whose presence in China would permit continued Japanese influence and many of whom, if permitted to remain, would strive secretly for the resurgence of Japanese power and influence on the continent of Asia. It was also recognized, however, that the Chinese authorities in several areas had expressed a need for the services of Japanese technicians and that the expulsion of all Japanese technicians from China, without an adequate number of trained Chinese to take their places in industry, communications, mining and other fields, would result in injury to the economic life of the country. The Department of State had originally expressed the opinion that the retention of Japanese, including "technicians," in China was highly undesirable and inconsistent with U.S. policy for the elimination of Japanese influence from China, including Formosa, but it was realized that the repatriation of Japanese civilians from China was a matter of domestic concern to China and one in which the United States could not properly force the acceptance of her wishes in the matter.

At the Joint Conference on repatriation of Japanese, held at Tokyo on October 25-27, 1945, in which Chinese representatives participated, it was agreed that the Chinese Government would be responsible for the repatriation of Japanese disarmed military personnel and civilians from the China Theater and that consonant with the terms of the Potsdam Declaration, as indicated in the President's statement of U.S. policy toward China on December 15, the United States Government would assist in this repatriation program.

On February 6, 1946, a Repatriation Plan for the China Theater was agreed upon by SCAP, CINCPAC, COMGEN-CHINA, the Chinese National Military Council and the Supreme Headquarters of the Chinese Army. In this plan, it was stated that "the Chinese National Government is responsible for the repatriation of all Japanese, civilian and military, with the specific responsibility of disarming and delivery of all repatriates to port areas and processing preliminary to the water lift." Direct responsibility was placed upon the Supreme Headquarters, Chinese Army, for the processing and movement of Japanese to the ports of embarkation. It was pointed out in the Plan that the role of the U.S. Forces, China Theater,* in this connection was to render advice to the Chinese National Government and to maintain liaison between the Supreme Headquarters of the Chinese Army, the Chinese National government, the U.S. Navy's 7th Fleet, SCAP and SCAJAP. The 7th Fleet was given responsibility for the water lift of Japanese involving the use of U.S. Navy vessels and SCAJAP for water lift by Japanese-manned ships.** The U.S. Forces, China Theater, under the Plan, were empowered to establish the order of priority for repatriation from the various repatriation ports in China and to allocate shipping from sources available to that command.

The question of the repatriation of Japanese from China was closely related to the cessation of hostilities, as the continued presence of Japanese armed forces in north China represented a very definite threat to peace in that area. This was particularly true because of the continued use by the National Government of armed Japanese units in garrisoning certain points along railway lines in north China and the Communist Party's insistence on the right of its forces to accept the Japanese surrender. With these circumstances in mind, the subject of Japanese repatriation was introduced into the discussions of the Committee of Three regarding the cessation of hostilities and the establishment of the Executive Headquarters. In the agreement for the establishment of the Executive Headquarters, provision was made for the submission by the Headquarters of recommendations for measures for the disarmament of Japanese forces and the coordination of the movement of those forces to the coast for repatriation.

On February 16, 1946, the head of the Repatriation Section of the U.S. Forces, China Theater, presented to the three Commissioners of the Executive Headquarters and the Headquarters personnel concerned a summary of the repatriation situation as of that date. The Executive Headquarters role in this task was expected to be that of facilitating the movement of Japanese to be repatriated to the ports of embarkation at

*This included the U.S. Marine Forces in China.

**SCAJAP vessels, consisting of LSTs, Liberty ships and captured Japanese shipping, were manned and operated by Japanese crews.

Tangku and Tsingtao. The Supply and Logistics* Section of the Headquarters was given the responsibility within the Executive Headquarters for such functions as would entail action by Headquarters in the repatriation program. The report of the head of the Repatriation Section indicated that the repatriation of Japanese from south China, Hainan Island and Formosa would be completed by May 1, that repatriation from central and north China was expected to be completed by June 1 and that repatriation from Manchuria, where little information was available regarding the actual number and location of Japanese, was expected to begin on May 1 and to be completed by September 30. Of particular concern to the Executive Headquarters were the estimates given of the total number of Japanese to be repatriated from north China and Manchuria: 307,000 in north China and 1,603,000 in Manchuria.

On February 18, the three Commissioners of the Executive Headquarters agreed upon and issued a general directive[29] to all field teams, all members of field teams and all National Government and Communist Party military commanders in north China regarding the repatriation of the Japanese. In this directive it was pointed out that the orderly movement of Japanese from their present locations to ports of embarkation was a matter of direct concern to the Executive Headquarters and that available information indicated that there were in north China approximately 120,000 Japanese military and 189,000 Japanese civilian personnel to be repatriated through the ports of Tangku and Tsingtao. Executive Headquarters' responsibilities in this connection were described as: to arrange for the establishment of food dumps and for the movement of Japanese repatriates to ports of embarkation in coordination with the Chinese Government and the China Theater; to take steps to ensure the availability of coal for use of the railways in connection with these movements; and to determine the priority of Japanese movements from areas, based upon the availability of rail facilities, or living conditions along the route of evacuation, and food availability in present locations. It was stated that the shipping and port facilities were then able to handle a rate of flow of 3,000 a day through Tangku and 1,500 a day through Tsing-

*Later changed to Railway Control and finally to Communications Group.

[29]See Volume Two, Appendix H, Document 1, for the full text.

tao and that the repatriation of Japanese from north China would be effected at the maximum rate consistent with the availability of shipping. It was explained in the directive that repatriation of Japanese from the Laoyao and Hsuchow areas would require no action or coordination by the Executive Headquarters. (Japanese from these areas were being evacuated through Laoyao and Shanghai and the responsibility of the Executive Headquarters in the repatriation program was confined to north China and Manchuria.) All military commanders were ordered to assist, of their own initiative, in the repatriation of Japanese from or through their areas, the routes of movement and timing thereof to be established by the Executive Headquarters.

Subsequent to the issuance of this directive and the active participation of the Executive Headquarters in this task of repatriation, it became apparent that some difficulty would be encountered in obtaining the repatriation of all Japanese in the face of the Chinese desire to retain Japanese technicians. On April 2 it was decided, after considerable discussion between the highest Chinese authorities and the U.S. Forces, China Theater, that the Chinese Governor General of Formosa would be permitted to retain temporarily 5,600 Japanese civilian technicians and approximately 22,400 dependents of these technicians, or a total of 28,000. It was understood that the repatriation, prior to January 1, 1947, of these Japanese technicians and their dependents would be the responsibility of the Chinese Government* and that the United States would complete the repatriation from Formosa of all Japanese military personnel and all civilians, except the above-described 28,000, by April 15.

By April 12, of the original estimated 2,116,307 Japanese military and civilian personnel in China (excluding Manchuria), Formosa and northern Indochina 1,379,276 or 65 percent had been repatriated and by that date the repatriation of Japanese from south China and Formosa was nearing completion. Of the 706,427 Japanese remaining in China (exclusive of Manchuria) at that time 424,988 or 60 percent were in central China. Of the 60,215 Japanese military personnel then reported in north China about 54,000, over 90 percent, were in Shansi Province.

*The Chinese Government subsequently requested and obtained permission from SCAP for the use of Chinese shipping to begin the repatriation of these Japanese in September.

The situation in Shansi Province, with respect to the Japanese, was of some concern, inasmuch as some of this number were believed to be still armed or else in areas readily accessible to arms for possible use by the provincial authorities against the Communists. The Chairman of the Shansi Provincial Government was insistent upon the retention of Japanese technicians, and the lack of cooperation from the National Government military commanders in this area and in the Peiping area in the repatriation program had resulted in a situation where two ships had sailed empty from the port of embarkation due to non-availability of Japanese personnel to be repatriated.

In view of this situation, I, therefore, addressed a letter to the Chinese Minister for Foreign Affairs on May 16, 1946, in which, referring to the apparent desire of the National Government to retain certain Japanese technicians, I inquired regarding the Chinese wishes in this matter in order that definite plans might be made with respect to the shipping involved. Under date of June 5, the Minister for Foreign Affairs replied that in order to ensure the uninterrupted operation of certain enterprises in the liberated areas of China the National Government had found it necessary to retain the services of a number of Japanese technicians "during the present transition period." He said that the number to be retained in China, excluding Manchuria and Formosa, was approximately 12,000.[30]

Repatriation statistics compiled by the U.S. Forces, China Theater, on May 24 showed that the scheduled repatriation of all Japanese military and civilian personnel from south China was completed on April 25, from northern Indochina on April 21 and from Formosa on April 23, a total of 1,759,500 Japanese (992,054 military and 767,446 civilians) having been repatriated from the China Theater, including Manchuria,* as of May 22. On the latter date there remained to be repatriated the following numbers of Japanese (excluding those in Manchuria): from north China, 7,070 military and 14,970 civilian personnel; from central China, 240,333

[30]See Volume Two, Appendix H, Document 2, for the text of this letter.

*Repatriation of Japanese from Manchuria, through the port of Hulutao, began in late April.

military and 33,555 civilian personnel—a total of 247,403 military and 48,525 civilians from the two areas. On June 21 there still remained in north China approximately 14,500 Japanese, although the original target date for completion of the repatriation from north China had been May 15 and 10 LSTs had after that date awaited the arrival of Japanese repatriates for nine days at the port of Tangku and had finally sailed for Hulutao without taking aboard any Japanese for repatriation. At this time the U.S. Army authorities informed the Supreme Headquarters, Chinese Army, that shipping would not be available in north China after July 15, 1946, and that the repatriation program at Tangku and Tsingtao would be considered completed as of July 15. The Chinese authorities were asked to inform China Theater of the exact number of Japanese to be repatriated through these ports and the number to be retained in China.

Final figures compiled by the U.S. Forces, China Theater, for central China showed that the repatriation of Japanese from that area was completed on July 11, a total of 810,226 Japanese having been evacuated from central China (683,474 military and 126,752 civilian personnel). The Chinese were reported to have retained 4,910 Japanese, 2,083 military and 2,827 civilians.

On July 16 the Executive Headquarters officially assumed the responsibility for the repatriation of Japanese from north China and Manchuria, thus relieving U.S. Forces, China Theater, of any further responsibility in the repatriation program for those areas. Statistics compiled by the Executive Headquarters showed that the repatriation of Japanese from north China was officially completed on August 11, 1946, a total of 551,500 Japanese, 239,266 military and 312,234 civilian personnel, having been evacuated to Japan by that date. The Chinese authorities in north China stated that a total of 6,737 Japanese were being retained in that area, including war criminals, technicians and their families. It was estimated that an additional number of 1,500 Japanese (the proportion of military and civilian personnel in this group was not known) had not been able to reach the coast. These were to be concentrated in Peiping as they became available and transported via rail by the Chinese to Hulutao for repatriation.

In this general connection and in view of the circumstance that it was to the interest of the United States that all civilian Japanese be repatriated from China, the American Embassy at Nanking, acting on instructions from the

86

Department of State, on July 6, 1946, forwarded a formal note to the Chinese Minister for Foreign Affairs, in which were expressed the desire of the U.S. Government that all Japanese nationals should be repatriated within the near future and the hope that the Chinese Government would repatriate the great majority as soon as possible, including all Japanese who desired repatriation. It was also stated in the note that the U.S. Government felt it highly desirable that only those Japanese be permitted to remain in China who were clearly indispensible on the grounds of their professional or technical qualifications for which there was no Chinese equivalent and who were able to demonstrate by their past records that they did not represent any threat to the peace and security of China.

The absence of accurate information regarding the number of Japanese to be repatriated from Manchuria made it difficult to make firm plans for the repatriation of Japanese from that area, as shipping, rail transportation, food and processing problems required advance knowledge of requirements. This was particularly true of shipping, as China Theater was expected to coordinate the repatriation program in the light of shipping available to General MacArthur's Headquarters and that portion thereof which could be used in repatriation of Japanese from the China Theater. The efforts of the U.S. Army authorities to obtain from all available sources in late February information regarding the number of Japanese military and civilian personnel in Manchuria and their geographical locations resulted in figures ranging from 1,500,000 to 3,000,000. The U.S. Forces, China Theater, took as a tentative basis for their planning the figure of 900,000 military and 703,000 civilian Japanese to be repatriated from Manchuria. The continued occupation of Manchuria by the Soviet troops at that time and the lack of Chinese control over that area made it impossible to obtain from Chinese sources adequate information regarding the number and location of Japanese in Manchuria.

Subsequently, it became apparent that, according to repatriation schedules then being maintained, south China, Formosa, Hainan Island and northern Indochina would be cleared of Japanese to be repatriated by April 30 and that shipping for repatriation purposes would begin to be surplus as early as April 15. With these circumstances in view, it seemed advisable to prepare for the repatriation program in Manchuria by sending a U.S. Army repatriation team to

Manchuria to gather information concerning strength and disposition of Japanese military and civilian personnel in that area and communications, billeting and staging area facilities related to repatriation. The U.S. Forces, China Theater, therefore, informed the Supreme Headquarters of the Chinese Army that China Theater was planning to send a repatriation team to Hulutao (a port in south Manchuria held by the National Government) shortly after April 15 to begin repatriation from Manchuria on a skeleton basis in late April, pending the development of a complete repatriation plan for Manchuria. The Chinese authorities were asked to establish the necessary Chinese repatriation organization at Hulutao and to plan for the repatriation program. On April 18 the Supreme Headquarters, Chinese Army, informed China Theater that its Repatriation Organization had been established at Hulutao and had approximately 60,000 Japanese concentrated there ready for repatriation. The U.S. Army unit of five officers and eight enlisted men, designated the Hulutao Repatriation Team, proceeded to Hulutao in late April and arrangements were made for the arrival of ten SCAJAP vessels at that time to provide transportation for the repatriates.

A joint conference was held between U.S. Forces, China Theater, and the Executive Headquarters at the beginning of the repatriation program for Manchuria in order to ensure action by Executive Headquarters field teams in Manchuria in connection with the movement of repatriates to the port of embarkation similar to that performed by the field teams in north China. U.S. Forces, China Theater, made provision for the necessary processing of Japanese repatriates and assumed responsibility for the coordination of repatriation schedules and procedures with SCAP. The processing procedures were handled by U.S. personnel, as had been true in other parts of China, because of the lack of trained Chinese personnel to perform these duties.

In connection with the repatriation of Japanese from Manchuria, on March 9, 1946, with the concurrence of the Secretary of State,* I addressed a letter[31] to the Soviet Am-

*It was felt that this procedure would make unnecessary a formal approach on this question by the Department of State to the Soviet Government in the midst of other more pressing negotiations.

[31]See Volume Two, Appendix H, Document 3, for the text of this letter.

bassador to China, in which it was stated that shipping for Japanese repatriation purposes would be gradually liberated beginning April 15 and that it would be appreciated if the Ambassador would ascertain the views of the Soviet Government regarding th evacuation of Japanese military and civilian personnel from Manchuria. It was pointed out that if such Japanese personnel could be made available at Manchurian ports beginning April 15 the shipping available could be devoted to the repatriation of increasingly larger numbers of Japanese as the evacuation from China neared completion. It was explained to the Ambassador that an early reply would be helpful as the shipping involved had either to be designated for repatriation purposes or for demobilization.

On April 2, Lieutenant General A.C. Gillem, U.S.A., serving as my representative on the Committee of Three during my absence in the United States, addressed a letter, in accordance with my telegraphic instructions, to the Soviet Ambassador, in which he stated that General MacArthur would have available on April 15th 75 Japanese-manned Liberty ships for repatriation of Japanese from Manchuria. Referring to my letter of March 9 to the Ambassador, General Gillem asked whether any decision had been reached by the Soviet Government in regard to the repatriation of Japanese from Manchuria. The need of an early reply was stressed in connection with the disposition of the shipping involved. No reply having been received to either of these letters, on April 15 Colonel J. Hart Caughey, member of my staff in China, addressed a further inquiry, on behalf of General Gillem, to the Soviet Ambassador in this regard.

On April 27, after my return from the United States, I addressed another letter[32] to the Soviet Ambassador, informing him that shipping had become available and that an American repatriation team was proceeding to Hulutao for purposes of coordinating the movements of Japanese from south Manchuria for repatriation through that port. I also informed the Ambassador that reports from the Supreme Headquarters of the Chinese Army indicated the presence of large numbers of Japanese in the Mukden-Dairen corridor and that in order to facilitate the repatriation of these Japanese it would be helpful to locate temporarily in Dairen an American

[32]See Volume Two, Appendix H, Document 4, for the text of this letter.

repatriation team for the sole purpose of coordinating the movements of the Japanese repatriates. The Ambassador was requested to advise me as soon as possible of the attitude of his Government in this regard. He was also informed that if it was desired that this matter be taken up on a higher level I should appreciate being notified accordingly.

In view of the continued lack of acknowledgment of or reply to these various communications to the Soviet Ambassador, on May 14 I requested the U.S. Ambassador to Moscow by radio to approach the Soviet Government in regard to the matter and pointed out that it was purely a business matter of economical use of shipping without unnecessary delays. On May 29 the U.S. Ambassador to Moscow informed me by radio that he had approached the Soviet Foreign Minister in regard to the sending of an American repatriation team to Dairen and that the Foreign Minister had agreed to inform him of the Soviet Government's decision at the earliest possible moment. Under date of June 29, the U.S. Ambassador to Moscow forwarded to me by radio via the Department of State a translation of the Soviet reply to his inquiry. The Soviet Government proposed that Japanese located in Dairen and the Port Arthur naval base area be repatriated through Dairen in a manner similar to that proposed by the Soviet representative in Tokyo for the repatriation of Japanese from northern Korea. The reply also stated that the Soviet military authorities at Port Arthur would be responsible for the movement of the Japanese to Dairen, their physical processing and embarkation, while General MacArthur's Headquarters would be expected to be responsible for their transportation from Dairen to Japan on vessels at the disposal of that Headquarters. It was suggested that the details be worked out in Tokyo. The reply concluded that Japanese outside Dairen and the naval base should be repatriated through other nearby Manchurian ports. Under date of July 4, the Soviet Ambassador to China forwarded to me a letter[33] of similar import.

At about this date, the Executive Headquarters was informed by the Japanese Headquarters in Mukden that there were 364,000 Japanese south of Ta Shih Chiao along the Kwantung Peninsula, distributed as follows: 250,000 at Dairen, 100,000 in the Port Arthur naval base area and 14,000 on

[33]See Volume Two, Appendix H, Document 5, for the text of this letter.

90

the Peninsula north of Dairen. Since the repatriation of this group of 14,000* would entail a long journey via Mukden by rail, cart and foot and would probably be difficult to complete through the one port of Hulutao prior to winter, I sent a further radio message on July 22 to the U.S. Ambassador to Moscow, suggesting that he approach the Soviet Government with a view to obtaining its consent to repatriate the entire group of 364,000 Japanese in this area through Dairen.

On August 19, no information having been received from SCAP at Tokyo** regarding further developments in this matter, I send a radio message to SCAP asking whether the above-described Soviet proposals had been accepted and what schedule of repatriation had been prepared. It was felt that such information was necessary in order to facilitate planning for the winter and that it was conceivable that the 350,000 Japanese in Dairen and the Port Arthur naval base area might be moved north and thus place an additional heavy burden upon the Executive Headquarters in its repatriation program, already handicapped by the congestion at the port of Hulutao.

SCAP subsequently informed me that the general question of the repatriation of Japanese from Soviet-controlled areas was then being handled by the Department of State on the highest governmental levels and indicated that the Soviet representatives in Tokyo were unable under their instructions to discuss the repatriation of military personnel in addition to civilian personnel, had confined their discussions to certain areas under Soviet control and were unable to agree on the provision of fuel supplies for the repatriation vessels.

Although no progress was made in connection with the evacuation of Japanese from the Soviet-held areas of Dairen and Port Arthur, the flow of civilian Japanese repatriates from Chinese-controlled areas in Manchuria continued at a steady rate. Arrangements were made by the Executive Headquarters for the repatriation of Japanese from Communist-held areas in northern Manchuria and these Japanese were sent across the line between National Government and Chinese Communist territory and transported south via Mukden

*This group was reported to be outside Dairen and the naval base area and thus, according to the Soviet proposal, were to be repatriated through other nearby Manchuria ports.

**SCAP had been kept informed of all developments regarding the repatriation of Japanese from Manchuria.

to the port of embarkation as rapidly as the available facilities would permit. By September 6 a total of 682,629 Japanese had been evacuated from Manchuria, and the Executive Headquarters estimated that an additional 722,598 Japanese remained to be evacuated from that area.

According to the Executive Headquarters' figures, only 9,575 of the total 682,629 Japanese repatriated from Manchuria as of September 6 were military personnel. CINCAFPAC figures for Japanese repatriation from Manchuria for the period ending September 1, however, show a total of 38,914 Japanese military and 952 naval personnel included in the overall total for Manchuria. It is believed that Japanese military personnel have in some cases exchanged their uniforms for civilian clothes and that upon their arrival in Japan such persons have admitted their military affiliations in order to be mustered out of the service and have thus been counted as military by CINCAFPAC. This reluctance of the military personnel to admit their identity has probably arisen in some cases from a fear of being retained by the Chinese if they were recognized as military personnel and in other cases from a desire to qualify as a civilian and thus be permitted to retain the larger sum of Japanese Yen allowed civilians as opposed to military personnel. The Executive Headquarters' figures for military personnel have included only those uniformed Japanese repatriated in organized military units.

The foregoing does not, however, offer an adequate explanation of the small number of Japanese military personnel evacuated from Manchuria approximately four months after the commencement of repatriation from that area. The location of the elements or personnel of the Japanese Kwangtung Army since the end of the war is not known. It has been assumed that large numbers were moved into Siberia. Small numbers were reported to be serving with the Chinese Communist forces at the time of the latter's capture of Changchun in April. A Japanese source in Manchuria asserts that a large force of well-armed Japanese are still in Manchuria. This source states that radio communication is maintained between units, that morale and discipline are high and that, while these troops remain neutral, they tend to favor the Chinese National Government. We have been unable to obtain any confirmation of this report or any partial evidence of its authenticity. It is mentioned here merely as an indication of a possible but not seemingly probable complication in the Manchurian situation.

Final figures* for the repatriation of Japanese from the China Theater, including those for Manchuria through September 6, were as follows:

Area	Total Repatriated	Total Military	Total Civilian	Reported by the Chinese as Retained
North China	551,500**	239,266	312,234	6,737
Central China	810,226***	683,474	126,752	4,910
South China	134,830	113,660	21,170	972
Formosa	454,152	157,976	296,176	28,000
Manchuria****	682,629	9,575	673,054	
North Indochina	30,888	29,198	1,690	
TOTALS:	2,664,225	1,233,149	1,431,076	40,619

*As compiled by U.S. Forces, China Theater, and the Executive Headquarters.

**At the time of the official completion of the repatriation program for north China, an additional 1,500 Japanese remained to be repatriated via rail to Hulutao by the Chinese authorities.

***Approximately 600 Japanese (the categories were not known) were reported by the Executive Headquarters as being expected to be available for repatriation through Shanghai in September.

****The figures for Manchuria are as of September 6, 1946, and the Executive Headquarters' estimate of the Japanese remaining to be repatriated from Manchuria as of that date was 722,598. No information had been obtained from the Chinese authorities regarding the number of Japanese they expected to retain in Manchuria.

The total number of Japanese repatriated from China as of September 20 is 2,711,951, 1,231,251 of this number being military and 1,480,700 civilian personnel.* By this date the major portion of the task of Japanese repatriation from Chinese territory had been accomplished. This task was one of great magnitude, involving the movement of Japanese repatriates from various inland points via inadequate lines of communications to the ports of embarkation. It required careful and close coordination between the Executive Headquarters Communication Group (charged with carrying out Executive Headquarters' responsibilities in this program), the field teams, the U.S. Navy authorities and SCAP, which controlled the bulk of the shipping used for repatriation purposes. It involved the timing and regulation of the flow of repatriates from the interior to the ports of embarkation in such a manner that there would be a minimum of delay in the departure of repatriation vessels without an overloading of the processing and billeting facilities available to the repatriation teams. It required the establishment of food dumps and billets at the necessary points en route. It is a tribute to the effectiveness of the planning and execution of the repatriation program that the evacuation from the China Theater of this tremendous number of Japanese was accomplished within a relatively brief period of time.

What role the Japanese remaining in China may play and to what extent their influence may be of importance is a debatable question, but it seems unlikely that Japanese influence on the Chinese scene through direct participation in Chinese affairs by the remaining Japanese will in the near future emerge as a factor of importance, unless such developments arise due to the possible presence of large numbers of Japanese military personnel in Manchuria.

*Additional information regarding the repatriation program will be forwarded as further statistics become available.

XIX.
ENTRY OF THE EXECUTIVE HEADQUARTERS
FIELD TEAMS INTO MANCHURIA; THE
SITUATION IN MANCHURIA

In accordance with the agreement reached on March 27 for the entry of the Executive Headquarters field teams into Manchuria, General Byroade and a small number of American personnel proceeded to Mukden via Chinchou on March 29. At the time of the receipt by the Executive Headquarters of notice of this agreement, General Byroade encountered difficulty in obtaining the consent of the two Chinese branches to despatch field teams to Manchuria. The Communist Party stated that it lacked sufficient personnel at that time and the National Government branch stated that the Generalissimo's Field Headquarters at Chinchou had not been informed by the Generalissimo of this new agreement and could not, therefore, deal with the Executive Headquarters. General Hsiung Shih-hui, Director of the Generalissimo's Field Headquarters in Manchuria, informed National Government representatives in the Executive Headquarters on March 28 that teams should not enter Manchuria. There was an inevitable suspicion that the National Government officials were delaying in this matter in order to prevent the entry of teams into Manchuria until the Government should have time to occupy Changchun, a suspicion apparently confirmed by a high ranking member of the National Government branch of the Executive Headquarters in a conversation with General Byroade. The National Government military leaders feared that field teams would stop their troop movements and thus prevent Government occupation of Changchun, from which the Soviet troops were expected to withdraw shortly. Following an approach made by General Gillem to General Chang Chih-chung and the Generalissimo in this regard, orders were issued by the latter on April 1 to General Hsiung to cooperate fully with the Executive Headquarters teams in Manchuria.

On March 30 the U.S. and National Government sections of the field teams for Manchuria proceeded to Mukden and on April 2 forty members of the Communist Party field team personnel arrived at that city. Shortly thereafter, agreement

95

was reached between the Communist Party and U.S. team members at Mukden for the despatch of teams into the field. On April 3, however, the National Government members of the teams said that they had no authority to act, as their team leaders were still in Chinchou. Although General Byroade, as Director of Operations, had authority to send teams into the field as specified by the orders issued, the teams could not well leave Mukden without National Government representatives. Faced with this continued obstruction of the operation of the teams in Manchuria, General Gillem on April 7 addressed a memorandum to the Generalissimo, in which he described the foregoing situation, referred to press reports that the Government was purposely delaying in order to allow time for its occupation of Changchun and asked the Generalissimo to issue immediately appropriate instructions to ensure the cooperation of the National Government team members at Mukden.

The situation in Manchuria at this time was complicated by developments connected with the Soviet withdrawal from that region. Subsequent to their withdrawal from Mukden, the Soviet military authorities in Manchuria refused to approve the National Government's use of the rail line north toward Changchun for the transportation of Chinese troops, alleging that it was prohibited by the terms of the Sino-Soviet Treaty. It was also reported that the Soviet authorities had rejected a request from the Chinese Government for the retention of small Soviet garrisons in the points then being evacuated by Soviet troops until the National Government troops should arrive to take over sovereignty at such places. Sino-Soviet relations were further complicated by the status of economic negotiations which had been begun by Soviet request in Changchun but had been broken off by the Chinese through the departure of Chinese negotiators from Changchun as a result of the continued Soviet occupation of Manchuria beyond February 1, the date on which the Soviet forces were expected to have evacuated Manchuria. Subsequently the Soviet Government had asked the Chinese authorities to continue discussions on economic matters in Manchuria at Changchun, but the latter had refused to participate in such discussions unless they were transferred to Chungking. There the matter had rested, until on March 25 the Soviet Ambassador to China informed the Chinese Government that the Soviet Government was willing to enter into discussions at Chungking on the question of economic cooperation in Manchuria.

It was against this background of Sino-Soviet relations in Manchuria that the Executive Headquarters field teams proceeded to Mukden. On April 5 the Chinese authorities forwarded to General Gillem a schedule of Soviet withdrawals from Manchuria, furnished the Chinese Government by the Soviet authorities in Manchuria, which provided for the progressive and complete withdrawal of Soviet troops from Manchuria, beginning April 6 and ending April 29. In view of the continued presence of Soviet troops in Manchuria, even though the agreement of March 27 had clearly stated that field teams should not proceed to points under Soviet occupation, General Byroade suggested to General Gillem the advisability of official notification being conveyed to the Soviet military authorities in Manchuria of the presence of the teams in that region. General Gillem accordingly recommended to the Generalissimo on April 1 that the National Government inform the Soviet authorities of the presence of the teams and the purpose of their mission in Manchuria—that is, to implement the agreement of March 27. On April 4 General Gillem was informed by the Chinese authorities that the Generalissimo had instructed General Hsiung Shih-hui to notify the Soviet Headquarters in Changchun of the sending of field teams into Manchuria and of the directive under which they were to operate.

Another phase of the Manchurian situation, one which was the subject of frequent propaganda attacks by the Chinese Communist Party, was that connected with the transportation by U.S. facilities of National Government troops. It was during this period that the Communist Party for the first time endeavored to find justification for its contention that the number of National Government troops in Manchuria was limited to five armies and that this limitation was provided for in the agreement reached on February 25 for the reorganization and integration of the Chinese armies. On March 28 the Communist Party Commissioner in the Executive Headquarters protested the movement of Government armies into Manchuria and on March 31 General Chou En-lai, in his capacity as the Communist Party representative on the Committee of Three, forwarded a protest to General Gillem against the further transportation by U.S. vessels of Government armies into Manchuria, stating that the military reorganization plan of February 25 restricted the number of Government troops in Manchuria to five armies. General Gillem replied that the basis of this contention was incorrect since the limitation of Government armies in Manchuria, set forth in the

97

military reorganization plan, was to be effective at the end of 12 months and the movement of Government armies into Manchuria was provided for in the Cessation of Hostilities Order of January 10. This made an exception in the prohibition against troop movements to allow the movement of Government troops into Manchuria for the purpose of restoring Chinese sovereignty. General Gillem also drew attention to the fact that even though the five army limitation applied to a yet distant period, the total strength of troops then in Manchuria was far below that authorized on the five army basis. While the subject was dropped for the time being, this question was to be referred to again and again by the Communist Party and was to play an important part in its propaganda attacks against what it termed American aid to the Kuomintang.

At the time of the reaching of the agreement for the entry of field teams into Manchuria, it was contemplated that the Committee of Three would visit Mukden in order to assist in determining the critical areas and in making such readjustment of the field team locations as the Committee would find necessary. It was not, however, until April 8 that agreement was finally reached by the field teams at Mukden for the sending of teams into the field in Manchuria and on that day two teams were despatched to areas north and southeast of Mukden, respectively. On April 14 the Acting Committee of Three (each branch had a representative acting on behalf of the original members of the Committee), together with the three Commissioners of the Executive Headquarters, departed from Peiping for Mukden on a tour of investigation of the situation to allow for a presentation of the actual conditions in Manchuria to the Committee of Three at Chungking subsequent to my impending return from the United States. The tour actually resolved itself into a fact-finding trip, as the teams had been in the field for too brief a period to permit any effective results. The Acting Committee of Three returned to Peiping on April 16 and departed on April 18 for Chungking

On April 14 the Soviet troops withdrew from Changchun north along the rail line to Harbin and within an hour after this withdrawal the Chinese Communist forces in that area opened an attack on the airfield. The following day the Chinese Communists launched an attack on Changchun and captured the main points in the city that day, although scattered fighting continued until the 18th when all National Government resistance ceased. The Communist forces were reported to have numbered some 20,000 to 30,000 well-equipped and well-disciplined men, against whom the National Government opposed about 15,000 troops, the majority of them ex-puppet Manchurian troops flown to Changchun from Peiping during the time of Soviet occupation. The Communists were reported by an official U.S. observer to have employed a small number of Japanese in the engagement, these consisting chiefly of tank crews. This observer also reported that prior to the fall of the city, National Government troops killed over 30 Soviet citizens, these murders accompanied in some cases by torture and mutilation, and that the Soviet officials and the majority of Soviet civilians of importance left the city for Harbin subsequent to the Communist occupation of Changchun.

The action of the Chinese Communists in attacking and occupying Changchun was a flagrant violation of the Cessation of Hostilities Order and an act which was to have serious consequences, as shown by subsequent developments. It made the victorious Communist generals in Manchuria over-confident and less amenable to compromise with the National Government, but even more disastrous was the effect upon the Government. It made my position in the negotiations and my efforts to persuade the Generalissimo and National Government leaders of the advisability of certain compromise courses of action much more difficult. It greatly strengthened the hands of the ultra-reactionary groups in the Government, who were now in a position to be critical of my previous advice and to say that the Communists had now demonstrated that they never intended to adhere to the agreements reached, which had always been the contention of these Kuomintang leaders.

It is difficult to explain with certainty the reason for the Communist attack on Changchun. One possible explanation is that the Communists were endeavoring to force the National Government to put an end to hostilities in Manchuria, cease the movement of its troops north from Mukden and negotiate for a settlement. This explanation is strengthened by the determined stand made by the Communist forces at Ssupingchieh, an important junction on the railway north of Mukden, where the Communist troops successfully stood off strong Government attacks for more than a month, the city finally being captured by the Government forces on May 19. This action may also be connected with the general situation in north China, where railway reconstruction, after a successful and promising beginning, had bogged down in argument over the question of the destruction of fortifications. The political situation had also definitely deteriorated with indications that the Kuomintang was endeavoring to obtain revision of important PCC decisions reached in January. Therefore, the Communist Party may have hoped that successful military operations on its part at this moment in Manchuria, coupled with a deteriorating situation in north China and an effort on the part of the Communists to prevent the movement of additional Government armies into Manchuria, might make the National Government more amenable to negotiation for a solution of the issues in Manchuria. But, whatever the reasons for the action, it was clearly a serious tactical blunder on the part of the Communists and an action which was to plague them time and time again.

General Chou En-lai's explanation of the Communist attack on Changchun was that at the end of 1945, when the Government armies were advancing along the railway from Chinchou toward Mukden, the Communists had urged the Government to proceed to Mukden to negotiate with the Soviets regarding the taking over of sovereignty and had informed the Government that, if the Government troops were advancing toward Mukden for the purpose of taking over sovereignty of places under Soviet control, the Communists would offer no obstruction. General Chou explained that the Government had been warned that if its troops moved to the west to attack Communist forces there would be danger of hostilities. He further stated that the Government had altered the course of its advance and had launched an attack west toward Jehol and that even after the signing of the cessation of hostilities agreement in January the Government had to be asked again not to attack the Communists. As late as March 15, said General Chou, the Communists had urged the Government to take over Mukden and the Changchun Railway and on March 27 he himself had stated that if hostilities were ended in Manchuria "the Government could be assured of the status of Changchun, Harbin and others." He concluded that the Communists had consistently promised the Government that Changchun could be preserved until April 15th if the Government would end hostilities, but the Government was unwilling to do so—under these circumstances the Communists had no alternative but to take Changchun.

XX.

THE DETERIORATION IN THE SITUATION AT THE TIME OF MY RETURN TO CHINA; EVENTS LEADING TO AGREEMENT FOR A TEMPORARY TRUCE IN MANCHURIA

It was against the background of a general deterioration of the situation that I returned to China on April 18. After a brief stop-over in Peiping, in order to acquaint myself with the situation in relation to the functioning of the Executive Headquarters, I proceeded to Chungking.

In my first conference with the Generalissimo immediately on my return to Chungking, he made a frank statement of the over-all situation to the following effect: That it should be clear to me now that I had been wrong in contending that the Communists would live up to their agreements, as evidenced by their failure to present the list of their divisions required to be submitted within three weeks of the signing of the army reorganization agreement of February 25, and by their attack on Changchun and refusal to go ahead with the reestablishment of communications in north China; that Government divisions in Manchuria were in danger of annihilation; that he did not feel that further advance could be made in Manchuria and that some withdrawal would be necessary; that he was even considering the complete evacuation of Manchuria, turning the issue over to international settlement.

To this, I replied that while I realized the critical situation in Manchuria, and considered that the Communist attack on Changchun was a glaring violation of their agreements, at the same time I felt that, having in mind the deep distrusts and suspicions inherent in the situation in China, the Government's procedure had been fatally provocative and at times inexcusably stupid. I deplored the procedure which had been followed in Manchuria by the military commander along with the Government's long refusal to permit teams from Executive Headquarters to enter that area. I opposed his view that he might decide to evacuate Manchuria or to make a serious withdrawal. I thought that there still remained a fair hope for a compromise which would be far more to the advantage of

101

the Government than a possible withdrawal. I stated that I did not concur with his statement regarding the Communist refusal to proceed with the reestablishment of communications because, in my opinion, there was much to be said on their side in criticism of the attitude of his people in the Ministry of Communications.

As a result of this conversation, I drafted a proposal for a compromise arrangement in Manchuria, particularly as related to Changchun and the region to the north. When I saw the Generalissimo the following evening, however, he made no more mention of the dangers of the situation (annihilation of divisions) or of possible withdrawals, but seemed to be contemplating an aggressive policy. My compromise proposal, which had been based on the statement of his views the previous day, was therefore inappropriate and was dropped by me. It included the clearance of two additional armies (the 60th and 93rd) for Manchuria, (one largely aboard ship and the other just starting its embarkation) which were subsequently transported by American vessels to Manchuria. The Generalissimo objected to limitations on the movement by U.S. facilities of National Government armies to Manchuria and insisted that an additional two armies (in addition to the 60th and 93rd) be transported by the U.S. Navy. Incidently, I declined to authorize this movement then or later, drawing the line here between agreed U.S. assistance to the National Government by transporting armies into Manchuria to reestablish the sovereignty of the National Government and assistance in a fratricidal struggle. I had to weigh the Government's justified (in my opinion) requirements in taking over sovereignty in a vast region against the Communist increasing military concentration in the north with a parallel increase in armament obtained from dumps or depots of Japanese materiel in that area.

In my initial discussions with the National Government officials after my return, I endeavored to emphasize the seriousness of the existing state of affairs, the difficulties of finding a solution and my own estimate of the situation. It was my opinion, as stated to Government representatives, that many of the existing difficulties could have been avoided earlier by the National Government but that the situation was now reversed; that there was a complete lack of faith and a feeling of distrust on both sides and each side saw behind all proposals from the other an evil motive; that the National Government had blocked the sending of field teams into Manchuria, which might have been able to control the situation; that while the Communists said that the Cessation of Hostilities Order applied to all of China, the National Government resisted its application to Manchuria; that when the National Government troops moved into Manchuria they took the ill-advised action of attempting to destroy the Communist forces in the hinterland; and that the Generalissimo's military advisors had, I was forced to the conclusion, shown very poor judgment. In many instances the National Government authorities had offered opportunities to the Communist Party to make accusations against their good faith: (1) the Hankow situation, where Communist troops were surrounded by large Government concentrations; (2) the movement of Government troops toward Chihfeng, Jehol Province, in violation of the cease-fire order (orders had been issued by the Government military headquarters at Chungking for this operation); (3) the refusal of General Chang Fa-kuei, the Commanding General at Canton, to recognize the Communist troops in that area as well as the orders of the Executive Headquarters and the National Government at Chungking; (4) the failure of General Ho Ying-chin's army headquarters to submit daily reports of the troop movements south of the Yangtze, as was clearly required by the Cessation of Hostilities Order; (5) the search of homes of Communist Party personnel and closure of Communist newspaper offices at Peiping; (6) the "buzzing" of the airfield at Yenan by Government planes; (7) the detention of Communist team personnel at the airfield at Mukden. All these were stupid acts which were of no benefit to the National Government but which not only served as ammunition to the Communists, but, what was far more serious, stimulated their suspicion of the Government's intentions. The Kuomintang had had an opportunity to have peace in Manchuria but it did not utilize this chance. Now the Communists were taking advantage of the existing situation and were becoming stronger daily, thus placing the National Government in a very dangerous military position with over-extended lines and a constantly increasing dispersion of forces.

In a conversation with General Hsu Yung-chang, Director of the Board of Military Operations of the Ministry of War, who was appointed by the National · Government on April 23 to serve as its representative on the Committee of Three and the Military Sub-Committee, I expressed views similar to those above-described and pointed out the tragedy of the situation—the Government had had several opportunities to resolve matters satisfactorily since the beginning of negotiations in December 1945 but the Communist Party was now in a position to present excessive demands on the Government. The National Government blunders were described to me as including an adamant attitude on minor matters which served no useful purpose and were provocative of serious dilemmas.

In my first conversation with General Chou En-lai following my return to China, he pointed up the difficulties of finding a solution by elaborating on his lessened ability to negotiate. He said that the Communist leaders in Manchuria were now concerned over the manner in which they would fit into the army reorganization plan and that the Yenan authorities felt that the ratio of one Communist division to 14 Government divisions in Manchuria, provided for at the end of 18 months in the military reorganization agreement of February 25, was no longer appropriate. Yenan, he said, wished to reconsider the ratio of troop strength in Manchuria and was adamantly opposed to the movement of additional Government troops into Manchuria.

In an effort to clarify the position of the United States in relation to the movement by American vessels of National Government troops into Manchuria, I gave General Chou the exact data regarding Government troops moved by U.S. shipping into Manchuria: the 13th, 52nd, New 1st, New 6th, and 71st armies or a total of 145,000 troops had already been transported; the Northeast Garrison Command Headquarters of 6,500 men and 12,000 service troops had also been moved for the establishment of a major supply base at Chinhuangtao and/or Hulutao; and the 60th Army (32,000 men), 93rd Army (30,000 men) and the 1st Army Group Headquarters (2,600 men) remained to be transported by U.S. vessels under present commitments—when the latter movements were completed, a total of 228,000 Government troops would have been moved by U.S. facilities by June 1, the date scheduled for the completion of such movements. (It should be pointed out that according to the military reorganization agreement of February 25 the National Government was to have five armies of three divisions each in Manchuria at the end of the first 12 months, each division to consist of a maximum of 14,000 men. The agreement also provided for supporting troops not to exceed 15 percent of the total strength and thus, in accordance with the agreement, the total National Government strength at the end of the first 12 months would be approximately 240,000 men, more than the number already moved and due to be moved by U.S. facilities in accordance with previously made commitments to the Chinese Government.)

In further conversations with General Chou En-lai on April 27 and 29, I communicated to him new proposals given to me by the Generalissimo for a settlement of the Manchurian situation, which by that time was governing the entire situation in China. The Generalissimo posed as the essential condition to the cessation of hostilities the evacuation of Changchun by the Communist forces and its occupation by Government troops and said that after such occupation that Government would be willing to have the various aspects of the military and political situation considered by the Committee of Three. The Generalissimo specifically proposed: (1) the carrying out of the cease-fire order; (2) the fixing of troop strengths in accordance with the military reorganization agreement of February 25; (3) the reestablishment of Chinese sovereignty in Manchuria by Government control of the railways named in the Sino-Soviet Treaty together with a 30 *li** strip of territory on each side of the rail lines; and (4) further discussion of political matters.

It was during this period that Democratic League representatives entered the discussion regarding a settlement of the Manchuria problem and submitted a proposal, the chief points of which were: the appointment of three non-partisan representatives to the Northeast Political Council, and the dismissal of the National Government military commander from the chairmanship of the Council; the reorganization of the Northeast Political and Economic Councils; the stationing of Government representatives at key points, such as Harbin, Changchun and Tsitsihar and other cities along the railway lines; a prohibition against Government troop movements on the railways; and the withdrawal of the Communist forces to points 30 *li* from the rail lines—a joint commission to investigate the situation in Manchuria after the issuance of a cease-fire order. The Generalissimo rejected these proposals and General Chou, himself, seemed to think them superficial, stating that the main problem had to do with the control of the railways, which could be achieved either by (1) local civilian garrisons, (2) full military control or (3) the establishment of a commission.

*Three Chinese *li* equal one mile.

On April 29, General Chou informed me that he had forwarded to Yenan the proposals of the Generalissimo and of the Democratic League and that he was inclined to accept the idea of a joint commission to investigate the situation in Manchuria after the issuance of a general cease-fire order, this commission to take up the problems of (1) separating the armies, (2) control of communications, (3) reorganization of the political and economic councils and (4) consideration of the status of the various provincial governments. The Communist Party, he said, was strongly opposed to further Government troop movements and wished to obtain the issuance of a cease-fire order prior to negotiations. General Chou felt that the National Government, as indicated by its insistence on the occupation of Changchun, wished to fight first and talk later, while the Communist Party wished to cease fighting and discuss the over-all problems. He said that the Communist Party could accept the Generalissimo's proposal for the occupation of Changchun prior to negotiation and suggested the following points for a settlement: (1) separate the two armies from close contact; (2) prohibit troop movements by both sides; (3) solve the communications problem; and (4) send Executive Headquarters field teams to points of close contact between the two forces and along the main railways. General Chou suggested immediate action on these four points and subsequent discussion of four additional points: (1) review military dispositions in Manchuria; (2) carry out the plan for demobilization; (3) redispose the opposing forces; and (4) readjust army strengths.

In reply to these proposals from General Chou, I informed him that in my opinion the fundamental difference between the positions of the two sides lay in the question of sovereignty in Manchuria; that sovereignty implied control and control could not be held by the Government unless it occupied Changchun; and that the Generalissimo had made a great concession to the Communists by his willngness to hold open for negotiation problems relating to the remainder of Manchuria provided the Communist forces evacuated Changchun. I further stated that after giving careful and deep consideration to the discussions during the past few days, it was with regret that I felt it necessary to make General Chou the following oral statement:

> "I have done the best I can in an effort to
> negotiate this critical situation. The matter,
> with this statement, virtually passes out of

my hands. I do not see anything more I can do in the way of mediation and I think it best this be understood. I've exhausted my resources in an effort to compromise the various positions and views and I cannot see how I could gain any more by further discussion of this particular issue with the Generalissimo. As I told you before, my position is greatly changed because in all previous agreements I was continually confronted by the statement of the Government that whatever agreement I brought about would not be carried out by the Communists. At the present time my position in endeavoring to persuade various lines of action by the Government has been heavily compromised by the Communist action in Manchuria. I repeat again, I am intimately familiar with your resume of actions of the Government not in accordance with agreements. For instance: the Canton situation; the question of jurisdiction of Executive Headquarters in Manchuria; the action by Government troops in fighting in Manchuria without recourse to the presence of teams to stop fighting. But the fact remains I've exhausted my resources and I have tried to give you the basis of what I think could be a Government agreement."

General Chou in a lengthy exposition of the Communist attitude toward the existing situation said that the Generalissimo's attitude of fighting for Changchun had caused the difficulties and that it was difficult to convince the Generalissimo—first, he would not recognize the Communist forces in Manchuria; second, he desired to use military force when he failed at negotiations; and, third, he desired to exercise the authority of the Government and made concessions only when forced to do so. General Chou stated that the Generalissimo had entered into previous agreements with reluctance and that he was at one with the "irreconcilables," a belief supported by his lack of criticism of, or efforts to rectify their actions. General Chou pointed out that an easy occupation of Changchun would tempt the Government to attempt the capture of Harbin and that the problem of sovereignty in Manchuria had changed considerably in that both Japanese and Soviet troops were no longer in occupation of the Northeast and the basic considerations involving the establishment of

Chinese sovereignty no longer existed. In explanation of Communist attacks on the granting of a loan to the Chinese Government by the United States, General Chou said these attacks were made in good faith and were based on the firm conviction that temporary suspension of action in this regard was one of the surest means of averting civil war in China and that the continued movement of Goverment troops and the granting of a loan would tend to create an effect opposite to that desired by the United States.

It was at this point that I withdrew from mediation between the two parties for a settlement of the Manchurian problem. An impasse had been reached and it was my opinion that my withdrawal from mediation might serve to exert pressure on both sides to make compromises in their respective positions. I did, however, continue to hold conferences with representatives of the two sides in an effort to prevent the deterioration of the situation in North China.

In a conversation with General Hsu Yuang-chang on May 4, I advanced for the first time my idea of a possible solution of the Manchurian problem, taking into consideration the insistence of the Government on the occupation of Changchun and the adamant stand of the Communist Party against evacuation of that city. It was suggested to General Hsu, for use in his discussions with the Generalissimo, that it might be agreeable to both sides for the Communists to evacuate Changchun and for an advance echelon of the Executive Headquarters to be established at Changchun for the purpose of maintaining peace, a mayor to be appointed who might organize a peace preservation corps to maintain local order and security. On May 8, I again brought up this plan in a conversation with General Yu Ta-wei, Minister of Communications, and my liaison with the Generalissimo, suggesting that the Communists evacuate Changchun, that an advance echelon of the Executive Headquarters be established at that city and that provision be made for the entry of National Government troops into Changchun in approximately 6 months.

On May 10, in accordance with a request from Generalissimo Chiang Kai-shek that I furnish him my ideas of a possible basis for agreement regarding Manchurian issues, I forwarded to him a memorandum setting forth certain considerations and suggestions, the gist of which is as follows:

Military. The deployment of the National Government forces in Manchuria should be based: first, on the Government's uncertainty regarding the future actions of the Chinese Communist Party and the possible reaction of the Soviet Union in connection therewith, and, secondly, on the facilities for supply and maintenance—these two considerations indicating a concentration of Government troops in south Manchuria with major concentrations in the Mukden area and north of Hulutao. A third consideration would be the Communist Party's demand for increased army strength in Manchuria—if they insist on one army the National Government might increase its strength by one division and thus retain the 5 to 1 ratio. The National Government should hold its strength in Changchun and at points south of that city and accept the Communist forces, as a future part of the National Government Army, to the west of Harbin and toward Manchouli. The stationing of Government forces between Changchun and Manchouli as a symbol of Government authority would probably block negotiations and, even if agreed to, would be a constant source of trouble.* There is danger in the northward advance of Government troops before reaching a basis for agreement for the cessation of hostilities. There would be small prospect for agreement except by the destruction of the Communist forces in Manchuria, action not within the Government's power. If an advance is continued and defeated, the Government's position would then be seriously compromised. It is not known whether the Communist Party would agree to evacuate Changchun and to permit eventual occupation of that city by Government troops, but it is hoped that the Communists would agree and would accept some compromise arrangement for Government oc-

*National Government representatives had been strongly insistent on the stationing of symbolic forces in the areas west of Harbin, although I continued to warn them of the uselessness of such action in demonstrating Government authority and of the danger of possible incidents attendant upon the stationing of troops in areas dominated by the Communists.

cupation of Changchun. If that should materialize, it is suggested that the Executive Headquarters establish an advance section at Changchun to control the city during negotiations. Although the Generalissimo has stated that no compromise regarding his proposals is possible, it is to the interest of the Government to find an acceptable basis of compromise, as time is to the advantage of the Communists and the situation in north China is also serious—all this might lead to general civil war.

Political. The Communist Party and the Democratic League desire the reorganization of the Political and Economic Councils for the Northeast and their removal from military domination, and the appointment of both Communist Party and Manchurian representatives would facilitate all other negotiations. The Communist Party has definitely stated its insistence on having its local self-governments in Manchuria, elected under its supervision, continued in effect pending the settlement by negotiation of future political arrangements in Manchuria. They will also probably insist on representation in these local governments, as well as in the provincial governments—this might be arranged through compromise related to the disposition of Communist troops. The present Communist control of almost all of Manchuria from Changchun north makes it likely that they will be inclined to drive a hard bargain, but this problem must be faced unless the larger part of Manchuria is to be abandoned, which would also involve a complete breakdown in north China.

Conclusion. The Government's military position is weak in Manchuria and the Communists have the strategical advantage there. The psychological effect of a certain compromise on the part of the Government to achieve peace would not injure its prestige but would indicate that the Generalissimo was making every effort to promote peace. The proposal to utilize Executive Headquarters in Changchun would bolster the conviction that the

Generalissimo was striving for peace. Finally some compromise must be achieved as quickly as possible or China will be faced with a chaotic situation, militarily, financially and economically.

On May 11, at the request of General Yu Ta-wei for his use in discussions with the Generalissimo, I prepared a summary of my proposals for a compromise solution of the Manchurian issues, the four points of which are as follows:

"1. General Marshall suggests that he propose that the Communists withdraw from Changchun and that an advance echelon of Executive Headquarters be established therein as a basis for terminating the fighting preliminary to entering into negotiations.

"2. When arranging for acceptance of (1) above, General Marshall would have an understanding with the Communist representative that Government troops *would subsequently* occupy Changchun, within a maximum time of six months, preferably a much shorter delay.

"3. Also, General Marshall would reach a preliminary understanding with the Communist representative regarding a revision of the troop ratio in Manchuria on the basis of not to exceed one Communist Army to five National Armies.

"4. General Marshall would use his influence to preclude occupation of key cities north of Changchun by Communist forces."

As I continued to point out to the Generalissimo and the National Government representatives, the time element was of great importance. The situation in north China was becoming more serious with two major irritants affecting the situation there—the unsettled question of the destruction of railway fortifications and the failure of the National Government to report its routine troop movements to the Executive Headquarters. The situation in north China was, of course, dominated by the outcome in Manchuria and continued failure to find a solution in Manchuria would, it was feared, make the Executive Headquarters completely ineffective. A solution was made more difficult by the repeated insistence of the Generalissimo that he would not sign or agree to any settlement that did not provide for evacuation of Changchun by the Communists and its occupation by the Government and that he would accept nothing less than complete National Government sovereignty in Manchuria. In the light of the foregoing, I felt it unwise for me to re-enter the negotiations in the capacity of mediator, knowing that there was no basis for agreement by the Communist Party and not wishing to be placed in a position where I would have no power to avert an otherwise certain stalemate.

On May 12, the Generalissimo, referring to my memorandum regarding a possible basis for settlement of Manchurian issues, informed me that he agreed in general with the suggestions therein related to military terms, but, he added, there must be a specific proviso that the Communist Party should not occupy Harbin. In regard to the political factors, the Generalissimo said only that the National Government military headquarters in Manchuria (presumably the Generalissimo's Field Headquarters headed by General Hsiung Shih-hui) and the Northeast Political and Economic Councils should be abolished and that the National Government would then exercise its control direct through the nine provincial chairmen. Although I emphasized the critical state in north China and said that delays would be dangerous and might involve irreparable breakdowns, the Generalissimo asked that no efforts be made to initiate discussions with the Communist representatives, preferring that the initial overtures come from them.

In connection with the deteriorating situation in north China, General Chou En-lai informed me on May 13 of his desire to end the spread of trouble and difficulties in that area. He felt that the Communists were being unjustly accused of violations of the truce agreement and that the Kuomintang was trying to stir up trouble and bring about a civil war, at the same time putting the blame on the Communist Party. I replied that the diminishing effectiveness of the Executive Headquarters field teams was a matter of particular concern; that the lowered prestige of the Headquarters and its teams was most serious; that the Executive Headquarters' reports of the past few weeks revealed the complete opposition of Communist members, at the operations level in the Headquarters and in the field teams, toward any common sense action which should be taken by the teams; that U.S. Army officers had originally been impressed by the high degree of cooperation by the Communists but that the present

Communist policy of blocking action had lowered American confidence in them; and that all these actions merely served to increase suspicion and distrust.

This question of the ineffectiveness of field teams when required investigations were blocked by the failure of the team members to reach unanimous decision had for some time impaired the efficiency of the teams. Frequent efforts to reach an agreement for decision by the American team chairman for team investigations or by majority vote of the three team members had been blocked by Communist opposition. General Chou En-lai had recently submitted a six point counter-proposal in reply to General Byroade's proposal for agreement on a document to allow for U.S. determining voice in the movement of teams for purposes of investigation. I pointed out to General Chou that his proposal was too complicated in that it provided for investigation of troop movements only when they involved certain strengths and for an involved procedure of punishments for false reports. It was extremely important at this time that some change be made in the teams' operating procedure to provide for the removal of the restrictions on immediate action involved in the existing system of operation. Agreement was reached by the Committee of Three on May 14 on a document[34] designed to ensure more prompt investigation of reported violations of the Cessation of Hostilities Order, the pertinent portion of which required the U.S. member of a field team, in case of disagreement, to report the disagreement immediately to the three Commissioners of the Executive Headquarters, who within twenty-four hours would either reach a unanimous decision or report their disagreement to the Committee of Three. This was a far from satisfactory arrangement, though the National Government branch of the Executive Headquarters desired to permit the U.S. member of the team to have the power of decision regarding the investigations to be made, but the Communist representatives would not yield on this point. This matter is reported in some detail because subsequent developments made the question of decision by U.S. members of the Executive Headquarters field teams of some importance.

On May 13, during the above-described discussion with General Chou, I suggested to him for the first time the possibility of solving the Manchurian problem by the Communist

[34]See Volume Two, Appendix I, Document 1, for the full text.

evacuation of Changchun and the establishment of an advance section of the Executive Headquarters there, with Government troops to remain in their present positions and further negotiations regarding military dispositions and political problems to begin at that time. I stressed that I must have a general knowledge in advance of the Communist Party's demands regarding the readjustments in the military and political situation in Manchuria, if General Chou agreed to my proposals, as I would not act as a mediator unless I saw a fair prospect of reaching an agreement. It was also pointed out that whatever agreement was reached on Manchurian problems parallel solutions must be found for the problems of the destruction of fortifications along the railway lines in north China and free movement of the field teams (as described in the preceding paragraph, a compromise agreement was reached on this point the following day)—in short, an over-all solution. General Chou replied that he would transmit these proposals to Yenan and said that he did not wish me to resign my efforts at mediation.

On May 17, in further discussion of the situation, General Chou described a three point proposal advanced by the Democratic League as follows: (1) Reorganization of the Northeast Political and Economic Councils on a ratio of three Government, three Chinese Communist and three non-party representatives from Manchurian groups, the office of the reorganized councils to be located at Changchun; (2) appointment of a non-Government, non-Communist mayor of Changchun, with representatives of both parties in the Municipal Council; and (3) control of local security to be vested in police organized by the mayor or magistrate, such police to be essentially neutral in character. General Chou described his views regarding Manchuria as follows: (1) The Political Council in Manchuria and the various provincial councils should be reorganized; (2) self-government should be introduced in the *hsien* in accordance with the PCC program; (3) all communications should be restored and placed under an interim administrative council of Manchuria; and (4) a military reorganization plan for Manchuria should be based on actual conditions and must provide for adjustment of garrison strengths of the two parties in Manchuria. In regard to China proper, General Chou said that it was his understanding that a solution of the Manchurian problems would be taken up in connection with the Cessation of Hostilities Order, the PCC decisions, the army reorganization plan, the draft constitution and guarantees for the various freedoms—all these to be solved together with the problems in Manchuria as the overall solution. To that end he suggested the possiblity of having the PCC Steering Committee meet to seek a solution of the problems relating to China as a whole while the Manchurian problems were being discussed by the Committee of Three.

I replied to General Chou that I had endeavored to explain to him previously my withdrawal from the position of mediator in connection with Manchurian issues, as my position vis-a-vis the Chinese Government had been made so difficult as a result of the Communist attack on Changchun that I must not involve my Government in another stalemate. It was pointed out that, unless I could be reasonably sure of the position of the Communist Party on military and political issues, it would be impossible for me to resume the role of mediator and that I could not again place myself in the position of being a party to an agreement which included provision for negotiations regarding vital or fundamental differences unless I had reasonable assurance as to a favorable outcome.

My views on the Manchurian problem were explained to General Chou: once a state of oral agreement had been reached by the two parties, General Chou would have to make arrangements for the immediate reception at Changchun of the advance section of the Executive Headquarters. At the same time, the National Government and the Communist Party should issue orders to field commanders that arrangements were about to be made for the termination of hostilities and that in the interim there would be a neutral prohibition against advances, attacks or pursuits. The advance section of the Executive Headquarters would be established at Changchun and procedures for the withdrawal of Communist forces from that city would be initiated. As they withdrew, the advance section would take steps to form an orderly city government. At the same time at least three or four field teams would be deployed from Changchun to carry into effect at an agreed time the complete cessation of hostilities and the necessary readjustments of troops to ensure a termination of hostile contact. The duty of the advance section would also include the authority to direct teams throughout Manchuria to bring about the cessation of fighting and the necessary readjustments. In regard to military problems, agreement would be reached in subsequent negotiations and it would be necessary for me to know the Communist demands in regard to future troop dispositions—in what areas and under what conditions and strengths. It would be necessary to reach agreement on supervision, as neither side trusted the other and there would be no reduction of troops unless each had positive evidence of reduction by the opposing party. It would be necessary to expedite action in this matter in order to arrange for troop dispositions in the near future rather than at the end of 18 months. In regard to the political aspects, it would be necessary to have detailed understanding of the Communists' demands and it must be remembered that the Generalissimo had not welcomed the proposal of the Democratic League for the reorganization of the Political and Economic Councils in Manchuria.

I informed General Chou that I felt it useless for me to attempt to influence the Generalissimo to abandon his fixed idea regarding Changchun and that it was probably not desirable that there be continued hope that I was still in a position of possibly bringing about a solution. I emphasized my unwillingness to be involved again in a stalemate and concluded that it was my opinion that another stalemate would not only still more lessen my influence but would also inevitably result in the resumption of hostilities. In reply, General Chou charged that the National Government was even then engaged in laying plans for war, including an offensive against Changchun, and that Government leaders had recently attended a conference directed to that end.

On May 21, General Chou informed me that he had referred to Yenan my comments on the Manchurian situation. The Communist authorities had expressed a certain hesitation regarding the withdrawal of their forces from Changchun and had inquired of the Communist Party leaders in Manchuria on this point. They felt that they must consider two possibilities: (1) If the Government felt that it could capture Changchun within a short time, the Communists feared that it would not agree to my proposal, and (2) if the Government occupied Changchun, it might raise the question of other places, such as Harbin. The Communist authorities, therefore, doubted that the Government would consider such a proposal. General Chou described the Communist attitude on other problems as follows:

> *Political.* Points for consideration were the reorganization of the Northeast Political and Economic Councils into an administrative council on a 3-3-3 ratio, the appointment of a non-partisan mayor of Changchun and participation in the "magistrates council" by both

parties. It was strongly desired that Changchun be a peaceful city and secret police must not be allowed to infiltrate—this was of importance in connection with the organization of the police by a neutral mayor, rather than the adoption of the Government system of police under the National Government's control. Once the army reorganization plan had been determined and implemented and the disposition of troops had been decided upon, military matters should be separated from civil administrative affairs, military reorganization being placed under the control of the Executive Headquarters and civil affairs under the administrative council. This would ensure separation of political from military affairs and should give reassurance to all concerned.

Military. Demobilization should be carried out in accordance with a reorganization plan to be agreed upon and a procedure should be adopted to distinguish the National Government army from local forces. The Communist Party wished to have five divisions under the army reorganization program for Manchuria and would accept an earlier date for completion of the army reorganization plan. National Government and Communist troops would garrison different areas, with the Communist forces stationed in the major cities now under Communist control.

It was my opinion, I informed General Chou, that in order to avoid the possibility that he envisaged—the National Government attack on Changchun—an agreement had to be reached quickly, this being made equally urgent because of the situation in north China. With respect to the fear of Yenan that the Government occupation of Changchun might lead to the raising of other points, such as Harbin, I said that my attitude toward the National Government would be the same as it was now toward the Communist Party following its seizure of Changchun. Commenting on the Communist Party's desire for five divisions in Manchuria, I pointed out that this was five times the number provided for in the original military reorganization agreement and would inevitably result in a demand from the Government for a corresponding increase in its strength. It was suggested to General Chou that it would be preferable to hold down the total strengths and provide for one Communist army to five National Government armies in Manchuria, thus keeping in line with the five to one ration previously established in the military reorganization plan for the 12 month period. It was pointed out to him that the critical factor was the method and rapidity with which readjustment of the strengths and the decision regarding disposition of troops could be made. In the matter of troop deployments, it was observed that the Communist Party might wish to have its main strength north of Changchun in view of the present deployment of Communist forces and inasmuch as the Government had few units in that area, but that the Government would eventually insist on actual occupation of Changchun if its troop deployments were confined to areas south of Changchun.

For several days prior to May 22 I had almost daily discussions with the Generalissimo regarding the detailed terms for a military settlement, the redistribution of troops as a condition precedent to the issuance of a cease-fire order and tentative arrangements whereby the Communists would voluntarily evacuate Changchun and an advance section of the Executive Headquarters would assume control of the city, pending further settlement of problems relating to Changchun and areas north of that city. On May 22, the Generalissimo informed me that he had not heard from his military commanders in Manchuria for three days and feared that following their success at Ssupingchieh (captured by Government troops on May 19 after fighting lasting over a month) they were advancing toward Changchun. The Generalissimo expressed his agreement with me that occupation of Changchun by Government forces at a time when the basis of an agreement with the Communists was practically completed would be inadvisable and said that he was leaving for Mukden on May 24 in order to keep control of the situation. I pointed out that if the situation was as he described it, a delay of two days was too long. The Generalissimo replied that he had a prior engagement that he must keep and that he would go to Mukden on May 24 and return as soon as possible in order that we might proceed with the negotiations to completion. The Generalissimo and Madame Chiang Kai-shek departed for Mukden on May 23, this trip starting a chain of events which were almost completely disastrous in their effects on the situation.

On May 23, I conveyed to General Chou En-lai three points given to me by the Generalissimo prior to his departure as conditions precedent to any general agreement: (1) The Communist Party must make every effort to facilitate the restoration of communications; (2) in any agreement regarding Manchurian issues, provision must be made for carrying out the military demobilization and reorganization plan within specified dates; and (3) the Generalissimo would not commit himself to further agreements without an understanding that when members of field teams or of higher staff groups reached an impasse, the final decision would be left to the U.S. member.

In elaboration of these points, I explained to General Chou that I had informed the Generalissimo that the question of all other communications, as well as railways, had been insisted upon by the Communist Party and that the problem of railway fortifications had long been a stumbling block. The Generalissimo had expressed his willingness to leave these points to discussion between General Chou and General Yu Ta-wei, National Government Minister of Communications. It was further explained that while the Generalissimo did not commit himself definitely regarding readjustment of military strengths, it was my impression that he did not exclude reconsideration of this point. It was stressed to General Chou that the Generalissimo had been most insistent on the third point and that someone had to be trusted in order to prevent difficulties which might negate all that was being done in an effort to reach a solution—I would guarantee the impartiality of the U.S. members. While the Generalissimo did not analyze this point, it was my assumption that he meant routine matters, such as movement of teams, and I told General Chou that I did not think that the Generalissimo had in mind the Commissioners or the Committee of Three and that he would certainly not delegate to a U.S. member the final decision regarding political reorganization.

At the time of his departure for Mukden, I suggested to the Generalissimo that he consider the advantages of reaching a decision while in Mukden in order that he might make a statement there regarding the termination of hostilities—if he found my suggestions acceptable in principle, he could so inform me, and if it was possible to obtain from the Communist Party similar agreement, I would inform him accordingly. Immediate action could follow in the form of issuance of orders forbidding advances, attacks or pursuits, followed by the entry of the advance section of the Executive Headquarters into Changchun. The Generalissimo promised to send me a letter by courier from Mukden, and, as I informed General Chou, that was the extent of my knowledge of developments at that time.

General Chou was asked whether the Communist Party would agree to my proposals: that is, the evacuation of Changchun by the Communist troops, the entry into Changchun of the advance section of the Executive Headquarters and the cessation of further advances of Government troops. I told General Chou that I should also like to know his reaction to the three conditions of the Generalissimo and suggested that we forward a joint message to the Generalissimo on this basis.

General Chou stated that he could assure me of the Communist Party's acceptance of the arrangement for the evacuation of Changchun by its troops, the establishment of an advance section of the Executive Headquarters at that city and the cessation of advances by Government troops toward Changchun, with the issuance of orders by both sides for the cessation of advances, attacks and pursuits. He added, however, that the Generalissimo's three conditions were new and offered comment as follows: General Chou would endeavor to solve the communications problems with General Yu Ta-wei along the lines of destruction of fortifications excepting those essential to protection of railways from banditry, the restoration of all kinds of communications, the lifting of censorship by both parties on postal and telegraphic communications and participation by the Communist Party in railway administration. General Chou had no objection to abiding by the second condition. The third condition—that of the authority for decision by U.S. members—was new and he would try to convince his associates, but he would need time before being able to give his reply. General Chou expressed his fear that the Generalissimo had gone to Mukden in order to be absent at this time from negotiations and that it might still be the intention of the Generalissimo to employ force to settle the Manchurian issues. He also indicated his concern that the National Government military commanders in Manchuria would persuade the Generalissimo to seek a settlement by force.

On May 23 the National Government forces entered Changchun, following a Communist withdrawal from that city and little or no opposition from the Communist forces after the Government's capture of Ssupingchieh on May 19.

The absence of the Generalissimo from Nanking at this time and the difficulty of communications between that city and Mukden, together with the impossibility of direct contact with him, made for an extremely unsatisfactory situation at a most critical moment. The expected brief visit to Mukden eventually lengthened into 11 days before the return of Generalissimo and Madame Chiang Kai-shek to Nanking. In spite of my urgent appeals by radio to the Generalissimo for the issuance of an order for the termination of offensive operations, he took no action toward that end, although his earlier insistence had been on the evacuation of Changchun by the Communist troops and occupation by Government forces as a precedent to further negotiation and the issuance of a cease-fire order. To make matters more serious, the Government troops, after their occupation of Changchun, continued to advance north along the rail line toward Harbin and toward Kirin in the east, and the result was to increase Communist suspicion and distrust of the Government's promises and to place my own impartial position as a possible mediator in a questionable light insofar as the Communists were concerned. The positions were now reversed. Where formerly difficulties arose from the Communist attack on Changchun in open violation of the cease-fire order and the consequent stronger stand taken by the Communist generals in Manchuria, the present situation played directly into the hands of the National Government military commanders in Manchuria, who now felt sure that they could settle the problem by force and were therefore disinclined to compromise with the Communists.

The situation during this period had been made considerably worse through an unbridled press and radio campaign of propaganda attacks by both parties. I felt that the atmosphere in which discussions for the termination of hostilities were being held had grown so bitter that some steps had to be taken to moderate this propaganda campaign and that I was probably the only person in a position to take any action in this regard. It was realized that I might be critically attacked for appearing to tell the Chinese how to run their own affairs but some such action seemed imperative at this time. On May 20, therefore, I issued a statement[35] to the press, in which attention was called to the gravity of the existing situation,

[35]See Volume Two, Appendix I, Document 2, for the full text.

both in Manchuria and in north China, to the efforts being made to restore peace and to the serious dangers attendant upon "the reckless propaganda campaign of hate and suspicion" being engaged in by both sides. On the day this statement was released to the press the Kuomintang Minister of Information called on me to assure me of his cooperation and to ask what he could do to help in abating the propaganda campaign. I informed him that I could not advise the National Government without knowing what the Communist Party's action would be and pointed out that the effect of this propaganda was harmful to both sides and served to convince the American public that this was a free-for-all fight in China with little regard for the actual facts. I admitted that I did not know the effect of such propaganda in China but I did know that it made the negotiations for peace almost impossible. General Chou En-lai informed me on May 21 that he agreed with my statement and had telegraphed the text to Yenan. He said that he would call on the Kuomintang Minister of Information and discuss the matter with him with a view to deciding upon measures for the cessation of the propaganda attacks. Subsequent conversations between the Minister of Information and General Chou resulted in at least a temporary understanding between them regarding a cessation of the propaganda campaign and distortions of reports on military activities and for a brief period there was a very decided lessening of the propaganda attacks by both sides.

The propaganda attacks by the Communist Party broadcast from Yenan were later centered on the American position in China and served to indicate the suspicion engendered among the Communists both toward the U.S. Government and toward me personally by the failure of the National Government to halt the northward advance of its troops after the occupation of Changchun. My position was seriously compromised in the subsequent negotiations as a result of having presented my own proposals for the evacuation by the Communists of Changchun and the reopening of negotiations on Manchurian and other issues and my representation of the Generalissimo's conditions.

A detailed account of my exchange of messages with the Generalissimo during his absence from Nanking and of related matters is essential to an understanding of the developing situation at this time.

In accordance with the understanding at the time of the Generalissimo's departure from Nanking for Mukden on May

23, there was forwarded to me, in a letter from Madame Chiang under date of May 24, the following conditions offered by the Generalissimo as a basis for an understanding with the Communist Party:

1. The Cessation of Hostilities Order is to be carried out in spirit as well as to the letter.

2. The demobilization and reorganization of the armies is to proceed according to program.

3. The restoration of communications must be effected.

4. Method of procedure; (a) The Communist Party should not obstruct or impede the National Government in taking over sovereignty in accordance with the Sino-Soviet Treaty; (b) the Communist Party should not interfere with or obstruct the National Government's efforts to repair railways in all parts of China, the resumption of traffic along such railways to be begun within a specific time limit to be set by the Executive Headquarters; (c) in carrying out the three agreements (Cessation of Hostilities Order, military reorganization plan and the restoration of communications agreement),U.S. officers in Executive Headquarters or on the field teams must have the determining voice and the authority both in the execution and in the interpretation of views held in divergence by the two parties.

The letter concluded with the request that the Generalissimo be informed whether the Communist Party agreed with these terms and whether the U.S. representative would be willing to "guarantee" the good faith of the Communists. No mention was made in the letter of the Generalissimo's intention or willingness to issue an order halting advances, attacks and pursuits or to agree to the establishment of an advance section of the Executive Headquarters at Changchun, both of which had been envisaged at the time of his departure for Mukden.

In a second letter from Madame Chiang at Mukden, under the date of May 24, it was stated that the Generalissimo was willing for me to inform the Communist Party, in the event of their acceptance of the proposals described in the previous letter, that there was a possibility of his acceptance of my suggestion that the Communist Party have three divisions in Manchuria, as compared with 15 divisions for the Government—these increases to come out of the total number in the military reorganization plan. The Generalissimo also stated that the Communist troops in Manchuria should be stationed in the new boundaries of Heilungkiang Province, and, with respect to political questions, said that chairmanship of the provincial governments in areas where Communist troops would be stationed could be settled when military problems were decided upon.

On May 25, prior to the receipt of the two above-described letters from Madame Chiang, I discussed the situation with General Chou En-lai and, expressing my desire for an immediate cessation of hostilities, pointed out that my fears then were identical with those of the preceding month—at that time it was feared that the successful Communist generals at Changchun would hold out for conditions unacceptable to the Government, as they felt themselves in a strong position after the capture of Changchun; now the National Government generals would adopt the same attitude and the result would be the same. It was a case of the local commanders thinking only in terms of the local situation and losing sight of the over-all situation. It was pointed out to General Chou that until we had received the Generalissimo's letter there was no basis for negotiation beyond the previous three point proposal made by the Generalissimo.

On May 26, after General Chou had learned of the terms proposed in Madame Chiang's first letter from Mukden, he forwarded to me his reply, the substance of which is as follows:

> After the National Government's entry into Changchun, if the Government is willing to resume negotiations on the basis of its month-old statement that once Changchun is occupied an immediate truce can be effected, this is the moment to do so. The Executive Headquarters should immediately send a detachment to Changchun to take up the task of terminating hostilities.
>
> The Communist Party agrees in principle to the immediate implementation of the three agreements mentioned in Madame Chiang's letter but there should be included a fourth

agreement—that of March 27 for the entry of field teams into Manchuria. With regard to the question of sovereignty in Manchuria, if this refers to taking over from the Soviet Union, the latter has withdrawn and the procedure of taking over sovereignty has already been completed. If this implies the disposition of troops, this is a matter for decision by the Committee of Three in discussions on demobilization and reorganization of armies in Manchuria. If this implies civil administration in Manchuria, it is suggested that the Northeast Political and Economic Councils be reorganized into a democratic Northeast Administrative Council. Regarding the restoration of traffic, the Communist Party is willing that the repair of railways be immediately expedited in accordance with the restoration of communications agreement and General Chou will begin talks with General Yu Ta-wei on the detailed measures which will later be presented to the Committee of Three for approval. In regard to the question of authority for decision by U.S. officers, General Chou will exert further efforts on the basis of General Marshall's previous proposal that the U.S. representative on field teams be given the determining voice in the procedure of making the investigations.

On May 26, after the discussion with General Chou of the terms presented to the Generalissimo, I despatched to the latter at Mukden a message along the following lines:

General Chou is preparing a statement of agreements and commitments on certain details involved in your statement of general terms, but is unable to commit himself on details regarding the matter of procedure of the Government in taking over sovereignty and the extent of authority proposed for U.S. officers.

In the meantime, I make the following recommendations and observations: (1) General Chou and I propose the immediate establishment of an advance section of the Executive Headquarters at Changchun; (2) I urge that you immediately issue orders terminating advances and pursuits by National Government

125

troops within 24 hours of the time of the issuance of such order, publicly announcing such order and stating that this is done in furtherance of your desire to end fighting and to settle matters by peaceful methods of negotiation.

To press your present military advantage will invite a repetition of the unfortunate results of early National Government experience in Manchuria and the result of the more recent belligerent attitude of the Communist leaders at Changchun. In any event, to do otherwise would be contrary to your recent proposal to the Communist Party.

In regard to the proposal for decision by U.S. officers, I do not feel that the U.S. Commissioner at the Executive Headquarters should be put in the position of deciding on major matters shortly to arise and suggest restricting U.S. decision to specific matters—such as, when, where and how teams should proceed, whom they should see and decisions covering local situations, as well as final decision in the advance section regarding all immediate arrangements and matters in Manchuria pertaining to the termination of hostilities. This should also include decisions in the Executive Headquarters regarding matters referred to the Commissioners by the teams or the team chairmen and matters related to the restoration of communications. In all these decisions, there should be no authority to decide on political matters unless provided for in specific stipulations in later agreements. I conclude with a request for an explanation of the phrase "guarantee the good faith of the Communists."

Under date of May 28, Madame Chiang forwarded to me from Mukden a letter, the chief points of which are as follows:

The Generalissimo is replying to your message of May 26 through Dr. T.V. Soong. (The Generalissimo had asked that I communicate with him during his absence from Nanking through Dr. Soong.) The Generalissimo is irritated over the statement by General Chou (contained in the latter's letter of May 26 to

126

me) that he agrees "in principle" to the implementation of the three agreements and says that if both you and the Government stand firm the Communist Party will come to terms. In the event the Communists do not do so, the Generalissimo states that the only course left open is to occupy the strategic centers in Manchuria and the Communists would thus be forced to carry out the agreements.

In a letter from Mukden, under date of May 28 (received in Nanking May 30), the Generalissimo informed me:

I am "fundamentally in agreement" with your proposals of May 26 and set forth the following points for implementation of your proposals and in order to make their meaning and purpose clearer. I find it necessary to be more precise and definite in my dealings with the Communist Party as a result of my experience of the past five months. The points are:

(1) It is my desire and the object of my visit to Mukden to issue orders for halting advances and pursuits but you must obtain Communist assurances that the plan for military reorganization will be immediately put into effect and first carried out in the Northeast. You must formulate immediately and inform me of the concrete measure for the enforcement of the military reorganization plan. The advance section of the Executive Headquarters will be established on the day of the issuance of the cease-fire order.

(2) The National Government cannot abandon the right to take over any area but may, however, agree to send, after the National Government advance has halted, only administrative officials and such military and police forces as are absolutely necessary for the maintenance of local order and communications. These representatives are to take over the administration of various areas not yet taken over and areas which were once taken over but later seized by the Communist Party —the latter must not obstruct such action.

(3) The U.S. representative must be empowered with the authority for decision regarding the restoration of railways and other communications and regarding the time limit of the completion of this task.

(4) It is agreed that the U.S. representative's authority should be confined to specific matters but all executive matters regarding the restoration of railways and communications must be included in the scope of such authority.

(5) Regarding the guarantee of the good faith of the Communists, you are expected to set time limits for carrying out all agreements in which you have participated and to assume responsibility for supervision over strict observance of such agreements on the part of the Communist Party.

On May 29, having received no reply from the Generalissimo to my letter of May 26 (the above-described letter reached Nanking on May 30) and in view of the continued National Government advance in Manchuria and the absence of any action by the Generalissimo to end fighting, other than the general terms contained in Madame Chiang's letter of May 24, I felt that I must clarify my position in relation to the situation and requested Dr. T.V. Soong to forward the following message to the Generalissimo at Mukden:

"The continued advances of the Government troops in Manchuria in the absence of any action by you to terminate the fighting other than the terms you dictated via Madame Chiang's letter of May 24 are making my services as a possible mediator extremely difficult and may soon make them virtually impossible."

Discussions with General Chou on May 30 of the Generalissimo's proposals in his letter of May 28 revealed Communist fears that the National Government had no intention of halting the advance of its troops but instead was trying to settle the issue by resort to force. The Communists feared that, although the Changchun problem was now solved, the National Government planned to continue the war, particularly in Manchuria, until they should capture the large cities and occupy the rail lines. General Chou expressed his belief that the Government would then consider the resumption of negotiations and that it had organized to carry out its plans even without further U.S. aid to the Government. I informed General Chou that it would be necessary for me to discuss various issues with the Generalissimo personally before I would be in a position to estimate the prospect of successful negotiations at present. The Generalissimo had stated that he would agree to have only the Committee of Three as negotiators regarding military revision and deployment and political reorganization and had rejected the Democratic League's proposal for the reorganization of the Northeast Political Council and for the League's participation in the reorganization of local governments. As participation of the Committee of Three in discussion of Military and political questions definitely involved me, I was determined not to reenter the negotiations as a mediator unless there was a reasonably certain basis of compromise and so informed General Chou.

Regarding the situation in Manchuria, I pointed out to General Chou that the National Government generals now had access to the Generalissimo and I, of course, did not and asked him to remember that the action of the Communist Party in launching a full-fledged attack on Changchun in April had almost destroyed my powers of negotiation with the National Government and that while the prospects of ending the hostilities appeared gloomy I would not quit in the middle of a fight and that I was not a pessimist. I repeated that I must, however, talk with the Generalissimo in order to obtain an idea of his intentions.

On May 31, after the receipt of a message from the Generalissimo, sent through the U.S. Commissioner of the Executive Headquarters, advising me that he expected to remain in Peiping for two or three days before returning to Nanking, I forwarded a further message to the Generalissimo, the pertinent portion of which is quoted hereunder:

> "I have not received a reply to my message to you of May 29th. I must therefore repeat that under the circumstances of the continued advance of the Government troops in Manchuria my services in mediation are becoming not only increasingly difficult but a point is being reached where the integrity of my position is open to serious question. I

therefore request you again to issue immediately an order terminating advances, attacks or pursuits by Government troops, and also that you authorize the immediate departure of an advance section of Executive Headquarters to Changchun."

On June 1 the Generalissimo replied to my previous messages as follows:

"I have just received your telegram sent through Mr. Robertson. I surmise that you have received my message of May 28 sent through Dr. Soong. You may rest assured that in all my decisions I have kept in mind the difficulty of your position and am doing everything in my power to facilitate and assure the success of your word. I shall be returning to Nanking tomorrow or Monday when I shall tell you in person the Manchurian situation as I saw it. I am ready to agree to your proposal to send an advance party of the Executive Headquarters to Changchun for preliminary work in the event of my not being able immediately to issue orders to Government troops to terminate advances and so forth."

On June 3 the Generalissimo returned to Nanking. After a detailed discussion with him of the situation, I forwarded to General Chou En-lai a memorandum, under date of June 4, in which were set forth the Generalissimo's proposals for a settlement:

The Generalissimo has authorized the immediate despatch of an advance section of the Executive Headquarters to Changchun, to get established there in preparation for carrying out whatever agreements may be reached for the cessation of hostilities. The delay in the establishment of this advance section has been due to mistranslation of my request on this subject. I am ordering the Executive Headquarters to act in this matter.

The Generalissimo is willing to issue orders immediately to the National Government armies in Manchuria to cease advances, attacks and pursuits for a period of 10 days to afford the Communist Party an opportunity to complete negotiations with the National Government on:

(a) Detailed arrangements to govern the termination of hostilities in Manchuria; (b) definite arrangements, including time limits, for complete resumption of communications in north China; and (c) the basis for carrying out without further delay the plan for military reorganization.

In his conversation with me regarding the above-described proposals, the Generalissimo had originally stipulated a period of one week during which the negotiations for an over-all settlement should be completed and later agreed to an extension to 10 days. He also stated very emphatically that this was his final effort to deal with the Communists, as the economic situation in the country was deteriorating at such a rate with communications disrupted and general economic stagnation that even all-out war was preferable to this condition.

General Chou informed me on June 4 of his acceptance of the Generalissimo's proposal but objected to the 10 day period for negotiations as too brief to permit the reaching of agreement on the several vital problems to be discussed. General Chou suggested a period of one month and I was subsequently able to persuade the Generalissimo to extend the period to 15 days.

Prior to the actual issuance of the order for cessation of advances, attacks and pursuits, it was arranged that General Chou would discuss with General Yu Ta-wei and Colonel Donald C. Hill, U.S.A., Chairman of the Executive Headquarters Communications Group, the problem of the restoration of communications. I had already had prepared a draft proposal on the subject of the authority of U.S. officers to have the determining vote under certain circumstances and this had been presented to both sides for study and later discussions by the Committee of Three. The other question of importance was that of the reorganization of the armies and I pointed out to General Chou, who was at this time preparing to return to Yenan for discussion of the Generalissimo's proposals with the Communist leaders, that no information was available regarding Communist troop dispositions, thus making it difficult to draw up a draft statement on military reorganization and redispositions in Manchuria. General Chou said that he would obtain detailed data in Yenan on this question.

In a conversation with General Chou on June 6, prior to his return to Yenan, I again stressed the difficulties created because of the deep distrust prevailing on both sides and the many stupid and unnecessary actions of each side which had contributed to building up that suspicion. I emphasized to him, as I had done to the National Government representatives, the great desirability of avoiding measures which had little effect and which at the same time would cause great damage in arousing suspicion during this extremely critical period and also the desirability of making concessions without waiting for the submission of the other party's proposals —this would tend to build up confidence and faith and was very necessary in view of the limited time for negotiations during the truce period established in the new agreement.

XXI.

ANNOUNCEMENT OF TEMPORARY TRUCE PERIOD IN MANCHURIA; ESTABLISHMENT OF ADVANCE SECTION OF THE EXECUTIVE HEADQUARTERS AT CHANGCHUN

On June 6, 1946, the Generalissimo issued a press release announcing the temporary truce period in Manchuria. The text of this announcement is as follows:

> "I am issuing orders at noon today to my armies in Manchuria to halt all advances, attacks and pursuits for a period of 15 days commencing noon Friday, June 7th. I am doing this to give the Communist Party an opportunity to demonstrate in good faith their intention to carry out the agreement they had previously signed. In taking this action the Government in no way prejudices its right under the Sino-Soviet Treaty to take over the sovereignty of Manchuria.
>
> "The following matters must be satisfactorily settled within the 15 day period:
>
> "a. Detailed arrangements to govern a complete termination of hostilities in Manchuria.
>
> "b. Detailed arrangements, and time schedules, for the complete restoration of communications in China, and

"c. A definite basis for carrying out without further delay the agreement of February 25, 1946, for the demobilization, reorganization and integration of the armed forces in China."

General Chou En-lai, on behalf of the Communist Party, issued an announcement to the press of the truce period in Manchuria on the same day, although he indicated that he regretted the lack of a joint statement by the two parties as he feared that the Government announcement would be viewed as an ultimatum. I had earlier prepared a press release in the form of an announcement by the Committee of Three of the truce in Manchuria but the Generalissimo declined to enter into a joint press release on this matter. The following is the text of the Communist release:

"The Chinese Communist Party is advocating all the time an unconditional and true termination of civil warfare, which applies to hostilities in China proper and in Manchuria as well. It is due to the persistence of the Chinese Communist Party, the aspiration of the Chinese people, and the efforts exerted by General Marshall, that the Generalissimo's issuance of orders to halt all advances, attacks and pursuits in Manchuria for a period of 15 days and negotiations on the following matters are secured:

"(a) Detailed arrangements to govern a complete termination of hostilities in Manchuria.

"(b) Detailed arrangements and time schedules for the complete restoration of communications in China, and

"(c) A definite basis for carrying out without further delay the agreement of February 25, 1946, for the demobilization, reorganization and integration of the armed forces in China.

"Though we feel concerned over the shortness of the 15 day period, and that the inevitable involvement of political subjects pertaining to Manchuria, or even China as a whole, into the forthcoming negotiation would call for a longer period for discussion, we concur with the 15 day cease fire arrangement, having in mind that no opportunity for the realization of peace should be skipped over. In doing so, we will exert out best efforts toward bringing the negotiations to a success. We hope that the Kuomintang, in compliance with the desire of the Chinese people as well as nations abroad, would demonstrate in good faith their intention to carry out the agreements they had previously signed, and make the temporary armistice a lasting truce, with advances, attacks and pursuits stopped forever."

It should be noted that each of the press releases carried undertones of the distrust and bitterness between the two Parties and, by implication, blamed the other for the failure to carry out previous agreements.

Upon receiving the Generalissimo's agreement for the establishment of an advance section of the Executive Headquarters at Changchun, on June 4 I informed the Executive Headquarters by radio of this agreement and instructed that this action should be carried out "with the understanding that the special instructions to govern the functions of this advance section will be issued later." On June 5 the Committee of Three authorized the issuance of a press release announcing the establishment of the advance section "in preparation for carrying out whatever agreements may be reached for the cessation of hostilities." It was also announced that General Byroade would be the senior American officer in this advance section and that Brigadier General Thomas S. Timberman would temporarily take over General Byroade's duties as Director of Operations in the Executive Headquarters. On June 5, General Hsu Yung-chang, Government member of the Committee of Three, informed the Government military authorities in Manchuria of the impending establishment of an advance section at Changchun and instructed that "in the preparatory period you should render every assistance and convenience to the said office." The actual functioning of this advance section was limited by the stipulations contained in a letter to me from the Generalissimo under date of June 6, in which he stated: "As regards the despatch of an advance section of the Executive Headquarters to the Northeast, as proposed by Your Excellency and the Communist representative, it may be sent to Changchun for preparatory work, but of course does not start work until concrete measures are settled."

General Byroade, with a small group of U.S. officers, officially opened the Advance Section of the Executive Headquarters at Changchun at noon on June 6. The handicap under which the limitation of the functions of the Advance Section placed the field teams in Manchuria was soon revealed when fighting broke out at Lafa, northeast of Changchun, where the Government military commanders charged the Communists had attacked after noon on June 7, the time at which the truce period began. Under the circumstances, there were four teams in Manchuria being directed by the Executive Headquarters at Peiping, rather than by the Advance Section on the spot. General Byroade immediately sent a U.S. officer to the scene of reported fighting as an observer, but it was clearly desirable that the Advance Section have control over the teams purely as a matter of administrative efficiency and in the interest of immediate action. On June 10, therefore, I addressed a memorandum to General Hsu Yung-chang asking that he obtain the Generalissimo's agreement for the Advance Section at Changchun to exercise direct control over the teams in Manchuria, but strictly in accordance with the limiting terms of the agreement of March 27. On June 11, I discussed this problem with General Hsu and pointed out that the sole question was that of administrative efficiency and that the matter was brought up as a result of an appeal from the Government military commanders, who asked for aid in settling the Lafa fighting. General Hsu emphasized repeatedly that the Generalissimo did not wish the Advance Section to operate during the 15 day truce period. The Executive Headquarters was, therefore, informed, in reply to its inquiries on this subject, that specific instructions from the Generalissimo precluded the functioning of the Advance Section until agreements should have been reached.

In the meantime, pursuant to my request, General Byroade forwarded to the Executive Headquarters and the Committee of Three on June 9 a proposed plan of operation[36] for the Advance Section and the field teams in Manchuria, which envisaged the initial use of eight teams in Manchuria and the immediate despatch by General Byroade of the members of those teams to designated points to make arrangements for

[36]See Volume Two, Appendix J, Document 1, for the full text.

135

the reception of the Chinese team members as they should become available. On June 15, the Committee of Three approved this plan and instructed the Executive Headquarters to put it into effect without delay, the instructions issued pointing out that the field teams in Manchuria would operate under the agreement of March 27 for the entry of teams into Manchuria.[37]

XXII.

NEGOTIATIONS DURING THE 15 DAY TRUCE PERIOD IN MANCHURIA

The first few days of the truce period were marred by disturbing incidents in Manchuria and Shantung Province. The Government military commanders in Manchuria charged that the Communist forces had launched an attack on Lafa, a city northeast of Changchun, at the beginning of the truce period, and, in the absence of teams under the direction of the Advance Section, General Byroade immediately despatched an American observer to that area. This incident was soon settled by the withdrawal of the Communist forces from Lafa but was complicated by the despatch of a message by General Tu Li-ming, National Government commander in Manchuria, to the Generalissimo, in which he stated that "if they (the Communists) show no sign of good faith and keep on attacking the Government troops, then it is my intention to instruct the troops under my command to resume attack and pursuit." It was my opinion that this was a serious matter in that General Tu was taking upon himself to interpret the measures to be taken to deal with the situation and, although General Tu would have been justified in adopting defensive measures or in ordering a counter-attack in a sector under Communist attack, the situation might again get completely out of hand if he ordered the resumption of advances, attacks and pursuits, which had been specifically prohibited under the orders for the temporary truce. As a result of my representations, the Government issued orders to General Tu instructing him to remain strictly on the defensive.

[37]See Volume Two, Appendix J, Document 2, for the full text of the instructions.

Additional difficulties were created by the opening of an attack on June 7 by Communist forces in Shantung Province along the Tsinan-Tsingtao Railway and at points north and south of Tsinan along the Tientsin-Pukou Railway. The Communist commander in that area attempted to justify his action by saying that it was in retaliation for attacks by Government forces in north Kiangsu on Communist-held towns and that his attacks were made only against points under puppet-occupation. The attacks, of course, had been conceived and ordered before the local commander had any knowledge of the truce. The continuation of these attacks after June 8 became a serious matter having later repercussions in the form of retaliatory action on the part of the Government, which moved two armies into Shantung—one to Tsingtao and the other to Tsinan—to meet a possible Communist threat to those cities; also, they furnished the Government with an example of Communist disregard of a formal agreement—the truce.

The possibility of a Communist attack on Tsingtao also brought up the question of the involvement of the U.S. Marines stationed at that city, where the U.S. Navy was training units of the Chinese Navy. General Chou En-lai stated categorically that the Communist armies would not attack Tsingtao and Tsinan, as the Communist attacks had been made only against towns held by former puppet troops, but there was much speculation in the press regarding the possible role of the U.S. Marines in the event of a Communist drive on Tsingtao and there were indications that the Government authorities at Tsingtao were desirous of having American aid in defending the city.

These incidents, leading to retaliatory action and the usual bitter recriminations, added to the difficulties of the situation and were followed almost immediately by the Government's occupation of Faku, a city northwest of Mukden, which the Communists charged was occupied by Government forces on June 9. Against this background of charges and countercharges, which were reflected in the press and which led to a breakdown of the temporary and short-lived propaganda truce, the discussions began looking toward agreement within the 15 day truce period on the points at issue between the two parties.

In separate discussions with the Chinese representatives it was decided that during the 15 day truce period the communications problem would be the first to be dealt with, followed by detailed arrangements for the cessation of hostilities and later by the question of revision of the army reorganization plan. General Chou En-lai would hold initial conferences with General Yu Ta-wei and Colonel Donald C. Hill on the communications question, and points on which agreement could not be reached would be referred to the Committee of Three. In discussion with General Chou of the Agreements to be reached, I expressed the opinion that there should be a detailed agreement regarding the readjustments of armed forces in Manchuria during the next six months, that this should be incorporated in a special annex to the agreement of February 25th for reorganization of the armies and that it should cover monthly periods for the first three months and quarterly periods thereafter. I pointed out that this part was more difficult of settlement than the problems of communications and cessation of hostilities and was the most essential problem for consideration.

In connection with the settlement of the political factors involved in the agreements to be reached, it was my opinion that the positions of the local governments in relation to the military redispositions were exceedingly important and might prove to be a stumbling block to the military revision. Several members of the PCC had called on me to suggest that the PCC Steering Committee be convened at this time to work simultaneously on political problems while the Committee of Three handled the military problems. I had informed them that this did not come within the scope of my authority, but I subsequently passed this information along to General Hsu Yung-chang. The Generalissimo had often stated that he would not negotiate on political problems until he had occupied Manchuria; he had, however, later said that after the Government's occupation of Changchun he would be prepared to negotiate both political and military questions. The Communist attitude toward the discussion of political matters at this time was described by General Chou En-lai as including four possible formulas: (1) While discussing military reorganization, it would be preferable to omit discussion of political matters and to preserve the *status quo* in the various areas. (2) It had been suggested in the past that a provisional administrative council for the Northeast be formed to be charged with political, economic and communications problems—although the Generalissimo had not approved, this should still be given consideration. (3) The Generalissimo had suggested that the Committee of Three be empowered to solve adminis-

trative problems and, although General Marshall had been reluctant to accept this proposal, General Chou felt that it should
be given further consideration—as General Marshall did not
wish to be involved in political decisions, this could be solved
by the use of a platform approved by the coalition government and the Committee of Three could make an inspection
tour of Manchuria at the end of the 15 day truce period. (4)
At the end of the 15 day truce period, there would be immediate discussion of the reorganization of the government and
the government in Manchuria would be dealt with as a part of
the over-all solution of the reorganization of the government;
with regard to local governments, General Chou felt that once
the government was reorganized, the magistrates would proceed with reorganization of the local governments through the
medium of elections in accordance with the PCC platform and
that prior to elections they would maintain the *status quo.*

(a) *Restoration of Communications*

Colonel Donald C. Hill, U.S.A., Chairman of the Communications Group of the Executive Headquarters, prepared a
draft proposal for the restoration of communications, which
was presented to the two Chinese parties for study and discussion in the Committee of Three meetings.

General Chou En-lai informed me on June 14 that those
portions of Colonel Hill's draft which dealt with the reopening
of communications were generally acceptable but that sections
on the administration and operation of the railways, while in
principle seemingly all right, contained certain points which
needed reconsideration. General Chou agreed with General Yu
Ta-wei, National Government representative, that work
should first be begun on the Lunghai, Tientsin-Pukou and
Tsinan-Tsingtao lines, but pointed out that General Yu had
suggested revisions of the draft—these revisions to include the
deletion of the first paragraph, which was a general statement
on the reopening of communications, and to make provision for
armed railway police instead of the unarmed train guards.
General Yu, said General Chou, had also refused to accept the
draft proposal regarding administration and operation.

I explained to General Chou that the general statement
regarding the reopening of communications represented no
difficulties as this was included in another general document
prepared by General Yu covering the principles desired by
General Chou. With regard to the question of railway police,

General Yu had said that the guarding of installations along the rail lines had always in the past been the responsibility of the railway police and to use troops for that purpose would represent a change in a long-used system. I told General Chou that I had explained to General Yu that the Communist objection to the use of railway police arose from their fear of the use of secret police agents for purposes other than guarding the railways, but that General Yu did not discuss this point. Colonel Hill at this point of the conversation pointed out that the original communications agreement had provided for protection of the rail lines by the local troops in the areas through which the lines ran and that the introduction of new railway guards into Communist-held areas would involve another type of guard not previously agreed upon. Colonel Hill also explained, in regard to railway administration and operation procedure, that General Yu did not desire to discuss this question at present because of the insufficient time in the 15 day truce period to permit a decision on a subject which did not require immediate decision; General Yu had suggested that work could be started on a plan for administrative control but that discussion should be postponed until there was sufficient time for full discussions and a final decision. In commenting on this point, General Chou stated that he would wish to have General Yu's views on the following three points before he made any decision: (1) The present railway agencies should be maintained pending the reaching of a new agreement and in the meantime the *status quo* should be preserved; (2) arrangements would have to be made prior to the establishment of through traffic; and (3) when the problems of administration and operation were discussed, Colonel Hill's draft should be used as the basis for discussion. In conclusion, I observed that the difficult point seemed to be the character of the railway and the railway guards in the Communist areas and that the difficulty was bound up in the suspicion entertained by the Communists—all other details being seemingly easy to adjust.

On June 23, the Committee of Three met for discussion of the draft proposal for the restoration of communications. General Yu Ta-wei brought up four points for discussion: (1) the destruction of fortifications; (2) employment of Communist Party personnel in the railway administration; (3) the desire of the Communist Party that the Government not send railway police to the sections repaired; and (4) the wish of the Communist Party to restore all communications, as well as railways. General Yu commented that the Government agreed in principle with the last point but laid special emphasis on the restoration of railway lines as the first step. General Yu stated that the Government was prepared to destroy all fortifications, blockhouses, et cetera, lying within 1,000 meters on either side of the rail lines but agreed to the compromise solution suggested by General Marshall that installations needed to defend railway stations, bridges, tunnels, workshops, storage depots and water points should be exempted. Colonel Hill commented that agreement had apparently been reached that fortifications should be destroyed, except those required for the defense of vital railway installations, but that the definition of what constituted vital installations had not been agreed upon. Colonel Hill suggested that vital installations be defined as railway stations of the first, second and third classes, all tunnels and bridges with a total span of more than five meters.

General Chou En-lai commented that agreement had been reached in February on the restoration of communications but that the carrying out of this agreement had been blocked by the question of the destruction of fortifications; that while many field teams had decided that fortifications should be destroyed, the Chinese branches of the Executive Headquarters could not agree on an interpretation of this question; that in April the Commissioners had referred this matter to the Committee of Three, which, because of the Manchurian situation, had not been able to enter into discussions on this problem; and that as a result the restoration of railways and the destruction of fortifications had been delayed up to the present time. General Chou continued that he agreed that railway repair should be given priority and that he and General Yu had agreed on three railway lines for initial restoration. He did not insist that all fortifications on and along the railway lines should be destroyed. Commenting on the question of railway administration, General Chou felt that an interim arrangement had to be worked out prior to the reorganization of the government and expressed agreement with the points set forth in Colonel Hill's draft: (1) railway control will be unified under the Minister of Communications and (2) the National Government recognizes that in Communist-held areas the Communist Party will nominate personnel to take examinations to be given by the Railway Control Teams of the Executive Headquarters, the Communist Party to have the right to be represented in the administration and control of those railway lines which concern the Communists. With regard to the question of railway police, General Chou said that this was an entirely new proposal never before mentioned in the agreement on the restoration of communications, protection for railway lines previously having been made the responsibility of the local troops of each party and of the unarmed train guards. As this proposal was contrary to the previous agreement and since the Communist Party strongly objected to the organization of railway police as such, General Chou found this proposal unacceptable.

Further discussion followed on the question of the various railway stations, during which it was revealed that about three-fourths of the stations on the Tientsin-Pukou Railway were third class stations and that only a few were fourth class, those being flag stops. General Chou agreed to accept the provision for the retention of fortifications lying within 1,000 meters of first and second class stations, a compromise distance of 200 meters for third class stations and the definition of five meters span for bridges (this was explained by Colonel Hill as the approximately maximum span that could be repaired by timber girders, a longer span requiring steel girders very difficult to obtain). General Chou, while expressing his agreement to this provision, pointed out that the result would be that no fortifications would be destroyed, to which General Yu replied that these fortifications would be used only to protect the lines against bandits and that no new fortifications would be constructed unless the lines were attacked. It was suggested by me, and approved by the Committee, that provision be made in the agreement for the construction of new fortifications only to meet attacks against the railway line itself and only when approved by a communications team.

On June 24, in further discussion of the problem of the restoration of communications, a compromise agreement was reached on the destruction of fortifications on the Lunghai Railway west of Hsuchou, the date for such destruction to be settled later between General Yu and General Chou because of its connection with the army reorganization plan. In commenting on the question of Communist participation in the operation of the railway lines after the reopening thereof, General Chou pointed out that on some lines, such as the Peiping-Suiyuan Railway, a large part of the line was in Communist territory and the Communists had their own separate and independent administration for the operation of this line. He felt, therefore, that Communist personnel should not only participate in the operation of the line over the reopened sectors but should also participate in the over-all administration of the line. General Yu replied that he had no authority to agree to this proposal and this question was finally resolved with the inclusion in the agreement of a statement that "qualified railway personnel of the Chinese Communist Party may be taken into the employ of the Ministry of Communications in accordance with a plan to be determined." The agreement further stated that the qualifications of such personnel would be determined by examinations conducted by the communications teams or by the Communications Group of the Executive Headquarters.

At the end of this discussion agreement was reached on a document[38] entitled "Directive for Reopening of Lines of Communications in North and Central China." The document provided for the opening of lines of communication in north and central China without delay; for definite time limits, ranging form 30 days for the Hsuchow-Haichow sector of the Lunghai Railway to 150 days for the Yuanshih-Anyang sector of the Peiping-Hankow Railway, for the repair of 11 sectors of the Tientsin-Pukou, Tsinan-Tsingtao, Lunghai, Peiping-Suiyuan, Peiping-Hankow, Peiping-Kupeikou and Tung-Pu Railways; for the supervision of construction by the communications teams under the control of the Ministry of Communications; for the destruction of fortifications, as described above; for the use of Communist Party personnel in the railway administration; and for future discussion of the restoration of all other lines of communications.

Agreement was thus reached on the first of the three major points at issue, which were to be settled during the 15 day truce period, it being understood that all documents on which agreement was reached were to be signed at the same time, in accordance with a stipulation to that effect by the Generalissimo.

(b) *Termination of Hostilities in Manchuria*

General Byroade prepared a draft proposal for the termination of hostilities in Manchuria which was presented to the two Chinese representatives for study and later discussion in the Committee of Three. An effort was made to produce as simple a document as possible, since the complications would

[38]See Volume Two, Appendix K, Document 1, for the full text.

143

appear in the document providing for revision of those sections of the military reorganization plan affecting Manchuria.

In discussion of this draft proposal with me, General Chou En-lai expressed a desire to include the March 27th agreement for the entry of teams into Manchuria as well as the Cessation of Hostilities Order of January 10, since the former was specifically drawn up for Manchuria. He pointed out that the situation had changed and that parts of both of these agreements had become obsolete. He expressed particular concern over the provision in the Cessation of Hosilities Order relating to the movement of Government troops into Manchuria for the purpose of reestablishing Chinese sovereignty and his desire that terms of the Order, such as this one, which was no longer effective due to the complete withdrawal of Soviet troops, should be excluded from the Order. He felt that this point must be covered, as otherwise the Government might insist on sending troops to places, such as Harbin and Tsitsihar, now under Communist control, on the ground that these places had formerly been occupied by the Soviet troops and that the Government has thus not yet completed the process of restoring sovereignty. I pointed out to General Chou that the question of Government occupation would be covered in the agreement regarding troop redisposition in Manchuria within prescribed periods and that this document referred only to the immediate details of termination of hostilities. It was my opinion, therefore, that matters of this kind should not be contained in the document for the termination of hostilities.

In discussion of this draft proposal in a meeting of the Committee of Three on June 22,* General Chou En-lai suggested that there be omitted from the document any provision regarding the question of decision by the senior officer of the Advance Section, as had been originally incorporated in General Byroade's draft, and that a separate document on all matters regarding field teams and the question of decision by U.S. officers be prepared for application both to Manchuria and to China proper. This was agreed to by General Hsu Yung-chang, who pointed out that the three problems of restoration of communications, the termination of hostilities in Manchuria and the revision of the military reorganization plan constituted the over-all problem and that these would be solved all together and the documents embodying agreement on these

*This was the first meeting of the Committee of Three since March and marked my formal reentry into the negotiations as mediator.

problems would be signed at the same time.

On June 24, the Committee of Three approved the document,[39] which was entitled "Directive for the Termination of Hostilities in Manchuria," with the proviso that paragraph "c" of the Directive was agreed upon with the understanding that the matter of details and the question of decision by U.S. officers would be covered in separate documents. I explained to the Committee that I had written paragraph "f" of the document with the idea of avoiding unfortunate propaganda against the movement of Government troops into Manchuria. This paragraph, as adopted, reads: "The Government and the Communist Party will move no additional combat units to Manchuria. However, individual replacements of the Government are authorized for the purpose of bringing up to approved strength those units authorized in the basic plan for the reorganization and integration dated February 25, 1946, as hereafter amended."

This Directive, in the form of instructions from the Committee of Three to the Commissioners of the Executive Headquarters for the termination of hostilities in Manchuria, provides for the application to Manchuria of the Cessation of Hostilities Order of January 10, 1946, except as modified in the Directive or later by the Committee; for the separation from contact of troops in close or hostile contact; for the readjustment of troops on the basis of the situation believed to have existed at noon of June 7, 1946; for the cessation of all tactical movements; for the punishment of commanders who fail to carry out the terms of the Directive; and for the submission by both sides to the Advance Section, within 15 days of the effective date of the Directive, of lists of all units, strengths and locations in Manchuria.

Agreement on this document marked the settlement of the second of the major issues to be decided during the 15 day truce period, which, as explained in the discussion of the subject of revision of the military reorganization plan, was extended to noon on June 30.

(c) *Authority for Decision by U.S. Representatives*

As indicated in previous sections of this report, the question of authority by U.S. members of field teams had long been a subject for debate, and proposals to permit the U.S. team

---

[39]See Volume Two, Appendix K, Document 2, for the full text.

chairman to decide on the priority of team investigations had been brought up in the meetings of the Executive Headquarters Commissioners and of the Committee of Three. The National Government had supported such proposals and the U.S. representatives had urged such a solution as a means of ensuring prompt action to investigate reported violations of the Cessation of Hostilities Order. The Communist representatives in the Executive Headquarters and General Chou had opposed these proposals as a departure from the principle of unanimous agreement under which both the Executive Headquarters and its field teams had operated from the beginning. As a result it had been possible to obtain only a compromise solution of this problem, which was incorporated in a document signed by the Committee of Three on May 14, providing that in the event of continued disagreement by the team members, the U.S. member should report directly to the three Commissioners, the latter to reach a unanimous decision within 24 hours or report the matter to the Committee of Three for decision.

This question had again been brought into prominence by the Generalissimo when, prior to his departure for Mukden on May 23, he informed me that he would be unwilling to commit himself to further agreement without an understanding that when team members or corresponding higher staff groups reached an impasse the final decision would be left to U.S. members. While the Generalissimo did not at that time analyze in detail this condition, it was clear that it went beyond previous proposals for decisions on priority for team investigations.

In meetings of the Committee of Three during the truce period, the question first arose in discussion on June 22 of the draft proposal for the termination of hostilities in Manchuria. This draft provided that, in the event of disagreement, the decision of the senior officer in the Advance Section of the Executive Headquarters at Changchun would be accepted. General Chou En-lai had earlier proposed that this be altered to read: "The senior American officer at Changchun will report the situation to Executive Headquarters at Peiping or to the Committee of Three at Nanking, depending upon the urgency of the situation." In discussions during this meeting, however, he suggested that a separate document on all matters regarding field teams and the question of decision by U.S. representatives be prepared and that such a document be made applicable both to Manchuria and to China. This proposal was approved and General Chou subsequently prepared two draft proposals, one regarding action by field teams and the other

146

regarding the resolution of disagreements among field teams and the Executive Headquarters.

On June 24, in a meeting of the Committee of Three, General Chou's draft proposal regarding action by field teams was presented for discussion. The proposal was in the form of instructions from the Committee of Three to the Commissioners of the Executive Headquarters prescribing action by field teams, in four specifically described cases, for the purpose of assisting the teams to effect a uniform application of the terms of the agreement for the termination of hostilities in Manchuria. It was also expected to be applicable in all cases where troops were found in close contact or actually engaged in hostilities. This document[40] was not discussed in this meeting, as General Yu had not previously had an opportunity to study the proposal, and it was reserved for future discussion.

In this same Committee of Three meeting on June 24, agreement was reached on a document[41] entitled "Stipulations for the Resolution of Certain Disagreements among the Field and Communication Teams, and Executive Headquarters in Changchun and Peiping," although proposals for additions to the document were left for further study and discussion at a later date.

General Chou proposed that an additional paragraph be added as follows: "In case of disagreement as to the interpretation of the directive for the reopening of lines of communication, the senior American officer of the Communication Group of the Executive Headquarters is authorized to render the decision." No action was taken on this proposal.

General Yu Ta-wei presented a proposal for two additional paragraphs as follows: (1) In case of disagreement regarding where and when to send field teams, the U.S. Commissioner in Executive Headquarters in Peiping has the authority to render the decision; and (2) in case of disagreement concerning the interpretation of all agreements and the manner of execution of the agreements, a majority vote of the Committee of Three will be decisive. I immediately said that General Yu's second paragraph was a matter for negotiation between the two Chinese parties and that discussion of this ques-

[40]See Volume Two, Appendix K, Document 3, for the text of this document.

[41]See Volume Two, Appendix K, Document 4, for the full text.

tion should not be carried on in my presence. General Chou, in commenting on the first paragraph, pointed out that when the Committee of Three issued instructions for the despatch of field teams, the U.S. officer, in case of disagreement, was authorized by paragraph IIb of the document already agreed upon to direct the execution of the order and to despatch the team; he further stated that if no previous instructions had been issued for the despatch of a team, the U.S. Commissioner by virtue of paragraph IIa of the document was to render a report to the Committee of Three and ask for instructions. General Chou, therefore, asked for further time to permit him to study these two paragraphs proposed by General Yu.

The document, as agreed upon, provided for: (1) in case of disagreement regarding matters of urgency, the U.S. representative of a field or communication team may render his own report of the situation direct to Executive Headquarters at Changchun or Peiping requesting instructions; (2) in case of disagreement, the U.S. member of a field team is authorized to make the decision regarding where and when the team will proceed within his area to investigate military activities; (3) in case of disagreement regarding matters relating to cessation of hostilities and separation of forces, the U.S. member of a field team is authorized to issue orders in the name of the executive Headquarters to the local commanders of both sides; (4) in case of disagreement, the senior U.S. official of Executive Headquarters in Peiping or Changchun may render his own report to Executive Headquarters in Peiping or the Committee of Three requesting instructions; and (5) in case of disagreement regarding the implementation of orders or instructions from the higher level, the senior U.S. official of the Executive Headquarters in Peiping or Changchun is authorized to direct the execution of that order or instruction unless amended or rescinded by the higher level itself.

At this point, the Committee of Three had reached agreement on the problems of restoration of Communications and the termination of hostilities in Manchuria and had agreed on a document regarding the question of decision by U.S. representatives, with the possibility of additions to this document after further study and discussion. There remained only the important problem of the revision of the military reorganization plan.

(d) *Revision of the Basic Plan for Military Reorganization of February 25*

The problem of reaching agreement on revision of the basic plan for military reorganization of February 25 was the most difficult task facing the Committee of Three during the truce period, as it involved questions of troop distributions, troop strengths, demobilization and related political considerations which could not be divorced from the problem of revision of the basic plan.

On June 14, General Chou En-lai repeated the Communist Party's desire to have five divisions in Manchuria and suggested that under the redistribution plan the Communists would like to have one division stationed in each of five large cities (unnamed) in Manchuria. He said that Communist troops should be stationed in areas then under Communist control, but pointed out, in regard to the question of redistribution of troops, that the National Government held the most important, the best-developed and most densely populated areas of Manchuria. The National Government was thus in a position of having more food and supplies available for its troops than was the case with the Communists—the latter being in occupation of north Manchuria, which was sparsely populated and where food supplies for troops would be more of a problem. General Chou, therefore, felt that there were four factors to be considered in relation to redistribution of troops: (1) the number of troops, (2) the distribution of areas, (3) the transportation facilities and (4) supply facilities.

I informed General Chou that I had told the Generalissimo of the Communist Party's desire for five divisions and that, while the Generalissimo had made no definite statement, I believed that the Government would be willing to accept a 5 to 1 ration in Manchuria to replace the 14 to 1 ratio provided for in the military reorganization agreement of February 25. I said that this could be achieved by increasing the strength of the forces in Manchuria to six armies, three divisions of which would be Communist and 15 divisions National Government. I pointed out the unavoidable relationship between political considerations and military redistribution and suggested that the disposition of Communist troops might be related to the question of provinces where Communist Party members were chairmen of the provincial government. I added that I did not know what those provinces would be. I also said that, while I wished to avoid all political complications, it appeared that

149

the Communist Party's decision regarding the redistribution of its troops would be related to whether or not any commitment was made regarding the nature of the local district councils.

General Chou offered no comment on the redistribution of Government troops or on the question of comparative strengths but suggested that it should be possible to arrive at a figure for Communist troop strength in Manchuria somewhere between the five divisions desired by the Communists and the three divisions suggested by me. He felt that the concentration of each division at one point should provide reassurance to the Government.

On June 17, I informed General Chou that, while I could not at present say what the Government's terms or proposals were in regard to revision of the military reorganization plan, my greatest difficulty was that the Communist Party had not yet made any definite proposals. It was feared, therefore, that I might find myself in a position where my efforts of persuasion for moderation of terms might be handicapped by lack of knowledge of what the Communist conditions were. I pointed out that I expected to see the Generalissimo that evening and learn the Government's proposals, but I could only guess at what the Communists might consider as an equitable adjustment and was not, therefore, in a position to influence matters at this critical moment. I reminded him that he had given me only one very general statement and that was the extent of my knowledge of the Communist position.

General Chou replied that he had in previous discussion with me tried to convey a general impression and understanding of the Communist attitude on this question and that he had not made concrete statements because during the present negotiations the Communist Party had assumed the attitude of being willing to make concessions in order to reach a settlement. On political issues the Communist Party would have certain proposals to advance but had preferred to delay such proposals to a later date for fear that they would at the present time affect negotiations on the matters for immediate decision. In brief, said General Chou, the Communist Party advanced no proposals because it was willing to make concessions.

On June 17, after a conference with the Generalissimo, I forwarded to General Chou a memorandum to which were attached three papers constituting the principal proposals of the National Government for the agreements to be reached during the truce period: (1) Government Stipulations regarding North China in Connection with Proposed Readjustment of Troops in Manchuria[42]; (2) Manchuria Annex[43] (to be an annex to the amended agreement of February 25, 1946); and (3) Restoration of Communications.*

The first proposals for the revision of the basic military reorganization plan were presented to me by the National Government on June 12. Because of the unreasonable nature of some of the proposals, particularly in regard to Manchuria, I prepared a draft for revision of the basic plan on June 15, which I presented to the Generalissimo and discussed with him on the following day. On June 17 General Hsu Yung-chang forwarded to me the Government's proposed amendments to this draft and I incorporated these amendments and others given to me orally by Government representatives in a document for discussion. This document included the Government Stipulations for North China, the revision of the basic plan, a Manchuria Annex and a North China Annex. The Government Stipulations regarding North China and the Manchuria Annex, as stated in the preceding paragraph, were forwarded to General Chou for study. Full discussion of the revision of the basic plan** [44] [45] [46] was, however, held up at

[42]See Volume Two, Appendix K, Document 5, for the full text.

[43]See Volume Two, Appendix K, Document 6, for the full text.

*This document has been discussed above.

**See, in Volume Two, the following enclosures related to the revision of the basic military reorganization plan of February 25:

[44]Appendix K, Document 7—the National Government's "Draft of Supplemental Methods to Real Application regarding the Basic Plan of Army Reorganization and Integration of Communist Army into the National Army," presented to me on June 12.

[45]Appendix K, Document 8—a memorandum of June 17, 1946, from General Hsu Yung-chang to me enclosing suggested Amendments to the Army Reorganization and Integration of the Communist Army into the National Army Plan. This memorandum indicates the areas in which the Government wished Communist troops concentrated.

[46]Appendix K, Document 9—draft proposal as of June 17, 1946, for revision of the basic plan, based on the Government's original proposal and incorporating amendments suggested by General Hsu Yung-chang's memorandum of June 17 and by Government representatives orally. This enclosure includes only the revision of the basic plan, the Government Stipulations regarding north China and the Manchurian Annex (constituting part of this draft proposal) having been attached to this report as enclosures Nos. 42 and 43.

this time to permit completion of the documents regarding the restoration of communications, the termination of hostilities in Manchuria and authority for decision by U.S. representatives. When later discussions revealed the impossibility of reaching agreement for revision of the basic plan prior to the expiration of the extended truce period on June 30, negotiations were centered on a preliminary agreement covering only the principal points at issue, with the understanding that formal revision of the basic plan would be negotiated after the completion of the preliminary document.

On June 18 I held a conference with General Chou in regard to the Government proposals forwarded to him on June 17. The first of these papers required the evacuation of Communist troops from Jehol and Chahar Provinces before September 1, 1946; the occupation by Government forces of Chefoo and Weihaiwei in Shantung Province; the reinforcement of Tsingtao with one National Government Army to permit the withdrawal of the U.S. Marines stationed at that city; the evacuation by the Communists before July 1, 1946, of all localities in Shantung Province forcibly occupied by the Communist troops after noon of June 7, 1946, and their withdrawal a minimum distance of 30 *li* from such localities; the immediate occupation of these localities by Government garrisons; and the reinforcement of the Tientsin region by one Government army, commencing September 1, 1946, to permit the withdrawal of the U.S. Marine forces in that area.

In commenting on these papers, General Chou expressed his surprise at these portions related to China proper, described in the Stipulations regarding north China, and his belief that this was entirely the Generalissimo's idea. He said that he was not in a position to consider this proposal except those portions regarding the restoration of conditions in Shantung prior to June 7. He described the other parts of the proposal as completely unexpected and said that it was a heavy blow to him as he had been trying to compromise in every way possible on the various issues under discussion. He felt that the Government's intention was not to seek a solution of the problems and that public reaction would be similar to his. General Chou promised that he would radio the proposals to Yenan and said that he felt it necessary that he return there to make a report on the development of negotiations. He explained that during the period of the truce he had tried to work along the lines of compromise suggested by General Marshall and had, therefore, assumed an optimistic attitude in his reports to Yenan. Now, with the receipt of these new proposals, General Chou felt embittered, although there had been indications during the past few days of some change in the Government's attitude, as revealed by rumors and General Yu Ta-wei's attitude in the negotiations on the problem of restoration of communications.

General Chou, referring to specific points contained in the Government's proposals, said that except for the restoration of the status in Shantung prior to June 7, none of the other points could be considered by him, and pointed out that this date should be applied to Manchuria only, while the restoration of original positions in China proper should be based on the Cessation of Hostilities Order and the Executive Headquarters' directive—these would entail the use of January 13 as the date of the beginning of the truce and the establishment of positions. General Chou, replying to Government charges of Communist attacks on Government-held areas and Communist troop movements, pointed out that Kuomintang attacks had been made on Communist-occupied points off the railway lines, which had thus drawn no attention, and added that Communist Party troop movements could not be compared with those of the Government, as Communist troops moved on foot and on a small scale while the Government had moved 118 divisions since the issuance of the cease-fire order in January. General Chou charged that the Government had staged a publicity campaign regarding the Communist attack on Lafa in Manchuria, but had in the meantime occupied Faku and that, while the Communists had evacuated Lafa, the Government troops were still in occupation of Faku. He continued that the Communist attack in Shantung was in retaliation for the National Government's occupation of 5 or 6 towns during May and June and that they were directed solely against puppet-held places. Referring to the Government's demand for the Communist evacuation of Chahar and Jehol Provinces, General Chou said that the Government could produce no basis for such a demand and that the demand for the Government's occupation of Chefoo and Weihaiwei was equally without foundation. General Chou said that if the Generalissimo would not make adjustment of these demands, it would be useless for him to return to Yenan.

Referring to the draft proposal by the Government set forth in the Manchuria Annex, General Chou pointed out that under this proposal Government troops would enter many places then held by the Communist forces, such as Harbin,

Mutankiang, Paichen, Antung and Tunghwa. He had two points in mind in regard to Manchuria: (1) the strength of the Communist forces, which was still open for discussion, and (2) the distribution of troops. His suggestion had been that the Communist troops would be stationed in areas then under Communist control and that point had apparently been given consideration in drawing up this proposal. The other aspect of this question was that certain points would be left ungarrisoned and that National Government troops should not enter places under Communist control at this time. General Chou said that the crux of the situation now seemed to be whether the Generalissimo really wished to solve the problems or whether he wished to complicate matters to the utmost. He pointed to the concessions he had already made in the agreements for the restoration of communications and said that the Government was now trying to force the Communist Party to make concessions far beyond the agreements of January and February, at the same time giving no assurances regarding political questions at issue. General Chou concluded that, were he simply a representative of the Communist Party and not concerned about his position as a Chinese citizen and the question of Sino-Soviet cooperation, he would resign, because the negotiations conducted by him seemed to have been a complete failure.

In conversations with General Hsu Yung-chang and General Yu Ta-wei on June 18, I informed General Yu that in my opinion the Generalissimo's terms were too harsh and asked whether the latter would recede from these terms. General Yu said that the Generalissimo had indicated to him that he was willing to give the Communists more generous areas in the troop redistribution program. General Yu also showed me a map of the areas where the Communist forces were to be concentrated, under the Government's proposals, within four months time. I informed him that if the Communists agreed to such a proposal they would be completely under the Government's military dominance and that I felt, therefore, that there was no probability of Communist acceptance of this proposition. In connection with the redisposition of Communist forces in Manchuria, General Hsu said that the Government favored the stationing of two Communist divisions in the Tsitsihar and Hailar regions and one division on the border near Korea.

On June 20, in a discussion of this subject with General Yu Ta-wei, I informed him that it would probably be necessary as a basis of further discussion to consider the following points: the deletion of the stipulations regarding Jehol, Chahar and Shantung and the inclusion of these provinces in the program for the redistribution of troops; the movement of one additional Government army into north China during the first phase and a second additional army during the second phase, rather than both during the first period; granting control of certain railways to the Communists; Communist retention of Chihfeng; and the extension of the 15 day truce for at least five days.

In discussion of the extension of the truce period, General Yu suggested that it be extended one day. I replied that this was not sufficient, as many unresolved matters remained for discussion, and that his approach was not realistic and was probably based on his feeling that the United States would support a civil war in China. I informed him emphatically that the United States would not support a Chinese civil war, as his questions in this regard seemed to indicate a definite interest in the probable attitude of the United States in the event of civil war in China.

In further discussions on the Government's proposals with General Chou on June 21, I informed him that I had proposed to the Generalissimo that (1) the Stipulations regarding north China be dropped as such and that they be incorporated in the amended military reorganization agreement in the redistribution of troops in north China and that (2) the temporary truce period, which was due to expire at noon on June 22, be extended. While I could obtain no firm commitment from the Generalissimo on the first point, I did have an understanding that there was a possibility of the Government's acceptance of my proposed modification and thus there seemed to be a better basis for negotiating the details with General Chou. I again called to General Chou's attention the difficulty of negotiating without a definite outline of the Communist Party's proposals, which had embarrassed me throughout the recent discussions. I explained that the Government's stipulations regarding north China had grown out of modifications I had managed to obtain on the Government's original proposal concerning Manchuria—each time that the Generalissimo made a concession in the original proposal, he attached a stipulation regarding north China. I also pointed out that I had enlarged the areas of Communist troop dispositions established by the Government for the first period as the Chinese Army Staff had not taken into account the large numbers of troops involved in this period. Both National Government and Communist dispositions were complicated by the fact that little demobilization had taken place in north China; the National Government had confined its demobilization to south and west China and further demobilization would be largely confined to north China and Manchuria. This demobilization had been carried out by reducing divisions which lacked full strength to brigades, the officer personnel of divisions headquarters and headquarters troops having been demobilized. The real point was that under this proposal there would be involved very heavy troop demobilization on both sides between July 1 and January 1, 1947.

General Chou replied that he opposed discussion during the 15 day truce period regarding troop dispositions in north and central China, as this should be worded out by the Military Sub-Committee and the staffs of the two parties. He explained that this was the first time this had been discussed with him and that he had made no preparation on this question. He pointed out that this was a unilateral proposal of the Government and that under this arrangement the Communist forces would be concentrated in places away from the railway lines except in the Kalgan area. He charged that this was the Generalissimo's idea so that with the Communists in areas constituting the least threat to his position he could wipe them out at his leisure. It was his opinion that if the Communists accepted such a proposal, the Generalissimo could achieve his aim by peaceful means; if they rejected the proposal, the Generalissimo would achieve his goal by force—the sole difference being the methods employed. General Chou said that he could not accept this proposal and that the Communist authorities at Yenan had instructed him to propose: (1) The Committee of Three should immediately stop the fighting in Manchuria and China proper and a new order for the termination of hostilities should be issued with the additional stipulation that U.S. members of field teams should have the power to execute this order and to decide upon investigations to be made by the teams; (2) after the cessation of fighting, the Committee should work out a plan for the restoration of communications and the Communists pledged that the repair of railways would have first priority; (3) after the cessation of hostilities, the Committee should work out arrangements for the reorganization and demobilization of armies in all China, including Manchuria, and the staffs of both parties under the leadership of the American staff should work out a plan for the Committee of Three's approval; and (4) a second session of the Committee of Three should be convened to discuss the reorganization of the Government, the protection of the people's rights and a solution of the people's livelihood, and local governments should be reorganized and elections held. General Chou expressed the belief that the Generalissimo was most concerned over the problems of army reorganization, integration and training and thus he presented demands which caused concern to the Communist Party, because if these were accepted there would be no assurances on the many other points which had not been discussed. This, said General Chou, was the crucial point at issue. He suggested, therefore, that during the period of army reorganization the Communist troops be reorganized in Communist areas and Government troops in Government territory and that training be carried out by U.S. officers, who were trusted by both sides, the two forces to be brought together and integrated after this interim period.

I pointed out to General Chou that the Generalissimo had stated very clearly, in his announcement of the truce period on June 6, that there should be established a basis for carrying out without further delay the agreement of February 25 for the demobilization, reorganization and integration of Chinese armies and that the Generalissimo had this in mind when he presented these proposals. I emphasized that we must have a definite understanding of Communist demands regarding the redistribution of troops in north China and that this should have been decided upon in March and April, when the Communists were to have submitted a list of their troops for demobilization. While the National Government had submitted such lists the Communist Party had not done so. In the absence of these lists, the staffs had been unable to draw up a plan for troop redistribution in north China. I concluded that I did not, therefore, think the Generalissimo's insistence on the settlement of troop dispositions in all of China was illogical, particularly in view of his public statement in this regard.

At this point in the conversation, a telephone message was received from the Generalissimo stating that he had issued orders to his military commanders extending the suspension of advances, attacks and pursuits until noon on June 30. (I had not been able to get a firm commitment from him the preceding evening on this point.)

In view of this extension of the truce period, I urgently appealed to General Chou not to wreck this last possibility of reaching preliminary agreement on military considerations in this period ending June 30. I informed him that I would exert every effort to persuade the Generalissimo to make an announcement or definite commitments regarding the PCC resolutions and certain other matters connected with the reorganization of the government. I also stated that I had in mind for immediate action by the Generalissimo several other proposals regarding governmental matters of a political nature, which I was not at the time prepared to discuss but which were of a practical nature—that is, they could be put into effect immediately without debate or delay.

XXIII.
EXTENSION OF THE TRUCE PERIOD IN MANCHURIA UNTIL June 30; NEGOTIATIONS DURING THIS PERIOD

On June 21 the Generalissimo publicly announced the extension of the 15 day truce period in Manchuria in the following statement:

> "To afford the Chinese Communist Party once again an opportunity to obtain a satisfactory solution of the problems of military conflicts, restoration of communications, army reorganization and redisposition, I have ordered my army commanders to extend the effective period of my previous order to cease advances, attacks and pursuit to noon on June 30, 1946."

Although I had not been able to obtain a firm commitment from the Generalissimo on the preceding day for this extension, General Yu Ta-wei telephoned to my Headquarters on June 21, to inform me of the Generalissimo's decision in this regard and of two additional points for transmission by me to the Communist Party: (1) Communist forces along the Tsinan-Tsingtao Railway must be withdrawn to areas 30 kilometers away from either side of the Railway before August 1, 1946, and (2) the procedure of reaching a decision by a unanimous vote of the Committee of Three and of the Executive Headquarters must be revised before June 30, 1946.

On June 21, after learning of the Generalissimo's decision to extend the truce period, General Chou En-lai informed me that although he had not previously been prepared to discuss the redistribution of troops in north and central China he would agree to include these questions in the agenda and prepare a statement of Communist proposals on the subject. He pointed out that the greatest gap between the two parties was this problem. He also expressed the belief that the Generalissimo wished to have the Communists evacuate the places now garrisoned by them and concentrate in the poorer areas; that under the military district system the Government side would increase its areas; and that although the Generalissimo was forcing concessions from the Communists in military matters, he was offering no assurances for the settlement of political questions.

I then described to General Chou the difficulties in the present situation: A number of leading Government officials were of the firm opinion that the Communist procedure was to drag out negotiations, to add new points to the discussion and, if agreement were reached, to find a method to obstruct its implementation. The Government also feared that Communist policy was either coordinated with or directed by Soviet Russia. On the other hand, the Communist leaders were equally convinced that the Government would not carry out agreements reached or else would force the acceptance of terms threatening the continued existence of the Communist Party. The Communists feared that this would be achieved by the Government's failure to carry out the measures agreed upon for the reorganization of the government in a democratic manner; by the use of secret police to terrorize or obstruct the Communist Party; by the control of the press and news agencies; and by the actions of some of the Government military commanders, who were convinced that a policy of force would settle matters. I informed General Chou that I had talked just as frankly with Government representatives in a final effort to remove the deep suspicions which had made agreement on even the simplest matters almost impossible.

General Chou replied that he hoped this would not be the final effort as it appeared likely that many matters would be settled within the eight days of the extended truce period and many questions would not, thus making it necessary to reach a solution after that time. He asserted that the Communist Party had made no new demands during these negotiations and had not tried to delay the negotiations, while the National Government continued to present new demands, such as the power of final decision by U.S. representatives, the railway police and the revisions of Colonel Hill's draft on the restoration of communications. He felt that the situation was very critical and that the Generalissimo would run a great risk if he expected to achieve his aims within six months by the use of force. He suggested that the Generalissimo might be thinking of American support, but at the same time he should keep in mind the possibility of not receiving American support in the event of civil war. On the other hand, he said, the Communists should keep in mind the possibility that the United States would continue to aid the Government. He felt, therefore, that the reaching of a settlement would be far easier if both parties would keep these possibilities in mind. Regarding the fear of Soviet influence on the policies of the Communist Party, General Chou said that such a charge was entirely groundless and that the Communists were at this time seeking cooperation from the United States and would welcome the sending of American representatives and people, after the termination of hostilities, to investigate areas under Communist control. He pointed out that this, as well as other aspects, showed the difference between the Chinese Communist policy and that of Soviet Russia.

I reminded General Chou that, in judging the present situation and in saying that the Government did not desire a successful conclusion of the negotiations, particularly when referring to the attitude of the Government military commanders in Manchuria, he should remember what I had previously said about the Communist generals in Manchuria at the time of the occupation of Changchun. He should also remember that he himself had frequently used the expression "conditions have changed" in justifying some proposal and this expression was now being used by the Government in presenting its new stipulations. I said that I resented such a point of view and that my effort was to erase as many suspicions as I could prior to the final discussions.

As described in the preceeding section of this report, agreement was reached shortly after the beginning of the extended truce period on documents covering the restoration of communications, the termination of hostilities in Manchuria and the authority for decision by U.S. representatives, leaving only the question of revision of the military reorganization agreement of February 25 to be settled prior to June 30.

On June 26, I informed General Chou En-lai that the Government had agreed to a 5 to 1 ratio as the basis of troop strength in Manchuria but that I did not think the Government would agree to five Communist divisions in Manchuria and a total increase of Communist divisions to 20. I also said that it was my opinion, from discussions with the Government, that it would not agree to continued Communist occupation of north Kiangsu until a point was reached in reorganization and unification of the armies which would indicate a peaceful basis of negotiation without prospect of renewed hostilities and that the continued Communist occupation of Chengte (capital of Jehol Province) was a point considered of great importance by the Government.

General Chou replied that the Communist Party's difficulty was that, while it was making concessions and reaching agreements on military affairs, it did not know what the Government's attitude would be later in regard to political questions. It was the Communist view that army units would have no connection with civil administration; that after the reorganization of the government and local governments, the Communist armies would be assembled in areas under Communist control and Government armies in areas under its control; and that the army would be separated from civil administration through the establishment of local self-government and elections. He felt, however, that the Government's views were that political administration should be adjusted according to the identity of the troops in control of a particular area and that this was a violation of the principle of subordination of the army to civil administration. Everywhere the Government armies entered Communist territory they abolished the existing local civil administrations and replaced them with their own governments. It seemed that under the Government's proposals Government troops would in many cases move into Communist areas with the result that civil administrations would be changed. General Chou could find no reason for the movement of Government armies into Communist-held areas for the purpose of demobilization, as this would mean occupation of Communist territory through negotiations as a substitute for occupation by force. This procedure was incompatible with the PCC resolutions on this subject and with the general agreements. General Chou stated that the Communists were willing to withdraw from some areas in order to erase the Government's fear of a Communist threat, but he felt that such places should be left ungarrisoned. He explained that both Jehol and Shantung were largely under Communist control and it was more logical to expect the Government to evacuate these provinces than it was to demand that the Communists do so. He continued that if the Communist Party did not accede to Government demands regarding evacuation of points in Jehol and north Kiangsu and along the Tsinan-Tsingtao line and the Hsuchow-Tsinan line, the Government would use force to occupy these points and had already made plans for this eventuality.

I pointed out to General Chou certain fundamental conditions governing the situation: The Communist Party felt that it must not allow itself to be placed in a position militarily which would so weaken its defensive power that it would adversely affect the efforts of the Communist Party in the political negotiations to follow. On the other hand, the National Government feared a Communist effort to influence the course of the political discussions through military force. To this was added the freely expressed desire of certain Government military officials to settle matters by force.

General Chou replied that the Communists were willing to make concessions on military matters in order to get the Government to make political concessions looking toward democratization of the government and nationalization of armies, but at present the discussions were confined to military matters and the Communists feared the outcome of the political settlement. The Communist fears were: If the Communists weakened their military strength, they might lose their bargaining power in political matters; the National Government would enter Communist areas and dissolve their local administrations, while the Communists wished to leave such places ungarrisoned. General Chou went on to say that for the Communists to make concessions which would allow the Government to enter Communist territory and wipe out the reforms instituted by the Communists for the benefit of the peasants would mean the failure of the Communist Party. He then suggested two alternatives: (1) First, implement those agreements which have points which can be readily agreed upon—that is, termination of hostilities in Manchuria and the restoration of the railways—and there would then be time for discussion of the army reorganization plan; (2) establish a few principles regarding military reorganization (if the Government insisted on solving all problems simultaneously)—for example, it could be specified that during the army reorganization period each party's armies would be stationed at points not threatening each other, that civil administration would be decided by the reorganized government and would not be subject to army interference, that certain places in both Government and Communist areas could be left ungarrisoned during the period of reorganization and that arrangements could be worked out initially for Manchuria.

I informed General Chou that I felt certain that the Government would not agree to his first suggestion, as it had insisted on the simultaneous solution of all three major problems, but that it might consider the second suggestion. I pointed out that there was no time left for maneuvering and further delays and that the extension of negotiations was not practicable because of the growing unrest and the constant threat of disturbances and vicious propaganda.

On June 27, I had a conference with Generalissimo Chiang Kai-shek, during which he described Communist tactics of delay and obstruction since the PCC session and the military reorganization agreement of February 25 and ascribed to the Communist Party the failure to carry out the reorganization of the government and the demobilization and reorganization of the armies. He said that political adjustments were now difficult, if not impossible, unless military readjustment were effected as a means of avoiding clashes. He then presented specific proposals for such readjustments: The Communist Party should, within 10 days, evacuate north Kiangsu Province, the Tsinan-Tsingtao Railway, Chengte and Kupeikou, Antung Province and Harbin, these places to be occupied by Government troops within one month; the Communists should withdraw in one month from other places to be evacuated, but the entry of Government troops might be delayed for two or three months; and as a compromise measure, I might propose Communist officials in Hsin Heilung-chiang, Hsingan and Nenchiang Provinces in Manchuria, and Chahar Province, who might be accepted by the Government as a temporary arrangement which would receive consideration at the time of political reorganization.

I informed the Generalissimo that while his charges against the Communists were on the surface correct other factors had exercised profound influence on the course of events during this period. The Kuomintang Central Executive Committee decisions had caused grave doubt regarding the intentions of the Government to carry out the PCC resolutions and many violent demonstrations had taken place in Government areas against Communist individuals and offices. I said that these were either Government acts or acts permitted by the Government and that they had militated against the implementation of the agreements. I stated that the Government was now laying down very severe terms for the Communists in north China, terms which it was highly improbable that that they would accept or could accept without feeling that the continued existence of their party would be seriously jeopardized. I concluded that the Generalissimo's terms regarding Kiangsu, Jehol and Harbin in particular would not be accepted by the Communists and that it would, therefore, be necessary to find some basis for compromise.

Following the above-described conversation with the Generalissimo, I informed General Chou En-lai on the same day of the terms presented by the Generalissimo and of the particular insistence of the Government that the Communists evacuate north Kiangsu. I added that the Generalissimo, in referring to Communist Party claims of the benefits it provided for the peasants, said there were no indications of refugee movements from Government territory into Communist areas, while the movement of about five million refugees from Communist areas into National Government territory would indicate that conditions were more satisfactory in areas under Government control.

General Chou went into a detailed reply to the Generalissimo's charges that the Communists had been responsible for the failure to carry out the reorganization of the government and the demobilization and reorganization of the armies, stating that after the Communist representatives had compromised on three points in the PCC constitutional principles the Government had insisted on further revision and that the Communist Party could not submit lists of its troops in Manchuria while hostilities were continuing in that area. He also stated that millions of refugees had gone into Communist areas from Government territory, but that the Communist procedure was to assist them in rehabilitation and not, like the Government, to use them for propaganda purposes and the creation of disturbances. He described Communist aims as: the reduction of rentals and interest rates, the increase of productivity among the peasants and the increase of the number of those owning land. These reforms, he pointed out, caused an exodus of landlords from Communist areas, who were hostile to such a program. They and secret police agents, who infiltrated into Communist areas, spread rumors of Communist massacres and terrorism.

Commenting on the Generalissimo's terms, General Chou stated that garrison troops must not interfere with the local administration in areas where they were stationed. He said that, while the Communist Party was willing to consider a readjustment regarding Harbin and the detailed problems involved in stationing Government and Communist troops in specified areas, it was not in a position to accept the Government's claim to the Tsinan-Tsingtao Railway, Chengte, Kupeikou and the other places. However, if the Government felt that the Communist forces in north Kiangsu and Shantung (along the rail line) constituted a menace to the Government, the Communists would be willing to reduce their forces in such areas or withdraw them altogether, but the Government troops should not enter Communist areas; the Communists had agreed to discuss military questions before political matters but it would not expose the people in its areas to oppression by Government troops, as this would constitute the failure of the Communist Party and would result in turning the people against the Party. General Chou stated specifically that the Communists would garrison north Kiangsu with a small force by reducing the number of troops provided for in the military reorganization agreement of February 25; that they would withdraw their troops from the Tsinan-Tsingtao Railway, if the Government would agree to garrison only Tsinan, Weihsien and Tsingtao; and that all Communist troops would be withdrawn from the Tsaochuang coal mines, leaving no garrison troops and freeing the railway line for operation in connection with the coal mines, the latter to be controlled by a committee established for that purpose. He emphasized that these withdrawals should, however, in no way prejudice the local administrations established by the Communists in those areas.

On June 28, the Generalissimo informed me of his views regarding certain Communist troop dispositions:The Communists should evacuate Tenghsien (north of Hsuchou on the Tientsin-Pukou Railway); he took exception to the stationing of Communist troops in Hotse (southwest Shantung), Taming (south Hopei) and Wenhsi (southwest Shanshi on the Tungpu Railway), and he accepted the stationing of Communist troops at Hsingtai (south Hopei on the Peiping-Hankow Railway).

In explaining these views to General Chou En-lai on the same day, I pointed out that it was my impression that the Generalissimo also accepted the stationing of Communist troops in Changchih (southeast Shanshi), but that his reaction to the presence of Communist troops north of Huaian (Kiangsu) and the evacuation of Kiangsu and Anhui Provinces west of the Grand Canal and south and east of the trace of the old Yellow River bed between Huaiyin and Tunghai, with the understanding that Communist forces would be stationed at Huaiyin and Suchien (both in north Kiangsu), was not clearly indicated. I stated that I was proceeding on the basis that this would be accepted and that I had told the Generalissimo that I would endeavor to persuade the Communist Party to evacuate the region south of the railway from Pingchuan (Jehol) to Chengte and along a line through Fengning (southwest Jehol) and Kuyuan (southeast Chahar), thence south of the outer wall through Kalgan to the Suiyuan border. At the conclusion of our conversation the Generalissimo had still been adamant regarding his demand for the Communist forces in eastern Manchuria at Yenki and would not agree to the total evacuation of Harbin, insisting on having sizeable Government forces garrisoning that city.

I informed General Chou that I had pointed out to the Generalissimo that it would be impossible to reach agreement on the exact wording of a document for formal modification of the military reorganization agreement by June 30 and that I had, therefore, proposed the drawing up of a special document in which would be set forth the agreements on critical factors now under discussion—this document to be the basis for a detailed amendment of the military reorganization agreement which would be negotiated after June 30. I had also informed the Generalissimo that in my opinion further extension of the truce would not be a workable arrangement because in the present confused and highly dangerous state of affairs among troops and in the civil population there would be fatal ruptures involving the general spread of hostilities, which would militate against the progress of negotiations.

General Chou expressed agreement in principle with this proposal and said that we should continue to work on the detailed arrangements for military reorganization. He pointed to the danger of the present situation and charged that the Generalissimo had issued orders to his military commanders at Chengchou and Hankow to annihilate the Communist forces north of Hankow and that as a result of this order such an attack had begun on June 26. I agreed with him that the situation was critical but pointed out that I heard both sides of the picture and that the Government was fearful of large Communist concentrations in the vicinity of Tatung.

Commenting on the Generalissimo's views regarding Communist troop dispositions, General Chou said that it was clear that the Generalissimo did not accept the basic principle proposed by the Communists—that is, that areas evacuated by the Communists during the period of army reorganization would not be occupied by the Government forces. General

Chou said that the Communist Party could consider proposals only in accordance with that principle; that Communist agreement to evacuate certain areas was an entirely unilateral concession, as the Communists had not proposed that any place under Government control should be left ungarrisoned and had even proposed that Government troops be permitted to garrison all strategic points under its control; and the Communists had not proposed that their troops should be stationed in areas under Government control. He pointed out that the Generalissimo had given no indication that local civil administrations would be permitted to continue their functions until the reorganization of the government was carried out. General Chou charged that the result of the Communist withdrawals in accordance with the Generalissimo's demands would be the separation of the Communist forces into five isolated areas, with only two points on the railway lines (at Kalgan and Hsingtai) and only two large cities—Tsitsihar in Manchuria and Kalgan in China proper. If the Communists evacuated all the railway lines and highways, their communication lines would be abandoned and the Communist areas cut into pieces which would be easily surrounded. He concluded that he would, however, agree to work out certain stipulations regarding army reorganization which would serve as a preliminary document pending the reaching of agreement on the detailed revision of the military reorganization plan.

I then informed General Chou that I had prepared a draft of a preliminary agreement to govern the amendment and execution of the military reorganization plan of February 25 and that this would represent a special memorandum of conditions to be agreed to by the Committee of Three. It was explained that this was not a complete directive and was prepared in order to avoid the difficulty of attempting to place all stipulations in a formal amendment of the military reorganization agreement. This draft covered the highly disputed points and the issues involved therein would determine whether the Communist Party and the National Government could get together in the brief time remaining. It was suggested that a summary of this document might be released to the press and the details thereof announced when formal amendment of the February 25 agreement was agreed upon. I concluded that it seemed to me that the principal Communist considerations were the assignment of troops to specific places rather than to areas, the prohibition against the movement of Government troops into areas to be evacuated by the Communists and the continuation of the present local governments.

On the same day (28 June), pursuant to the Generalissimo's request for my views regarding the status of negotiations, I forwarded to him a memorandum, the substance of which is as follows:

In compliance with the Generalissimo's request for my views on the present status of negotiation and distribution of troops under the February 25th agreement, I find National Government demands and the Communist position irreconcilable at present on the following points: total Communist evacuation of Kiangsu, Communist evacuation of Chengte and the Communist insistence that local governments in areas evacuated should not be disturbed until the establishment of the reorganized government. The Generalissimo recently informed me that he would not consider any political discussions for three or four months following the successful conclusion of military agreements. It is my belief that such a delay would almost inevitably have serious consequences. While, from the Generalissimo's viewpoint, the delay would be for the purpose of testing the good intentions of the Communist Party, it would actually result in all probability in a renewal of hostilities through rather normal reactions to the present tense political state of affairs.

It seems apparent to me that formal detailed amendments to the February 25th agreement cannot be produced prior to noon of June 30 and I do not think that a prolongation of the truce period beyond June 30th could be carried out without a complete breakdown in the situation. I propose, therefore, that a special agreement be reached covering a settlement for the critical areas in enough detail to protect the Government's interests sufficiently to permit the issuance of instructions for the cessation of hostilities on June 30th.

On June 29 I discussed with the Generalissimo a compromise solution regarding the special document prepared to make possible an agreement prior to noon on June 30th. The Generalissimo refused to modify the conditions he had demanded in regard to Communist troop dispositions. Specifically, he insisted on Communist evacuation of Chengte, of all of Kiangsu Province (rather than all of the area south of Huaian) and of Antung Province (in Manchuria) and on the removal of the existing local governments in areas to be evacuated by the Communist forces.

I told the Generalissimo that I was left with no basis for further negotiations because the Government had confined itself to demands in north China and had made no compromise in these demands except for slight modifications. When the Generalissimo again referred to his past experience with the Communists and the necessity for permanent and not temporary measures, I replied that the same logic could be carried to the point of justifying complete elimination of the Communist Party and Army as the only measures possible for the maintenance of peace in China. I also pointed out that the negotiations were made particularly difficult by the freely and publicly expressed opinions of high Government officials, particularly those in commanding positions in Manchuria; they were saying that even if agreement were reached, it would be of no importance and they were determined to resort to a policy of force. The political leaders in the Kuomintang had expressed similar opinions, were opposing the negotiations and favored the use of force to settle matters. I stated that, whatever might be thought on the basis of past evidence, the Government of China would be judged by world, and certainly American, public opinion as having unnecessarily plunged the country into chaos by implacable demands and its evident desire of pursuing a policy of military settlement of the issues. In reply, the Generalissimo expressed his regret that the negotiations had failed and his appreciation of my efforts and produced a draft of a statement referring to me (apparently for release to the press), in which he voiced his hope that I would continue my efforts at mediation. I thanked him for the complimentary references in the statement but said I would prefer to have no such references, and further, that I would not act as an umpire on a battlefield. I concluded that I would see General Chou En-lai immediately but there seemed to be no probability of reaching any satisfactory agreement.

On the afternoon of June 29, I had a conference with General Chou and informed him of the Generalissimo's comments on the draft proposal entitled "Preliminary Agreement to Govern the Amendment and Execution of the Army Reorganization Plan of February 25, 1946."[47] The Generalissimo had been unwilling to agree to confine paragraph 5* of the document to Manchuria only. Regarding paragraph 6, which dealt with the status of Harbin, the Generalissimo had agreed to appoint a civilian mayor and to name a person acceptable to the Communist Party. In regard to paragraph 7,** the Generalissimo had first expressed complete disapproval and his final attitude was not clearly indicated—he agreed to Communist local governments but could not accept such an arrangement in Kiangsu Province because of the numerous refugees, who, he felt, would be mistreated by the existing local governments there, and he accepted the idea of peace preservation corps on the basis of strengths similar to those of local security troops in a *hsien*. The Generalissimo would not accept partial occupation by the Government of north Kiangsu but had insisted that the Communist evacuation should be carried out as far north as Huaian within six weeks and at a later period, three to six months, north of the Lunghai Railway. He had also stipulated that the Communist evacuation of the Tsinan-Tsingtao Railway should include the coal mines along that line, particularly Poshan (on a spur running south from Changtien). He had been unbending in regard to the Communist evacuation of Chengte and had said that the Communists should evacuate areas in Jehol south of the latitude of Chengte within one month and the city itself within three months. He had stipulated that Antung Province should be

[47]See Volume Two, Appendix K, Document 10, for the text of this proposal in its fourth draft, as of July 2, 1946.

*Paragraph 5 of the 3rd draft of this document on June 29 reads:
"5. The Executive Headquarters will immediately determine the localities occupied by the Government or Communist forces in Manchuria after noon of June 7th, 1946, and will require the troops involved to vacate those localities within 10 days after the signing of this agreement unless specifically directed otherwise."

**Paragraph 7 of the 3rd draft of this document on June 29 reads:
"7. The Chinese Communist Party has agreed to concentrate its troops in specified localities, it being understood that the Government troops will not move into the areas thus vacated in China proper and that the present established civil governments and the Peace Preservation Corps for the maintenance of local security will be continued. It is further agreed that in these areas no restrictions will be imposed on imports or exports, and free communication with adjacent regions will be assured."

evacuated within one month and had concluded that a paragraph should be added to the document requiring the completion of amendments to the military reorganization agreement of February 25 within 10 days. In regard to the Manchurian Annex, which the Generalissimo had approved, he stated that the entire demobilization and integration program in Manchuria should be completed before November 1, the original document having provided for its completion by January 1, 1947.

General Chou replied that he could not agree to the Generalissimo's desire to make an exception of north Kiangsu, as the Communist Party could not turn over the 20 million people in that area to Kuomintang rule in the absence of a coalition government. He added that the Communists would be willing to station only minimum forces in that area, which would be limited to two divisions during the second phase. As this division would be integrated with Government forces under a Government army commander, it did not seem that the Government should feel threatened by such a Communist unit. When I pointed out that the Generalissimo felt that the peace and security of the large number of refugees who had fled from that area would be menaced if they returned while this region was under Communist control, General Chou said that the number was not as large as charged by the Government and that in any event the number of those subject to oppression by Government troops, if the latter should return to that area, would be far larger than the number of refugees scattered in the Nanking-Shanghai area. General Chou then suggested a solution through the holding of elections under the supervision of the Kuomintang and other parties either during the present year or after the reorganization of the National Government.

Commenting on the Annex to the Preliminary Agreement, General Chou said that he was not in a position to accept the time limits desired by the Generalissimo because he was not sufficiently informed of actual conditions to know how much time would be required to effect the concentration of Communist troops in the areas indicated. He, therefore, suggested a period of one to three months—in some cases it would require the minimum and in others more. General Chou continued that, as Shantung Province was almost entirely under Communist occupation, the Communists should have some cities on the Tientsin-Pukou line if they withdrew entirely from the Tsinan-Tsingtao Railway. He did not feel that the stipulation that the Communists should give up all the

171

coal mines along the Tsinan-Tsingtao Railway was acceptable in principle even though the Communists had no intention of stationing troops there. This demand seemed to indicate that the Generalissimo was trying to strangle the Communists. General Chou found further concessions regarding Chengte impossible and said that he had made many concessions to the Government without presenting any demands from the Communists, except the proposal for an increase of a few divisions in Manchuria, and that he was now asking Yenan for authorization to withdraw that proposal. In regard to Antung, General Chou said that he had previously thought that this demand for Communist evacuation referred to the city rather than the province and he would now be compelled to refer the matter to his colleagues in Manchuria before giving his reply.

General Chou expressed his appreciation of my efforts but said that the Generalissimo's proposals were keeping him hard pressed in that he had made all the concessions he was able to offer and it would be necessary to obtain approval regarding several points from Yenan and Manchuria prior to commitment. If agreement were not reached on the preliminary document, he feared that a complete breakdown might follow with the Government resuming its attacks and at the same time attempting to continue negotiations. He warned that the Generalissimo had completed his preparations for an attack in Shantung, Jehol and Kiangsu Provinces and said that, while he had done all he could possibly do and was moved by my strong desire for peace, the Communist Party could not under the circumstances accept the Generalissimo's terms.

I pointed out to General Chou the serious trouble created for me in the negotiations by the Communist aggressive actions in Shantung and near Tatung, which had made it difficult for me to persuade the Government to alter its position. I added that I was aware of Government actions which threatened the Communist positions and that all of these circumstances had made my task very difficult. I did not feel that the negotiations were going to be concluded successfully by the end of the extended truce period and I did not know what the Government's procedure would be. My impression had been that the situation was so tense that it might get out of control if the present loose so-called truce basis were continued. It had been my hope, therefore, to obtain agreement on this preliminary document in time to ensure the issuance of a document for the termination of hostilities in Manchuria and orders to stop fighting in China proper.

In reply to my request for his suggestions, General Chou said that he was ready to consider any formula except that for civil administration involving the withdrawal of the Communists from north Kiangsu and the Government occupation of that region. He suggested that I confer with Dr. Wang Shih-chieh, Chinese Minister for Foreign Affairs, General Chen Cheng, National Government Chief of Staff, and Mr. Shao Li-tze, leading Government member of the PCC, and added that he would also talk with these officials in an effort to obtain acceptance of the main text of the document by the Government prior to noon on June 30. He said that the main text was almost entirely acceptable to the Communists except for one or two minor points. If these efforts proved unsuccessful, said General Chou, arrangements could be worked out for the immediate cessation of hostilities, with a time limit established for the settlement of the chief issues in this preliminary document and with further discussion to follow during that period; in that case, the Government would still be free to take action at the end of the time limit.

On June 30, the Generalissimo informed me that he was willing to compromise somewhat in the matter of Chengte but insisted that the evacuation of Kiangsu by the Communists to the north of the Lunghai Railway be completed within one month.

In reply to the Generalissimo's inquiry regarding the possibility of the Communist Party's willingness to compromise under those terms, I said that I did not believe the Communists would do so. I informed him that the issue in Kiangsu was serious; that it would be impossible logistically to evacuate to the north of the Lunghai line in one month; and that if the Communist evacuation north to Huaian were accepted by the Generalissimo on a one month's basis, I might possibly be able to persuade the Communists to evacuate to the north of the Lunghai within three months. I pointed out that the most serious factor was the Communist insistence on the continuation of their local governments and a Peace Preservation Corps. I said that I, therefore, desired to see a compromise solution on the basis of the continuation of the local governments, including the calling of a political or some specially selected group to arrange an agreement regarding a modification of these governments and the matter of the Peace Preservation Corps. When the Generalissimo expressed his concern regarding peace unless his requirements were met, I pointed out that all demands regarding north China had been made by the Government and no compromise had been offered to the Communist Party except in some modification of the terms. Furthermore, I said, the situation was being dominated by the military group in the Government: General Ho Ying-chin, whose position in regard to the negotiations was well-known, though retired as Chief of Staff, had been visiting the critical areas, including Peiping, Mukden, and Changchun; a public statement on the situation had been issued by the Government Chief of Staff in Manchuria; and a statement had also been issued by Chen Li-fu, the Kuomintang political leader. All this indicated to me that the Government was washing its hands of any democratic procedure and was pursuing a dictatorial policy of military force. I informed the Generalissimo that the comparison with the army dictatorship in Japan, which led to the destruction of that nation, with the present procedure of the Chinese military leaders would be inevitable. The Generalissimo disclaimed any responsibility for the speeches of Chinese officials who were, he said, using their right to freedom of speech but spoke of his responsibility for the hundreds of thousands of refugees. He concluded that he had already issued orders to his armies not to undertake any offensive action except in defense and he expressed his hope that by this further stay of fighting the negotiations could be successfully completed. He asked that I use my influence to that end.

I told the Generalissimo that I thought it imperative that we introduce some political discussion at this time and referred to the proposal made on the preceeding day by General Chou En-lai, which I had originally suggested, that three high Government officials, two civil and one military—the Minister for Foreign Affairs, the Chief of Staff and a leading member of the PCC—should meet with a corresponding Communist group and endeavor to word out an arrangement regarding local civil governments and any other points in the present negotiations that they might be able to compromise. The Generalissimo agreed to suggest to General Chou En-lai the meeting of this special group and, in reply to my proposal that he see General Chou personally, also gave his assent.

In the afternoon following the above-described conversation, I informed General Chou that the Generalissimo had issued orders that his army should not engage in any aggressive action but should defend their present positions and that he had also expressed his intention of proceeding with the negotiations. I added that I had made no suggestion regarding the prolongation of the period of restraint from aggressive action, as I feared mere prolongation would result in violent rupture due to the tense situation. I pointed out that I had advised against a time limit in the order but did not know whether the Generalissimo had established any such limitation in his orders to his troops. I explained that it was the desire of the Generalissimo and myself to complete the negotiations as soon as possible but that I feared that we might be overtaken by the critical and tense situation. I informed General Chou of the Generalissimo's willingness to talk with him and suggested that he discuss the preliminary special agreement as the entire amendment of the basic plan of February 25 would require too much time.

In discussion of the existing situation and the difficulties confronting the negotiations, General Chou described the fighting and preparations for fighting and said that the main difficulties lay in north Kiangsu and Jehol and along the Tiensin-Pukou Railway as the Generalissimo was very stubborn on the problems related to these three places. I expressed the belief that the question of the local government was equally difficult, that is, the local governments in those areas which the Communists were expected to evacuate. The immediate problem seemed to me to be the prevention of further hostilities in north China and this was made difficult because the Government felt that Communist actions in Shantung from June 9 to June 13 or 14 had been very hostile and aggressive, and that Communist concentrations around Tatung were now of a threatening nature and that the recent destruction of bridges by Communist forces were not evidences of good faith. On the Communist side, I continued, the Communist party felt that the Government action in north Hupeh and along the Tungpu Railway in Shansi constituted aggressive action. The situation was thus being complicated by retaliatory action being taken by both sides to regain what had been lost since June 7.

On the afternoon of June 30 the Kuomintang Minister of Information publicly announced that, while the truce period had expired at noon on June 30 and although no satisfactory agreement had been reached between the two parties, the Government had requested me to continue mediation with a view to reaching a peaceful settlement and that the Government would not initiate any attacks against Communist forces but would order its troops to remain on the defensive and await the settlement of pending issues. The Government furnished me a copy of the Generalissimo's order, under date of July 1, to his military commanders, in which they were instructed as follows: "If the Communist troops do not attack our forces, then our troops will not attack the Communist forces. Should the Communist troops advance against our forces, then our troops, for the sake of self-defense, protecting lives and properties of the people, and to keep local law and order, will concentrate their strength and counter-attack them. . . ."[48]

General Chou En-lai subsequently handed me a copy of an order which he said had been issued on July 1 by Chairman Mao Tze-tung and General Chu Teh, Commander-in-Chief of the Communist Armies, to the Communist forces in much the same vein as that issued by the National Government to its armies.[49]

This stay of fighting without any accompanying time limit offered a prolongation of the period for negotiations without, however, being accompanied by the issuance of any formal order for the cessation of hostilities. Agreement had been reached on several vital issues separating the two parties and the breakdown had come after partial agreement had been reached in regard to revision of the military reorganization plan, a breakdown caused chiefly by failure to find a formula covering local civil governments which would be acceptable to both sides. Whatever the reasons therefor, it seemed clear in the negotiations during the truce period that the Communist Party had been the more desirous of reaching an agreement for the cessation of hostilities, the Government posing such harsh conditions that acceptance by the Communists was improbable. It also appeared that the power and authority of a number of Kuomintang civil and military leaders was directed toward a solution by force in the belief that all-out war was preferable to the existing state of half-war accompanied by economic and political stagnation.

[48]See Volume Two, Appendix K, Document 11, for the full text.

[49]See Volume Two, Appendix K, Document 12, for the full text.

XXIV.

CONVENING OF THE FIVE MAN CONFERENCE FOR DISCUSSION OF THE LOCAL GOVERNMENT PROBLEM; SPREAD OF HOSTILITIES AND DETERIORATION OF THE SITUATION

In my last conference with the Generalissimo (on June 30) prior to the expiration of the extended truce period, I had pointed to the danger of the situation inherent in the plainly evident and strong pressure from his military leaders to pursue without delay a policy of force, for which they had made all plans, toward the settlement of the issues. Faced with this critical aspect of the situation and the impasse in the negotiations, I forwarded a telegram to the Undersecretary of State on July 2, in which I asked that he inform me of his and Mr. John Carter Vincent's frank and informal appraisal of the situation and the issues that might suddenly arise. In making this request, I explained that I had been so closely involved in the developments that I feared that I might lack the proper perspective. The Undersecretary, in his reply of July 4, generally confirmed my own estimate of the situation and expressed agreement that the meeting of a high level group to discuss a political solution of the problem appeared to be a sound tactical move.

During the above-mentioned conference on June 30, the Generalissimo said that he would consider my suggestion for the calling of a special group of Government and Communist representatives to discuss the problem of local government in areas from which Communist forces might evacuate in accordance with the Government's demands. He agreed to see General Chou En-lai personally and said that if my suggestion were approved he would himself propose such a procedure to General Chou.

The calling of this special group, known as the Five Man Conference, was approved by the Government and the first meeting of the Conference was held on July 3. Government representatives on this group were: Dr. Wang Shih-chieh, Minister for Foreign Affairs, General Chen Cheng, Chief of Staff, and Mr. Shao Li-tze, leading member of the PCC. The

Communist Party was represented by General Chou En-lai and Mr. Tung Pi-wu, the latter a member of the Communist Party's Central Executive Committee and a delegate to the PCC. The task of this Conference was to settle the problem of local government, which was the only serious issue standing in the way of a settlement between the two parties and which had led to the impasse in the negotiations at the end of June.

On July 9 I discussed with the Government representatives of the Five Man Conference the results of their meetings. They pointed out that the Government was insisting that Communist troops withdraw from four areas: south of Chengte (including Chengte) in Jehol Province, Antung Province in Manchuria, the Tsinan-Tsingtao Railway and north Kiangsu. It was explained that the Government did not demand that the Communist Party surrender local government control as well as military control in all areas to be vacated by its troops, but only in the four specifically named areas; this in order to eliminate any threat to and provide security for the Government. The representatives said that local government in all other areas vacated by the Communist forces could be discussed and solved either by the PCC or the PCC Steering Committee, but that the problem of local government in these four areas must be solved for the interim period before a permanent cessation of hostilities order could be issued. Mr. Shao Li-tze explained that after three meetings of the group no agreement was reached and that the Conference had adjourned on July 6 without setting a date for further negotiations, it being understood that the Government representatives of the group would report to the Generalissimo and the Communist representatives would report to Yenan. The Generalissimo had first said that he needed time for consideration of the situation and had subsequently instructed the Government representatives to continue the negotiations with the Communist Party, but no decision had yet been reached regarding the manner in which these negotiations would be conducted.

I expressed my pleasure that the Generalissimo had permitted further discussion by the Five Man Conference and emphasized the extreme importance of settling the problem of local government, which was the only serious question now preventing the issuance of an order for the cessation of hostilities, and I pointed out the danger of the spread of hostilities unless some agreement were reached. Contrary to the Government's belief, it was my opinion that the Communist

Party was intensely anxious to obtain agreement on a temporary arrangement which would permit the immediate issuance of a cease-fire order. I said that General Chou En-lai feared that the Government intended to abandon the PCC entirely and that one approach to the present problem might be to agree to the convening of the PCC, or its Steering Committee, at a specified date in the near future for discussion of the local government question, thus providing assurances for the Communist Party. I concluded that agreement had now been reached on documents covering the termination of hostilities, the restoration of communications and the authority of U.S. representatives to settle disagreements among the Executive Headquarters teams and that the only important issue unsolved was that of local government.

On July 11, in a conversation with General Yu Ta-wei, I expressed the opinion that the answer to the immediate problem lay in obtaining results from the Five Man Conference, which was working on the local government issue. I suggested that it might be advisable to approach the problem by establishing groups composed of National Government, Communist Party and American civilian representatives in the key areas in Kiangsu. These groups would act as courts of appeal to rule on equitable distribution of property and to prevent violation of agreements reached for the control of local government and civil administration thereunder.

This same idea was broached by me to General Chou En-lai on July 13. I said that the present stalemate seemed to arise from what appeared to be the fundamental issue between the Government and the Communist Party—that is, the agrarian problem, the question of land, taxation and relations between the peasantry and the land owners. Pointing out that I was not sufficiently familiar with all these problems to propose a settlement of this fundamental issue in China, I suggested that it might be possible to establish an interim policy for the return of refugee land owners and to set up a special agency composed of one National Government, one Communist Party and one American civilian commissioner, with a China background, for over-all supervision of this policy. This special agency could in turn have subordinate agencies for the various *hsien*, which could control the rate of return of the refugees and arbitrate or interpret policies regarding land adjustment for the time being until the entire problem should be decided by a constitutional convention.

General Chou replied that there was danger that many disputes would arise, not only in the four specific areas but also in other areas, because the whole question of land policy was involved. He explained that the Communist Party's land policy and the Government's land laws differed little, as both were based on Dr. Sun Yat-sen's principles that peasants should own their land and that the rights of land ownership should be equalized. He asserted that the Kuomintang's chief interest was not in the land problem but rather in the question of control of local government and pointed to three possible solutions of the present stalemate: (1) deal with the refugee problem—this, he said, had not been approved by the Government; (2) solve the land problem—this was extremely complicated and would require much time; and (3) permit the National Government to take over local government in the areas vacated by Communist troops—this was not acceptable to the Communist Party. General Chou said that he believed it advisable to persuade the Kuomintang to settle military problems first and leave the question of local government for later settlement.

In my conversation with General Yu Ta-wei on July 11, I expressed my disappointment that the Five Man Conference had failed to find a solution to the problem of local government and pointed out that failure to reach a solution, even if on a temporary basis, would at this time inevitably lead to civil war, particularly in view of the critical military situation. I said that it appeared that the Generalissimo had consented to this conference to please me but at the same time had issued such definite and detailed instructions to the Government representatives that they were committed to an unyielding attitude in the discussions with no basis for compromise. General Chou En-lai informed me later on the same day that the Five Man Conference had met on July 9 and 10 and that on the second of these two days the Government representatives had indicated that they could not alter the essence of the Generalissimo's instructions regarding the local government and civil adminstration of the four areas. They could only promise that when the Government took over such areas they would take into consideration the existing Communist agencies in those areas. This basis had not been acceptable to General Chou, who had suggested a general discussion regarding local government in all Communist controlled areas in order to reach a solution on the four specific areas as well as all others. The Government representatives, he said, had replied that the problem of the other Communist-controlled areas could be discussed only after the reorganization of the National Government. General Chou, fearing that if the Communist Party surrendered these four areas without obtaining any guarantee for the other Communist-held areas, said that while the Communist Party might consider a further reduction of its forces in the four areas it could not accept a complete withdrawal of Communist troops and Communist local government from such areas.

During this period in July, there began a gradual worsening of the military situation with the spread of hostilities to various points in China proper. The Commissioners of Executive Headquarters had endeavored to keep the situation under control by despatching a message on July 5 to all field teams and to the Advance Section at Changchun, in which it was stated that the National Government and Communist Party had announced that the truce was to be continued throughout China pending the outcome of further negotiations. The Commissioners directed all commanders to refrain from aggressive action, including advances, attacks and pursuits. The effect of this order was short-lived and other events occurred which gave indication of further deterioration in the situation, both militarily and politically.

On July 8 General Chou En-lai forwarded to me a memorandum to which was attached a manifesto issued by the Central Executive Committee of the Chinese Communist Party on July 7, the anniversary of the outbreak of Sino-Japanese hostilities. This manifesto constituted a strong and bitter attack on American policy toward China and a protest against what the Communists termed American military and financial aid to the National Government, which encouraged the civil war policy of the Kuomintang. I had previously refrained from comment on such propaganda attacks but the coincidence of events led me to inform General Chou En-lai of the serious blow to my negotiations with the Government that such propaganda attacks represented, paralleling as they did similar propaganda releases from Moscow, and of the impossibility of my serving any useful purpose in mediation and in the termination of hostilities while such attacks continued.*

With no results from the discussions of the Five Man Conference and the discontinuance of its meetings, it was clear that my mediation efforts would become increasingly

*A separate section of this report will deal with the subject of the attitude of the Communist Party toward the United States.

difficult. Matters were not helped by the departure of the Generalissimo from Nanking on July 14 for Kuling, which meant that negotiations during his absence would be greatly handicapped.

There were increasing signs of the gravity of the situation from a military standpoint. The Government continued to press its pursuit of the Communist troops which had broken through the encirclement north of Hankow and had fled to the northwest. After the Communist attack on the Tsinan-Tsingtao Railway (begun on June 7) had subsided, the Government forces counter-attacked along that line with the avowed intention of recovering those places occupied by the Communist forces since June 7. On July 11 the Communists charged that Government forces from the Sian area had entered south Shansi and were advancing north along the Tung-pu Railway against Communist areas. The Government charged that Communist forces had begun an attack in north Kiangsu on July 13, while the Communists counter-charged that the Government had launched an attack in this region on July 15 and exhibited to me what purported to be a copy of the order for such an attack. Government representatives said that the Communists were preparing an offensive in east Hopei and charged that Soviet advisors and pilots were serving with the Communists in various areas. The problem was, as usual, one of the serious effects of retaliation on the part of the two parties. I had told the Government that it was wrong to continue its campaign along the Tsinan-Tsingtao Railway, particularly as it involved places not occupied by the Communists after June 7, and had also informed them that it would probably have been possible very quickly to obtain agreement from the Communists to evacuate the places occupied since June 7 without engaging in a campaign to recapture them. In the meantime, as I informed Chou, the Government brought to my attention threatening movements of Communist troops west of the Grand Canal not very far north of Nanking and against the Tsinan-Tsingtao railroad line from the north and south and also Communist operations against the Tsientsin-Pukou Railway between Tehsien and Tsanghsien (south of Tientsin).

Accompanying the deterioration in the military situation were evidences on the part of certain Kuomintang officials to suppress open criticism of their party government. Two well-known Chinese liberal members of the Democratic League at

Kunming were assassinated by unknown persons (later revealed to be members of the Kunming Garrison Headquarters' secret police) and there were indications that Kuomintang secret police were intimidating leading Democratic League members and Chinese liberals in other parts of the country. Communist activities during this period, in line with the Yenan attack on the United States policy toward China, began to be centered on the U.S. Marines in China and in mid-July occurred the first serious incident involving the Communists and U.S. Marines, the kidnapping of seven Marines in east Hopei and their detention by the Communists for several days before being released. This was followed at the end of the month by the deliberate Communist attack on a U.S. Marine-escorted motor convoy bound from Tientsin to Peiping, during which three Americans were killed and 12 wounded.*

In a discussion of the situation with General Yu Ta-wei on July 13, I pointed out to him that the Committee of Three was facing a difficult period during which it might not be possible to conduct negotiations in view of the Generalissimo's impending departure for Kuling and that every effort must be directed toward stabilizing the military situation in order to avoid civil war. I referred to the evident unwillingness of the Government to despatch field teams to the critical area north of Hankow and expressed my concern at this attitude, as the only apparent reason therefor would be to permit military action by the Government to be carried on unobserved during this critical period. If this were the case and if aggressive military actions developed, I would be forced to withdraw from the negotiations, adding that I could not, of course, make any specific charges unless a definite course of hostile action developed from the Government's operations.

General Yu, commenting on the present state of negotiations, informed me that the Generalissimo would again enter into discussion of the problem of local government if General Chou En-lai so wished, but that the Communist Party would have to withdraw its request for retention of Peace Preservation Corps in the areas to be evacuated by Communist troops. (The Generalissimo had previously agreed to the retention of such units.)

On the same day, 13 July, General Chou En-lai pointed

---

*This incident will be described in a subsequent section of this report.

out to me the urgent need for an over-all truce. He explained that if the National Government carried out its plans for an attack in north Kiangsu on July 15, as he feared would happen, fighting would be certain to break out in Shantung, as the two areas were both under the same Communist commander, and also that the same danger was involved in the situation in south Shansi Province, where Government troops under Generals Hu Tsung-nan and Yen Hsi-shan were on the verge of an offensive, in which case the Communists would retaliate with an attack on Tatung. General Chou felt that local truces were ineffective and that if retaliation were to be avoided there must be an over-all truce. Referring to the question of local government, General Chou said that this issue could not be settled without the reorganization of the National Government. He also said that the stand of the Government was inconsistent in that it had stated that it would not take up political matters until military affairs had been settled, although at the present time, it was insisting on the settlement of the problem of local administration, a purely political question.

General Yu informed me on July 16 that the Communist forces in Kiangsu just north of the Yangtze River had on the previous day launched an attack in an effort to wipe out crack Government troops in that area. I expressed disagreement with General Yu, as I did not believe that the Communist forces were capable of doing so, and pointed out that this was contrary to Government statements that it could destroy all Communist forces in China in from three to six months. I suggested that the attack might have been made to offset attacks which they feared the Government was preparing to initiate in north Kiangsu. I described to General Yu the weakness of the financial and economic structure of the country which argued strongly against civil war and said that if the Generalissimo continued in his present attitude toward negotiations civil war was inevitable. It was my opinion that the Generalissimo believed that the military situation might develop favorably for the Government during this lull in the negotiations but developments might not occur in accordance with his belief. I pointed out that an agreement for the complete termination of hostilities had been prepared and agreed to in June and that its implementation was waiting only for settlement of the question of local government, on which the Generalissimo continued to delay. I said that the Generalissimo's military commanders were leading him into an uncontrollable situation and when such a situation materialized these same commanders would be appealing for aid which would not be forthcoming. In further discussions with General Yu on succeeding days, I mentioned the assassinations of the two Democratic League members at Kunming and the circumstances under which other Chinese who believed their lives to be threatened were given refuge by the American Consulate at that city and stated that negotiations could not be conducted in an atmosphere of this kind. When General Yu said that the Communists had begun the fighting in Kiangsu and would have to take the consequences, I pointed out that a continuance of this attitude would certainly lead to civil war and warned him that further Government advances in south Shansi would probably result in Communist attacks in the vicinity of Tatung. I concluded that the efforts of Executive Headquarters were apparently stalemated along with the negotiations, but that I was willing to make a last desperate effort to bring about a solution.

Later on July 16, in a discussion of the situation with General Chou, I said that we had come very close to a solution regarding military dispositions and I felt that an extra effort must be made to find a solution to the local government problem. I informed General Chou that, while he apparently feared that if he agreed to a decision on the question of local government the PCC resolutions might be eliminated from further consideration in a general political settlement, he should bear in mind that I might be able to obtain agreement for a meeting of the PCC; and that, if the situation degenerated into a civil war, the PCC would serve no useful purpose whatsoever. I explained that I could not persuade the Generalissimo to issue a cease-fire order unless we were able to reach agreement on the special preliminary document. I added that the issues were small from a military standpoint but very difficult from a political viewpoint. I then advanced a proposal for General Chou's consideration: The Communist Party to retain the *hsien* occupied prior to the Japanese surrender and withdraw from those *hsien* occupied subsequent to the surrender and permit the Government to take over the latter; some temporary agreement to be reached regarding land problems in the *hsien* thus taken over by the Government and the question of land adjustments in those *hsien* long under Communist control to await the reorganization of the National Government.

On July 17, General Chou informed me that due to the

spread of hostilities and the political assassinations he had found it more and more difficult to convince his people to accept the Government's demands regarding the north Kiangsu question. Referring to my suggested solution, he said that prior to the PCC session, the Kuomintang had presented a proposal similar to mine. He pointed out that during the Japanese occupation Japanese troops were in control of only some of the cities and a few main lines of communication while the areas surrounding the cities and communications line and many villages were in the hands of Communist regular and guerrilla forces. He said that at present, the Communists had local governments in the places evacuated by the Japanese and therefore, if the Communists vacated such places and Government troops entered, the forces of the two parties would be in such close contact that clashes were certain to occur. General Chou continued that since the Communist evacuation of Changchun, the Communist Party had found the military formulas proposed by me almost entirely acceptable. He added, however, that if the Communist Party were driven into a corner by the Generalissimo's efforts to achieve his aims by force and intimidation or by forcing concessions, the Communists would resist rather than capitulate, since to capitulate would mean higher and higher demands from the Generalissimo.

The deterioration of the situation in China and what appeared to be the decisive influence of the reactionary political and military group around the Generalisimo had convinced me of the desirability of obtaining the assistance of an American of unquestioned character and integrity and with long experience in China in the mediation effort. With this view in mind, I recommended the appointment of Dr. J. Leighton Stuart, then President of Yenching University at Peiping, as United States Ambassador to China. On July 11 the United States Senate confirmed the nomination of Dr. Stuart as Ambassador to China. Shortly thereafter he proceeded to Nanking to present his credentials and entered into discussions with representatives of the two parties. Dr. Stuart's knowledge of China and the psychology of its people, his thorough command of the language, and the regard in which he was held by Kuomintang and Communists alike, admirably prepared him for participation in the mediation effort. His presence would offset the criticism of my lack of knowledge of things Chinese.

On July 26, shortly after Dr. Stuart's arrival at Nanking, General Chou, referring to the spread of hostilities and the terroristic activities of the Kuomintang secret police, suggested that there were only two ways out of the existing dilemma: (1) An order for the unconditional cessation of hostilities should be issued immediately and at the same time the arrangements worked out during the truce periods in June should be put into effect, particularly the termination of hostilities in Manchuria and reiteration of the cease-fire order for China proper. If agreement could be reached on those two documents, other agreements should be carried out, such as the restoration of communications, the authority for settlement of disagreements among field teams and in the Executive Headquarters, and the supplementary arrangement on army reorganization embodied in the special preliminary document — these documents to be placed in force without touching on the question of local government. Discussions could then be held regarding the reorganization of the government in accordance with the PCC resolutions and subsequently regarding the problem of local government. General Chou said that he would be glad to discuss the detailed procedure along these lines and suggested that Government and Communist Party representatives meet with Dr. Stuart for preliminary discussion of the reorganization of the government and local government problems. When agreement should be reached in these preliminary discussions, it would be necessary to convene the PCC Steering Committee to obtain its approval of such an agreement, as the reorganization of the government in accordance with the PCC resolutions required the approval of all parties. General Chou continued that I should deal with the question of the cessation of hostilities while the above-described group was engaged in discussion of the reorganization of the government. (2) The only alternative to the above-described procedure, General Chou said, was a full general civil war. In that event, it was his opinion that the United States would be forced to reconsider its policy toward China and would not aid a nation torn by civil strife.

In further discussion of the first of these two ways out of the existing dilemma, General Chou expressed fear that the Generalissimo might, after consulting the various parties about the reorganization of the government, make an announcement in his own name that the government would be reorganized rather than through convening of the PCC Steering Committee. Such action would constitute further indication of the Generalissimo's intention to drop the PCC resolutions bit by bit until the point might be reached where they were discarded altogether.

On July 31, I had a frank discussion of the situation with General Yu Ta-wei and endeavored to impress upon him that the principal loss as seen in the American press reaction to the China scene was, in my opinion and that of Dr. Stuart, the lowering of the Generalissimo's prestige and that this was tragic as the Generalissimo represented perhaps the greatest asset China possessed at this time. His advisers were giving him such narrow and prejudiced advice that the situation seemed hopeless and I had been told by the Generalissimo's own people of things which they could not say publicly. I insisted that the political situation was now more important than the military situation and that the deterioration of the situation toward civil war demanded a solution on the highest level. One of the critical factors in the present situation was the secret police, who were keeping under surveillance many individuals who had expressed any liberal views. The most recent death was that of an American university Ph.D., who had been driven into hiding in two different places by the pressure of the secret police and had finally died of apoplexy. An outrageous attack had been made upon a peace delegation from Shanghai upon its arrival at Nanking and had lasted for more than five hours without any positive action being taken for its suppression. When I brought such matters to the Generalissimo's attention he stated that he was in a difficult position because he had to have many liberals kept under surveillance lest something happen to them for which the Government would be blamed. I mentioned to General Yu that I had been advised by an informed American some time prior to the assassinations in Kunming that such a campaign would begin. To Americans the evident persecution of the most highly educated and most liberal minded people in China and the suppression of newspapers and publications were antagonistic to every conception of democracy.

On August 1 General Chou En-lai described to me the continued pursuit of the Communist forces in north Kiangsu, Shantung and Shansi and indications of Government preparations for operations against Harbin and Antung and said that these activities seemed to indicate that the Government's military plans were based on the demands made by the Government at the end of June for Communist evacuation from certain areas. He stated that if these attacks continued, the Communists would unquestionably counter-attack and also launch attacks in other areas thus permitting the civil war to spread. He felt that the war-minded members of the Government favored a full scale civil war so that the mediation efforts would end. General Chou asserted that the Communists wished to avoid civil war and that he had in mind three alternative courses: (1) As civil war had assumed wide proportions, a nationwide truce should be announced immediately and all documents drawn up prior to June 30 should be signed and published, the problem of local government to be left for future discussion. (2) The conflict might be settled piece-meal by dealing first with the most serious areas of fighting, such as north Hupeh, north Kiangsu and Shantung; teams should be sent to those places to settle the conflicts one by one so that a general truce could eventually be effected. (3) Military questions should be resolved along with political problems.

General Chou said that he had suggested to Dr. Stuart that if a general truce could not be reached immediately it would be advisable to discuss political matters and to work out a procedure for the reorganization of the government so that both political and military questions could be solved simultaneously. He added that if the Government rejected all three of the proposals described in the preceding paragraph, it would then be rather obvious that the Government was inclined to extend the civil war and that would leave the Communists only two possible courses of action: (1) Since the Government continued to attack and occupy Communist-controlled areas, the Communists must launch counter-attacks in those and other places, the result of which would be the spread of civil war. (2) The Communist Party would issue public statements, addressed both to the people of China and of the United States, announcing that a general civil war existed in China and that the situation would deteriorate further. General Chou was of the opinion that if the issues were eventually to be resolved through negotiations on the basis of positions held on January 10 in China proper and on June 7 in Manchuria, the armies of both sides would be required to withdraw to positions held on those dates. He could not, therefore, understand the Government's intentions of continued delay in negotiations unless it was to retain possession of the places now being occupied. General Chou said that if both

189

parties persisted in this attitude, then a deadlock would ensue and the whole purpose of the truce would be nullified. General Chou concluded with a suggestion that, in view of the recent incidents involving U.S. Marines in north China, a plan could be prepared for their evacuation to include provision for Executive Headquarters teams to protect the railway between Peiping and Shanhaikuan and for Government assurances that its troops would not use the railway as a basis for attacks on adjacent Communist-held areas.

I informed General Chou that, serious as was the military conflict carrying China to the verge of chaos, I had come to the conclusion that while a military settlement was an immediate necessity in order to stop the fighting, the immediate agreement for the initiation of a first step in the formation of a coalition government seemed necessary to save the situation. Dr. Stuart and I were of the opinion that an agreement for the organization of the State Council represented the only practical move at this time.

On August 3 I informed General Chou that Dr. Stuart had had a long conference with the Generalissimo on August 1 at Kuling and had proposed the organization of a special committee, including Government and Communist representatives, with Dr. Stuart as Chairman, for the purpose of reaching agreement for the immediate organization of the State Council. I explained that the Generalissimo had agreed to Dr. Stuart's proposal in principle but wished to defer his decision until he had an opportunity to discuss the matter again with Dr. Stuart and me and that I had, therefore, asked Dr. Stuart to remain in Kuling until my arrival there. (During the Generalissimo's residence at Kuling from July 14 until late September, I visited Kuling nine times, my visits lasting for several days in each case.)

General Chou replied that he felt it desirable that we endeavor to settle the question of Government reorganization while negotiating for a truce agreement, but he suspected that the Government was trying to stall by initiating political discussions while at the same time it was waging a full scale civil war. He referred to reports he had just received of the bombing of Yenan by Government planes on August 2 and indications of Government plans for an offensive north from Hsuchow towards southern Shantung. He feared that, should the Communists retaliate, this might give the Generalissimo an opportunity to maneuver in such a way that if the Communists acceded to his demands in the negotiations he would

190

obtain occupation of the disputed areas, thus putting an end to the fighting; that if he did not obtain these areas through negotiations, he would announce a general civil war. General Chou emphasized that if the problem were not approached from a standpoint of first getting a truce agreement we might face a situation where, while discussions were going on in regard to political matters, the fighting would become more and more intensified and the situation might get completely out of control. He felt, therefore, that we must find some means of effecting a truce while the political discussions were going on.

I reminded General Chou that the proposal for political discussions at this time had been suggested by Dr. Stuart and not by the Government and that we were aware of the rapidly disintegrating military situation. The problem was how to get an agreement for the termination of the fighting. It was for this reason that I had especially deplored the Anping incident involving the Communist attack on U.S. Marines, as I had felt sure that the Government would react to the incident in a manner not conducive to a cessation of hostilities.

Commenting on Dr. Stuart's proposal, General Chou said that he shared my view on the desirability of having an informal meeting regarding the reorganization of the Government and thought that the whole plan should be submitted to the PCC Steering Committee as soon as a suitable basis for reorganization had been found. In conclusion, he expressed a desire that Dr. Stuart get in touch with the other minority parties in the course of the discussions so that they would not feel completely detached from the negotiations.

It now seemed, at the beginning of August, that the chief hope of saving the situation lay in the meeting of the small informal committee, under Dr. Stuart as chairman, for the purpose of reaching agreement on the organization of the State Council envisaged in the PCC resolutions. In view of the apparent impossibility under existing circumstances of obtaining the Generalissimo's agreement to the issuance of an order for the termination of hostilities, Dr. Stuart and I had felt it advisable to approach the problem from another angle —that of this committee. It was our belief that if some progress were made by this committee the Generalissimo would be willing to agree to a cessation of hostilities, which were at this time increasing in extent throughout north China and were threatening to spread into Manchuria.

XXV.

NEGOTIATIONS DURING AUGUST: UNSUCCESSFUL EFFORTS TO CONVENE THE FIVE MAN COMMITTEE UNDER DR. STUART'S CHAIRMANSHIP; EXCHANGE OF MESSAGES BETWEEN PRESIDENT TRUMAN AND THE GENERALISSIMO; CONTINUED DETERIORATION OF THE MILITARY AND ECONOMIC SITUATION

On August 5 the Generalissimo informed Dr. Stuart of his concurrence with the latter's proposal for the forming of a small informal committee, to be composed of Government and Communist representatives, under Dr. Stuart as chairman, for the purpose of reaching an agreement for organization of the State Council. On the following day, however, the Generalissimo stipulated certain preliminary conditions which must be accepted by the Communist Party. The Generalissimo said that the objectives of the committee (hereafter known as the Five Man Committee*) were to be: (1) to put into effect the Cessation of Hostilities Order of January 10; (2) to put into effect the restoration of communications agreement of February 9; and (3) to carry out the military reorganization plan of February 25. He set forth the following stipulations to be carried out within one month's to six weeks' time: (1) The Communist forces in north Kiangsu should withdraw north of the Lunghai Railway; (2) Communist forces should withdraw from the Tsinan-Tsingtao Railway; (3) Communist forces should withdraw from Chengte and areas in Jehol Province south of that city; (4) Communist forces should withdraw into 2½ provinces in Manchuria (Hsin Heilungchiang, Nenchiang and Hsingan); and (5) Communist forces should withdraw from places in Shansi and Shantung Provinces occupied after June 7.** The Generalissimo said that if

---

*To be composed of 2 Government and 2 Communist representatives, with Dr. Stuart as Chairman.

**These five stipulations became known as the Government's five conditions.

192

in the first meeting of the Five Man Committee the above-described five conditions were accepted, fighting would be stopped immediately and the Committee would meet again and resume negotiations.

On August 6 Dr. Stuart communicated these terms to General Chou En-lai. The latter pointed out that the Generalissimo made no mention of local government, which problem, after the Communist evacuation of north Kiangsu and other areas, should be solved in accordance with the PCC resolutions. He explained that the refusal of the Communists to accept the Government's demands for the taking over of the local administration in these areas, which led to the impasse in the negotiations at the end of June, was based on the contention that such a procedure was contrary to the PCC resolutions.* General Chou continued that during the negotiations in the Five Man Conference, headed by Dr. Wang Shih-chieh, during July fewer areas were mentioned by the Government than were now being brought up by the Generalissimo and that the Government representatives in this Conference had finally conceded that if the issue of local government could be settled first for one area (this was presumably north Kiangsu) the matter could be considered as satisfactorily arranged. General Chou felt that the Government should also evacuate areas occupied by its forces in Shansi and Shantung since June 7 and said that it should be noted that the tentative agreement at the end of June contained stipulations regarding troop disposition in areas in both Manchuria and in China proper. He stated that the demands now being presented were greater than all those made previously and that he could agree to none of the Generalissimo's conditions. General Chou charged that the Generalissimo held three views regarding the existing situation: (1) He desired to accomplish his aims by force and then negotiate; (2) he could continue to fight on one hand and negotiate on the other; and (3) if the Communist Party refused to negotiate, he could place responsibility for the civil war on the Communists. General Chou said that

*Annex 1 of the PCC resolutions entitled "Program for Peaceful National Reconstruction" reads:

"In those recovered areas where the local government is under dispute the *status quo* shall be maintained until a settlement is made according to Articles 6, 7 and 8 of Chapter III on Political Problems in this Program by the National Government after its reorganization."

the Generalissimo was in a more favorable military position than at the time of my arrival in China and that he (the Generalissimo), therefore, believed that he could accomplish his aims by force within three months or so. The Communist Party, said General Chou, still demanded an unconditional cease-fire order and the convening of the PCC Steering and Constitution Reviewing Committees and could not accept any of the Generalissimo's five conditions.

General Chou went on to say that the American attitude had been to look for some democratic elements to lead both the Government and Communist authorities but that China actually had no such elements. He also expressed his opinion that the United States had begun to feel that the Communists were growing too strong and that this might not be beneficial to the United States. General Chou felt that such fears should be banished, as otherwise two results might follow: (1) The civil war would be prolonged and aggravated, a condition not beneficial to the United States, and the latter would not be able to render open aid to the Kuomintang, the consequence thus being permanent civil war in China; (2) there might be international intervention or the United Nations Organization might institute an investigation, neither of which courses would benefit China. He felt, therefore, that the United States should continue to arbitrate the issues in China but should also give consideration to the question of whether the Communists were to be feared and whether cooperation with them was impractical. General Chou agreed with the American policy formulated at the time of my arrival in China and expressed hope that the United States would continue to implement that policy.

Commenting on the question of the veto power in the State Council, General Chou said that the use of the veto power would be limited to preventing the overthrow of the PCC program, a change in which would require the approval of two-thirds of the Councillors, and pointed out that other matters were not subject to this restriction.*

*Item 6 of Section I (Concerning the State Council) of the PCC resolution entitled "Government Organization" reads:

"General resolutions before the State Council are to be passed by a majority vote of the State Councillors present. If a resolution before the State Council should involve changes in administrative policy, it must

(Continued on following page.)

General Chou expressed hope that I would continue to strive for peace in China but added that if the United States should change its policy by assisting the Kuomintang in annihilating the Communist Party there would be no need for my services along such lines; General Chou did not, however, believe that the United States would act in such a manner. He stated that the Communists would agree to allow military and political discussions to be held simultaneously but could not accept the five conditions as a proviso which must be agreed to prior to political discussion; he explained that if he accepted these conditions, they could be considered only as an unsolved problem in connection with military matters and that if it were intended to make them a subject for discussion in the political talks, they could not be regarded as a proviso that must be decided in advance. It was his opinion, he said, that the question of local governmental authority should be included in political talks.

On August 8 I had a very frank talk with the Generalissimo at Kuling. I first informed him that no progress had been made by Dr. Stuart in his discussions with General Chou; the latter considered that the five conditions represented a return to the impasse of June 30 and that the terms had been made worse by the inclusion of additional harsh stipulations. I then outlined to the Generalissimo my estimate of the situation: Fighting in north China would soon be completely out of control; and, once it spread to Jehol Province, Manchuria would be aflame and then fighting would become general in all areas. My objective beyond that of a unified and rejuvenated China was not what some of the Generalissimo's advisers seemed to think—that is, put the Communist Party in Control—quite the contrary. I differed from the Generalissimo and his immediate advisers in that I thought their pres-

(Continued from preceding page.)

be passed by a two-thirds vote of the State Councillors present. Whether a given resolution involves changes in administrative policy or not is to be decided by a majority vote of the State Councillors present.''

It should be noted that ''administrative policy,'' mentioned in the above-quoted item, is in the Chinese text rendered as ''Shih Cheng Kang Ling.'' This is also the title given to the second of the PCC resolutions, the English equivalent of which, in the official translation issued by the Kuomintang Ministry of Information, is ''Program for Peaceful National Reconstruction.''

ent procedure would probably lead to Communist control in China and the chaotic condition now developing would not only weaken the Kuomintang but would also afford the Communists an excellent opportunity to undermine the Government. It would also afford an exceptional opportunity to Soviet Russia to intervene, either directly or under cover, in a manner favorable to the Chinese Communists. My information from a wide variety of sources indicated a serious lowering of Kuomintang prestige, and criticism of Kuomintang Governmental procedures was increasing daily. Even more serious consequences were impending at this time. Recent events in China had created a body of American opinion that freedom of the press and freedom of speech were being denied and that intellectual elements, especially those educated in foreign universities, were under deliberate persecution and certainly under repressive measures intended to intimidate them and prevent them from expressing views unfavorable to the Government. The most serious consequence of this was its profound injury to the prestige of the Generalissimo, which was perhaps China's greatest asset. There was a feeling among intellectuals in the United States that the suppression of liberal opinion in China was a procedure identical to that followed in Germany, a procedure which had shocked and outraged the world. I reminded the Generalissimo that the Communists had thoughout the past two months asked continuously for the cessation of hostilities to be followed by negotiations for a settlement of the disputed points. I pointed out that the Communists were intensely anxious to have the decisions and procedures of the PCC followed and that they believed that the Government was deliberately by-passing the PCC. I referred to the extremely narrow point of view of certain Kuomintang military leaders, who saw only the immediate military objectives in their own areas and were completely oblivious of measures which might serve to control the developing situation; this was particularly true in Manchuria, where Government military activities were calculated to promote rather than curtail communism among unemployed workers—no measures were being taken to train them in technical positions left vacant by the Japanese nor were there any indications that their future was of concern to local military commanders.

Referring to the assassinations at Kunming, the Generalissimo said that the only course was to locate the guilty persons and to punish them, action which he was determined to carry out. He felt that many of the Communist and Democratic League accusations in this case were deliberate misrepresentations of the Government's purpose, which was to protect individuals against harm that would inevitably be charged against the Government.

I pointed out that there were other factors which threw quite a different light on the Government's actions and intentions and called his attention to a report I had just received that morning of the suppression of six newspapers or magazines at Kunming. While the Minister of Information had informed me that these suppressions were due to the failure of the publications to register properly, I felt that the Government was ill-advised to suppress publications in Kunming at this particular time and that no one in the United States would accept such an explanation, which would serve to convince the American public that a campaign of intimidation was being carried out by the Government against the most highly educated group in China. The American people were certain to contrast such action with the broad educational limitations of some of the most aggressive Government military leaders, who, in my opinion, were precipitating civil war. The conversation concluded with the Generalissimo's request that I inform him of the results of my discussion in Nanking with General Chou En-lai if there seemed to be any possibility of an agreement.

On August 9, after my return from Kuling, General Yu Ta-wei informed me that the over-all military situation not only showed no improvement but indicated a deterioration, the most striking feature being the serious situation in Shansi Province, where the Communists had advanced on Tatung and had occupied the airfield and city power plant. Communist forces, he said, had also destroyed sections of the rail lines between Taiyuan and the Shansi-Hopei border and south of Taiyuan on the Tungpu Railway.

In reply to General Yu's query, I informed him that no results had been achieved from the Generalissimo's five conditions presented by Dr. Stuart to Communist representatives since they were even harsher than the terms dictated at the end of June. It was my opinion that the situation was most serious and the feeling on both sides was at such a pitch that it almost precluded the development of any procedure which would permit a peaceful settlement; the situation within the Government itself was such that I had difficulty in seeing my way clear even to suggesting a reasonable approach.

On the same day (August 9), Dr. Stuart described to me his conversation with General Chou, during which he had communicated to him the Generalissimo's conditions: General Chou had appeared shocked and had said that the whole matter should possibly revert to the discussions for the complete termination of hostilities, which were in progress in June, as items of unfinished business. He had objected to each and every one of the conditions, commenting only on one aspect, this having to do with the possibility of a Communist withdrawal from those places in Shantung and Shansi Provinces occupied after June 7. Dr. Stuart informed me that he had pointed out to General Chou that, if the Communists accepted the Government's conditions, he (Dr. Stuart) would see that the Communist Party received fair treatment with respect to the implementation of the conditions and that by the acceptance of these conditions the Communists would indicate to the world their sincerity in wishing peace in China.

Matters were much complicated during this period by Communist obstruction to procedure at Executive Headquarters in the investigation of the Anping incident, in which Communist forces had ambushed a motor supply train convoyed by U.S. Marines between Peiping and Tientsin. Both the Yenan authorities and the Communist branch of the Executive Headquarters were apparently endeavoring to color and confuse the issue by charging that the United States and Chinese Government branches were delaying the investigation while the Communists were pressing for prompt action. The situation was so intolerable that I gave serious consideration to the issuance of instructions to the United States branch of Executive Headquarters to withdraw from the investigation, at which time I would make a public statement of what I believed to be the facts in the case. I was deterred only by the fear of the effect such a statement would have on the possible successful conclusion of the general negotiations to terminate the fighting. It would serve to convince the ultra-conservatives in the Kuomintang of the accuracy of their oft-repeated charges that the Communist attitude was always one of delay and obstruction and that it was impossible to carry on normal negotiations with them or operate the administration of the Government if they were a party to it.

On August 9, in commenting to me on the Generalissimo's conditions presented to him by Dr. Stuart, General Chou En-lai gave a lengthy resume of his view of the negotiations during the recent months: The Generalissimo and the

Government had adopted a course of action and regardless of the situation the Generalissimo would not alter this course. This line had been developing ever since the last meeting of the PCC Steering Committee in April, at which time it had been decided to postpone the National Assembly. Disputes over the carrying out of the PCC resolutions had continued since this last meeting of the PCC Steering Committee; despite the existence of differences over the question of sovereignty in Manchuria, there was for a long time a possibility of reconciling the differences on the Manchurian issues—this ceased when the Generalissimo moved from Chungking to Nanking in late April as the Generalissimo then changed his whole attitude in this regard. From the latter part of April on, General Chou continued, the Generalissimo had pursued definite objectives: When he could achieve them by negotiations, as in the case of Harbin, he stopped military operations; when negotiations failed, as in the case of north Kiangsu, he resorted to the use of force. His objectives were now growing more extensive—he was making an amendment to the condition regarding the restoration of positions as of June 7 which would require the Communist forces to withdraw to such positions, but not the Government troops. Everything pointed to his disregard of the PCC resolutions and to his intention to reorganize the government without consulting the other parties; this procedure might lead to a national split. In all this the Generalissimo was trying to place the Communists in the position of causing civil war and a national split; this was aimed to deceive the Communists and the United States representatives and every step in this course of action was designed for propaganda and not for peaceful settlement. General Chou said the Communist Party had attacked United States policy toward China and, while I must have felt that some of this criticism was directed against me, it had been, rather, against that phase of United States policy which had resulted in continued American aid to the Government prior to a peaceful solution in China. General Chou added that he had had full confidence in my proposals and firmly believed that I had been working for peace. However, Kuomintang military power had been strengthened as a result of American aid, and when American-armed Government troops attacked the Communist forces and when Government troops were transported by American ships into areas in the vicinity of Communist forces, the Communists were suspicious. It was for this reason that the Communist Party had been reluctant to submit a list of its military units to the Executive Headquarters prior to the establishment of a real truce. The Communist Party had never wavered from the basic agreements reached with my assistance and it still proclaimed its adherence to these agreements. General Chou stated that the Government, however, had an entirely different scheme and planned to place the Communists in such a position that they would be forced into surrender or attacked. During the past six months General Chou had placed complete confidence in the mediation efforts of the United States and, while in some cases the Communists had attacked American policy, the basic attitude of the Communists had never deviated from the statement of policy announced to President Truman. General Chou felt that the United States had a moral responsibility toward the Chinese people and that after leading China into such a dilemma the United States should find some means of settlement. Its mediation efforts would be required to solve the problem. The Communists desired cooperation with the Kuomintang and the United States and did not desire to change the indisputable first place which the United States now occupied in China, but Communist relations with the United States were approaching a dilemma and were placing the Communists in a very difficult position. General Chou indicated that he could not accept the Generalissimo's terms and explained that he had not made counter-proposals because he felt certain that they would not meet the Generalissimo's approval. He concluded that to go into details on the various conditions would merely result in increased delay and that in the meantime the Generalissimo would carry on the civil war, begin the reorganization of the Government and call the National Assembly, thus causing the Communists to be confronted with the question of what steps it should take.

I informed General Chou that Dr. Stuart and I had explored every possibility in an effort to find a way in which we could exert pressure to force a decision for the termination of hostilities and from our combined knowledge of the situation we had a fair basis for reaching such conclusions as were possible in this complicated and tragic situation. I concluded that personalities, suspicion and bitterness, however, played an important part and there was the normal attitude of the party out of power opposed by the inevitable attitude of the party in power to fight to avoid losing individual or party power—all these were aspects of the situation and of the difficulties involved.

On the following day (August 10), Dr. Stuart and I had a long discussion with General Chou En-lai. The latter described three possible procedures for settlement of the issues: (1) the issuance of an immediate nation-wide truce order, after which all documents prepared prior to June 29 could be signed and implemented, leaving for later discussion the problem of local government; (2) a simultaneous solution of government reorganization and military problems, with approval by the PCC Steering Committee of any agreement reached for reorganization of the government; and (3) if the first two alternatives could not be achieved, then, in the process of negotiations, the cessation of hostilities could be settled piece-meal in order to prevent the spread of fighting. General Chou expressed the belief that the Government had no intention of settling the differences and merely presented conditions which it knew would not be acceptable to the Communists; these conditions now went beyond those brought up prior to June 20 and those discussed in the Five Man Conference in early July. He did not, therefore, see any way in which these conditions could be carried out. General Chou charged that the Generalissimo had informed his military leaders in June that he felt completely assured that the military issue would be settled within a year and General Chen Cheng, his Chief of Staff, had stated at a press conference that the Government would resort to force to settle the situation. Stating that the Government was employing most of its military forces north of the Yangtze in its offensive against the Communists, General Chou said that if the Generalissimo's demands for Communist evacuation from certain areas were not met, fighting would break out over this entire region north of the Yangtze River. He repeated his previous statements regarding the Government's intentions of reorganizing the National Government without consultation with the other parties and said that the Communists favored government reorganization through discussions with the minority parties and along the lines proposed by Dr. Stuart.

Commenting on the role of the United States in China, General Chou expressed the belief that the Kuomintang hoped that during the next two or three months the United States would stand aside and not take any action to terminate the hostilities, thus leaving the Government a free hand in its attempts to occupy additional Communist-held areas and in its plans to proceed with the reorganization of the government and the convening of the National Assembly. General Chou felt that it would be extremely unfortunate and disadvantageous to China if the United States should stand aside and that it was most desirable from the standpoint of China that American mediation in line with President Truman's statement be successfully carried on. He further stated that if American mediation failed there were only two alternatives: The first would leave China to the chaos of civil war, which would be a complete tragedy, and the second would be "international intervention," which was highly undesirable. General Chou referred to a recent editorial in a Kuomintang newspaper, which, he said, indicated that the Government did not fear intervention and implied that it would be pleased to have me out of the way for the time being—by this means the Kuomintang hoped to force the Communist Party into a corner and leave it no way out. General Chou pointedly remarked that the Government could not expect the Communist Party to find itself cornered without endeavoring to find a way out of its difficult position. He continued that the Communist Party had abandoned plans made the previous year for the calling of a conference in its liberated areas and had endeavored to avoid a national break, but that if the Kuomintang were given a free hand for the next few months the Communists would be forced to consider what measures they should adopt, in which case China might be virtually divided into two parts. This, he said, would be contrary to Chinese interests as well as detrimental to the world and the United States. It was for this reason, said General Chou, that he was so anxious for Dr. Stuart and me to continue our mediation efforts and he wished us to redouble our efforts during the present critical period.

Dr. Stuart then presented to General Chou, for his consideration, an informal proposal as the joint recommendation of Dr. Stuart and myself: The Communist forces would withdraw (1) from all of north Kiangsu to a point north of the Lunghai Railway, (2) from the Tsinan-Tsingtao Railway, (3) from the city of Chengte and all of Jehol Province south of that city, and (4) into the 2½ provinces in Manchuria previously named (Hsin Heilungchiang, Nenchiang and Hsingan). If the Communist Party would agree to these points, Dr. Stuart and I would urge the Government to arrange, at the earliest possible moment, for the proposed informal Five Man Committee. This would be followed by the convening of the PCC Steering Committee and the establishment of the State Council, which would in effect form a reorganized government in which the Communists would be represented. This reorganized government could take up all matters, such as the problem of local government, not only for areas now under consid-

202

eration but for all areas. Dr. Stuart and I would further recommend to the United States Government that plans for a reformed and reorganized government be assisted in every possible way.

General Chou replied that the points raised by Dr. Stuart were all old issues that had been under discussion prior to June 29 and also in the Five Man Conference. He explained that insofar as the military aspects were concerned he had previously proposed that the Communists retain only a small force in north Kiangsu and withdraw their troops from the Tsinan-Tsingtao Railway and from south Jehol; that the Harbin issue had been solved*; and that he was willing to discuss the Antung issue, the only unsolved problem from a military standpoint. He added that the political aspects of the situation were more difficult, as the Government insisted on taking over those areas vacated by the Communists—a procedure contrary to the PCC resolutions, which the Generalissimo had repeatedly said he would observe. These resolutions specified that discussion regarding local government in the disputed areas would be held after the reorganization of the National Government. He said that he would agree that the informal Five Man Committee be called to hold preliminary discussions on the whole issue of local government in the Communist areas prior to government reorganization but said that the discussions should not be confined to only a part of these areas as was envisaged in the Government's conditions. General Chou concluded with the suggestion that there be a division of issues: Any proposal regarding military affairs which was not settled prior to June 29 should be settled at this time; local government issues should be referred to the PCC Political Sub-Committee, which should discuss this problem in the over-all sense and not piece-meal—the alternative would be the handing over of such areas to the Government, tantamount to the cession of territory by the Communists.

On the afternoon of the same day (August 10), I discussed the situation with General Yu Ta-wei and informed him of Communist fears that they were being pressed into a corner by the Generalissimo's five conditions because of the severity of the terms and of their feeling that the Generalissimo did not wish to reach an agreement, but was merely negotiating to

---

*It was agreed in June that the Government would garrison Harbin with a force of not more than 5,000 men and that it would appoint a mayor acceptable to the Communist Party.

gain time for military operations. The chief fear of the Communists, in my opinion, was that the Government was not only not interested in implementing the PCC resolutions but also sought to conceal any implications thereof.

General Yu described the general deterioration of the situation and placed the responsibility on the Communists in that while their theory regarding the implementation of the PCC resolutions was correct their actions belied such theory.

I expressed the opinion that the deterioration in the general situation was due rather to the fact that both sides entered into retaliatory military operations and each failed to evaluate the opposing side. I pointed out that, while the Generalissimo did not want communism in his Government, the present tactics being followed by the Government were such that in its efforts to prevent communism the Government was creating conditions favorable for a communist regime—for example, the present financial and economic situation would be made more serious by a continuation of the present military operations, and civil war, accompanied by economic chaos, would provide fruitful breeding grounds for communism.

The situation at this time had again reached an impasse with the Communist Party refusing to participate in the informal Five Man Committee proposed by Dr. Stuart and the Government refusing to recede from its insistence on the Communist acceptance of the five conditions prior to the Committee's actually engaging in discussions on the matters with which it was to deal. The military situation had shown no improvement and charges and counter-charges were made by each party of military activities in violation of the agreement reached in January. The Communists had undertaken an attack in the Tatung area in north Shansi and in early August were besieging that city. The Government charged that the Communists were also seriously threatening Taiyuan; that Communist forces had destroyed a mine north of Chinhuangtao; that the Communists were breaking the dykes of canals and rivers in many places in north Kiangsu, Shantung and north Honan; and that Communist troops were launching a large scale attack on the Lunghai Railway between Hsuchou and Chengchou. The Communists counter-charged that the Government was attacking Communist forces in the Peiping-Tientsin area; that Government planes were bombing and strafing cities in Communist-held areas in Hopei, Shantung and Honan; and that their military operations in Shansi were due to provocative attacks by Japanese and former puppets under General Yen Hsi-shan, to Government attacks in south Shansi along the Tungpu Railway and to the Government offensive in the Anhui-north Kiangsu area and along the Tsinan-Tsingtao Railway.

Faced with this critical situation and the impasse in the negotiations, Dr. Stuart and I issued a joint statement regarding the situation to the press on August 10[50] with a view to bringing public opinion to a realization of the crisis and impending chaos and to arousing that opinion toward exerting pressure on both parties for a settlement of their differences.

In the statement we described our efforts to terminate the conflict and to initiate a truly democratic government and the almost unanimous desire of the Chinese people for a peaceful solution. We pointed out that it appeared impossible for the two parties to reach an agreement on those issues which might permit the issuance of a general order for the cessation of hostilities; that certain of these issues were related to the redisposition of troops; and that the fundamental issue which had deadlocked the negotiations was that of the character of local governments in the areas to be evacuated as a result of military redispositions pending a basic decision in this regard by the National Assembly.

During this period Dr. Stuart and I had also given consideration to the possibility of the issuance of a statement on American policy toward China but had felt that it would not at this time be as helpful as a personal confidential message from the President to Generalissimo Chiang Kai-shek. We, therefore, prepared a draft of a suggested message for such use and forwarded it to the President for approval and appropriate action. I was subsequently informed that the Department of State had on August 10 handed to the Chinese Embassy at Washington a letter, under that day's date, from the President to the Generalissimo, the text of which was similar with that suggested in our draft.[51]

In this letter, the President expressed his regret that my efforts had apparently proved unavailing. He stated that he was certain that I had reflected to the Generalissimo the overall attitude and policy of the American Government and of informed American public opinion. He spoke of the concern of

[50]See Volume Two, Appendix L, Document 1, for the full text.

[51]See Volume Two, Appendix L, Document 2, for a paraphrase of this letter.

the American people over the deteriorating political and military situation in China and of the responsibility of extremist elements in both parties in preventing a solution of the situation. He described the disappointment in the United States at the failure to achieve implementation of the PCC resolutions, of the growing conviction that an attempt was being made to settle major social issues by resort to force, military or secret police, rather than by democratic processes, and of the continued desire of the United States Government and the American people to assist China in achieving peace and a stable economy under a truly democratic government. The President pointed out that unless convincing proof was shortly forthcoming indicating that genuine progress was being made in settling Chinese internal problems peacefully, it must be expected that American opinion toward China would not retain its generous attitude and he would find it necessary to give an explanation and redefinition of the position of the United States Government to the America people.

General Chou En-lai gave the first indication of Communist reaction to the joint statement released by Dr. Stuart and me, when, on August 11, he informed Dr. Stuart that this statement was a definite indication that Americans felt that my mission had failed. Dr. Stuart replied that this was definitely not the case. General Chou then outlined the terms under which the Communist Party might accept the Generalissimo's five conditions: (1) *North Kiangsu*—According to the military reorganization agreement of February 25, the Communists were to have initially in this area three divisions; the Communist Party would now consider the allocation of one division in north Kiangsu. (2) *Tsinan-Tsingtao Railway*—The Communists would withdraw completely from this line. (3) *Jehol Province*—The Communists would withdraw their forces from south Jehol provided they were permitted to retain troops in Chengte itself. (4) *Manchuria*—Antung was the only major issue involved and that could probably be resolved satisfactorily. (5) *Shantung-Shansi*—The Communists would agree to evacuate their troops from towns and cities occupied since June 7 if the Government would take similar action. General Chou continued that most of the military problems could be solved but at the same time the question of local governments always cropped up, a problem which was creating an increasingly greater divergence of views. He explained that the Communists could not surrender north Kiangsu because of the large population involved and because of Communist belief that if this concession were made the Government would demand greater concessions elsewhere in China.

On August 16 I had a long talk with the Generalissimo at Kuling. He had just received the message from President Truman, which had been delayed in transmission, and had urged me to return to Kuling. While the Generalissimo did not, in this conversation, make specific mention of the President's personal message, his discussion and his questions were directly related thereto. He charged that the Communists were violating all aspects of the truce agreement by offensive operations in Kiangsu, in the Tatung area and along the Lunghai Railway, that their proposals were not sincere, that they treated negotiations as a means of prolonging matters in order to gain military advantages, that they were working closely with the Soviet Government, and that they would not carry out any arrangement for the organization of a coalition government. He further charged that the Government had no assurance that the Communists would cease fighting if a formal order for the cessation of hostilities were issued. He concluded with the statement that the Communist aim was to overthrow the Government and seize power and, apparently referring to the President's message, asked the following question: If the Chinese Government were broadened by the inclusion of minority party representatives and of other individuals of high standing, without the inclusion of the Communist Party or its representatives, would the United States consider this as bona fide action toward the formation of a coalition government?

The Generalissimo did not amplify this question, but it was evident that the inclusion or exclusion of the Communists could result either from Government action or from Communist refusal to participate in the Government unless certain terms were met. General Chou En-lai had been contending for some time that the Government was moving unilaterally toward a situation where it would be in a position to say that the Communists had been given an opportunity to participate in the Government, but that the conditions would be such that the Communists probably could not commit themselves to such participation without condoning the continuation of a government under complete Kuomintang control.

I made no reply at that time to the Generalissimo's above-described question, but, in response to his request, gave my estimate of the situation: The views expressed to me by the Communists were almost exactly opposite to those expressed by the Generalissimo. The Communists insisted that the Government had begun offensive operations and that the Communist reaction had been defensive to avoid being squeezed into a corner. The events during the weeks following my final talk with the Generalissimo prior to his departure for Kuling corresponded almost exactly with my predictions at that time— the Generalissimo had said that he could control the situation in Manchuria and that fighting in north China would be local, and that if I were patient, the Communists would appeal for a settlement and would be willing to make the compromises necessary for such a settlement. I reminded him that I said that the situation in north China would spread beyond control and that fighting would probably be resumed in Jehol, which might light a conflagration in Manchuria and thus result in general civil war beyond his or Communist control. I said that this would be a catastrophe in that it would afford an ideal opportunity for the Communists to spread unrest and for the Soviet Government to support the Communists either secretly or openly. I pointed out that the Government had much to lose and little to gain from hostilities at this time, which might end in the collapse of the Government and of the country's economy, and that it must be remembered that the long lines of communications in China and the bordering mountains favored the employment of Communist guerilla tactics. I urged the Generalissimo to agree to Dr. Stuart's proposal to nominate one or two men to meet with a similar number of Communist representatives, with Dr. Stuart as chairman, in an effort to obtain agreement on precise terms for the inclusion of Communists in the State Council as a first step toward a genuine reorganization of the government. When the Generalissimo said that the Communists declined to nominate members for the Council, I reminded him that this had been true during the discussions at Chungking, but that Democratic League leaders now told me that the Communists were ready to name their members and were exchanging views regarding the coalition government and the question of mixed ministries.

At this time the Generalissimo seemed clearly inclined to a policy of force as the only possible solution, although I had made very plain my belief that political negotiations were impossible while fighting continued and that the fighting could be terminated unless it were allowed to spread to a point where it would be beyond control. On August 14, the first anniversary of the Japanese surrender, the Generalissimo had issued a public statement,[52] which was indicative of his attitude. The entire blame for the breakdown in the negotiations and the economic distress in the country was laid at the door of the Communists. He stated that "we must put down rebellions" and described the Government's policy as: (1) the ending of the period of political tutelage and establishment of constitutional government, to which end the National Assembly would definitely be held on November 12; (2) adherence to the PCC resolutions; (3) broadening of the basis of the Government by the inclusion of members of all parties and nonparty persons to carry out the PCC Program of Peaceful National Reconstruction; (4) adherence to the January 10 cease-fire agreement, with the proviso that the Communists withdraw from areas "where they threaten peace and obstruct communications"; (5) the use of political means to settle political differences, but only if the Communists gave assurance and evidence that they would carry out the various agreements reached; and (6) the protection and security of the people and their properties and the removal of any threat to peace. The statement was not in a conciliatory tone.

On August 17, following the above-described conversation with the Generalissimo, Dr. T.V. Soong called on me and said that in his opinion the Generalissimo's stand was correct and that he (Dr. Soong) had no faith whatever in the willingness of the Communists to proceed on a normal basis with the reorganization of the Government.

In view of the Generalissimo's statement that the Communists would not nominate their representatives to the State Council, on August 17 I instructed my representative in Nanking to inquire of General Chou En-lai whether he would take such action. After discussion of the matter with General Chou, my representative informed me by radio that General Chou had said that he had always been ready to nominate the Communist members of the Council when two conditions were met: (1) When the PCC resolutions were implemented and (2) when cease-fire arrangements were implemented. General Chou added, however, that since the Government appeared to be reluctant to proceed with government reorganization without a more practical understanding he was willing to modify these conditions as follows: (1) When the terms of the cease-fire agreement should have been arranged and (2) when the

[52]See Volume Two, Appendix L, Document 3, for the full text.

Five Man Committee under Dr. Stuart should have worked out the basis for government reorganization. General Chou also commented that three political problems would have to be discussed in the Five Man Committee: (1) elaboration of the first PCC resolution regarding seats on the State Council*; (2) definition of veto powers as provided for in the PCC resolutions**; and (3) reorganization of the Executive Yuan to include other parties.*** General Chou added that there was

---

*Pertinent portions of the PCC resolution entitled "Government Organization," which deal with the matter of seats on the State Council, are as follows:

"1. There will be forty (40) State Councillors, of whom the Presidents of the Executive, Legislative, Judicial, Examination and Control Yuan wil be ex-officio members.

"2. The State Councillors will be chosen by the President of the National Government from among the Kuomintang members as well as non-members of the Kuomintang."

"Note: A. The appointment of State Councillors by the President of the National Government willbe made on the nomination of the different parties concerned. In case he does not consent to the candidature of any given individual, the party concerned may nominate another one for the office.

B. When the President of the National Government nominates any individual with no party affiliations as State Councillor whose candidature is opposed by one third of the other nominees, he must reconsider the matter and make a different nomination.

C. Half of the State Councillors will be Kuomintang members and the other half will be members of other political parties and prominent social leaders who are to serve as State Councillors will form the subject of separate discussions."

**Pertinent portions of the PCC resolution entitled "Government Organization," which deal with the question of the veto power, are as follows:

"5. If the President of the National Government is of opinion that any decision of the State Council is difficult to be carried out, he may submit it for reconsideration. In case three-fifths of the State Councillors, upon reconsideration, uphold the original decision, it shall be carried out accordingly.

"6. General resolutions before the State Council are to be passed by a majority vote of the State Councillors present. If a resolution before the State Council should involve changes in administrative policy, it must be passed by a two-thirds vote of the State Councillors present. Whether a given resolution involves changes in administrative policy or

(Continued on following page.)

also the problem of local government, which, according to the PCC resolutions, should be decided upon after the reorganization of the national government, but that he was now willing to have this matter also dealt with in the Five Man Committee. He felt that these matters should be agreed upon by the Committee, then referred to the other minority parties and finally presented to the PCC Steering Committee for approval.

On August 19 I had another conversation with the Generalissimo at Kuling, during which he repeated his previously expressed views regarding the situation and said that he was willing to proceed with the action proposed regarding the formation of the State Council. He did not, however, wish the Five Man Committee to discuss any other matters involved in the PCC agreements and he would not agree to the issuance of an order for the cessation of hostilities until agreement should have been reached regarding the State Council. He added that this was a great concession on the part of the Government and that it was taking a decided risk in such action.

I replied that I failed to understand what added risk the Government ran in agreeing to cease fighting, since in my opinion the exact contrary was true and added delay would, in the long run, be to the disadvantage of the Government.

The following day (August 20), General Yu Ta-wei informed me that the Generalissimo was particularly insistent that nothing should be said in my discussions with the Communist representatives which would give the impression that the Generalissimo had proposed that efforts be made to form the State Council and, even more important, that, while there should be no discussion by the Five Man Committee of other matters, the fact that such a prohibition was imposed by the Generalissimo should not be made known. General Yu explained that should this become known the Communists would inevitably charge that the Generalissimo was voiding

(Continued from preceding page.)

not is to be decided by a majority vote of the State Councillors present.''

***Pertinent portions of the PCC resolution entitled ''Government Organization,'' which deal with the Executive Yuan, are as follows:

''II. Concerning the Executive Yuan.

1. All Ministers of the Executive Yuan are *ipso facto* Ministers of State. There may be three to five Ministers of State without portfolios.

2. Members of all political parties as well as individuals with no party affiliations may become Ministers of State with or without portfolios.''

211

the PCC resolutions; the Generalissimo, however, was prepared to go through with the PCC resolutions at the proper time.

On August 21, shortly after my return to Nanking, Dr. Stuart informed me that General Chou En-lai had that day inquired of him whether the five conditions imposed by the Generalissimo as a proviso for the termination of hostilities would apply in the event the Five Man Committee met with the object of resolving certain of the outstanding political aspects of the present situation. I replied that I had not specifically discussed this matter with the Generalissimo but that it was my understanding that these conditions were still applicable. Dr. Stuart continued that General Chou appeared to be optimistic regarding a solution and to be confident that the necessary arrangements could be worked out, but definitely desired that the agreement reached in the Committee be sanctioned by the PCC Steering Committee and that assurances be obtained from the Generalissimo that agreements reached in the Five Man Committee would be accepted in higher governmental levels.

Although I felt certain that the Generalissimo had not withdrawn his five conditions, on August 22 I inquired of Dr. T.V. Soong, who had at this time been introduced into the negotiations, whether these conditions would be set aside while a political solution was being sought in the Five Man Committee, at the same time pointing out that this was General Chou En-lai's chief concern. Dr. Soong seemed to be insufficiently familiar with the course of negotiations to be in a position to answer this question. I pointed out the conditions under which the Communists were willing to nominate their members to the State Council, which the Communists had in the meantime released to the press, and said that it should not be too difficult to reach agreement on the military issues, if early agreement was reached on the State Council, unless additional conditions were introduced. Dr. Soong said that he would discuss the situation with General Chou, an action in which I concurred.

Dr. Stuart also attempted to discover whether the Generalissimo's five conditions still held firm and on August 22 inquired of General Yu Ta-wei in this regard. Dr. Stuart pointed out that a solution had almost been reached and that it was very important to continue to explore all possibilities as long as there was hope for peace.

General Yu replied that since the Communist forces had launched an attack along the Lungchai Railway the entire military situation had so changed that even complete Communist acceptance of the Generalissimo's five conditions would not help matters materially. He added that the Generalissimo, however, appeared willing to try to settle the political differences, but stated with some reluctance and hesitation that his interpretation was that the Generalissimo wished to continue fighting while at the same time efforts were continued toward a settlement of the political issues. General Yu emphasized the Generalissimo's desire that particular care be taken to guard against any intimation that he was taking the initiative in proposing the establishment of the State Council. The Generalissimo, explained General Yu, desired to avoid giving the Communists any opportunity to charge that while they would be participating in the State Council they had been, in effect, barred from participation in the Executive Yuan.

Dr. Stuart suggested that it would be a good idea to explore the political approaches to the issues regarding the State Council and said that it was his hope that with political differences settled both sides would have a better understanding, even though the military situation remained unchanged. He pointed out that General Chou had indicated to him that he was willing to take up matters regarding the State Council and permit everything else, such as problems concerning the Executive Yuan, to be deferred to a later date, but General Chou had been insistent that there should be a clear understanding in regard to the five conditions.

General Yu pessimistically observed that there was no chance for peace in China and that Soviet Russia constituted a menace to the nation. He explained that the Generalissimo's five conditions were essentially bargaining points for the Government and that the Generalissimo was apparently willing to accept Communist action in Manchuria as a *fait accompli*, being willing to concede 2½ provinces in Manchuria to the Communists although he stamped it as a violation of the PCC agreements. The Generalissimo was willing to do this provided the Communists were willing to pay the purchase price of the five conditions.

On August 22 General Chou En-lai informed Dr. Stuart that he was willing to discuss the State Council issues, such as, the number of members for each party and the veto arrangements to be established. When he informed me of this agreement, Dr. Stuart suggested that I ask the Generalissimo to appoint the Government members of the Five Man

Committee and to take all possible steps to pave the way for the organization and operation of the State Council. He felt that I should continue to press the Generalissimo to issue an order for the cessation of hostilities, as it would not be appropriate for fighting to continue while efforts were being made to settle political differences by peaceful means. Dr. Stuart said that, while the five conditions would undoubtedly again be brought up, General Chou was willing to proceed with discussion of the political problems if the discussions of military matters made progress. I agreed with Dr. Stuart's suggestion and decided to leave the following day for Kuling in an effort to obtain the Generalissimo's agreement to name the Government members of the Five Man Committee to discuss the organization of the State Council, but pointed out to Dr. Stuart that the question of the issuance of a cease-fire order would immediately involve the problem of local government.

The following morning (August 23), in discussion with General Yu Ta-wei, I was informed by him that, while there was no connection between the Generalissimo's five conditions and the political negotiations to be conducted by the Five Man Committee, the Government was not waiving these conditions but was willing to set them aside until that Committee had been able to reach agreement. I informed General Yu of General Chou's agreement to participate in the Committee and pointed out that in the meantime the situation continued to deteriorate. It was possible that the Communists would be driven to seek outside support, such as Soviet aid, which would ultimately make more difficult the task of reaching a peaceful settlement.

Shortly before my departure for Kuling on August 23 I had a lengthy discussion with General Chou En-lai. The latter said that he felt that certain points should be clarified, as the Government apparently had not yet decided on its stand in regard to the State Council and the question of the Generalissimo's five conditions, to judge from his (General Chou's) conversation with Dr. Soong and Dr. Stuart's talk with General Yu Ta-wei.

I informed General Chou that I had suggested that Dr. Soong see him since he was the President of the Executive Yuan and was concerned with the economic situation, which bore relation to local affairs. I then explained to General Chou the matter of the surplus property transaction, which Dr. Soong was then discussing in Shanghai with Mr. Thomas B. McCabe, Foreign Liquidation Commissioner, and representatives of the War and Navy Departments. These American officials had come to China because the time had arrived when a final settlement was mandatory and because a settlement had not previously been possible due to difficulties which had arisen, such as: the War and Navy Departments forced action in shipping selected items of surplus property in the Pacific back to the United States; it had been impossible to obtain an accurate inventory of the masses of material due to the rapid demobilization of the American armed forces and their evacuation of the islands; and UNRRA and the Philippine Islands had had priority on purchase rights to the property. All this made it difficult to ascertain what would be available for purchase by the Chinese Government. A settlement on the surplus property question was then being discussed by the McCabe delegation at Shanghai, in which the War and Navy Department representatives had been included to prevent an agreement reached in China being disrupted by those departments in Washington. I pointed out that munitions were not included in the surplus property to be acquired by the Chinese Government in this transaction, which consisted only of machinery, motor vehicles, rations, medical supplies and items for civilian use. (I took this occasion to explain the surplus property transaction to General Chou to forestall any fears the Communists might have that the United States Government was making available to the Chinese Government military materiel.)

Referring to the Five Man Committee, I pointed out that Dr. Stuart and I had proposed the formation of this Committee without regard to the military situation in an effort to get something done immediately which might make other settlements easier to reach. I explained that in one sense it had no relation to the Generalissimo's five conditions and in another sense it represented, in our opinion, a probable avenue to a peaceful adjustment. We were endeavoring to have the Committee begin its discussions in the hope that as soon as the Committee reached agreement we would be able to find an immediate basis for settling the military stalemate, the important point being to break this stalemate and avoid further civil war. I suggested to General Chou that there be as few conditional arrangements as possible, as these in the past had caused the most difficulty.

General Chou replied that the organization of the State Council seemed to be a simple question because the chief problems were settled in the PCC with the exception of the two points: (1) the distribution of the seats in the Council among the parties and (2) the veto power in the Council in connection with the carrying out by the reorganized government of the Program for Peaceful National Reconstruction, agreed upon by the PCC and contituting one of the PCC resolutions. The reorganized government, said General Chou, should carry out this program and the ⅓ veto power applied to this program or platform. General Chou said that he also felt that agreement on government reorganization would aid in bringing about a cessation of hostilities, which was a necessary factor in the successful reorganization of the government, and that the Communist representatives could not be expected to participate in the Government if civil war were going on. He said that he had been informed that large scale fighting would begin in the next two or three weeks and felt that immediate action was necessary. He had also been informed that the Government was preparing to use gas in its military operations and this, like the Government use of planes, would cause increased resentment among the Communists, who had neither.

I pointed out to General Chou that, while there had always been a wealth of accusations on each side regarding the evil purposes of the other, I had never seen such complete contrast in views of the situation as existed at this time: The Government stated that the Communists were provoking the fighting and using the negotiations as a means of gaining military advantages, and the Communists made exactly similar charges against the Government. I said that I had tried every method possible to put an end to hostilities and that I was now turning to the State Council. Up to the present I had had to confine my efforts to matters concerning military affairs and the Generalissimo had insisted on certain conditions of a military nature before he would agree to consider the political aspects, including the issue of local governments in Kiangsu and certain other stipulated areas. Now I had prevailed on him to agree to the Five Man Committee under Dr. Stuart as a means of establishing the State Council. It would have to be done quickly and once the candidates were named, we might be able to reach a prompt understanding for the termination of fighting. I agreed with General Chou that it was inconceivable that actual political discussions in a newly created Council could proceed while fighting was going on and said that it was my objective to obtain agreement for the naming of the members of the Council and then with this evidence of conciliation on both sides to turn to the problem of terminating hostilities.

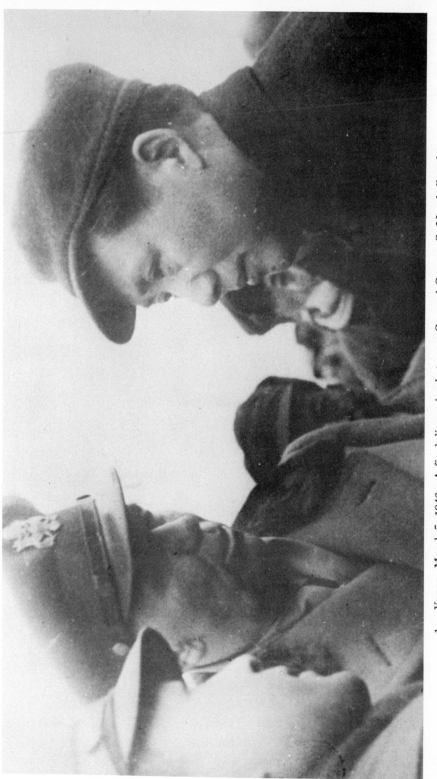

1. Yenan, March 5, 1946: A final discussion between General George C. Marshall and Chairman Mao Tse-tung prior to Marshall's departure [for the U.S. for consultation (March 11-April 18) ed.].

2. Yenan, March 5, 1946: General George C. Marshall and Madame Mao Tse-tung (Chang-Ching).

3. General Chou En-lai, General Marshall, General Chu Teh, General Chang Chih-chung (Nationalist Army), and Chairman Mao Tse-tung review Communist troops at Yenan airfield.

4. Yenan, March 4, 1946: Chairman Mao Tse-tung asking General Marshall to have tea. (Taken in the reception room of the Communist Military Headquarters).

5.   Tangshan, North China, November 1945: U.S. Marine sergeant examines the papers of three Japanese soldiers leaving Tangshan to be repatriated.

6. Chinwangtao, October 24, 1946: Two Chinese Nationalist Army sentries prepare to relieve the last two Marines on Bridge 105 of the Peiping-Mukden Railway (note fortifications in background).

7. China, March 1947: Nationalist Chinese train with armored car, which is the protection afforded every train that must pass through territory possibly infiltrated by Communists.

8. Tientsin, 1946: Fortification on Tientsin-Peiping Highway. The Chinese Nationalist Army maintains a string of similar fortifications all along the highway.

9.   Mukden, Manchuria, April 8, 1946: The Russian Army of Occupation erected this monument to the Red Army dead, during a six-day war with Japan, in front of the Mukden railroad station.

10. Mukden, Manchuria, April 6, 1946: Chinese accused Russian occupation forces of the damage to this formerly large textile mill in Mukden industrial region.

11. Chihfeng, Manchuria, April 8, 1946: Marine Colonel Pressley with Nationalist Lieutenant Colonel Kwang (left) and Communist Major Gen. Twang Shu Chuan (right) toast to the success of the cease-fire program.

中華民族經過艱苦的八年抗日戰爭,才戰勝了日本法西斯強盜,蔣介石為了請美國反動派幫助打內戰就又把美帝國主義份子請到中國來了,讓美軍在中國長期駐紮讓美國艦艇在中國領海內河自由航行,中國才戰勝了日本,郤又要變成美國的殖民地了!

我們要求國家民族的獨立!

我們反對美國幫助蔣介石屠殺自己同胞!

中央軍華兄們你們快覺悟吧不要跟着蔣介石出賣國家民族利益的事!

12. Sian, 1946: Chinese Communist Party Propaganda Poster. (Translation) After 8 bitter years in the War of Resistance, the Chinese people finally defeated the fascist bandits of Japan. Now, to get the help of American reactionaries in fighting a civil war, Chiang Kai-shek turns around and asks American imperialists to come to China. He lets the American army be stationed indefinitely in China; he lets American warships sail freely on China's territorial waters and rivers. Even though China at last defeated Japan, it is about to be turned into an American colony!

We demand the independence of the nation and her people!

We oppose America's helping Chiang Kai-shek butcher our countrymen!

Brethren in the Central Government armies, come to your senses! Don't go along with Chiang Kai-shek's sellout of the nation and the interests of her people. [Ed. tr.]

13. Nan Tuan, Shansi Province, May 1946: Sino-American cease-fire team returning from a ride into Communist-held territory.

14. China, 1946: U.S. Marine-manned Peace Team in China prepares for trip into interior.

15. Hsuchow, 1946: General Chang and General Marshall inspect troops.

16. Yenan, March 1946: The Big Three of the Chinese Communist Party; left to right: General Chou En-lai, Chairman Mao Tse-tung, and General Chu Teh.

General Chou replied that the military initiative was in the hands of one side at one time and at other times in the hands of the other side, and that when the Government launched attacks the Communists counter-attacked. He added that in two respects the Government and Communist attitudes differed greatly: (1) Since April of this year the Government had occupied many more places in Manchuria and China proper than had the Communists; the latter had maintained that the positions held by each side on January 13 in China proper and those of June 7 in Manchuria should be restored, but the Government desired Communist evacuation of places taken after those two dates and was not willing to withdraw from places it had taken during the same period. (2) The Communist Party had continually advocated an unconditional truce without any accompanying military conditions, while the Government attached conditions to its truce terms, which were becoming more and more severe. The Government also seemed to be willing to enter into a truce when circumstances were adverse, and reluctant to do so when the situation was to its advantage. General Chou believed that the Government's attitude was that the longer the hostilities lasted the more places the Communists would lose, and that the Government was thus determined to carry on the war to the end. It was for this reason, said General Chou, that the Communist Party had recently broadcast a total mobilization order. This order, he explained, was aimed at total resistance, which would be conducted in all places where Communist troops were stationed and which included the mobilization of the civilian population. He added that this was a defensive measure and that the Communists had no intention of striking out from the Communist-held areas or of attempting to overthrow the Government, but warned that should the fighting continue indefinitely the situation might change, thus forcing the Communists to wage a nation-wide war. He concluded that, if the Kuomintang convened a National Assembly without Communist participation, the Communist Party would be compelled to call a conference of the liberated areas under its control.

As I feared might happen in spite of my efforts to explain to General Chou in advance, the Communists immediately misinterpreted the surplus property transaction being negotiated at Shanghai and on August 26 General Chou had, through my Headquarters at Nanking, forwarded to me at

Kuling a message protesting against this deal.[53] He had apparently proceeded to Shanghai in an effort to prevent its consummation and the Communist spokesman there had issued a public statement attacking the United States for extending aid to the National Government. As I pointed out to him on August 29 after my return from Kuling, the major charge, and probably the most serious one, he made was that related to a civil aviation agreement. In this charge the Communists had endeavored to show that the Chinese Goverment was contemplating "sharing Chinese aerial sovereignty" in return for American war materiel. I told General Chou that the only connection between the McCabe mission and the aviation agreement consisted of Mr. McCabe's consenting, the night prior to his departure from Washington, to give passage on his plane to a State Department representative without relation to the surplus property transaction, who had come to China to conclude a long range civil aviation convention with the Chinese agreement—such a convention had grown out of the international aviation conference recently held at San Francisco.

In view of the reports appearing in the Shanghai press charging that the McCabe mission had come to China to arrange for the delivery to the Chinese Government of large quantities of war material, the McCabe mission, with my concurrence, issued a statement[54] to the press on August 27, explaining the surplus property transaction and refuting the Communist charges of secret negotiations for the sale of large amounts of military equipment to the National Government. The reaction of the Communists to the surplus property deal was indicative of the deep distrust and suspicion of that party toward every act which might be interpreted as American aid to the Chinese Government, and apparently no explanation could convince the Communists that the surplus property in this transaction did not include vast quantities of munitions, planes and military materiel.

On August 27 I held another lengthy conversation with the Generalissimo at Kuling in an effort to obtain his agreement to the naming of the Government members on the Five Man Committee under Dr. Stuart. The Generalissimo finally gave his assent and said that he would direct Dr. Soong to select the Government members on the Committee. Referring

[53]See Volume Two, Appendix L, Document 4, for the full text.
[54]See Volume Two, Appendix L, Document 5, for the full text.

to recent public statements issued by General Chou En-lai and the Democratic League leaders that they desired the issuance of a cease-fire order and the reconvening of the PCC, the Generalissimo stated that a cease-fire order was unnecessary as that was already provided for in the January 10 truce agreement and that it was necessary only for the Communists to stop fighting. With regard to the PCC, he said that this organization had discharged its functions by reaching agreement on the PCC resolutions and that there was no purpose in its being reconvened, although he did accept the necessity for the PCC Steering Committee for the purpose of settling some details involved in the implementation of the PCC resolutions. Referring to our discussion on August 23, when I had orally communicated to the Generalissimo a written statement from General Chou En-lai charging offensive military operations by the Government in Shantung and against Chengte and Government plans for the use of poison gas in the Hsuchou area, he said that as long as the Communists attacked they must expect Government military operations and that the recent Communist mobilization order was a declaration of open rebellion against the Government. He pointed out in this connection that Chengte was in the same war zone as Tatung, which the Communists were at this time besieging.

I informed the Generalissimo that, while I had not seen the statements by General Chou and the Democratic League leaders to which he referred, it was my opinion that their desire was not so much the reconvening of the PCC as it was to obtain acknowledgment by the Government that it was committed to carrying out the PCC resolutions. General Chou had indicated such an attitude in regard both to the Five Man Conference in early July and to the Five Man Committee under Dr. Stuart, when he insisted that any agreement reached should be submitted to the PCC Steering Committee for approval. I pointed out that the Communists believed that the Generalissimo was endeavoring to by-pass the PCC procedures and commitments and they were insisting on positive evidence that the PCC resolutions were still being considered. The Communists also feared that the Government was ignoring the other minority parties while they, the Communists, desired participation by these parties in the agreements reached. Referring to the Generalissimo's statement that the issuance of a cease-fire order was unnecessary because of the January 10 agreement, I questioned him regarding the great changes in military dispositions since that date and the application of this agreement which required the Government to withdraw from all the places taken since January 13th. He informed me that he did not intend to withdraw the troops from those places. I also called to his attention the question of points already agreed upon in the document for the termination of hostilities in Manchuria during the June negotiations and pointed out that this involved evacuation of places in Manchuria occupied after June 7.

I referred to the Generalissimo's five conditions as precedent to the cessation of hostilities, and to his other stipulattion which would allow the Government to take over the local governments in Kiangsu and other areas, in contradiction to the PCC agreements, from which the Communists were to withdraw. I asked whether he now meant that these issues should be settled by the State Council after its organization, as General Chou had always contended should be done, or whether he had in mind exceptions to his general statement regarding the immediate functions of the State Council.

The Generalissimo in reply made clear that he still insisted that the Government take over local governments in Kiangsu, along the Tsinan-Tsingtao Railway and from Chengte south in Jehol Province (and probably in Antung Province, although he made no mention thereof), but that the issue itself could be settled later in the State Council along with this same problem in other areas.

I pointed out that his views regarding the issuance of a cease-fire order in relation to the organization of the State Council seemed to imply that while the Council was in session discussing general matters fighting would continue and that this was in my opinion quite impractical. I said that he possibly had in mind procedure along the following lines: Agreement would be reached by the Five Man Committee under Dr. Stuart and the members of the State Council would be duly named, followed possibly by the formal opening of the Council; at this point the fighting should be terminated in the manner previously prescribed and tentatively agreed to in June in the document for the termination of hostilities in Manchuria.

The Generalissimo replied that this was a good idea to which he would give careful thought and that he would also consider whether troop redistributions could be decided by the State Council. Referring to the situation in Manchuria, he said that if the Communists felt they had the power for successful military action in Manchuria there would be hostilities there at this time. When I reminded him that this was inconsistent with his statement several months ago that neither the Chinese Communists nor the Soviet Government wished to come out in the open in Manchuria but wished to accomplish their purpose or gain control under cover of the National Government, the Generalissimo made no reply.

On August 28, after my return from Kuling to Nanking, I described my conversation with the Generalissimo to General Yu Ta-wei and pointed out that the Generalissimo made statements that seemed to provide a solution but careful questioning of his meaning developed the continuation of the several conditions or stipulations he had previously made. This had happened in reference to the State Council's authority to resolve all political issues, to which the Generalissimo had added an exception for the local government issue in Kiangsu and other areas to be evacuated by the Communists. The same exception had been made in regard to the application of the January 10 cease-fire order, when the Generalissimo had said that Government forces had not occupied any places since January 13 which were properly Communist areas. When I had expressed disagreement with this statement, he had said that he would make a check on this point. In reply to General Yu's query, I stated that it was definitely my opinion that the Communists desired a cessation of hostilities, as had been their contention for a long time. I did not feel that they intended to make strong demands for the reconvening of the PCC, but it was my opinion that they feared that the Generalissimo was endeavoring to get away from the PCC and the PCC resolutions. They, therefore, were insisting on positive evidence that the PCC resolutions still obtained and this explained their insistence on having agreements in the Five Man Committee confirmed by the PCC Steering Committee. I concluded that there was no doubt in my mind that the Communists wished to stop the fighting and that on the other hand there was no doubt in my mind that Government military leaders wished to continue the fighting in an effort to gain local advantages.

General Yu pointed out that the Communists should be well aware that the Government would not accept a cease-fire arrangement as long as the Communists continued to occupy certain areas without giving up those held illegally and asked if I knew what areas they would be willing to surrender. (He did not explain the meaning of "illegally," which might have been those areas now occupied after the January 10 cease-fire agreement or those areas occupied between the time of the Japanese surrender and January 10.)

I replied that I did not now know what areas the Communists would be willing to give up but that they would probably be willing to continue on the basis of the January 10 agreement, to which the Government had never given a fair trial. I pointed out that there would be little point in delay and investigation for another month until the situation passed the stage of negotiations. I explained that Dr. Stuart and I had proposed this Five Man Committee in order to achieve one basic step and that we would confine the discussion in this Committee solely to the organization of the State Council and would avoid entering into the ramifications of the PCC. If the Communists brought up other matters, it might be necessary to make a statement to this effect, but we did not wish to do so at the present time. I told General Yu that there were two main points for him to consider: (1) The State Council should be established at the earliest possible moment as a lead up to the negotiations for a peaceful settlement; (2) there was no doubt that the Communists wanted a cessation of hostilities but there was also no certainty how long they would continue to feel this way—if the fighting spread to Manchuria, it might mean inviting the Soviet Government to enter into Chinese affairs and that would prove to be the undoing of the Government.

Later in the same day (August 28), General Yu called on me to say that, subject to confirmation by the Generalissimo, the Government had nominated the following members of the Five Man Committee: General Wu Tien-chen, Secretary-General of the Kuomintang, and Mr. Chang Li-sheng, Minister of Interior. He also said that the Generalissimo had informed him by telephone from Kuling that nothing that the Generalissimo had told General Marshall should in any way prejudice the former's stand on the five conditions.

Upon my return from Kuling, I had described my conversation with the Generalissimo to Dr. Stuart, who had subsequently informed General Chou En-lai of the Generalissimo's statement that a cessation of hostilities order was unnecessary in view of the January 10 agreement and that it was necessary only for the Communists to stop fighting. The Generalissimo's exceptions were not mentioned. General Chou took this statement to mean that if the Communists issued a cease-fire order to their troops the Government would be willing to do likewise. He indicated to Dr. Stuart that Chairman Mao Tze-tung might issue such an order to the Communist field commanders directing a cessation of hostilities for a stipulated period provided I would bring pressure on the Generalissimo to take similar action.

General Chou called on me the following day to discuss this matter. I informed him that he had apparently not been fully informed as to the Generalissimo's statement, that the five stipulations still stood.

I gave General Chou a general outline of my last conversation with the Generalissimo at Kuling and informed him that it was only during this conference that I had obtained the Generalissimo's full agreement to the Five Man Committee under Dr. Stuart and to the confirmation by the PCC Steering Committee of any decisions reached by the former Committee. I then described my estimate of the Communist position at present as being useful in an interpretation of my part in this conversation with the Generalissimo: I had assumed that the Communists had practically reached the conclusion that the Government intended to pursue military operations in order to gain at least more favorable positions and was proceeding to follow a general policy of force; I had assumed that the Communists were endeavoring to prevent the Government forces from placing them in a weak position and were at the same time endeavoring to strike all possible blows in the hope of convincing the Government that a policy of force was not profitable; and I had assumed that, if the foregoing were correct, the Communists wished to proceed without the embarrassment of any negotiations with which I was concerned and that this was the reason for the propaganda attacks against me. My estimate of the Government position was: I had assumed that individuals in the Government, particularly the military leaders, were firmly convinced that a policy of force was the only practical course of action and that they were capable of carrying out such a policy; I had also assumed that certain political groups in the Government agreed with the military group and that there was a considerable liberal group with divergent views.

Referring to the question of Communist issuance of a cease-fire order, General Chou said that his suggestion was made on the spur of the moment and had not been reported to or discussed with the Yenan authorities. Now that he had heard my explanation of this matter, he felt that his suggestion was superfluous, although it might still be given consideration. He continued that he had originally approved the calling of the Five Man Committee under Dr. Stuart and had accepted my suggestion that discussion be devoted first to the question of the reorganization of the government in order that, as soon as agreement should have been reached, fighting could be terminated. He now felt that in view of the circumstances his hopes were without foundation. While the Communists expected that, upon the completion of the discussion of the reorganization of the government and evidence of Communist good faith by participation in the government, the Government would agree to the issuance of a cease-fire order, it now seemed that the Generalissimo would still insist upon taking over north Kiangsu, the Tsinan-Tsingtao Railway and Chengte and those areas in Jehol south of that city after the reorganization of the national government and prior to any agreement regarding local governments. General Chou added that if the Generalissimo could not achieve this objective peacefully, he would do so by force—in which event, even if agreement were reached on the reorganization of the government and even if the Communists participated in the government, the resumption of hostilities could not be prevented. He felt, therefore, that if the Communists now complied with the Generalissimo's wishes, they would have no guarantee that fighting would cease; the Generalissimo's demands meant that (1) either the Communists yielded those places under dispute, in violation of the PCC resolution, or (2) the Generalissimo would take them by force, a result contrary to the original expectation of both Dr. Stuart and the Communists. With regard to the PCC, General Chou said that the reorganization of the government through the State Council should be worked out by the Five Man Committee, but that the draft constitution could not be taken up by the Council since the PCC itself had created a special body for that purpose. He added that the same was true regarding the delegates to the National Assembly, final arrangements for which were to be made by the PCC Steering Committee as these delegates were not under the jurisdiction of the State Council.

I pointed out to General Chou the many difficulties involved and said that I had sought to bring out such points in my conversation with the Generalissimo in order to provide a clear understanding. My present problem was to try to find one thing on which we could reach agreement and which would represent positive evidence of the beginnings of coalition government—hence the proposal for the Five Man Committee.

General Chou replied that it seemed easy to reach agreement on the reorganization of the government unless the Government intended to use the negotiations as a means of delay, but that it was still uncertain whether the Government would issue a cease-fire order after agreement on the State Council in the Five Man Committee. He feared, therefore, that by the discussions of that Committee there might be created a false optimism and an illusion of impending peace when there was actually no such prospect and that under such circumstances the United States Government might continue aid to China. The result would be that, while the Communist Party was making various commitments, the war-like elements in the Government would continue to enjoy every facility for continuing hostilities. General Chou said that he was considering the advisability of making a public statement on the situation, pointing out that elements in the Government insisted on war and would not come to terms even though the Communists had exerted every effort for peace. He hoped by thus revealing the situation that public opinion would be aroused against war and the United States Government would cease its aid to the Chinese Government. He said that he also hoped that Dr. Stuart and I would offer some kind of assurance that, in the event agreement were reached by the cease-fire order, I would make some explanation to show the responsibility of the Government for the continuation of the war—in other words, he hoped that the United States Government would clarify its own position in the situation. This, he concluded, was his attitude toward the Five Man Committee.

I emphasized to General Chou that I had with great difficulty persuaded the Government to agree to the Five Man Committee, as the Government was insistent that the Communists would not go through with any agreement and would follow an obstructionist policy, and that it was I who had pressed for this action and not the Government. Referring to his comment regarding American aid to the Government, I said that in my opinion he was confusing propaganda with fact and that Chinese propaganda was far from fact, consisting rather of exploiting any possible item regardless of the lack of actual basis for the circumstance involved. I informed General Chou that I thought that I had stopped almost every direct phase of military support of the Government and yet propaganda seemed to indicate that hostilities could not con-

tinue for so long as one week without American aid. I continued that the Communist propaganda campaign going on at
this time was directed against practically everything pertaining to the United States Government in relation to China;
that I accepted it as political propaganda because it had virtually no relation to the operations at the present time in its
actual effect, but that it had been said so often that those
who prepared it had probably begun to believe it; and that I
trusted that General Chou would not permit all these prepos-
terous statements to deceive him into decisions that in my
opinion would be fatal to the interests of the Communists. I
revealed that I noted Soviet propaganda attacks on me at
Shanghai, that Government propaganda was at times critical
of me, that the Yenan propaganda had attacked me and that
now Soviet propaganda, paralleling that of Yenan, was attacking me—in all this propaganda there was complete disregard for fact and almost in every case it was timed with other
considerations. I pointed out that I found myself in a difficult
position, with irreconcilable elements in the Kuomintang largely opposed to my efforts but rejoicing in Communist propaganda attacks on me as being to their advantage. I concluded
that my own position in this was purely impersonal—I did
that my own position in this was purely impersonal—I did not
take offense and I was not irritated but I was deeply concerned
at the extent to which this propaganda campaign made more
difficult or impossible the termination of hostilities.

On August 30, in a conversation with General Yu Ta-
wei, I informed him that while General Chou was not particularly hopeful in regard to the Five Man Committee and was
inclined to think that it would merely prolong the war and
lead the people of China to take too optimistic a view of the
situation, he had agreed to go ahead with the Committee. I
added that the Communists seemed to be victimized by their
own propaganda and continued to develop the theme that
every effort of the Kuomintang was and would continue to be
dependent upon the immediate support they received from
the United States.

At this point, General Yu informed me that the Chinese
Government had just been informed that the Department of
State had disapproved the granting of the necessary export
license for ammunition which the Chinese Government had
expected to purchase in the United States. The reason given
was that approval would be given only for ammunition intended for a representative national army under a coalition

government. General Yu said that this was the first really major evidence of restriction of American aid to China and that it would place the Government in a very difficult position.

I informed General Yu that this matter had been handled without reference to me and that I was glad that it had occurred in this way, since it confirmed exactly what I had been telling both him and the Generalissimo for some time. I concluded that I had anticipated some such action and had warned them that it was only a matter of time before such a step would be taken.

Earlier in the month I had been shown a copy of the message which Generalissimo Chiang Kai-shek proposed to send to President Truman in reply to the President's personal and confidential message of August 10. I had commented at the time in a message to the President and the Secretary of State that the Generalissimo's message might mean much or little, depending upon the development of the negotiations and the situation. This message from the Generalissimo was delivered to President Truman by the Chinese Embassy at Washington under date of August 29.[55] In the light of the existing situation at the time of the delivery of the message, it could be described as unsatisfactory. It placed the blame on the Communists and on their desire to seize power by force for the failure to achieve a peaceful settlement in China. It charged that the Communists were guilty of flagrant violations of the agreements reached, and, while admitting that "some subordinates on the Government side" had made mistakes, said that the Government dealt sternly with such offenders. It pointed to the policy of the Government to broaden the basis of the Government by the inclusion of all parties and non-party individuals in order to carry out the PCC program and said that "our success must depend upon the sincerity of the Communists in responding to our appeals."

After a month of negotiations devoted chiefly to efforts to convene the informal Five Man Committee under the Chairmanship of Dr. Stuart, we had not yet been able to bring about a meeting of this Committee. The Generalissimo's agreement to our proposal for the Committee had been accompanied by his reassertion of the five conditions, and his stipulation regarding the issue of local governments in the areas

[55]See Volume Two, Appendix L, Document 6, for a paraphrase of this message.

227

from which the Communists were expected to withdraw remained unsettled, although Government military occupation of certain of these areas served to accomplish in part his objective. The Communists expressed willingness to participate in the Five Man Committee but refused to do so unless the Government would agree to the issuance of an order for the cessation of hostilities as soon as a basis of agreement for the State Council should have been reached, action which the Government would not guarantee to take. The chief Communist concern was that the Government was endeavoring to by-pass the PCC resolutions and ignore the other minority parties. The Generalissimo attempted to meet this fear by agreeing to the Communist request that any agreement reached by the Five Man Committee would be submitted to the PCC Steering Committee for confirmation, action consonant with PCC procedures.

The military situation during this period continued to deteriorate. On the Government side it was highlighted by its occupation of important points in north Kiangsu, practically the whole of the Tsinan-Tsingtao Railway and Chengte (occupied on August 29, following a Communist withdrawal) and by the bombing of a plane on the airfield at Yenan. On the Communist side, the high points were the continued siege of Tatung by Communist forces and a Communist attack along the Lunghai Railway between Hsuchou and Chengchou.

The economic situation was also a cause for concern. The major portion of the Government's budget was being devoted to military expenditures. It was questionable how long the Government could survive under the existing situation. Dr. T.V. Soong had informed me in July that it was economically possible for the Government to carry on civil war for six months and in August he expressed the opinion that it could not survive economically under the existing state for more than two months. The Government was faced with the problem of feeding and clothing a huge army and of restoring the economic life of the country with inadequate and disrupted communications. When such problems entered into my discussions with the Generalissimo, however, the latter seemed to feel no great concern over the possibility of economic collapse.

The situation had not been made better during August by the continued efforts of the Communists to frustrate attempts for a proper investigation of the Anping incident, in which U.S. Marines had been killed and wounded as a result of a Communist ambush, by the increasingly bitter Communist propaganda attacks on the United States, by the Communist reaction to the surplus property transaction and by the campaign of terror and intimidation directed by the Government against liberal elements critical of the Government.

Dr. Stuart and I had resorted to various means in an effort to break the deadlock. We had issued a joint public statement on August 10 and, upon our recommendation, President Truman had addressed a personal confidential message to the Generalissimo on the same day. The Generalissimo's public statement on August 14 and his reply of August 29 to the President's message, however, gave indication of his attitude.

XXVI.

CONTINUED UNSUCCESSFUL EFFORTS TO CONVENE THE FIVE MAN COMMITTEE UNDER THE CHAIRMANSHIP OF DR. STUART; DEPARTURE OF GENERAL CHOU EN-LAI FOR SHANGHAI

In view of the generally unsatisfactory nature of Generalissimo Chiang Kai-shek's reply of August 29 to President Truman's personal message and the continued deadlock in the negotiations, the Department of State felt it advisable to forward an additional message from the President to the Generalissimo, in which it would be indicated to him that future American aid to China would be contingent upon the cessation of hostilities and the achievement of political unity in the country. A draft of a proposed message[56] of this nature was forwarded to me for approval and, upon my acceptance thereof, the message was subsequently forwarded to the Chinese Embassy at Washington for delivery to the Generalissimo. The message emphasized that the prompt end of the threat of civil war in China through the establishment of political unity would make it feasible for the United States to proceed with its plans to aid China in the rehabilitation of its industrial and agricultural economy in accordance with the final paragraph of the President's statement of policy issued in December 1945.

[56]See Volume Two, Appendix M, Document 1, for a paraphrase of this message.

In the meantime, Dr. Stuart and I continued our discussions with Government and Communist representatives at Nanking, interspersed with weekly trips by me to Kuling for conferences with the Generalissimo.

By September 3 the full membership of the informal Five Man Committee had been decided upon as follows: American —Dr. J. Leighton Stuart, Chairman; Government—General Wu Tien-chen (Secretary-General of the Kuomintang) and Mr. Chang Li-sheng (Minister of Interior); and Communist Party—General Chou En-lai and Mr. Tung Pi-wu (Communist delegate to the PCC and member of the Communist Party Central Executive Committee). Agreement on the composition of the Committee did not, however, mean that the Committee's meetings were assured. Discussions toward that end revealed the Communist Party's continued insistence on the receipt of Government assurances of the issuance of an order for the cessation of hostilities as a prerequisite to its agreement to participation in the Committee.

On September 4 General Chou En-lai described to me public statements made by the Kuomintang Minister of Information and a leading Government official, in which they charged that hostilities were due to Communist attacks, as the Government had made no attacks since the January 10 cease-fire agreement. He referred to a similar statement by General Wu Tieh-chen at Kuling, in which he had said that the question of a truce did not exist, as all fighting since January 10 had been initiated by the Communists, and that the Generalissimo's five conditions could not be abandoned. All this, said General Chou, meant that prior to the convening of the Five Man Committee the Government was already expressing its firm refusal to consider the questions of the cessation of hostilities and of the abandonment of its five conditions. General Chou continued that he had gone to Shanghai to find that the surplus property transaction had been completed and that he could only express the Communist Party's attitude in the press—in general, the Communists were highly critical of the conclusion of the deal at this critical stage of the negotiations, which had greatly strengthened the Government and had left the Communists in an embarrassed position. Referring to a visit to him by the Government representatives on the Five Man Committee, he quoted them as saying that the question of a truce did not exist in view of Communist responsibility for the initiation of all fighting and that the question was not whether the Generalissimo's

230

five conditions were to be dropped but was the "settlement of conditions in various areas." Today's newspapers, he said, quoted these Government members of the Committee as saying that all outstanding issues regarding the truce and the settlements in the various areas should be discussed by the State Council. General Chou expressed his surprise at these statements, as he had clearly told them that unless the fighting ceased there was no possibility that the Communist Party would submit a list of its members of the State Council.

Referring to our previous discussions regarding the possibility of the Communist Party's issuing a cease-fire order, I asked General Chou whether he had received any information concerning Yenan's decision in this matter.

General Chou replied that he had sent a message to Yenan in which he had cited four possible procedures: (1) The Communist Party might issue a cease-fire order to be followed by a similar order from the Generalissimo; this, he felt, might be embarrassing to the Generalissimo. (2) Both parties should simultaneously issue cease-fire orders, a procedure agreeable to the Communists. (3) The Government might wish to take the initiative in issuing such an order, in which case the Communists would issue a similar order. (4) If the Communist Party issued a cease-fire order, the Government might say that it was appropriate for the Communists to do so, as they had initiated all fighting, and it was thus not necessary for the Government to take similar action—this was not acceptable to the Communists since it would appear that the Communists alone were responsible for hostilities, and furthermore the Government would continue fighting and would charge the Communists with breaking their own pledge should they counter-attack.

I replied that I had informed Dr. Stuart that I would not mention the possibility of this action to the Generalissimo until I should receive word of Yenan's decision in this regard. My idea, I said, was slightly different from that of General Chou's, as I had thought that Chairman Mao Tze-tung would, without reference to the Generalissimo, issue a cease-fire order for four days to the Communist commanders without any agreement or joint action in connection with this procedure. I again reminded General Chou that he should not base his decisions and logic on propaganda, Government or Communist. Statements issued by Government spokesmen, such as those he had described, followed by the inevitable denials and counter-charges led only to misunderstandings and increased distrust. Referring to the State Council, I pointed out that he should keep clearly in mind that Dr. Stuart and I had proposed this procedure because of the impasse in the negotiations and that we had hoped that the meetings of the informal Five Man Committee and the organization of the Council would develop a different state of mind, which might make possible an agreement for the cessation of hostilities. We had been determined that this Committee should confine itself solely to discussion regarding the State Council and that Dr. Stuart would not continue as chairman if other matters were brought up, as this would automatically involve so many other considerations that nothing would be accomplished. I explained that it was only after insistence on our part that the Generalissimo had agreed to this Committee and now, to my great discouragement, I found that even prior to a meeting of the Committee conditions other than those regarding the State Council were being brought up and discussion was beginning concerning matters which were not stipulated for discussion by the Committee.

In reply to his comment on the surplus property transaction, I explained to General Chou that this matter had been under discussion since the previous January and had almost been settled at the time of my departure for the United States in March. During my visit to the United States I had ironed out most of the difficulties involved, and the failure to achieve agreement on this transaction in February had been due to the Chinese Government's efforts to improve the terms thereof. I continued that in the meantime certain complications arose: Due to a cut in military appropriations, the War and Navy Departments began to ship back to the United States the "cream" of this surplus property; the Philippine Republic acquired large amounts of the property as a result of a change in the policy of the United States; and the United States Government could not continue to safeguard this surplus property, which was rapidly deteriorating due to exposure in open storage. It was purely a question of completing negotiations with China or of immediately disposing of the "cream" of the property to other governments in the Far East and dumping the balance in the ocean—in either case the people of China would have received none of this material, which would be of vast importance in the economic rehabilitation of the country. I reminded General Chou that it was not an issue brought up three weeks prior to completion of the transaction but a matter which had been under negotiation for more than six months, and that, if the Communist Party's suggestions had been accepted, the Chinese people would have been denied the whole of this property. I concluded that propaganda had translated this transaction into every evil purpose possible and that all possible harm had thus been done; this I accepted as inevitable, although I was getting extremely tired of such propaganda, but I was greatly disturbed when a proposal such as that for the establishment of the State Council was being destroyed as a result of such propaganda.

After General Chou explained that he had attached importance to the Minister of Information's statement because it had been issued in accordance with the Generalissimo's instructions, I commented as follows on our proposal for the informal Five Man Committee: When this proposal was presented to the Generalissimo, the latter had said that it would not be an effective procedure, as the Communists would immediately introduce other matters which would so complicate the discussions that no progress would be made. I had replied that Dr. Stuart would function as chairman of the Committee only during discussion of State Council issues and if other issues were brought up, the only course would be to terminate discussions under Dr. Stuart's chairmanship. I had exerted every effort and every argument to break down the present impasse and obtain a cessation of hostilities, and I had ignored the attacks on me personally, both those of public knowledge and those made by individuals within the Government who were opposed to almost everything I had been trying to accomplish—it seemed now that propaganda would win the day, the result of which would be chaos. I had left Kuling at the end of my last visit somewhat encouraged, because I had engaged the Generalissimo in a detailed discussion of the question of preparation of the draft constitution under the PCC arrangements and of an approach to the National Assembly on a general rather than a unilateral basis. Throughout this discussion I had maintained that it would be quite impossible to have negotiations conducted by the State Council while fighting continued. It had been my hope that once agreement regarding the basis of the State Council had been reached, followed by confirmation by the PCC Steering Committee, the candidates would be named and would possibly be sworn in—by that time we would have found a solution to the problem of cessation of hostilities.

General Chou replied that he wished to repeat the basis on which the Communist Party had expressed its acceptance of the proposal for the Five Man Committee: He had told Dr. Stuart several times that the Communists would accept upon receipt of a guarantee that cease-fire arrangements would be made and that the Government would drop its five conditions after the reaching of a formula for government reorganization in the Committee. He had also told me that it was inconceivable that the Communist Party would nominate its Councillors while fighting continued. The Communists had agreed to discuss the State Council at this time because Government officials, including the Generalissimo, had said repeatedly that without a political settlement the Government would have no guarantee once the fighting stopped. Now, according to the procedure I had suggested, the State Council might even be convened before the fighting was stopped. This procedure was inconceivable and the Communists could not name their delegates to the Council under such conditions. He had explained this point to my representative, when the latter called to ask under what conditions the Communist Party would be prepared to nominate its delegates. At that time, said General Chou, he had posed two conditions: (1) When there was a cessation of hostilities and (2) when the reorganization of the government had been carried out in accordance with the PCC resolutions. He felt that it was the Generalissimo's idea that cease-fire arrangements should be left for discussion by the reorganized State Council.

When I asked General Chou where this suggestion had been made, he replied that the newspapers had carried an account of an explanation by the Generalissimo regarding the Government's point of view in this matter. He made further comment as follows: It was his opinion that cease-fire arrangements should be carried out in accordance with the Cessation of Hostilities Order of January 10 and the tentative agreements reached in June. If the matter were left to the State Council, the Kuomintang, together with the Youth Party, would have a majority of the votes and any agreement reached would be on Kuomintang terms. Under these circumstances it was desirable for the Committee of Three to handle cease-fire arrangements. If no guarantee were given for the issuance of a cease-fire order after discussion in the Five Man Committee, there would be little advantage in having such discussions. General Wu Tien-chen (Government member of the Five Man

Committee) had been quoted in the press as saying that cease-fire arrangements would be effected by the State Council after its organization.

I pointed out that the Communists had also issued public statements on this subject and that all this merely went to show the confusion into which everything was thrown by the general propaganda campaign. It now seemed to me that there was no prospect of a meeting of the Five Man Committee under existing circumstances.

General Chou, after stating that Dr. Stuart had informed him that there was still no assurance that the Government would issue a cease-fire order but that efforts would be made to obtain such a guarantee, went into a lengthy explanation of his views on several points: With regard to the Communist issuance of a cease-fire order, it had never been his idea that the Communist Party alone would issue such an order, because this would be seized upon by the Kuomintang to prove its contention that the Communists alone were guilty of offensive military operations. With regard to the question of the surplus property transaction, he did not agree with my view that it was profitable to the Chinese people at this time, since such items as trucks, communications equipment and army rations and clothing would be used for civil war purposes and other items would be sold on the markets and the proceeds thereof expended for war; the Chinese people would thus bear the responsibility for payment and it would not, therefore, be in the interests of the people. In April, when I had told him of this transaction, the Communists had felt that the reorganization of the government would soon take place and that all materials would be turned over for reconstruction purposes and not for war—now the situation was reversed and the Communists did not feel that this was a matter of fact. With regard to the connection between Chinese Communist and Soviet propaganda, he had previously avoided making any statement on this subject for fear of embarrassment. Quite often Communist propaganda had taken the same line as that of American public opinion and of the United States Government—the Communists had criticized the delay in the withdrawal of American troops from China, but this had also been criticized in the United States. He had also said at one time that the Communists favored the speedy withdrawal of Soviet troops from China, and it could thus be seen that the Communist attitude was the same on this point, regardless of whether the troops were Soviet or American.

General Chou concluded by saying that he was puzzled at the role of Mr. Philip Fugh (a Chinese acting as the private personal adviser to Dr. Stuart) in the discussions with Dr. Stuart. He said that Mr. Fugh revealed to the press the details of the discussions and had been critical of the Communist Party on several occasions, action which was not appropriate to Dr. Stuart's role as a mediator.

On September 5, in describing to General Yu Ta-wei my talks with the Generalissimo at Kuling, I said that the latter believed that the Communists would immediately demand the reorganization of the Executive Yuan while attempting to settle the State Council issue in the Five Man Committee and that he also felt that the Communists would not participate in the National Assembly until the Executive Yuan had been reorganized. The Generalissimo had said that he desired to have the State Council meet on October 10 and arrange matters so that at the time of the cessation of hostilities the Communists would submit the names of their delegates to the National Assembly. I had said that a delay until October 10 in bringing about a cessation of hostilities would result in general war beyond immediate control and that I did not think that the Communists attached first importance to the reorganization of the Executive Yuan, although I feel that they were determined not to participate in the National Assembly unless a draft constitution in accordance with the PCC principles was to be adopted. I pointed out to General Yu that the situation was also complicated by statements regarding the Generalissimo's five conditions made by Government spokesmen in Kuling, Nanking and Shanghai. The Generalissimo, I said, had made it clear that he did not wish military and political matters to be discussed simultaneously or to be correlated, while General Chou insisted on the two matters being discussed simultaneously. When General Yu said that so for as he knew the Generalissimo had not discussed the idea that military considerations would be connected with the political considerations agreed on by the Five Man Committee, I agreed that this interpretation was correct but pointed out that there was no question in my mind that the Generalissimo knew of the Communist attitude on this point. I explained that I had informed the Generalissimo of General Chou's statement on August 17 to my representative, in which he expressed willingness to participate in the State Council only after agreement should have been reached on both political and military considerations which were outstanding.

I then told General Yu that General Chou had now touched upon the crux of the surplus property transaction when he said that the Government was using the credit it obtained through this transaction, plus its gold reserves in the United States, to prosecute the war. I added that the Government military leaders and advisers were, in effect, using me through this means to create chaotic conditions in China and concluded that I could not, without completely disrupting the Kuomintang, make this phase of the matter known to the world, since I would be destroying the good faith which the United States was placing in the National Government through me.

General Yu thereupon brought up again the matter of the refusal of the Department of State to grant the necessary export license for ammunition recently requisitioned by the Chinese Government and expressed the opinion that the refusal to grant such a license, except for ammunition for an integrated army, in effect was a declaration of policy not intended by the United States.

Later in the same day (September 5), Dr. Stuart and I held a long conference with General Chou En-lai on the subject of the Five Man Committee. General Chou explained his views as follows: When Dr. Stuart proposed this Committee, he (General Chou) feared that the Kuomintang would not issue a cease-fire order as soon as the formula for government reorganization was agreed upon and that instead the Government and the Generalissimo intended to delay in the issuance of such an order so that the Government forces might occupy additional towns and cities, after which it would bring up the Generalissimo's five conditions for discussion in the State Council. When Dr. Stuart suggested the convening of this Committee so that at the end of the discussion a cease-fire order might be issued, General Chou had proposed that this point be made clear: that, after the discussion of government reorganization, a cease-fire order would definitely be issued and the five conditions would be dropped once and for all. The Government, however, had merely agreed to the meeting of the Committee and its reply regarding the cease-fire issue had been ambiguous. The two Government representatives on the Five Man Committee had informed him on September 3 that the Generalissimo had given them no instructions regarding a cease-fire order, and in a statement to the press they had repeated this remark and had added that the question of a cease-fire order could be taken up by the State Council, which procedure would mean that it could be brought up only after the inauguration of the Council. Dr. Stuart and I had led him to believe that the State Council would be useless without the assurance of a cessation of hostilities, but on the previous day General Chen Cheng, Government Chief of Staff, had made the same statement regarding the cease-fire order that had been made by other leading Government officials. From his talks with me on September 4 he had understood that the Generalissimo's idea in this regard was that a cease-fire order would probably not be assured until the convening of the State Council and it was his (General Chou's) understanding that the Generalissimo would bring up the five conditions again when the Council met. If this were true, the Kuomintang, together with the Youth Party, would be able by virtue of a majority in the State Council to approve proposals in the Council requiring the Communists to give up the places named in the five conditions; if the Communists did not surrender these places, they would be accused of breaking faith. The result would be that such procedures in the State Council would lead to a split and a resumption of fighting. While he did not feel that anything would be gained by discussion of government reorganization at this time in view of Government efforts to delay matters, he would, however, give the matter another chance. Government military leaders were now issuing warnings that the Government would attack Kalgan and Yenan and, therefore, while discussion would be devoted to government reorganization, the Government would attack one Communist area after the other. If the Government would give a guarantee that, as soon as discussion regarding the State Council was completed by the Five Man Committee, an order for the cessation of hostilities would be issued, he would be happy to enter the discussions and was even prepared to make concessions with the hope that the question of government reorganization might be settled in one meeting. If, however, no guarantee could be given, his concessions would be fruitless and it would be difficult to convince Yenan to make any commitment regarding reorganization of the government in the absence of any Government concessions and its insistence on the ratio of 8-4-4-4 seats among the minority and non-party members. If the Communists entered into the discussions, the Government would force them to name their candidates; if that demand were yielded to, the Government would insist on convening the State Council prior to the discussions of a cease-fire order—this meant that he would be forced into commitments step by step. It appeared that under such circumstances there was no point in entering into the discussions, which would lead nowhere, because he knew that there was no hope for settlement of the cease-fire problem. He, therefore, had favored simultaneous meetings of the Committee of Three and the informal Five Man Committee, but if no guarantee could be given for a cease-fire order until the State Council should convene, and if the Committee of Three were to discuss the question of a cease-fire order only at the time of the convening of the State Council, he could not agree to this procedure. The Generalissimo would in this case maneuver and delay in discussions on the State Council until the Government was in a favorable military position.

When I commented that this meant that an impasse had been reached, General Chou reiterated the Communist Party's stand that it would participate in the discussions in the Five Man Committee providing that, when a basis of agreement had been reached, a cease-fire order would be issued. He added that an unconditional cease-fire order should be issued or the Committee of Three should meet immediately to discuss this question. He further stated that a state of war actually existed even though the Government refused to admit it and then asked if I thought a state of war existed and what were my attitude and that of the United States Government. He also asked whether the American side could give a guarantee that a cease-fire order would be issued if the Communists participated in the discussions of the State Council issue. He felt that, if the war continued, my mission could not be considered as ended and that I should try to ask the Govenment side to stop the war and that the latter should give a definite reply. Otherwise, said he, it would be clear that the Government had definite intentions of carrying on the war and that the war could not be stopped; as the American side appeared to have no means of stopping the hostilities, it would seem to the public that the United States was actually favoring the Kuomintang. He concluded that the continuation of American aid to the Government caused much concern to the Communists.

In reply to these remarks, I said that I did not consider that a war was going on but that I could offer no guarantee of the cessation of hostilities. I said that I would not discuss the question of American aid to the Kuomintang, as that led to endless disagreement, but that I did wish to comment on one statement made by General Chou on the previous day—that money from the sale of surplus property might be used to further the Government's war effort. I told him that this was correct, but I wished to add that I had already taken up this matter with the Generalissimo in very positive terms before General Chou had ever referred to it; I had informed the Generalissimo that I would not only be opposed to such a procedure, but that I would take every measure to block it. I continued with comment on the State Council problem: Several statements made by General Chou regarding the Government's or the Generalissimo's stand were not in accord with the Generalissimo's statements to me personally. The Generalissimo had not told me personally that the State Council must actually be sworn in and would then determine the basis for the cessation of hostilities; he had referred in a general way to the fact that many matters in dispute, even military questions, would be discussed in the State Council, but he did not say that the State Council was to be sworn in before any other action would be taken. I had outlined to the Generalissimo a possible course of procedure, which I had later described to General Chou, in which I said that, assuming that an agreement was reached by the Five Man Committee and that this agreement was confirmed by the PCC Steering Committee and assuming that the various members of the State Council were named, we could then turn to the problem of cessation of hostilities. I had further said that we might even go so far as to swear in the State Council but that it was not conceivable to me that any negotiation could be carried on in the State Council while fighting was in progress. The Generalissimo had replied that this was an interesting statement which he would consider carefully, but he never said to me what General Chou had just indicated as being the Government stand. Dr. Stuart and I had proposed this Five Man Committee as the only way out of an impasse, which might break the stalemate and afford the possibility of reaching an understanding for the cessation of hostilities, and this proposal had been obscured by propaganda and complications. I then asked General Chou: "Are we to cease negotiations and let the war go on and abandon any possibility of agreement as a basis for the formation of the State Council?"

At this point, Dr. Stuart said that he had felt that the Five Man Committee provided the best possible means for Americans to help accomplish the thing they wanted very, very greatly—that was, the end of fighting. He explained that we could give no guarantee but that we could promise to do everything we could and that we could say that we wanted both sides to join in a coalition government, prior to which we wanted the fighting ended.

General Chou replied that the Government, including the Generalissimo, would not promise to stop the fighting after the completion of the Five Man Committee discussions and that the American mediators also could not give such a promise. He charged that the Government had continually raised its demands:Changchun, followed by Harbin and north Kiangsu, and in turn by the other four conditions. He said that the Communists were now willing to end the fighting and to discuss the issue of the State Council but must first have a guarantee that the fighting would definitely be stopped; he was ready to make concessions regarding the State Council so that the discussions might be concluded in one meeting. He said that it had been clear from the beginning that the Kuomintang would not offer a guarantee for the end of hostilities but that he had not expected that the American side would also be unable to give such a promise. He concluded that Dr. Stuart had said that such a guarantee must be obtained and that he (Dr. Stuart) would endeavor to do so with all his power as well as that of the United States Government; now it was realized that it was almost hopeless to expect to obtain such a guarantee.

Dr. Stuart expressed the belief that it was not hopeless and said that, if the Five Man Committee paved the way for the State Council and achieved results toward that end, there was hope of obtaining the desired guarantee. He added that he would go further and say that he thought such a guarantee ought to be given as soon as the Committee had accomplished some results. When General Chou asked for a definition of the term "results," Dr. Stuart replied that if the points of issue in the State Council—allocation of seats and the veto power— were settled in the Five Man Committee and approved by the Steering Committee, it would seem that he and I would have a very strong argument to use on the Government in regard to the question of the issuance of a cease-fire order.

I informed General Chou that neither the Generalissimo nor I had posed as a condition that the State Council members should be sworn in, but that if the negotiations reached the point of naming the Council members with the stipulation that they would not take their seats until the fighting had ceased, then Dr. Stuart and I would have greater chances of prevailing upon the Government to agree to the cessation of hostilities. I concluded by repeating my question regarding the possible course of action in the event the Five Man Committee were not convened.

General Chou replied that he did not know what the next step should be and that he would have to give further consideration to this question. He expressed his hope that we would continue our mediation efforts. He asserted that the Government's original reluctance to accept our proposal for the Five Man Committee arose from its fears that it might lead to a cessation of hostilities, but that the Government now felt that even if a formula were worked out by the Committee it could still continue to wage war and further delay matters; the Government was, therefore, trying to exploit this proposal and at the same time not commit itself to the issuance of a cease-fire order. He said that Dr. Stuart's statement indicated that he could guarantee only that he would exert further efforts to obtain the Government's agreement to a cease-fire order and could not guarantee the cease-fire order itself. He then went on to describe the ways in which he felt the Government could delay matters and avoid the actual end of hostilities. On his part, he said, he was making concessions one after the other without any result, and it was only today that he had realized that the American side could not give a guarantee for a cease-fire order. He concluded that the reason he wished to participate in the Five Man Committee had been to obtain such an order.

I emphasized to General Chou that if Dr. Stuart and I had been able to guarantee the issuance of a cease-fire order the fighting would have long since stopped and that I failed to understand his meaning. I pointed out that Dr. Stuart and I were not the Government of China and that I had previously rejected the Generalissimo's request that I furnish a guarantee of Communist action; I was not the head of the Communist Party; and it was not within the power of Dr. Stuart and myself to furnish such guarantees. I concluded with a reference to the concessions he said he had made, and pointed out that in this particular matter I didn't see that he had made any concessions.

General Chou replied that from the beginning the Communist Party had sought an unconditional truce and that in June he had made a number of concessions on various matters. He said that those concessions still stood but at that time he had said that no new subjects should be brought into the discussions. He felt, therefore, that his agreement to enter into the discussions of the State Council issue represented a further concession in that it was a subject not included in the June agenda. He added that Dr. Stuart had previously said that in case the discussions in the Five Man Committee were completed but were not followed by a cease-fire order he (Dr. Stuart) would "step out to criticize the Government."

I then made the following statement to General Chou in this connnection: "If an agreement had been reached as to the basis for the organization of the State Council and if it had been cleared by the Steering Committee and then the Communists stated they would not nominate their members until the fighting had ceased, I would confirm their action as being my understanding that they were under no obligation to nominate their members until the fighting ceased. In other words, to that extent I would endeavor to protect the Communist Party against the accusation that they were showing bad faith in refusing to go ahead with the State Council under those conditions, and therefore the Government was unjustified in making such an accusation." I added that whether I would go further than this statement would depend on the terms for the cessation of hostilities and that I was not referring directly to the Generalissimo's five conditions but to the confused state which had prevailed since early June; I would have to decide that at the time the Committee of Three met to discuss the redistribution of troops.

On September 6 General Yu Ta-wei informed me that the Generalissimo was interested in the progress being made toward the convening of the Five Man Committee and wished specifically to know whether General Chou En-lai was insisting on a simultaneous discussion of cease-fire arrangements. I replied that General Chou was insisting on a simultaneous discussion of political and military matters and wished to be assured of the issuance of a cease-fire order if the Five Man Committee reached a satisfactory solution in its discussions. I concluded that the Government propaganda campaign was making a solution increasingly difficult.

On the afternoon of the same day (September 6), General Chou En-lai indicated to Dr. Stuart and me his understanding that the discussions of the Five Man Committee were to be confined solely to the question of the State Council but said that when the agreement reached in the Committee was submitted to the PCC Steering Committee, the latter might go beyond that scope to discuss the Executive Yuan and other matters. General Chou then asked for clarification of two points; (1) Was it our understanding that the issue of the cessation of hostilities would be referred to the Committee of Three for settlement and (2) was it possible that the Government would wish to present certain demands, such as the five conditions, in connection with the cessation of hostilities?

I replied that it was my idea that the Committee of Three would discuss the cessation of hostilities but that the Government had made no definite statement to this effect. I said that I was of the opinion that the Government would present certain demands for the cessation of hostilities and gave the following explanation for this belief: The Generalissimo had once informed me that all that would be necessary would be for the Communists to stop fighting and that the terms of the January 10 agreement were still applicable. When I questioned him closely in order to obtain a complete understanding of his meaning, I found each time that he had not receded from his five conditions. It was our hope that Dr. Stuart and I might prevail upon the Government to moderate its demands to a point acceptable to the Communists and when we encountered a deadlock we had turned as a last resort to the settlement of one political phase of the matter—that is, the State Council.

During the conversation General Chou exhibited to Dr. Stuart and me a paper constituting a report he wished to send to Yenan concerning the state of the current negotiations. We discussed this paper with General Chou and I pointed to several inaccuracies therein, particularly in that portion reporting my statement of the action I would take regarding the possible failure of the Communists to name their delegates to the State Council under certain conditions, which I had made to General Chou on the preceding day. The substance of this paper is as follows:

> A state of civil war exists in China.
> While the Communist Party advocated an unconditional truce, accompanied by an immediate cessation of hostilities and the implementation of the terms agreed on during June, the Kuomintang insisted on the Communist acceptance of the five conditions as a prerequisate to the end of the hostilities.
> Dr. Stuart has proposed the formation of an informal five man group to discuss the question of government reorganization with a view to approaching the realization of the cessation of hostilities. General Marshall and Dr.

Stuart have promised to exert their utmost efforts as representatives of the United States Government to press for the realization of peace. The Communist Party is willing to participate in this informal group but first wishes to have the following three points clarified:

(1) Will the State Council be reorganized in accordance with the PCC resolutions? If this is the case, the formula for the State Council established in the informal group will be submitted to the PCC Steering Committee for final approval. This understanding is shared by the Government.

(2) Will the Government agree to the issuance of cease fire orders by both parties as soon as the formula for the State Council is worked out by the informal group?

(3) Will the Government agree to drop its five conditions?

The Government reply to the last two points is in the negative.

Both General Marshall and Dr. Stuart say that there is no assurance at this time that the Government would promise to issue a cease-fire order as soon as the discussion of the informal group shows results.

Both General Marshall and Dr. Stuart say that the American side cannot give a promise that cease-fire orders will be issued by both sides as soon as a formula for the State Council has been worked out by the informal group.

Dr. Stuart says that he will criticize the action of the Chinese Government in case the Government refuses to issue a cease-fire order when the formula for government reorganization has been approved by the PCC Steering Committee.

The last portion of this paper dealt with my above-referred to statement. After discussion of this paper and suggesting correction of some portions thereof, I told General Chou that with his permission I would inform the Generalissimo of the substance of the message and would explain that it was being sent to Yenan.

Shortly after this conversation I proceeded to Kuling for

further conferences with the Generalissimo, while Dr. Stuart remained at Nanking in constant touch with the Government and Communist representatives. It was Dr. Stuart's opinion at that time that the crux of the problem lay in whether the Generalissimo would give explicit assurances regarding the cessation of hostilities if the issues related to the establishment of the State Council were satisfactorily settled.

On September 10 I returned to Nanking after my conferences with the Generalissimo at Kuling. During those conferences the Generalissimo had yielded on one important point when he had said that the question of local government could be referred to the State Council after its establishment. It was my opinion that unless the Communists adopted new tactics designed to delay the negotiations this would permit progress to be made in the current negotiations. Dr. Stuart felt that General Chou was in a quandary regarding the next steps to be taken by the Communists in the negotiations, General Chou apparently fearing that if he took any positive steps the Government might raise new conditions.

On the day of my return from Kuling, I addressed a memorandum, under that day's date, to General Chou, in which I outlined the principal results of my talks with the Generalissimo. The pertinent portions of that memorandum are quoted hereunder:

"1. The Generalissimo agreed to the following:

a. The settlement of the military terms for the cessation of hostilities would be by the State Council if the Communist Party accepted the proposition that the Committee would carry into effect the agreement for the restoration of communications, the terms previously arranged for the termination of hostilities and the redistribution of troops in Manchuria, and an agreement for military reorganization of the armed forces which would stipulate the places where the Communist troops were to be stationed.

b. He agreed that the settlement of the question of local governments in Kiangsu would be effected in the State Council.

"2. The Generalissimo stated that:

a. He wished to see the Constitutional Draft Committee resume its task, and with the

246

evidence of an agreement being reached by the Stuart Group and confirmed by the Steering Committee of the PCC he would reconvene the Draft Committee.

b. He stated that before the promulgation of the order for the cessation of hostilities the Communist Party must designate their representatives for the National Assembly.

"3. While no statement was made regarding the following matters I gained the impression indicated below:

a. That the reorganization of the Executive Yuan would not be undertaken prior to the convening of the National Assembly.

b. That the Generalissimo had in mind continuing in governmental military occupation of the places recently occupied in Jehol, etc.

c. That, with the agreement to have the local government issue generally, and in Kiangsu in particular, settled by the State Council, and having in mind sub-paragraph b above, he felt that practically all of the issues covered by his five demands or stipulations would be automatically taken care of by the Committee of Three."

On September 11 General Chou and I had a detailed discussion of the above-described memorandum. General Chou commented as follows: Referring to paragraph 1a, in which were mentioned the agreement for the restoration of communications, the redistribution of troops in Manchuria and the stipulations of places where Communist troops were to be stationed, it was not clear to him whether the Generalissimo referred to the agreements tentatively reached in June. He recalled that full agreement (although not signed) had been reached on the restoration of communications but not on the other two matters and asked whether the Generalissimo meant that his five conditions presented in June were to be accepted at this time. Referring to the settlement of military terms for the cessation of hostilities mentioned in this same paragraph, General Chou asked if that meant the various agreements just described or did the Generalissimo desire a separate document covering military terms for the cessation of hostilities.

I gave the following explanation of my understanding of the Generalissimo's terms: The Generalissimo meant first that he was not demanding that the State Council should settle the military terms but was agreeing to General Chou's contention that the Committee of Three should settle such terms, the use of the expression "terms" being in contradistinction to political matters to be discussed by the State Council. With regard to the various points in paragraph 1a of the memorandum, the Generalissimo meant that he agreed to action by the Committee of Three with the understanding that it was not confined to an unconditional cessation of hostilities, although he did not use the word "unconditional"; this action by the Committee of Three was to include the various issues discussed by the Committee of Three in June and they were now to be carried to completion.

I went on to explain that the Generalissimo had made no such succinct statement as that set forth in my memorandum but had talked in general terms, following which I had asked specific questions to enable me to reduce his statements to definite terms. The Generalissimo, I said, had used the reluctance of the Communist Party to participate in the Five Man Committee as an argument to me that the Communists were opposed to this procedure. Referring to paragraph 1a of the memorandum, I reminded General Chou that we had reached certain agreements in June and had been stalemated by certain disagreements, which were largely a question of local government; it seemed to me that we were now clear of that issue, or at least I assumed this to be the case. My questioning of the Generalissimo had, however, revealed, as indicated in sub-paragraph 3b, another complication regarding military reorganization—that was the continued Government military occupation of areas recently taken over by the Government. I said that I had also informed the Generalissimo of the points in General Chou's message discussed by us on September 6, and of the statement made by Dr. Stuart and me that we would support the Communist position if agreement were reached in the Five Man Committee. I concluded that I had told the Generalissimo that the Communists would not nominate their candidates to the State Council until hostilities had ceased.

General Chou said that paragraph 3c of the memorandum was not clear to him—the Generalissimo had indicated that practically all the issues covered by his five conditions had been or would be automatically taken care of by the Committee of Three—did that mean that those points would again be raised in the Committee of Three? I replied that it was my impression that the Generalissimo meant "automatically" by his insistence on continued Government military occupation of places recently occupied by Government troops.

General Chou then commented at length on the Generalissimo's terms and the state of current negotiations: Previously, when the Communists realized that a cease-fire order could not be obtained because of the Generalissimo's feeling of insecurity, the Communists had made a suggestion that a formula first be worked out for the reorganization of the State Council—this in order to give him a sense of security and assurance of Communist cooperation. It subsequently developed that this could not be carried through because of the lack of assurances of a cease-fire order and the probability that the Generalissimo's five conditions would again be raised for discussion. This led to the reluctance on the part of the Communists to participate in the Five Man Committee and the Communist Party then turned to the Committee of Three as a vehicle for discussion of the cease-fire issue in order to expedite action. The Generalissimo's agreement to such discussion by the Committee of Three had now been obtained, but the subjects to be discussed by that Committee in connection with the cessation of hostilities had become more and more complicated—they included terms brought up by the Generalissimo in June on which agreement had never been reached. Considerable time would be consumed in such discussions and it should be recalled that in previous discussions in June the Generalissimo had said that places in Manchuria occupied since June 7 should be evacuated by both sides and that places in China proper occupied since January 13 should similarly be vacated—now the Government has changed this position and demanded that only the Communist forces should withdraw from such places. General Chou's idea of the appropriate procedure would be to have informal discussions first regarding the basis for reorganization of the government, any agreement thereon to be conveyed to other parties and groups and to the PCC Steering Committee for confirmation; the Constitution Draft Committee should also resume its task—this procedure would be that of reviving the PCC resolutions. It was the Generalissimo's intention to defer the reorganization of the Executive Yuan until after the convening of the National Assembly, a procedure not in conformity with the

PCC resolutions.* These resolutions provided that the State Council name the members of the Executive Yuan and if the latter were not reorganized until after the convening of the National Assembly the State Council could not exercise its proper functions—for example, the local governments were responsible to the Executive Yuan and, in the absence of appropriate control over the Executive Yuan by the State Council, the latter would immediately be powerless to enforce its decisions. It was General Chou's idea that the cessation of hostilities issue was the dominant question for solution. Therefore, the Committee of Three should be called to solve this important problem and it would be most practicable to

---

*Pertinent portions of the PCC resolutions relating to the Executive Yuan are as follows:

Government Organization

I. Concerning the State Council:

Pending the convocation of the National Assembly, the Kuomintang, as a preliminary measure preparatory to the actual inauguration of constitutionalism, will revise the Organic Law of the National Government in order to expand the State Council. The following are the salient points of the revision under contemplation:

    4. The State Council will be competent to discuss and decide on:

        E. The appointment and dismissal of Ministers of State with or without portfolios, and the appointment of members of the Legislative and Control Yuan.

II. Concerning the Executive Yuan:

    1. All Ministers of the Executive Yuan are *ipso facto* Ministers of State. There may be three to five Ministers of State without portfolio.

    2. Members of all political parties as well as individuals with no party affiliations may become Ministers of State with or without portfolio.

    Note: D. Of the existing Ministers under the Executive Yuan and the proposed Ministers of State without portfolio, seven or eight will be appointed from among non-Kuomintang members.

        E. The number of Ministries to be assigned to non-Kuomintang members will form the subject of separate discussions after the PCC has closed.

(N.B. The foregoing translation is that issued by the Kuomintang Ministry of Information. It should be noted that in Paragraph I, final sentence, the Chinese text does not contain the phrase "under contemplation"; nor does the Chinese text contain the phrase "be competent to" in Paragraph I, 4.)

accept the tentative agreements reached in June without introducing new terms. That now seemed impossible because of the Generalissimo's new terms, and the Government now felt that it could occupy additional places and was strong enough to introduce new demands. Since those demands would not be acceptable to the Communist Party and since the latter might bring up counter-proposals, it would be impossible to stop the fighting. At the present time, except for the proposal for the Five Man Committee to discuss the reorganization of the State Council, the entire procedure in connection with political considerations outlined by the Generalissimo was actually contrary to the PCC resolutions. In conclusion, he felt it advisable that the Committee of Three be convened immediately to find some basis for the issuance of a cease-fire order, a measure which would also facilitate action by the Five Man Committee.

I replied that General Chou seemed to be returning to the impasse of June, which Dr. Stuart and I had been endeavoring to break through by our proposal for the reorganization of the State Council. I saw no reason, I explained, why the Committee of Three should not meet, but unless it was paralleled or preceded by efforts to reorganize the State Council we had simply returned to our previous deadlock; in that event our proposal for the State Council seemed to be a futile procedure and I did not know where to turn under these circumstances.

General Chou repeated his previous arguments regarding reluctance of the Communists to participate in the Five Man Committee in the absence of assurances of the issuance of a cease-fire order and said that the Generalissimo's agreement for discussion of the cessation of hostilities issue by the Committee of Three was in conformity with the customary procedure. The real difference, he felt, was that many more terms were involved in both this issue and in that of the discussion of the State Council, such as the National Assembly and the Executive Yuan. He pointed out that he had found it difficult to convince the other minority parties, as they said that by following this procedure the result would be neither a cessation of hostilities nor the reorganization of the government in accordance with the PCC resolutions. He explained that in previous discussions with Dr. Stuart he had outlined certain possibilities: The Communist Party could make concessions regarding the reorganization of the State Council regardless of whether the Communists had eight or ten seats, as in any event the Communists, together with the Democratic League, would be in the minority and a change of one or two seats

251

would not affect this status. With regard to the veto power, as long as the Kuomintang adhered to the Program for Peaceful National Reconstruction, it would have a free hand in the State Council, as the veto power was applicable only when this Program was jeopardized. Assurance that this Program would be adhered to could be obtained in two ways—either the Communist Party and the Democratic League would have a veto power regardless of the number of seats or there could be provision for the withdrawal of members from the Council if the Program were infringed upon. If such a procedure could be worked out and if assurances could be given for the issuance of a cease-fire order, he would immediately discuss the matter with the other minority parties in the hope that the State Council issue could be decided upon in one meeting. If, however, no assurances could be given for the cessation of hostilities, he could "find no way to talk to the other parties" and ask them to make concessions nor could he make such concessions for his own party. General Chou concluded that if the Committee of Three were called there would still be hope for the cessation of hostilities, although he did not feel certain of this, but he could not think of any other course of action.

Our meeting concluded with my informing General Chou, in reply to his question regarding the local government issue, that it was my impression from my talks with the General-issimo that the entire question of local governments would be settled by the State Council and that this was certainly true with regard to Kiangsu.

On September 11, I described my most recent talks with the Generalissimo to General Yu Ta-wei, the substance of which had been as follows: The Generalissimo had agreed to permit discussion of military matters by the Committee of Three and to a settlement of the Kiangsu local government issue in the State Council; he had said that the cessation of hostilities would depend on the submission by the Commu-nists of their members in the National Assembly and that the Constitution Draft Committee should begin its work as soon as the State Council convened; and he had implied that the reorganization of the Executive Yuan would not take place prior to the convening of the National Assembly and that the various areas occupied by the Government since January 13 and June 7 would not be given up. I continued that General Chou En-lai's reaction had not been favorable, as he had ob-jected to the Generalissimo's attempt to connect the cessation of hostilities with the naming of Communist delegates to the

National Assembly. General Chou had described this as an entirely new demand and contrary to the PCC resolutions. The Communists seemed very apprehensive over the intentions of the Government and did not wish to submit their list until they felt certain of the conditions for the formation of the government and the National Assembly, since they feared being placed in the position of having acceded to the Government demands and then at a later date of having failed to carry out the agreed upon procedure. It was my opinion that the Communists were making a mistake in not going ahead with the proposed procedure for the reorganization of the State Council, but General Chou seemed to be filled with inhibitions.

General Yu said that he believed that the crux of the entire problem was the resolution of the ratio of Communist divisions to Government divisions—if an arrangement could be made to locate, geographically, the ten Communist divisions, the entire problem would be solved. I replied that attempts to solve this problem had in fact led to the present stalemate in that it had resulted in the Generalissimo's five conditions and the local government problem, which thus far remained unsolved.

On September 12, Dr. Stuart described to me a conversation he had had that day with General Chou En-lai. The latter had repeated his usual arguments in regard to the Communist position and had said that the Communists attached great importance to the reorganization of the Executive Yuan, which they felt must be dealt with at an early date in the PCC Steering Committee. In reply to Dr. Stuart's question whether he would be willing to give to him (Dr. Stuart) or to me in a sealed envelope a list of the Communist members of the State Council, General Chou expressed unwillingness to do so and again proposed a meeting of the Committee of Three to settle all military issues.

It was my feeling, as I said to Dr. Stuart, that this would in effect take us back to the end of June, when each side refused to recede from its position. I also felt that General Chou's stand was harmful to the Communists as the Government probably wanted all the time possible for military operations and time was thus to its advantage. I would not care to convene the Committee of Three as the Government representatives, if authorized to attend, would be so restricted by the Generalissimo's instructions that nothing would be accomplished and the meeting would, therefore, be abortive from the start. Dr. Stuart and I were both of the opinion that General Chou was interested primarily in stopping the fighting and that he definitely desired that we continue our mediation efforts. We decided, therefore, that it would perhaps be advisable to wait quietly for a few days, in view of the apparent impasse, and permit the Chinese sides to take the initiative in any approach to the situation.

On September 13 I again proceeded to Kuling for conferences with the Generalissimo, while Dr. Stuart remained in Nanking to be available for possible discussions with Government and Communist representatives.

During my absence the Communist representatives, in talks with Dr. Stuart, insisted on two points: (1) assurances from the Government that the Communists would be able to control 14 votes in the State Council, and (2) the early issuance of a cease-fire order. General Chou emphasized that the safety of the Communist Party lay in the PCC resolutions and that he, therefore, wanted assurances that the Communists would be able to veto any measures designed to alter the PCC resolutions. He presented to Dr. Stuart a demand that the Communist Party be given 10 seats in the Council, leaving only 2 seats for non-party members, and suggested that Dr. Stuart discuss this proposal with the Government representatives on the Five Man Committee. General Chou said that if this could be approved in the Five Man Committee, the meeting would be considered successful; if it could not be approved, there was no need for the Committee to meet. The Communists were also apparently considerably exercised over the military situation at this time, one of the Communist representatives having informed Dr. Stuart that the Communists could not stand up against the Government's all-out offensive very long. Yet, in spite of the repeated insistence of Dr. Stuart and myself that this was all the more reason for the immediate convening of the Five Man Committee, the Communists continued adamant in their stand regarding the calling of the Committee. Dr. Stuart also discussed with the Government representatives the issues involved and concluded that they would be unwilling to reopen the question of seats in the State Council and the veto power because the Generalissimo's instructions to them had been so specific. The Government representatives felt that the Communist Party would be better off if the Committee did convene, as even a cease-fire order would then become a probability and they would be able to present their instructions in a way that might lead to a better mutual understanding.

On September 16 Dr. Stuart suggested to a Communist representative that the Communists take advantage of the Government willingness to meet in the Five Man Committee, if only to have a direct exchange of views, and use this Committee as an approach to a solution with the understanding that if any headway were made the Committee of Three would meet to discuss the military issues. The Communists apparently feared being led into a trap and Dr. Stuart then suggested that he bring the Government representatives of the Five Man Committee to pay a social call on General Chou En-lai and discuss the State Council during the course of this call. This was made impossible by the departure of General Chou for Shanghai on the afternoon of the day of this conversation. Prior to his departure General Chou presented a counter proposal to Dr. Stuart along these lines: Would the Government representatives accept nine Communist and five Democratic League members on the State Council, or perhaps eight Communists and six Democratic League members, with some form of block voting procedure to provide the Communist Party with required assurances that it could prevent any changes being made in the PCC resolutions? If the Government representatives would agree to this procedure, the Communist members of the Five Man Committee would gladly participate in the Committee's meetings.

Dr. Stuart felt that the chief obstacle appeared to be the lack of satisfactory guarantee for the Communists that the PCC resolutions would not be modified and he, therefore, took up this matter with the Government representatives. The latter informed Dr. Stuart that the place to discuss all these matters was in the Five Man Committee.

On September 15, during my visit to Kuling, I informed the Generalissimo of the Communist attitude toward his proposals, which were set forth in my memorandum of September 10 to General Chou En-lai: General Chou had insisted that the cessation of hostilities was of first importance and that the meeting of the Five Man Committee was dependent upon the solution of that issue; he had described the Generalissimo's statement that hostilities could not be terminated until the Communists had named their delegates to the National Assembly as another condition to be added to the previously presented five conditions; and had charged that this was intended to delay the peace as a means of permitting the Government to carry on its planned military campaign. General Chou had then insisted on an immediate meeting of the Committee of Three.

The Generalissimo replied that he would agree to a meeting of the Committee of Three once the Five Man Committee gave indication of reaching an agreement for the organization of the State Council and all that it was necessary for the Communists to do in connection with the National Assembly was to submit a list of their delegates—any delay would be the fault of the Communist Party and not of the Government.

In further conversations with the Generalissimo during this visit, I learned that he would not agree to informal discussion of the State Council issues by Government members of the Five Man Committee prior to the formal meetings of that Committee, but he would agree specifically that the two questions of the number of seats in the Council and the veto power would be the subjects for that Committee to discuss and settle. He also informed me that he had not issued such precise instructions to the Government representatives on the Committee that they would not be able to discuss these two important points, although Dr. Stuart had gained that impression from talks with the Government representatives.

On September 16, during my absence at Kuling, General Chou En-lai departed from Nanking for Shanghai. Prior to his departure, he forwarded to my Headquarters three memoranda addressed to me: The first memorandum, under date of September 15, outlined American aid to the Chinese Government, describing it as contributory to civil war and as inconsistent with President Truman's statement of U.S. policy toward China, and concluded that General Chou was "again instructed on behalf of the Chinese Communist Party and the 140,000,000 population in the Communist-led Liberated Areas to lodge a formal protest through you (General Marshall) to the U.S. Government over this sale (surplus property) and demand that the U.S. Government would freeze up all supplies, shipping, etc., covered by this agreement pending a settlement at the time when peace and unity is restored and a coalition government is initiated in China.[57] The second memorandum, dated September 15, contained a lengthy outline of the fruitless efforts to break the deadlock in the negotiations

[57]See Volume Two, Appendix M, Document 2, for the full text.

and a request that I immediately transmit the Communist views regarding the situation to the Government and arrange for a meeting of the Committee of Three at the earliest possible moment to dicsuss the issuance of an order for the cessation of hostilities.[58] In the third memorandum, dated September 16, General Chou announced his impending departure for Shanghai and said that as soon as I should decide to convene the Committee of Three he would return to Nanking upon receipt of notice thereof.[59]

A summary of these memoranda was forwarded by radio to me at Kuling and I in turn described the situation to the Generalissimo. The latter said that he would not authorize Government participation in the Committee of Three until the Five Man Committee under Dr. Stuart had convened and had given some indication of reaching a basis for the formation of the State Council. He agreed to a compromise proposal I presented regarding the seats in the State Council, saying that I might introduce it in the event the Government members failed to obtain agreement on their initial proposals in regard to the Council membership. My proposal provided for nine Communist Councillors, four from each of the two minority parties and three non-party Councillors. I felt that this would give the Communists within one vote of a veto power and that in the group of non-Communist controlled votes in the Council there was certain to be at least one liberal minded, independent person who would vote independently.

The absence of the Generalissimo in Kuling, together with the departure of General Chou En-lai for Shanghai, presented physical handicaps to the process of negotiation. We were back, in effect, to the impasse at the end of June, since the Committee of Three could make no progress until the Generalissimo modified his conditions. I had strongly urged the Generalissimo to terminate the fighting but he was unyielding in his attitude that the Communist Party should first meet certain conditions to ensure the security of the Government military successes. At the same time, as the Government military campaign continued to develop its advantage, the Government had become the more implacable in regard to these conditions for the termination of hostilities. During this period of negotiations, I had frankly told the Generalissimo that the Government's present procedure involved me and the

---

[58]See Volume Two, Appendix M, Document 3, for the full text.
[59]See Volume Two, Appendix M, Document 4, for the full text.

United States Government indirectly in procedures which could not be tolerated: When I had directed the withdrawal of the U.S. Marines from a number of points along the railway north of Tientsin, the Government military authorities in that area had informed the Marine commander that it was impossible to relieve these Marines at that time because the available Government troops in that area were required for the campaign then in progress; since the Marines were keeping the rail line open and the line was becoming a factor in a campaign, I stated that this situation had to be terminated immediately, to which he agreed.

It was my opinion at this time that the Communists must rid themselves of the idea that the proposal for the Five Man Committee had been made by the Government and also that the Government representatives should realize that they were expected as a matter of course to discuss the questions of the number of representatives each party would have in the State Council and the veto power problem in the Council.

During this period of negotiations in September, at the end of which General Chou En-lai had departed for Shanghai, there had been little change in the position of the Communists. They continued to insist that a solution for the cessation of hostilities issue was a prerequisite to their participation in the Five Man Committee discussions looking toward the organization of the State Council, although they did finally agree to enter into the Committee's discusions provided the Committee of Three should meet simultaneously to discuss the cessation of hostilities; they demanded that the Generalissimo's five conditions be dropped after a basis for the State Council should have been reached in the Five Man Committee; they stated their refusal to name their members of the State Council, in the event of agreement on a formula for the Council, until hostilities should cease; and they indicated their desire that the PCC Steering Committee should discuss the reorganization of the Executive Yuan. The greatest concern of the Communists during this period was for the cessation of hostilities and for assurances that the PCC resolutions would not be modified; to this latter end they insisted on some formula in the veto power arrangement which would ensure that the PCC resolutions would not be changed, as they apparently felt that their safety lay in the retention of the decisions of the PCC.

The Government's position during this period was less fixed: The Government first placed the blame on the Communists for the initiation of the fighting and thus insisted that there was no need to issue a cease-fire order; the Government stated at the beginning of the month that it would not abandon the Generalissimo's five conditions; and Government spokesmen during this period indicated that all issues regarding a truce and the settlements in various areas were to be discussed in the State Council. Subsequently, however, after an earlier refusal to consider the convening of the Committee of Three, the Generalissimo agreed to permit that Committee to settle the cessation of hostilities issue provided the Communists would carry out certain tentative agreements reached during June and, in effect, abandoned the five conditions through agreement to permit the Kiangsu local government problem to be settled by the State Council. The Government's military advances had more or less made the carrying out of most of these five conditions a *fait accompli*. The Generalissimo also agreed to the summoning of the Constitution Reviewing Committee as soon as the Five Man Committee should have reached an agreement and this agreement should have been confirmed by the PCC Steering Committee, thus providing some assurance to the Communists of conformity with PCC procedures. He had, however, posed an additional condition by stipulating that he would not agree to the cessation of hostilities until the Communists should have named their delegates to the National Assembly, a procedure which the Communists characterized as not in conformity with the PCC resolutions; and he had indicated that the Executive Yuan would not be reorganized until the National Assembly should have convened, although the PCC resolutions envisaged the reorganization of the Executive Yuan prior to that time. The Generalissimo also indicated that he contemplated continued Government military occupation of the places occupied in its military campaign. Toward the end of this period of negotiations, the Generalissimo, who had opposed simultaneous meetings of the Committee of Three and the Five Man Committee, agreed to the convening of the Committee of Three when the Five Man Committee under Dr. Stuart should give evidence of having reached agreement on the State Council, but he would not agree to informal meetings of the Five Man Committee prior to its formal meetings.

The positions of the two parties thus continued irreconcilable. Dr. Stuart and I had endeavored to break the deadlock through our proposal for the Five Man Committee as a step leading toward the cessation of hostilities. We had exerted strong pressure on the Generalissimo in an effort to obtain his concurrence to our proposal only to meet with Communist refusal to participate in the meetings of the Committee. Propaganda campaigns, as usual, played a part in wrecking our efforts, as they led to confusion and misunderstandings. The most bitter of these campaigns was that directed against the United States Government and the surplus property transaction by the Communist Party. Communist distrust and Communist practices of distortion and disregard of the truth made of this transaction an evil purpose intended to further civil war in China, which was quite contrary to the facts.

XXVII.
THE POSSIBLIITY OF A NATIONAL BREAK AS A RESULT OF THE GOVERNMENT OFFENSIVE AGAINST KALGAN AND THE QUESTION OF THE TERMINATION OF THE U.S. MEDIATION EFFORT; COMMUNIST REJECTION OF THE KALGAN TRUCE PROPOSAL

The situation at the time of General Chou En-lai's departure for Shanghai was not conducive to a successful conclusion of negotiations. General Chou had stated that he would return to Nanking upon receipt of notice of the convening of the Committee of Three. The Communists charged that the Government forces had begun a drive toward Kalgan, an important Communist political and military center in Chahar Province. A Government representative informed me that all of the Tsinan-Tsingtao Railway in Shantung Province, except for 80 kilometers, was in Government hands; that Government forces had captured several important cities along the Grand Canal in north Kiangsu and were in a favorable position to occupy another strategic point in that area; and that, while the Communists still had the upper hand in Shansi Province, the Government had completed occupation of Chengte and was mopping up in Jehol province south of Chengte. The Generalissimo was insisting on formal meetings of the Five Man Committee under Dr. Stuart, while the Communists seemingly wished to avoid the convening of that Committee apparently lest they later be accused of obstructionist efforts in connection with the reorganization of the government if the Committee should make no progress. On the other hand, the Communists were anxious to convene the Commit-

260

tee of Three in order to obtain first a cessation of hostilities, by virtue of which they might be more likely to be assured of a State Council satisfactory to them. It was my belief that the Communists, by this attitude, were maneuvering themselves into a bad position, since in the meantime the Government forces were making substantial military advances as a result of which the Communists might soon find themselves in the position of having virtually accepted the Generalissimo's five conditions by losses in military operations. In my last talks with the Generalissimo at Kuling, the latter had said very frankly that the conclusion of an agreement for the termination of hostilities was his final trump card in forcing the Communist Party to name its delegates to the National Assembly. Since the Communists considered this as a sixth condition to be added to the previously announced five conditions, they were pressing for the more immediate issue, as they saw it, of terminating the fighting. It was a game in which the Communists were pressing for the cessation of hostilities to free their hands for political negotiations while the Generalissimo was trading on the continuance of hostilities to ensure representation by all parties in the National Assembly. Communist propaganda directed against American lend-lease aid to China, the surplus property transaction and American policy toward China was apparently intended to give the impression that Dr. Stuart and I were aligned with the Kuomintang and was perhaps accompanied by the hope that it would serve to exert pressure on the United States to force the Chinese Government's hand. It was also possible that the Communist propaganda was leading to an appeal to the United Nations Organization or that they were endeavoring to rid themselves of American mediation and at the same time obtain Soviet backing.

On the Government side there was concern over the stoppage of delivery of certain military equipment from the United States. On September 19, General Yu Ta-wei informed me that Dr. T.V. Soong had learned that the delivery of certain lend-lease air force equipment earmarked for China had been suspended and that he had told Dr. Soong that there was no hope of getting this equipment, except possibly a few spare parts. In this connection, General Yu again inquired of me regarding the matter of the Department of State's refusal to grant the necessary export license to cover the export of ammunition to China. I replied that this action had not been a low level decision, as General Yu had previously stated, but was the result of a policy decision issued on a high level.

On September 19, in response to a request from General Chou En-lai, transmitted orally to Dr. Stuart by a Communist representative at Nanking, I addressed to General Chou a memorandum[60] in acknowledgment of his memorandum of September 15; in this communication he had requested me as Chairman of the Committee of Three to forward to the National Government the Communist Party's view regarding the situation and to arrange for a meeting of the Committee of Three at the earliest possible moment. In my reply I informed him that I had transmitted a copy of his memorandum to the National Government and had presented his proposal to the Generalissimo. The latter, I said, had told me that he would not authorize the attendance of the Government member at a meeting of the Committee of Three until the Five Man Committee under Dr. Stuart should have met and some progress should have been made in this Committee toward agreement on the organization of the State Council.

On September 22, Mr. Wang Ping-nan, one of the Communist representatives at Nanking, presented to me a memorandum, dated September 21, from General Chou at Shanghai. The substance of this memorandum is as follows:[61]

> The key to the present serious situation is the immediate issuance of a cease-fire order and, since the sole legal agency dealing with such matters is the Committee of Three, it is requested that you convene this Committee. The present situation is similar to that existing in January at the time of the issuance of the Cessation of Hostilities Order and the only proper approach now is to effect the prompt cessation of hostilities. It is clear that the Five Man Committee would not itself bring about a termination of the fighting; it would only pave the way for discussion of a truce and this is far from our objective, the cessation of hostilities. The reorganization of the State Council would present no complications if the Government would give sufficient seats to the Communist Party and the Democratic League to guarantee against infringement of

[60]See Volume Two, Appendix N, Document 1, for the full text.
[61]See Volume Two, Appendix N, Document 2, for the full text.

the PCC program. The Government's insistence on the Five Man Committee as a prerequisite to the meeting of the Committee of Three is a pretext for the purpose of obstruction. If the Committee of Three is not convened, I can hardly convince myself that there is any other course leading to the cessation of hostilities. I would, therefore, feel forced to make public all the important documents in the negotiations since the truce in June in order to make clear the responsibility for the present situation and would thus appeal to the public for judgment. I wish, hereby, to serve notice of my contemplated action.

In discussion of this memorandum with Mr. Wang, I explained that the preliminaries to meetings of the Committee of Three usually involved individual talks with Government and Communist representatives in order to ensure a reasonable probability of agreement and pointed out that to call a meeting of the Committee of Three without a probable basis for agreement would result only in a further loss of prestige to that Committee. It did not seem to me, I said, that there was at present any probability of agreement. I emphasized that the Five Man Committee had been proposed not by the Government but by Dr. Stuart and me in an effort to break the deadlock, but that the attitude of the Communists had been, as indicated by General Chou's statements and Communist propaganda, that the proposal was originated by the Government for an evil purpose. I continued that Dr. Stuart and I had previously had good reason to believe that Communist agreement to the Five Man Committee had been obtained and that the difficulty would be in persuading the Government to accept out proposal. Now, however, the situation was reversed and it was difficult to know just what purpose lay behind the current Communist stand.

Referring to Communist propaganda attacks, I made the following remarks to Mr. Wang: It was noted from recent Communist publicity statements that the Communists were resentful of my bringing Government stipulations, conditions or agreement to General Chou En-lai from the Generalissimo. Acting as a middle-man was my unhappy duty and it was equally disagreeable for me to carry disagreements or stipulations from General Chou to the Generalissimo. One point I wished most emphatically to clarify concerned the vicious propaganda attack directed against my personal integrity and honesty of purpose, which was paralleled by repeated private requests from the Communists that I continue my efforts at mediation. This procedure would no longer be tolerated—if the Communists had lost faith in me, my efforts would, of course, be ineffective; if this were the case, the Communists needed only to notify me accordingly and I would immediately withdraw. Mr. Wang, in reply, said that he would transmit these statements to General Chou at Shanghai. Our discussion concluded with my reminding him of the necessity for the elimination of distrust and the advisability of utilizing our proposal for the Five Man Committee as a means of strengthening the good faith on both sides and of paving the way for real peace through discussions across a conference table.

On the same day (September 22), I forwarded a copy of General Chou's memorandum of September 21 to General Yu Ta-wei. I felt certain that should the Committee of Three be convened the Communists would insist on reverting to the positions held as of January 13 and that the Government would insist on carrying out the Generalissimo's five conditions—the two positions would thus be diametrically opposed. I felt it desirable to await the Generalissimo's return to Nanking so that I would be able to determine specifically what restrictions the Generalissimo would now insist upon in any agreement for the cessation of hostilities. (The Generalissimo had left Kuling but was visiting various points in south China prior to his return to Nanking.)

In discussion of General Chou's memorandum of September 21 with General Yu Ta-wei, I cautioned him not to make an issue of the point raised by General Chou concerning the possible publication of the documents in the negotiations since this was not the real issue or an important matter; the Government's reaction to General Chou's proposal for a meeting of the Committee of Three was the problem. I impressed upon General Yu the delicacy of the situation and the possibility that the Government's stubborn position might force the Communists into the Soviet fold. I pointed out that the Communists were definitely of the opinion that I had the power to force the Government to meet the various terms and that they used this in their propaganda in an effort to bolster their own cause; for this reason particularly, Government propaganda would aggravate the situation. Referring further to the Communist propaganda, I said that until very recently I had not mentioned the most damaging aspect of the surplus property transfers; that is, the funds made available to the Government in disposing of the surplus property for cash with which to support a continuation of the campaign of force. I stated that I was concerned over the fact that certain Government officials were abusing or taking advantage of my efforts to assist the people of China by utilizing these facilities to pursue their military campaigns—this was particularly true of shipping. I concluded that I would not take any action to support the Government in a campaign of force and that I had been willing to proceed with the various programs only because they were intended for the benefit of the people.

On September 26, as the Generalissimo was expected to return to Nanking on that day and since General Chou En-lai still remained in Shanghai, Dr. Stuart and I addressed a joint letter[62] to General Chou, in which we stated that, on the basis of our past friendly relations and our personal esteem for General Chou, we urged him to return to Nanking without further delay in order that we might together explore all conceivable ways and means to achieve the peaceful objective which we sought. It was felt that this joint letter would enable General Chou to return to Nanking without any loss of face involved in the possible feeling that his bluff had not worked; instead he could point out that he had returned because of special representations from the American mediators.

Under date of September 27, General Chou forwarded his reply to our joint letter. In this reply he said that he was "not unwilling to return to Nanking for a discussion of the ways and means to stop the civil war"; that the Government, however, not only gave no signs of a cessation of hostilities but instead was increasing the tempo of its military operations against Kalgan and other areas; that further negotiations would do nothing to bring about real peace but would provide a smoke screen to cover up the Government's full scale civil war; and that for these reasons he would prefer to wait in Shanghai for the convening of the Committee of Three.[63] He also stated that he was requesting Mr. Tung Pi-wu, leading member of the Communist delegation to Nanking, to approach us on behalf of the Communist Party.

The Generalissimo returned to Nanking on September 26 and on the following day I had a conference with him. I out-

[62]See Volume Two, Appendix N, Document 3, for the full text.

[63]See Volume Two, Appendix N, Document 4, for the full text.

lined the existing situation: General Chou was still in Shanghai and was insisting upon a meeting of the Committee of
Three prior to any other meeting—in other words agreement
for the cessation of hostilities should be reached prior to negotiations for the reorganization of the government. The Generalissimo commented on the general situation and said that he
must be prepared for two courses of action: (1) If General
Chou refused to return to Nanking and the negotiations ended, the Government must decide what steps it would take. (2)
What action should the Government take now to break the
deadlock? He said that he thought that some public statement
by him would be advisable and that he was giving careful
consideration thereto. He then asked that I consider such a
course of action and give him the benefit of my advice.

I replied that I had already considered such a course of
action and had taken the liberty of preparing a draft of a
statement which I thought would be appropriate for him to
make (Dr. Stuart had concurred in this statement). My principle purpose in preparing such a draft, I explained, was to il-
lustrate what I thought should be the attitude of the Government at this time in the negotiations. I emphasized that whatever was said should be in a tolerant spirit and should carefully avoid provocative or irritating statements and that it
was necessary to propose definite and positive action rather
that the usual course of generalities. I suggested that he have
the statement translated into Chinese and discuss it with me
later.

The substance of this draft statement is as follows:[64]

> The continuation of the present political
> and military situation in China will be destruc-
> tive of the interests of the long-suffering Chi-
> nese people and will render impossible the
> unification of the country; it will also threat-
> en the peace of the world. It is, therefore, nec-
> essary to find an early solution. In the past
> three months I have stipulated certain condi-
> tions that must be met by the Communists be-
> fore peace can be realized. They have refused
> to agree to these conditions and now demand
> the immediate convening of the Committee of
> Three. That Committee, however, reached an
> impasse in June and, unless certain prelimin-

[64]See Volume Two, Appendix N, Document 5, for the full text.

ary but vital agreements or understandings are reached in advance, a meeting of this Committee would not only be ineffective but its possible future usefulness would be fatally impaired. I have insisted on the Five Man Committee under Dr. Stuart meeting first in order to give evidence of the good intent of both parties in regard to the reorganization of the government in accordance with the PCC resolutions and have further said that, concurrent with the termination of hostilities, the Communists should indicate their intention of cooperating in the reorganization of the government by naming their delegates to the National Assembly.

In view of the seriousness of the situation and the misunderstanding, public confusion and suspicions unfortunately prevalent, I now make the following public announcement of the conditions under which the Government is prepared to act to secure the immediate cessation of hostilities:

The Five Man Committee under the chairmanship of Dr. Stuart and the Committee of Three under the chairmanship of General Marshall should immediately convene with the following understandings:

(a) Opposing troops in close contact to be separated in accordance with the terms tentatively agreed to by the Committee of Three in June for the termination of hostilities in Manchuria.

(b) The restoration of communications to be immediately resumed in accordance with the agreement tentatively reached by the Committee of Three in June.

(c) The method of settling disagreements among the team members and the Commissioners of the Executive Headquarters to be in accordance with the agreement tentatively reached by the Committee of Three in June.

(d) The implementation of the agreement for the reorganization and unification of the armies to be settled by the Committee of Three without delay.

(e) Whatever understanding is reached by the Five Man Committee to be confirmed by the PCC Steering Committee without delay.

(f) All questions of local government to be settled by the newly organized State Council.

(g) Concurrent with the cessation of hostilities, the Communist Party to announce its intention of participating in the National Assembly by publishing its list of delegates to the National Assembly.

On the evening of the day on which I had presented this statement to the Generalissimo, he informed Dr. Stuart that he had liked the statement and he indicated his intention of issuing it, after making some changes. That same evening, General Yu Ta-wei called on me for clarification of the statement, to which I replied that, if the Communists expressed agreement to the general terms and procedure indicated in the draft, an order for the cessation of hostilities should be issued immediately and the Five Man Committee and the Committee of Three should meet at once.

On September 29 the Generalissimo informed me that after study on the draft he had come to the conclusion that it should include a statement that the several agreements indicated should be completed prior to the cessation of hostilities— in other words the Committee of Three would have to reach complete agreement on the redisposition of troops for demobilization and integration of the armies and the Five Man Committee would also have to reach an agreement prior to the issuance of an order for the cessation of hostilities.

I replied that such a procedure would completely vitiate the entire purpose of my proposed statement and that, rather than amend or qualify the paper as drawn, we should have to consider an entirely new approach. When the Generalissimo asked whether I had such an approach in mind, I said that I did not as I had included in this draft conditions which I thought sufficiently protected the Government and which I also thought might well be accepted by the Communists. I added that his proposal would in effect transform the draft statement, in which I had endeavored to place him on a high level before the world, into a procedure which was merely a prolongation of "horse trading" methods.

The Generalissimo then said that he felt that the time for such a statement had not arrived and that he wished me to convey to the Communist Party his willingness to accept "my proposal" for simultaneous meetings of the Five Man Committee and the Committee of Three.

I replied as follows: In the first place, such a proposal would lead to no solution and, further, I would not carry such a message orally to the Communist Party. If it were handed to me in writing, I would transmit the message without comment. The proposal should not, however, be referred to as "mine," since the procedure indicated was merely one portion of a general proposal and other vital portions had been omitted. Furthermore, if the written proposal were given to me for transmission to the Communists, the Generalissimo should instruct his Minister of Information to avoid any reference to this proposal as mine. The Minister had in the past wrongly attributed certain proposals to me in public statements; if he did so in reference to this proposal, I would issue an official denial.* I thought that the Generalissimo's proposal could not lead to agreement for the cessation of hostilities and I could not under the circumstances continue in my role as a mediator. I would be forced to recommend to my Government that I should be relieved of further responsibility in this affair.

On the evening of September 30 the Generalissimo informed me during a dinner party that he had decided not to release any public statement at this time regarding simultaneous meetings of the two Committees.

On September 29, pursuant to the memorandum of September 27 from General Chou En-lai, Messrs. Tung Pi-wu and Wang Ping-nan, members of the Communist delegation at Nanking, called on me. Mr. Tung explained that they wished to confer with me on the possibility of simultaneous meetings of the Five Man Committee and the Committee of Three, regarding which Dr. Stuart had informed them on the

---

*The Kuomintang Central News Agency on September 30 reported that this proposal was "mine" and I, therefore, authorized the issuance of the following release on October 3:

"Bradley Connors, official spokesman for the American Embassy issued the following statement to the press this afternoon:

The statement released by the Central News Agency in Nanking dated September 30 to the effect that Generalissimo Chiang Kai-shek had agreed to accept the proposal of General Marshall for a simultaneous meeting of the Committee of Three and the Five Man Committee is incorrect in attributing the proposal to General Marshall."

previous day. They wished to know if the Government had given any definite indication of its attitude on this question.

I replied that I had had only one talk with the Generalissimo since his return to Nanking; during this conversation I had gone over the entire situation with him and had exerted every effort to persuade him to action which I thought would lead to a peaceful settlement. Simultaneous meetings of both the Five Man Committee and the Committee of Three were, I explained, included in my proposal to the Generalissimo. The latter had given no definite reply but had said that he would consult with his staff and inform me of his decision later.

I then gave to Messrs. Tung and Wang the following lengthy exposition of my attitude toward the situation and events related thereto, explaining during my talk that as this was the first opportunity I had had to discuss matters with Mr. Tung I wanted him to have a clear picture of what was in my mind: In all these negotiations, it was most important, in my opinion, that the Communists should know clearly the basic difficulties with which Dr. Stuart and I had to contend and which were at this time blocking all our efforts. At the beginning of the negotiations in Chungking in January, the trouble was, as I saw the situation, that on the Government side a fairly large and powerful group was convinced that the Communists did not intend to go through with any agreement reached for the organization of a coalition government. They said time and time again that the Communist aim was to disrupt the Government in favor of Soviet Russian influence— this I was referring to specifically because the same argument had continued down to the present time. I had taken the opposite view and had accepted the sincerity of the Communist statements and of the Communist intentions to enter a coalition government. As a result, I had been accused of knowing too little about China and about the Chinese Communist Party and had been attacked under cover in China and directly in the United States by Kuomintang members for misleading the Chinese Government. These attacks had continued until recently and had ceased only because of Communist propaganda directed against me. Resistance to my views from this group, however, continued unabated.

On the other hand, I continued, I recognized the Communist feeling or fear that the Government did not intend to establish a genuine coalition government but was maneuvering for military superiority in order to crush the Communists, for which purpose the Government would continue to employ the Kuomintang secret police, the Government secret police, railway guards and similar agencies to suppress political meetings and practically destroy the body of the Communist Party. I recognized the character of the organized demonstrations, which were hostile to the Communists and which indulged in violence against the Communists in various cities. I had made a reference publicly to this group on the occasion of the signing of the agreement on February 25 for the reorganization of the armies and the integration of the Communist forces into the National Army.* I had felt then that this Kuomintang group was endeavoring to incite the Communists to retaliation so that they could accuse the Communists of specific acts indicating intention of breaking agreements. I had, therefore, asked General Chou En-lai to refrain from any retaliatory statements or action; this he had done. During this period, therefore, we had apparently had an acceptance of good faith and very solid agreements. With my departure for the United States, however, there began a series of steps by one side or the other, which rapidly caused the complete disruption of all that we had struggled to achieve. Both sides had been guilty of bad judgment or mis-steps until we were now in our present tragic situation. I had been working not only for a coalition government but also for one which removed the arbitrary power of government from one party and evolved a democratic set up. This had naturally been opposed vigorously by those who were going to lose power and position. I had also been involved in persuading a considerable group in the Government, both political and military leaders, to a course of action which they felt dangerous for China because of their conviction that the Communist purpose was to disrupt rather than cooperate with the Government.

Mr. Tung was, I went on, familiar with actions of the Government which the Communists felt were in violation of the agreements reached—such as, General Tu Li-ming's early operations in Manchuria and the Government's refusal to admit the Executive Headquarters team into Manchuria, the continued Government advances after its occupation of Chang-

---

*At the conclusion of the signing of this agreement by the members of the Committee of Three, I stated in a brief speech: "This agreement, I think, represents the great hope of China. I can only trust that its pages will not be soiled by a small group of irreconcilables who for a selfish purpose would defeat the Chinese people in their overwhelming desire for peace and prosperity."

chun and active operations in Shantung during the later part of June. He was also familiar with the statements credited to Government leaders and to the Generalissimo himself that a policy of force was the only practical procedure. I would not, therefore, go into details of events with which he was familiar, but I wished to remind him of the series of events which had greatly weakened my position in dealing with the Government and which were continually held up to me by the Government. The first of this series of events was an inexcusable one which had weakened the Communist position ever since—that was the failure of the Communist Party to submit a list of its troops within three weeks after the military reorganization agreement of February 25. Refusal to submit this list was apparently used as a political weapon, but I frankly thought it a tragic error of judgment because it was a direct and serious violation of a very recently signed agreement. The next error, although not so great as the first, was the Communist attack on Changchun. This was serious because it was a violent action used to force a course of political action, which meant later that the Government would probably retaliate by utilizing similar successes to force its desired course of action and would excuse them accordingly. The last of this overt series of mistakes, as I saw them, was the Communist offensive operations in Shantung Province after June 7. I had had great difficulty in persuading the Generalissimo to agree to the truce agreement of June 7, and then in a campaign in Shantung, lasting until about June 15, the Communists had almost wrecked everything I was trying to do.

I pointed out further that I wanted the Communists to keep in mind that my representations to the Government had been in effect the opposite of what I was saying to them at this time, as I had emphasized perhaps even more to the Government leaders actions on their part which I considered wrong and inexcusable. This I had done because I thought the Government in its position was the more responsible and, with its more effective communications, was in a better position to control its people, and also because certain Government leaders were making provocative public statements, which, in effect, discredited or certainly discouraged what I was attempting to do. My lengthy statement was being made to Mr. Tung because it was the first opportunity I had had to talk to him direct and I was making it also in an effort to have him understand what was in my mind and to give him a picture, as I saw it, of what was in the minds of a number of Government leaders.

I continued that in early July Dr. Stuart and I had found ourselves at a complete impasse regarding military settlements and had thus sought some way to open up a new approach toward a basis for the cessation of hostilities. The Generalissimo had insisted that the Communists evacuate certain areas and that the Government take over the local governments in those areas. To this the Communists would not agree. I had then tried other means—the Generalissimo had agreed to see General Chou personally and the Five Man Conference under Dr. Wang Shih-chieh had met to consider the problem of local government, all without result. The military situation continued to deteriorate and Dr. Stuart and I then turned to the proposal for the Five Man Committee under his chairmanship as a way out of the impasse. It was our understanding that General Chou had accepted this proposal without a statement that the cessation of hostilities would be automatically determined at the end of the Committee's meetings. General Chou did not agree with us on this point, but the misunderstanding in this regard was merely a matter of opinion, mentioned here only to prevent any confusion regarding the Government's attitude—it was Dr. Stuart and I who misunderstood and not the Government. Then the situation became completely reversed—the Generalissimo, who had been difficult to persuade to agree to the Five Man Committee, now insisted on it and General Chou, who, we thought, had agreed, now insisted on convening the Committee of Three. It appeared logical to Dr. Stuart and me that it was to the advantage of the Communist Party to proceed with the Five Man Committee rather than to prolong discussion while military operations grew more and more serious. To add to the difficulties, propaganda campaigns had done much to influence the leaders of both parties, and a situation had developed where the actions of both the Government and the Communists were influenced by misinformation, those responsible for the propaganda having begun to believe their own misrepresentations.

I pointed out that this was particularly true regarding the surplus property transaction. I could hardly expect them to believe what I was going to say, because their suspicions were possibly too great. As a matter of fact, I had never discussed the surplus property matter with the Generalissimo or with any military leaders in the Government, and they had never brought any pressure to bear on me in regard to this matter. My only discussions had been with Dr. T.V. Soong,

President of the Executive Yuan, and they had been confined to the question of what reduction would be made from the original cost and related matters. Dr. Soong had never urged an early settlement of this matter; to the contrary, it was my duty in representing the interests of the United States Government to urge that the matter be settled and completed. Discussions relating to this transaction had gone on from January on down to August. The Government could have settled the matter in February, March, April or May but was trying to drive the best possible bargain. The deal came to a head in August because the Foreign Liquidation Commissioner, having completed the surplus property negotiations in Europe, came to this area to complete similar negotiations for surplus property in the Pacific region, following which his duties would terminate and he would resign. He was accompanied by representatives of the War and Navy Departments to ensure that his negotiations would not be upset by those Departments after his return to Washington because of their habit of taking over certain portions of the property. The transaction had to be completed at that time or China would have been left out of consideration; the cream of the property would have been sold to other governments and the balance left to deteriorate or be dumped in the ocean. The completion of this deal could not be held in abeyance while a struggle in China, which had gone on for 18 years, prolonged itself for an indefinite period. The alternative was to deny to China, that is to the Chinese people, the economic opportunity for rehabilitation that should result from this surplus property transaction. It could have little or no relation to the present military situation, as it would be months and months before the Government could really bring in to China any sizeable amounts of this non-military property. Propaganda, however, had converted this program into tremendous support of a current military campaign, which was entirely contrary to the facts. The same was true of the attack on the lend-lease transaction, which had resulted almost entirely from my efforts while I was in Washington to obtain materiel for the ten Communist divisions, and yet I had been bitterly attacked for this ever since that time. I had felt a moral responsibility to see that this materiel would be available and I had obtained it. I had organized the Military Advisory Group without awaiting for Congressional authority in order to provide myself with a staff to work out the details for the Communist training center at Kalgan. This was to have opened on April 15 but General Chou had asked that it be postponed until July; the materiel for this school had in the meantime been accumulated at Peiping.

In conclusion of this statement to Messrs. Tung and Wang, I said that if the Communists were sincere in their desire to participate in the reorganization of the government, which would naturally be accompanied by a desire for the cessation of hostilities, they must endeavor to quiet some of their suspicions and fears sufficiently to enable us to make a new start. When they were motivated by their fears of secret police and suppression of freedom of expression and various Government actions and statements, they should remember that many Government leaders were absolutely convinced that the Communists were not to be trusted. These leaders feared that the Generalissimo might make too many concessions, and they made public statements accordingly. When the Communists weighed such provocative statements they should remember that the Communist Party issued in English actually from Executive Headquarters, which had been established throught my efforts for the purpose of mediation and peaceful adjustments, provocative statements and also personal attacks on me, utilizing the Executive Headquarters for that end. I had given the Communists everything in my power to facilitate their movements about China, including communications and materiel for that purpose; I had virtually forced the Government into agreements for communications and materiel to facilitate the Communist Party's business in connection with the carrying out of the agreements reached. The only hope now lay in their ridding themselves of some of their suspicions and irritations in an effort to find a basis for compromise without continued delay which would permit the military situation further to deteriorate. As I had previously told Mr. Wang Ping-nan, if the Communists had lost confidence in me, they should say so and I would immediately withdraw from the mediation efforts. I had been told that the Chinese procedure would be for both sides to go along with me in order to save my face—I was not interested in face. My only interest was in peace and unity in China. I had no ulterior motive of any kind whatsoever.

The two Communist representatives expressed their appreciation of my frank statement and then gave their explanation of the propaganda campaigns, particularly that against the surplus property transaction. Mr. Tung emphasized the importance the Communists attached to the question of the cessation of hostilities and said that the Communists thought that if the Committee of Three were reconvened I would be able to promote peace and lead China toward democracy. He concluded that the Communists had confidence in my efforts at mediation.

Our conference ended with my explaining that a meeting of the Committee of Three without reasonable assurance that it would be successful might be fatal, as if this Committee met under present circumstances and failed, it would mean the end of the Committee of Three, the Executive Headquarters and the mediation effort.

During this period the Government military advance against Kalgan continued, Government forces moving from Nankou along the rail line and from Jehol toward the north of Kalgan to cut off a Communist retreat in that direction and from Suiyuan in the west. The Communists, who had been besieging Tatung (north Shansi) since early August, announced the formal lifting of the siege of that city in order to meet the Government charge that Kalgan was being attacked because the Communists were threatening Tatung. On September 30 the Kuomintang Central News Agency announced that operations had been begun by the Government forces for the purpose of capturing Kalgan. On the same day the Communists announced publicly their refusal to name their delegates to the National Assembly unless certain PCC procedures were observed.

It was against this background that General Chou En-lai addressed to me, under date of September 30, a memorandum, the substance of which is as follows:[65]

> Since the conclusion of the discussions in June, the Government has destroyed the cease-fire agreement of January 10, has ignored all previous commitments and has launched a large scale drive in China proper. During the last three months the Government has occupied many points, has destroyed the local governments and had conducted widespread air raids. It has advanced the five conditions; when they were rejected, as contrary to the PCC, it launched an all-out offensive. It used the Communist siege of Tatung as an excuse for announcing it would attack Chengte, Kalgan and Yenan. Chengte was

[65]See Volume Two, Appendix N, Document 6, for the full text.

taken followed by Chining and Fengchen, key cities on the Peiping-Suiyuan Railway, and a three pronged attack is now being launched against Kalgan. The Communist campaign around Tatung was intended merely to divert attacks launched by Kuomintang troops in Shansi under Generals Yen Hsi-shan and Hu Tsung-nan and most recently the Communists announced the formal lifting of this siege, thereby freeing Tatung from any kind of menace.

The Government attack, however, continues, and the attack on Kalgan, one of the political and military centers of the Communist areas, shows that it wishes to force Kuomintang-Communist relations into an ultimate break. I am duly instructed to serve the following notice, which I request you to transmit to the Government:

If the Kuomintang Government does not instantly cease military operations against Kalgan and the areas in that vicinity, the Chinese Communist Party feels itself forced to presume that the Government is thereby giving public announcement of a total national split and it has abandoned its announced policy of a peaceful settlement. If matters reach such a stage, the responsibility for all serious consequences should, as a matter of course, rest solely with the Government side.

On September 30 General Yu Ta-wei called on me primarily to discuss the conditions under which the Government would consent to enter into meetings of the Committee of Three and the Five Man Committee. General Yu repeated his idea of the key to the situation as consisting of the location of the Communist divisions. It was my opinion that matters pertaining to the PCC resolutions were more important and I told General Yu that, while I would agree to participate in the Committee of Three meeting, I did not think that the Communists would agree to simultaneous meetings or that the meetings would succeed under the conditions to be imposed by the Government. If the meetings did result in a stalemate, I said, I was finished—I would not continue to be involved in further delays and long dragged out procedures leading nowhere; I would not become a party to the Government's evident delays in negotiations while proceeding with the Kalgan campaign; and I could not sit in these meetings with good faith while such activity by the Government was under way.

At this time I was giving thought to the possibility of formally notifying the Generalissimo that the present procedure placed the United States in an untenable position which could not be accepted and that I was, therefore, considering my withdrawal from the present negotiations. I felt serious concern over the latest turn of events, especially since it seemed to me that the Government politicos were endeavoring to make "stooges" of Dr. Stuart and me. Dr. Stuart had informed the Government members of the Five Man Committee on September 30 of the strain being put upon the United States Government and of my responsibility for protecting the position and integrity of my Government. He had further told them that the situation was intolerable and that he and I could not continue to be a party to negotiations if the present situation continued. He pointed out that it might be necessary even to withdraw American mediation and in turn other U.S. support to China, which would naturally have to be accompanied by an explanation for such action.

I decided at this time that I would not carry verbal messages to the Communists but would transmit only written communications. My inclination was to force the Government leaders to recede from some of their contentions and I felt it was important that the Generalissimo be convinced that the U.S. mediators were adamant in their stand. The Generalissimo had been proceeding with his so-called local operations for three months. The United States Government, I felt, could no longer continue to be a third party to the present procedure. It was apparent that the Government was no longer in a dangerous military position and the campaign for Kalgan could be justified only on the basis of a policy of force. I felt that I could not put myself in the position of mediating during a continued series of military campaigns and that I must have positive assurances from the Government that there was a reasonable basis for compromise which offered possibility of success. I outlined the foregoing ideas to Dr. Stuart and added that it might be advisable to include in any memorandum along these lines the statement that if such assurances were not forthcoming it would be necessary for me to recommend to the U.S. Government that it terminate its mediation efforts, withdraw from the Executive Headquarters and suspend activation of the Military Advisory Group. Dr. Stuart expressed his agreement with this course of action.

278

On October 1, Dr. T.V. Soong mentioned to Dr. Stuart that the Government desired to capture Kalgan prior to any action for resumption of the negotiations. During the interview he handed to Dr. Stuart an outline of a suggested procedure for settling the current difficulties. This procedure would have required probably a month of negotiations to resolve, during which fighting would apparently continue.

On the same day (October 1), Messrs. Tung Pi-wu and Wang Ping-nan, Communist representatives at Nanking, called on me in connection with General Chou En-lai's memorandum of September 30 regarding the Government offensive against Kalgan. Mr. Tung reviewed the Government's successive attacks on various Communist areas since the end of June and said that the Government's public announcement of its attack on Kalgan had caused the Yenan authorities to instruct General Chou to forward the above-mentioned memorandum to me, a similar communication having also been sent to the Government. Mr. Tung continued that General Chou wished to wait for a reply indicating the Government's reaction toward the proposed simultaneous meetings of the Five Man Committee and the Committee of Three before making his decision in this regard, but that if the Government continued its drive against Kalgan, he (General Chou) would not consider convening the Committee of Three to discuss a cessation of hostilities while the Five Man Committee was holding simultaneous meetings. Mr. Tung pointed out that prior to this announcement by the Government of its attack on Kalgan, General Chou had felt that the Communist Party could participate in the meetings of the two Committees. Mr. Wang interrupted at this point to say that the cessation of the Government's drive against Kalgan was a prerequisite to Communist participation in the simultaneous meetings of the two Committees.

I replied that I wished to give them an explanation of my view of the present situation: I had made it clear to the Government, and wished to make it clear to them, that I was not in agreement with either the Government course of action or that of the Communist Party. The situation had almost reached the point where I would not continue in the position of a mediator. I could no longer continue to be a middle-man in a prolonged series of accusations and counter-accusations or of proposals and counter-proposals. I had about reached the limit of my endurance and I had to give first consideration to the position of the Government that I represented. While I was struggling with the Chinese Government in my effort to have terms proposed which I thought had a fair chance of being accepted by the Communist Party, the latter had come forward with an announcement regarding its delegates to the National Assembly. While I was struggling with the Communists in an effort to reach a basis for agreement, the Government had made a public announcement of its attack against Kalgan. This type of procedure had continued week after week and month after month. The point I wished to emphasize was that the procedure followed by the Communists was inevitably productive of long delay during which military operations continued—the very thing Dr. Stuart and I had been trying to prevent—until we had now reached the present grave crisis. I was willing to discuss General Chou's memorandum of September 30 with the Government and would do my best to prevail upon the Government to take action which would increase the possibility of peaceful settlement.

Mr. Tung stated that it was General Chou's opinion that the Government had no intention of stopping hostilities and that this was the reason General Chou wished to have some official expression from the Government in regard to the cessation of hostilities. In explanation of the Communist Party's announcement that it would not name its delegates to the National Assembly, Mr. Tung stated that the date on which all parties should submit their lists of delegates was approaching and that if the Communist Party did not make a public statement in this regard it would be understood that the Communists would attend the National Assembly. He concluded that this statement contained nothing that had not been previously said.

During this period the Executive Headquarters field teams were becoming increasingly immobilized as the fighting spread. There were increasing concentrations of Government troops in south Shansi, presaging a Government advance north along the Tungpu Railway; Government troops had moved into east Hopei and the Communists had withdrawn into rugged country in that area; Communist forces were strengthening their defenses in the Chihfeng area and were destroying the railway lines south of that city; the Communists had rendered airfields at Chihfeng and Kalgan temporarily unusable; the National Government had occupied Chining (east Suiyuan), a city over which there had been considerable argument at the time of the establishment of the Executive Headquarters; and Government planes were active in raids on Communist-held towns. As a result of the spreading hostilities and for reasons of security, the Executive Headquarters teams were being withdrawn from various points in the field and returned to Peiping.

In view of the situation, on October 1 I addressed a memorandum[66] to Generalissimo Chiang Kai-shek, in which, after stating that I was not in agreement with the present course of the Government or of the Communist Party, I concluded: "I wish merely to state that unless a basis for agreement is found to terminate the fighting without further delays of proposals and counter-proposals, I will recommend to the President that I be recalled and that the United States Government terminate its efforts of mediation." Earlier in the memorandum I said that I had carefully considered all the factors involved in the present status of negotiations and military operations and had also taken into consideration the most recent developments, such as, the Communist Party's announcement of its refusal to submit a list of Communist delegates to the National Assembly unless certain PCC procedures were met, the Central News Agency announcement of the Government operations against Kalgan, the informal suggestions presented to Dr. Stuart by Dr. T.V. Soong and the memorandum of September 30 from General Chou En-lai (the last two documents were forwarded to the Generalissimo as enclosures to my memorandum).

On the following morning (October 2), the Generalissimo sent for Dr. Stuart to have him bring me a verbal account of the reply he expected to forward to me in a letter later in the day. The Generalissimo said that he was aware of my embarrassment in the present situation and that he always kept in mind my problems. However, he felt it absolutely essential to the national welfare that the Government gain control of Kalgan. If the Communists would withdraw, that would be so much the better; if they refused to do so, it would probably take the Government troops 10 to 15 days to capture the city by force. The Generalissimo considered Kalgan essential to the welfare of both Manchuria and north China, and occupation of this city by the Government, he stated, would prevent considerably further military action by the Communists. The Generalissimo said that he would issue a cease-fire order as soon

[66]See Volume Two, Appendix N, Document 7, for the full text.

281

as the Kalgan battle ended provided the Communists would agree (1) to simultaneous meetings of the Five Man Committee and the Committee of Three, (2) to the disposition of the 18 Communist divisions and (3) to submission of their list of delegates to the National Assembly.

Dr. Stuart described to the Generalissimo my concern over the continuation of the fighting on an ever increasing scale and of my feeling that the current negotiations were merely a cloak for the military operations of the Government. Dr. Stuart explained that he personally sympathized with my views, that the United States Government could not continue to be a party to negotiations that might be alleged to serve as a cover-up for military campaigns and that the United States could not favor one faction in opposition to the other. He concluded that the United States had in fact now been placed in the position of seeming to favor the National Government side by the recent actions of the Government.

My reaction to the description of the Generalissimo's views was that I could not negotiate while a cold-blooded battle for Kalgan was going on and that the Generalissimo should not expect mediation under these circumstances. The Generalissimo's statement served to convince me almost completely that the time had come for the United States Government to recall me from China—the Generalissimo was certainly following a definite policy of force under the cover of protracted negotiations. He had now completely reversed his previous agreement to permit the Communists to retain possession of Kalgan, which he had agreed with me to do during the negotiations in June—now Kalgan was made a prerequisite to negotiation. I had taken issue with the Generalissimo on June 30 on practically everything he proposed. The later proposal by Dr. Stuart and me for the State Council was made purely to find some wedge which would open the way for progress in the negotiations.

On the same day (October 2), I emphatically told Dr. T.V. Soong that I would not continue with the negotiations during the conduct of a military campaign by the Government. Dr. Soong replied that he hoped that some formula for agreement could be found and presented his suggestions therefor. These suggestions, however, involved matters of lengthy complication regarding the redisposition of troops in China and Manchuria.

On the afternoon of October 2, I received a memorandum[67] from the Generalissimo, under that day's date, in reply to my memorandum of the previous day. Referring to my communication, the Generalissimo said that "with a view to saving time and showing its utmost sincerity, the Government hereby, with all frankness, expresses its maximum concessions in regard to the solution of the present problem." These "maximum concessions" were as follows:

> "1. The Chinese Communist Party has been incessantly urging the reorganization of the National Government. This hinges on the distribution of the membership of the State Council. The Government originally agreed that the Chinese Communist Party be allocated 8 seats and the Democratic League 4, with a total of twelve. The Chinese Communist Party, on the other hand, requested 10 for themselves and 4 for the Democratic League with a total of 14. Now the Government makes a fresh concession by taking the mean and offering 1 seat for the independents to be recommended by the Chinese Communist Party and agreed upon by the Government so that, added to the original 12, it makes a total of 13 seats. But the Communist Party should without delay produce the list of their candidates for the State Council as well as the list of their delegates to the National Assembly. This reassignment of seats should be decided by the proposed group of five to be confirmed by the Steering Committee of PCC.

> "2. For immediate implementaion of the program for reorganization of the army, the location of the 18 Communist divisions should be immediately determined and the Communist troops should enter those assigned places according to agreed dates. The above should be decided by the Committee of Three and carried out under the supervision of the Executive Headquarters."

The memorandum concluded that if the Communist Party

[67]See Volume Two, Appendix N, Document 8, for the full text.

were "willing to solve immediately the above-mentioned two problems, a cease-fire order should be issued by both sides, when agreement has been reached thereon."

In discussion of the situation with Dr. Stuart on October 3, I expressed the opinion that the Government had used American mediation to its own advantage and would evidently continue to do so—the attitude of the Government in regard to the attack on Kalgan was so definite that there was now no escaping this conclusion. The above-described letter from the Generalissimo had not been particularly helpful to the situation, as the second condition concerning the location of the Communist divisions involved a lengthy procedure during which the attack on Kalgan would be carried to its conclusion. Also it omitted any reference to the disposition of Government divisions which was a requirement of the February 25 Agreement. I would be opposed to this procedure and I felt certain that the Communists would not accept it. As I informed the President and the Acting Secretary of State at this time, I was aware of the delicacy of the position in which my memorandum of October 1 to the Generalissimo placed the United States in relation to the situation in the Far East, but I did not think that the United States Government could afford to be a party to a course of questionable integrity and I, therefore, felt that this fact should be made unmistakably clear to the Chinese Government.

Dr. Stuart informed me that one of the Communist representatives had called on him to inquire regarding the American position at this time. (I had forwarded the Generalissimo's memorandum of October 2, after deletion of some provocative portions, to General Chou En-lai without comment.) I suggested that perhaps the only thing to tell the Communists was that we had labored with the Government in an effort to get an acceptable proposal and that the Generalissimo's memorandum of October 2 was the result. When Dr. Stuart suggested that the Communists might agree to evacuate Kalgan, I said that I did not think they would do so nor could I personally insist on such action—the one thing the Generalissimo had agreed to some time ago had been that the Communists could retain Kalgan. The Communists had given considerable evidence of good faith in June, except possibly in their stipulations regarding the retention of Peace Preservation Corps in certain localities—only time could have determined their sincerity in this regard. In the present situation, it was plainly evident that the Government did not want to halt its advance and that it was so intent on capturing Kalgan that it could not see the other issues involved or else chose to ignore them. I then suggested to Dr. Stuart that he discuss informally with the Communist representative a course of action which would include Communist concessions to meet the Government's so-called concessions, accompanied by a Communist demand that the Government halt its drive on Kalgan. There were several concessions that the Communists might well make: naming of their delegates to the National Assembly, agreement to 9 Communist and 4 Democratic League members on the State Council, evacuation of the northern tip of Kiangsu without further discussion and evacuation of the vicinity of Tatung.

On October 4 Messrs. Tung Pi-wu and Wang Ping-nan called to discuss the Generalissimo's memorandum of October 2 and the above-outlined suggestions for Communist concessions, which Dr. Stuart had in the meantime conveyed to the Communist representatives.

Mr. Tung said that the Generalissimo's memorandum made no mention of a cessation of the Government advance against Kalgan, thus indicating that the Government had no intention of stopping the fighting or halting its advance toward Kalgan. He continued that the attack on Kalgan had been and still was the most serious problem of the situation and that both General Chou and the Yenan authorities desired a definite reply from the Government regarding the Kalgan issue. He described the public confusion resulting from a Central News Agency report that the Government had agreed to the proposal for simultaneous meetings of the Five Man Committee and the Committee of Three but that the Communists had not indicated their attitude, although the Communists had made clear to Dr. Stuart and to me repeatedly that the Communists had not rejected the proposal for simultaneous meetings of these two Committees. The matter was further confused by the publication of a statement attributed to an American Embassy spokesman that the Government had not expressed its agreement for these two Committees.

I replied that the only official reaction I had had was the Generalissimo's memorandum of October 2, which had followed my transmission of the Communist Party's statement. In reply to Mr. Tung's request for my comment on the Generalissimo's memorandum, I said that I had nothing to say beyond what Dr. Stuart had already probably said—we had done our best to find a basis for the termination of hostilities without delay and the Generalissimo's reply was the result to date. I agreed with Mr. Tung that the memorandum set forth certain conditions as a prerequisite to the cessation of hostilities, these conditions including the State Council issue, the Five Man Committee and the naming of delegates to the National Assembly. The last point, I said, had been transmitted by me in a memorandum to General Chou about three weeks ago. (This was my memorandum of September 10.)

Commenting on the question of the National Assembly, Mr. Tung stated that there were still unsettled questions in this connection—whether the number of seats should be increased and the fixing of the number of Communist delegates. The most important issue in this regard, however, said Mr. Tung, was the draft constitution, which had not yet been agreed upon in the Constitution Reviewing Committee. In the absence of agreement on the draft constitution, there seemed to be little reason, in his opinion, for summoning the National Assembly, and the action of the Government in posing the naming of the Communist delegates as one of its conditions served to indicate the Government's lack of desire for a settlement. Referring to the second point in the Generalissimo's memorandum, Mr. Tung asked whether the agreements reached on the special supplementary document in June were still effective and pointed out that in this paper provision was made for the restoration of positions held by both sides as of June 7 in Manchuria and January 13 in China proper.

I replied that I could not answer this question directly, but that, as I had stated to General Chou some time ago, it was my impression that the Generalissimo intended to continue in military occupation of the places in north China recently occupied by Government troops. I had received no definite statement in this regard, I said, but this was the stand I anticipated. In regard to Manchuria, I continued, I had gained from the general discussions the implication that the tentative agreement reached in regard to troop dispositions in Manchuria, both for the cessation of hostilities and for the reorganization and redistribution of armies, would be applicable. To this, Mr. Tung said that he hoped that if any of the tentative agreements reached in June were to be made effective all such tentative agreements should be applicable. Otherwise, he feared that the Government would accept only those portions which were to its advantage. I pointed out that, while I knew no more than I had already said concerning the Government's stand on this point, it might readily use the language employed by General Chou after the Communist capture of Changchun, when he wanted modification of the military reorganization plan of February 25 to permit additional Communist divisions in Manchuria: he had justified his stand by the statement "the situation has greatly changed." At that time I had pointed to the danger of similar reactions on the part of the Government and my predictions had been borne out by subsequent developments.

Mr. Tung, referring to the question of troop dispositions, said that the Government was now concentrating 85 percent of its total troops strength in north China and Manchuria and that even though a peaceful settlement were reached, it could be only temporary under such conditions. He felt, therefore, that this was a point for consideration and said that, subsequent to the discontinuance of the meetings of the Committee of Three, Yenan had instructed General Chou that if agreement were to be reached the Government must withdraw half of its forces from Manchuria and north China. He explained that this had probably not been brought up by General Chou because other issues had entered the discussions and the problem of the cessation of hostilities had not been brought into the discussions since the end of June.

I then described the planning that had been required to provide for demobilization and troop dispositions and my own efforts to have sufficient information regarding troop locations and strengths so that I would not in the negotiations commit myself to an agreement impossible logistically of execution. While Mr. Tung was now giving me an indication of Communist requirements in relation to troop dispositions in north China and Manchuria, I said, the Communists had never given me any data which would enable me to make any calculation of any kind on this question, although such data was due three weeks after the signing of the military reorganization agreement of February 25. When Mr. Tung offered the civil war as an excuse for the failure of the Communists to submit this data, I pointed out that the three weeks' period had elapsed before the civil war flared up and had almost expired prior to my departure for the United States in March. I added that this was, of course, beside the point but that he should keep this in mind in relation to the question of Government troop strength in north China.

Our conversation concluded with my suggesting that he submit in writing his request that the Communists be given a reply from the Government in regard to the Kalgan issue.

On October 4 I held a long conference with the General-issimo. Commenting on my memorandum of October 1, in which I had said that unless certain action was immediately taken I would recommend to the President that I be recalled and American efforts at mediation be terminated, the Generalissimo said that he had searched his mind for any action that might have been construed as lack of integrity on his part. He said that such action by him was unthinkable and that, aside from his position as the head of the Government, his own conscience as a Christian would forbid. He regretted exceedingly if anything had occurred to give rise to such belief and he could only assure me that I was mistaken. He did not feel that it was a matter that could be discussed. He further stated that my departure from China was unthinkable and that I could not possibly cease my efforts of mediation since the crisis in China was the most important in the world at this time and my efforts were of great historic significance. He concluded that nothing he could recall had affected, surprised or disturbed him so much mentally and that a satisfactory basis must be found for the continuation of my mission.

In reply, I made the following statements: I was not implying any question of the integrity of the Generalissimo. It was my own actions and position and those of the United States Government as represented by me which were in question. I was convinced that a campaign of force was in progress and that negotiations could be described as a cover for this campaign—under such circumstances I could no longer participate in the negotiations. In June the Generalissimo had acceded to my proposal that Kalgan be left to the Communists and at that time the Government was in a very much weaker military position than at this time—Chengte had now been captured, most of Hopei and Jehol had been taken over, his troops had advanced well beyond Peiping in the direction of Kalgan and Government forces were on the verge of occupying Chihfeng and Tolun, both important strategic points. To say now that Kalgan was of such strategic importance that the Government could not consider any arrangement whereby it was denied possession of that city was not consistent with his agreement in June to Communist retention of Kalgan, in view of the much weaker position of the Government at the earlier date. The present procedure clearly meant to me a campaign of force and not a settlement by negotiation. At the end of June, I had opposed the whole procedure in prospect for July and August when he declined to accept the agreements openly reached and stated that there would be only local fighting in China proper and no fighting in Manchuria. I had disagreed not only with that conception but had thought that it inevitably meant the development of a full-fledged civil war beyond his or Communist control for a long time to come. I had also felt that it might provoke a situation which would be tantamount to inviting Soviet military intervention in Manchuria.

When the Generalissimo asserted that his reference to Kalgan in June had not constituted an agreement and that the Communists had not accepted the proposal, I pointed out that it was not a question of agreement. What I had referred to was a statement of a condition that had existed then when he had said that he was willing to submit himself to such agreement as contrasted to the strong position of the Government at the present time. Now he was unwilling to halt the Government's operations against Kalgan unless the Communists agreed to its occupation by Government forces. The Generalissimo then made a lengthy statement, more or less repeating the matters above-described and referring to various aspects of the negotiations with the Communists, but he gave no indication that he would halt the drive against Kalgan.

In conclusion, therefore, I replied that I regretted to inform him that nothing had transpired in our discussion that caused me to alter my point of view—in fact, I was the more convinced that the United States Government was being placed in a position where the integrity of its actions could be successfully questioned, and I must, therefore, recommend to the President my recall.

On the day following (October 5) this conversation with the Generalissimo, I despatched a message to the President and the Acting Secretary of State suggesting that my mission be terminated and that I be immediately recalled. The gist of the pertinent portions of that message is as follows:

> I feel that despite the present vicious Communist propaganda of misrepresentation and bitter attacks and despite the stupid failure of the Communists to agree to the Five Man Committee under Dr. Stuart, actuated in our opinion through fear of the very delays which have resulted from this refusal, the United States Government can not afford before the world to have me continue as mediator and should confidentially notify the Generalissimo accordingly. I believe that this is the

289

only way to halt the military campaign and to dispel the evident belief of the Government generals that they can drag the United States along while carrying out their campaign of force. It is suggested for your approval that the following message be sent by the President to the Generalissimo:

General Marshall recommends that his mission be terminated and that he be recalled. He has explained to you that he feels that a continuation of mediation under present circumstances of extensive and aggressive military operations would place the United States Government in a position where the integrity of its actions as represented by him would be open to serious question. I deplore that his efforts to bring peace to China have been unsuccessful, but there must be no question regarding the integrity of his position and actions which represent the intention and high purpose of the United States Government. I, therefore, with great regret have concluded that he should be immediately recalled.

That same evening (October 5), the Generalissimo's Aide called on Dr. Stuart and during the course of the conversation the latter informed him that I was sending a message to the President recommending my recall. A half hour later the Aide telephoned to Dr. Stuart to say that the Generalissimo would like to see him immediately. When Dr. Stuart called on the Generalissimo, the latter said that he was willing to agree to stop advances against Kalgan for a period of five days, possibly even longer if the American mediators insisted, on condition that the Communists would immediately participate in meetings of both the Five Man Committee and the Committee of Three and that Kalgan would be the first issue negotiated. The Generalissimo concluded with a request that Dr. Stuart and I discuss the matter with him on the following morning.

Upon the receipt of information regarding the Generalissimo's offer of this brief truce period, which Dr. Stuart had communicated to me immediately after leaving the Generalissimo's residence, I despatched a message to the Department of State instructing that the delivery of my message to the President regarding the termination of my mission and my recall be delayed pending the receipt of further instructions from me.

As I informed Dr. Stuart at the time, I did not think that the Communists would agree to the cession of Kalgan and it was my opinion that they would immediately challenge the procedure on the basis that the Government was imposing a condition in regard to Kalgan which, although the Government was halting its offensive against that city, would give them their objective without a fight. We agreed, however, to see the Generalissimo the following morning.

In the meantime, Mr. Wang Ping-nan, member of the Communist delegation at Nanking, had conveyed to Dr. Stuart an official, verbal reply from General Chou En-lai to the four points suggested by Dr. Stuart on October 3: (1) Regarding the State Council, General Chou En-lai said that the Communists and Democratic League had the "original right" to 14 members divided between the two parties and that arrangements could be made by the two parties for an appropriate division of the seats—Mr. Wang repeated the previous Communist arguments regarding the necessity of a veto power to prevent infringement of the PCC resolutions. (2) Regarding a Communist withdrawal from north Kiangsu, General Chou said that this matter should be referred to the Committee of Three and settled in conjunction with the agreement for the reorganization and disposition of troops. (3) Regarding the naming of the Communist delegates to the National Assembly, General Chou said that certain points had first to be cleared up by the PCC Steering Committee, such as the number of non-party delegates to the National Assembly, and that when the number and allocation of the various delegates had been fixed, the Communists would then be ready to proceed. (4) Regarding the withdrawal of Communist forces from the vicinity of Tatung, General Chou said that the Communist Party had already made an announcement of such action.

My reaction to this reply to our suggested concessions on the part of the Communists was that the latter had accepted none of them. The Government was certain to deny that the Communist Party and the Democratic League had the original right to 14 seats on the State Council and this very point had remained in disagreement from the beginning. It was difficult to expect agreement in the Committee of Three on the north Kiangsu question as such action would require a unanimous vote and General Chou could object to the Government's terms and thus prevent agreement. Regarding the number of delegates in the National Assembly, the same rule of unanimity prevailed in the PCC Steering Committee and one vote could prevent any agreement being reached on this point. The result was that we had made no progress while awaiting General Chou's reply.

Pursuant to the Generalissimo's request, Dr. Stuart and I called on him on the morning of October 6 to discuss the matter of a truce in the Kalgan area. I informed the Generalissimo that I did not favor such a procedure. I said that in my opinion a short truce would not permit of successful negotiations, particularly with the threat of resumption of aggressive military action, and a long truce would be too difficult of control in view of the complications to be faced by the military commanders in the field and their own aggressive attitude. I brought up again for discussion the draft statement I had proposed that the Generalissimo make, which I had presented to him on September 27—this involved an immediate cessation of hostilities once the Communists agreed to the procedure specified.

The Generalissimo replied that he did not think it the proper time for such a statement and that he could not agree to this proposed statement since Communist agreement to the suggested procedure would mean an immediate cessation of hostilities. He then insisted that the cessation of hostilities must depend upon the successful completion of meetings of the Committee of Three and the Five Man Committee. When I pointed out that this would completely vitiate the purpose of the statement, he said that he could not issue such a statement without convening the Government military leaders from the field, as well as his political leaders, which procedure would consume much time. He said that he could, however, order a truce without such a meeting and then proposed that a truce of five days be announced on the basis of Communist agreement to meetings of the Committee of Three and the Five Man Committee "as outlined" in his memorandum of October 2. (See Appendix N, Document 8, for the full text of this memorandum.)

I insisted that a five days' truce would bring no useful result and would lead only to additional misunderstandings and added bitterness. When the Generalissimo agreed to extend the truce period to one week, I insisted that it should be for a minimum of ten days.

The Generalissimo then said that if, as the end of the 10 day period approached, it appeared that the Communists were in a mood to negotiate he would lengthen the period, but that no such intimation should be given to the Communists at the beginning of the truce. He requested that the announcement of this truce be made as a proposal from Dr. Stuart and me rather than from the Government. Dr. Stuart and I agreed to this request even though it was not our proposal—it merely represented the best terms we could obtain.

I pointed out that, if such a truce were to be carried out, several provisions would be essential: One related to responsibility for observation of the truce, which should be assumed by the Executive Headquarters and the special organization of field teams for this purpose; and another, on which I insisted, was agreement by the Government and the Communist Party that publication of the terms of the truce was to be left to Dr. Stuart and me without comment by either side.

Following this discussion with the Generalissimo, Dr. Stuart returned to the Embassy to request an immediate visit by Mr. Wang Ping-nan in order that the question of the truce and the conditions related thereto might be explained to him. I immediately dictated and sent a memorandum,[68] under date of October 6, to Dr. Stuart, outlining the conditions of the truce, as I understood them, in order to avoid any misunderstanding between Dr. Stuart and me regarding the matters agreed to by the Generalissimo. Upon the receipt of this memorandum, Dr. Stuart informed me by telephone of his agreement to the written statements contained therein and said that he had just concluded a conference with Mr. Wang. On the following day, I learned that Mr. Wang had not been shown a copy of the written statement of conditions relating to the truce and I, therefore, sent to him a copy of my above-mentioned memorandum to Dr. Stuart and forwarded an additional copy to General Chou at Shanghai.

In this memorandum of October 6 to Dr. Stuart I said that he was to notify Mr. Wang that, in accordance with arrangements agreed upon between ourselves and the Generalissimo, we proposed a 10 day truce for the operations against Kalgan under the following conditions: (1) "The purpose of the truce is to carry out the two proposals of the Generalis-

68See Volume Two, Appendix N, Document 9, for the full text.

simo in his communication to me of October 2"; (2) during the truce period Executive Headquarters field teams would check on its observance with teams at all critical points—teams within Government lines not to have a Communist member, teams between the two lines to have both Government and Communist members and the American members of the teams to have the authority to determine where and when the teams should go and to submit a report on violations of the truce; and (3) public announcement of the truce would be made by Dr. Stuart and me without any announcement from the two parties.

On the same day (October 6) I informed the President and the Acting Secretary of State of the latest developments in the situation and instructed my representative in the Department of State to cancel that portion of my message of the previous day regarding the termination of my mission and my recall but to hand it to the President and the Acting Secretary as information essential to an understanding of the current situation.

Immediately after the Generalissimo's agreement to the 10 day truce and prior to communication of this proposal to the Communist representatives, I sent an urgent, confidential message to the U.S. Branch of the Executive Headquarters, in which I described the truce proposal, and instructed that the necessary plans be made to carry out the functions envisaged in the proposal for the Executive Headquarters field teams, information concerning such action to be withheld, however, until receipt of notice of acceptance of the proposal.

On October 8, Mr. Wang Ping-nan of the Communist Delegation at Nanking called on Dr. Stuart to convey to him a verbal reply from Yenan, forwarded through General Chou En-lai at Shanghai, to the 10 day truce proposal. Dr. Stuart reduced the points enumerated to writing and verified them with Mr. Wang for accuracy. The substance of this reply is as follows:[69]

> 1. There should be no time limit on the truce period and the proposal would appear to be a strategic move unless Government troops are withdrawn to their original positions.

[69]See Volume Two, Appendix N, Document 10, for the full text.

2. The Communist Party desires to have meetings of the Committee of Three and the Five Man Committee but discussions in these Committees should not be limited to the two paragraphs of the Generalissimo's memorandum of October 2; discussions of these topics during a truce would be considered as negotiation under military coercion.

3. Failure to reply to the Generalissimo's memorandum of October 2 has been due to the hope for receipt of information from General Marshall and Dr. Stuart clarifying the situation. The latest proposal implies little change in the situation and General Chou, therefore, is preparing a written reply and sees no necessity for his return to Nanking.

The Communist rejection of the truce proposal placed me in a position entirely opposite from the one I had previously held in opposing continued aggressive military action. It was now the Government which had offered at least a temporary cessation of hostilities and the Communists who declined. I suggested to Dr. Stuart that we ask Messrs. Tung Pi-wu and Wang Ping-nan of the Communst delegation to call for a discussion of the matter, as a means of giving us an opportunity to determine whether their attitude differed from that presented by General Chou. Dr. Stuart said that he felt that the first thing to be done was to publish an objective statement regarding the negotiations, which would place the responsibility on neither side and would make no accusations. I then dictated a statement[70] for publication as a joint statement by Dr. Stuart and me on that day (October 8). The statement began with a description of General Chou En-lai's memorandum of September 30 in regard to the Government's military operations against Kalgan and the Communist attitude thereto, quoting the concluding paragraph of this memorandum. The statement explained that this memorandum was forwarded to the Generalissimo, who replied in a communication of October 2 to me, and quoted the two paragraphs in the Generalissimo's memorandum containing the Government's "maximum concessions" for a solution of the problems. It next described the call made on the American mediators by Communist representatives asking whether the Generalissimo's memorandum,

[70]See Volume Two, Appendix N, Document 11, for the full text.

which I had immediately transmitted to them, was in reply to General Chou's communication of September 30, pointing out that there was no mention of Kalgan by the Generalissimo. Then followed a reference to the discussions between the Generalissimo, Dr. Stuart and me and a description of the 10 day truce proposal for military operations against Kalgan agreed to by the Generalissimo. The statement concluded that this information was immediately transmitted to the Communist representatives and that on October 8 the Communist Party's reply was received verbally from Mr. Wang Ping-nan, the substance of which was quoted. As indicated in this description of the statement, it was a recital of the negotiations from the time of the receipt of General Chou's memorandum indicating the Communist Party's desire for a cessation of the attack on Kalgan to the time of the receipt of the Communist Party's rejection of the 10 day truce proposal for military operations against Kalgan.

Messrs. Tung Pi-wu and Wang Ping-nan called on the afternoon of October 8 for a conference with Dr. Stuart and me. After informing them that I had sent to the Generalissimo a copy of the Communist Party's reply furnished me by Dr. Stuart, I made the following comments: I was completely baffled regarding the Communist position at this time, Dr. Stuart and I had made exhaustive efforts to obtain the Generalissimo's agreement to halt the offensive against Kalgan and his agreement to as much as 10 days' truce for the military operations. What concerned me most was that when Dr. Stuart and I were utilizing every pressure at our command in an effort to halt the Government's advance against Kalgan, we were told frequently by the Government that the Communist reaction would be one of further complications and that General Chou's statement in the final paragraph of his memorandum of September 30 to me would be followed immediately by other complications. I had disavowed this because it seemed to me that the Communists evidently desired a cessation of hostilities against Kalgan. Judging from this reply, however, I was apparently wrong. Dr. Stuart and I had proposed the Five Man Committee in early August in an effort to provide through the meetings of that Committee a basis for forcing the cessation of hostilities, but Yenan had twisted this proposal into an effort on the part of the Government to provide cover for a military campaign through delaying tactics. As a result of the Communist attitude great delays followed, which could certainly not have been greater had our proposal been accepted. This 10 day truce period proposal represented further effort by Dr. Stuart and me to obtain what General Chou desired, an effort far greater than the Communists evidently understood. It was to be assumed from the correspondence and the Communist statements that the Communist Party desired an immediate halting of the offensive against Kalgan. Yet, two days had passed during which operations against Kalgan had continued and negotiations were made more difficult by General Chou's residence in Shanghai. My question now was: What now do you expect of Dr. Stuart and myself?

Mr. Tung then explained the Communist refusal to accept the proposal for the Five Man Committee, his statements indicating confusion over the matters for discussion by this Committee—this had apparently been caused by statements to the Communists by Government representatives concerning the scope of the latter's authority for discussion, although, as I reminded Mr. Tung, both Dr. Stuart and I had on several occasions endeavored to explain to the Communists that this Committee would be limited in its discussion to the question of the membership in the State Council and the veto power. Mr. Tung then went on to say that when the Communists learned that the Government and the American mediators could not guarantee the issuance of a cease-fire order the delay resulted through the Communist inability to participate in the Five Man Committee under those circumstances. Referring to the Communist rejection of the 10 day truce proposal, Mr. Tung stated that the Communists had expected a complete cessation of the Government attack on Kalgan and not a 10 day truce, during which the Government could reenforce its troops and be in position to resume the attack if the Communists would not accept their terms.

I pointed out that his argument was not sound, as I had made provision to guard against this very eventuality through the use of the Executive Headquarters field teams. This was a measure of protection against such violations and it should be remembered that the Government had advanced the same arguments—that is, the truce would allow the Communists to re-group and bring up reenforcements.

Mr. Tung again stated the Communist viewpoint: The Communist Party wanted a definite cessation of the attack on Kalgan and the only way for the Government to show its sincerity was to withdraw its troops to their original positions. He explained that General Chou's delay in replying to the Generalissimo's memorandum of October 2 had been due to his hope that Dr. Stuart and I would be able to make the

Government realize that it was assuming the role of a victor over the vanquished and that we would also be able to make the Government change its policy of war. The Communists had now lost hope. They appreciated very much the efforts of Dr. Stuart and myself and our position in mediation in Chinese internal affairs, but China was now in the midst of civil war. He concluded that the Communists hoped that Dr. Stuart and I could on the one hand have the United States Government stop its one-sided aid to the Chinese Government and on the other hand could "have a fair mediating process which would be acceptable to both sides."

I replied that I did not accept his statement regarding the United States Government and that I did not like the inference of the second portion of his final statement. I concluded, that at the present time I very much feared that my efforts in the negotiations had terminated and that this was all I had to say.

Dr. Stuart interposed to point out that the good faith of the Government in its military operations around Kalgan seemed amply provided for in the field team arrangements, which constituted protection for the Communists. He continued that if the discussions during the 10 day truce period went satisfactorily in regard to the State Council and other political issues, there would be continued discussion regarding military affairs; if both sides wanted to cooperate in a coalition government and in a plan for a constitution, then the cease-fire order would follow very quickly. He concluded that he felt, therefore, that the Communists had repudiated our proposal and he did not see that there was anything we could possibly try to do.

Mr. Tung stated that 10 days was too short a period to expect any results and that the Government condition that the Communists accept the 10 day truce and execute all demands could not be accepted by the Communist Party. Mr. Wang explained that the Communists could not accept the two conditions in the proposal—one, the 10 day truce, and, two, the condition that the Communists must carry out the two points in the Generalissimo's memorandum of October 2.

Dr. Stuart replied that there must be some misunderstanding. We had considered that this would be a conference where the American mediators would see that the truce was carried out in a spirit of cooperation in order to find a mutually satisfactory solution in matters like the State Council and the draft constitution; as the Government had evidence of Communist readiness to cooperate in these matters, it would naturally lead to a settlement of military issues, dealing with the cessation of hostilities around Kalgan and elsewhere on a permanent basis. We believed, he said, that this would be the outcome. He went on to point out that we had proposed the Committee of Five and the Communists had first wanted the Committee of Three and later the cessation of the Government offensive against Kalgan—our 10 day truce proposal included all three matters, both Committees to meet and the attack on Kalgan to halt. We had thought that this truce would be the beginning to the accomplishment of everything both sides wanted. Mr. Tung, at the conclusion of the meeting, stated that he would report the substance of our conversation to General Chou and added that General Chou was returning to Nanking in the future.

In view of the unsatisfactory nature of this conversation and with the desire to do everything possible at this critical period, I decided to fly to Shanghai to see General Chou En-lai. I arranged to have General Gillem invite General Chou to lunch on October 9 at the former's residence, without divulging to General Chou that I would be present. This enabled me to have three hours' conference with General Chou. Upon meeting General Chou at General Gillem's residence and after explaining to him that I had arranged the engagement in this manner in order to avoid publicity, I described the unsatisfactory nature of my conversation of the previous day with the Communist representatives at Nanking. I added that, in view of its serious implications and my desire to leave nothing undone which I might do to save the situation, I had decided to proceed to Shanghai to see him. I then handed him a record of the previous day's conversation and suggested he first read this before we began our talk.

After reading this document, he asked me whether I had anything further to say. When I replied that I had nothing to say at the moment, General Chou commented as follows: He had read the Chinese text of the joint statement released by Dr. Stuart and me and would like to point out that the Communist representatives at Nanking had not known of this statement at the time of their call on Dr. Stuart and me. There was a divergence between the joint statement and the terms for the 10 day truce contained in my memorandum to Dr. Stuart (a copy of which had been forwarded to General Chou at Shanghai). In the joint statement it was indicated that the two Committees would meet in order "to consider" the two proposals of the Generalissimo set forth in his memorandum of October 2; in my memorandum to Dr. Stuart, however, it was indicated that the purpose of the truce was "to carry out" the Generalissimo's two points. If it were understood that the two points were to be carried out, it would be still farther away from the Communist understanding and the terms would represent a document of surrender.

I replied as follows: I had dictated both these papers, one of them in five minutes and the other in ten minutes. What General Chou was now talking about was my English rather than the Generalissimo's intention. I sent Mr. Wang Ping-nan a copy of the memorandum to Dr. Stuart on my own initiative and then dictated the press release very hurriedly in the presence of Dr. Stuart and a member of my staff. The Government did not see the memorandum and saw the release only when it appeared in the press. In dictating the press release, I endeavored to condense several letters except for the final paragraphs thereof. The paragraph which I had not quoted and which apparently would have avoided this present confusion read: "With a view to saving time and showing its utmost sincerity, the Government expresses its maximum concessions in regard to the solution of the present problem." The issue raised by General Chou apparently reduced itself to the use of the expression "to carry out," this referring to the Generalissimo's two proposals in his memorandum to me of October 2. I might have said "consideration" of these two proposals or "to consider" these two proposals. The point I wished to make, however, was that the Generalissimo had never seen this memorandum, which was a communication from me to Dr. Stuart. It seemed to me, therefore, that the use of the two different expressions should not be a cause for concern to General Chou, except to the extent that the one to which he took the least exception was that used in the press release. Neither was a direct quotation from the Generalissimo and I did not think that they should be a matter of such apparent moment. The previous disagreement and misunderstanding, which had been mentioned by Mr. Tung on the previous day, revolved about General Chou's desire, as conveyed to me through Dr. Stuart, to reach an informal understanding regarding representation on the State Council prior to formal meetings of the Five Man Committee. The Generalissimo would agree only to formal meetings of this Committee and this had apparently led General Chou to believe that the Government members of the Committee would not be empowered to negotiate the questions of the seats on the Council and the veto power or to discuss the military aspects, particularly the question of the cessation of hostilities. General Chou's understanding regarding discussion of military affairs by the Committee was correct, and this had been my understanding from the beginning of the efforts to convene this Committee. General Chou's statement regarding the Government's members' lack of authority to negotiate the two State Council issues had been taken up by me with the Generalissimo. The latter had assured me that this was incorrect and had agreed with me that the only two questions to be considered by the Committee were the two State Council issues — naturally the Government delegates would have the power to negotiate within the Committee. I could not understand the dragging out of the negotiations while military operations went on and my great problem had been so to arrange matters that active military operations in the Kalgan region could be quickly terminated. To that end I had confidentially instructed the United States Commissioner and the Director of Operations of the Executive Headquarters to work out in detail complete plans for the rapid deployment of field teams. It was, therefore, difficult for me to understand why matters were permitted to drag on while the military campaign proceeded and the situation became more difficult to handle. Another factor in the situation was the serious concern exhibited by General Chou over the restriction placed on matters to be discussed during the truce period, as the Generalissimo had stipulated that only certain matters were to be taken up. There was probably complete misunderstanding on this point. I had tried to obtain agreement for the cessation of hostilities with the negotiations to follow, and I had tried to limit as far as possible the number of matters to be adjusted prior to the issuance of an order for the complete cessation of hostilities. As I now understood it, General Chou was concerned that other matters were not to be discussed. It was my assumption, however, that there would be general discussion the moment fighting ceased. I concluded that the reason for my visit to Shanghai was to ask General Chou whether we were to have a meeting or whether we were to continue with the various complications involved prior to the holding of a meeting.

After a recess for lunch, General Chou replied as follows: The reason he had attached importance to the use of the expression "to carry out" was that this had appeared in the only letter he had received relating to the 10 day truce. However, when he read the joint statement by Dr. Stuart and me, the wording had become less important as it indicated that the

301

proposals were to be considered. The question presented, however, was that the Generalissimo considered his two proposals as the maximum concessions he could make, but from the Communist viewpoint these were not concessions— they were rather unacceptable conditions. In the first point, it was stipulated that certain seats in the State Council were to be allocated to the Communist Party and the Democratic League, a procedure not satisfactory unless it provided for the desired veto power. At the same time, to count one of the non-party members as a part of the Communist-Democratic League group in the State Council was not in accordance with the PCC procedure, and furthermore the requirement that the Communist Party present a list of its delegates to the National Assembly prior to the completion of the draft constitution was also contrary to the PCC resolutions. The second point in the Generalissimo's proposals was a unilateral demand, which went beyond the truce in June. It was equivalent to saying that, while the Communist troop locations would be fixed, the Government's 90 divisions would be free to move and would be able to occupy Communist areas.

General Chou went on to say that he had not sent an immediate reply to the Generalissimo but had merely asked the Communist representatives at Nanking to make an oral reply to Dr. Stuart for transmission to me. This he had done because the two points were unacceptable and he had felt that Dr. Stuart and I might still find some means of halting the Government offensive against Kalgan and avert a national split. The effect of the Government proposals was to force the Communists to surrender; if the terms were not accepted in 10 days, the Government would continue its drive against Kalgan. The situation differed from that in June in that during that period questions were brought up for discussion, while the scope of discussion was now limited and the solutions were worked out beforehand—this was equivalent to an ultimatum.

I repeated my explanation that the limitation on the matters for discussion had resulted from my efforts to put as few difficulties as possible ahead of the question of the cessation of hostilities. I pointed out that both sides had presented terms and that, if in discussion over a conference table no agreement were reached, the proposals would be a failure; and that the proposal for the truce in no way represented a commitment to specific terms as outlined by the Generalissimo— such as the delegates to the National Assembly and the location of troops. These questions, I said, could not be decided without sitting down at a conference table for discussion of terms.

General Chou then offered the following comment: The same argument which I had advanced against calling a meeting of the Committee of Three without preliminary discussion to find a basis for agreement was equally valid with reference to the Five Man Committee. In the absence of such informal preliminary discussions regarding the State Council, it would be equally difficult to convene the Five Man Committee. Aside from this point, there was still the question of the lack of guarantee for the issuance of a cease-fire order. Prior to his departure from Nanking, he had tried to communicate to Dr. Stuart in every possible way his ideas regarding the Communist proposals for the reorganization of the State Council. The Government had, however, refused to discuss these questions informally. The Generalissimo's present proposal regarding the seats on the State Council appeared very ridiculous and would not be approved by the Democratic League. At the present time the Government was engaged in a large scale attack on Kalgan, which had formally begun at 2 p.m. on September 29, as announced by the Kuomintang press and Government military leaders in Peiping. At that time the Communists came to the conclusion that the situation had gone too far to be saved. While I agreed that the attack on Kalgan should be stopped, I did not consider that this move was tantamount to a national split. The Communists, however, still held that the Government attack on one of the few cities constituting a Communist political and military center, such as Yenan, Kalgan and Harbin, did represent a national split. It was his hope that I would understand that ever since the Communist withdrawal from Changchun, the Communists had been on the defensive while the Government had attacked at will in many areas. The Communists now felt that the continuation of this drive on Kalgan was a declaration of the Generalissimo'a determination to abandon the last prospect of negotiation and that this was the reason he was driving headlong toward a nation-wide split. On this question there was only one issue—whether hostilities should cease or not—it was not a question of a temporary armistice. Prior to the Generalissimo's reply of October 2 to General Chou's memorandum of September 30 in regard to Kalgan, the Standing Committee of the Kuomintang Central Executive Committee had held a meeting at which the Kuomintang political and military leaders decided upon a policy of settlement by force. The Generalissimo had immediately despatched his memorandum of October 2, in which there was no mention of Kalgan and in which were set forth proposals that he knew would be unacceptable to the Communist Party. The Government thus used this proposal as a cover for war. The Communists had learned a lesson from the two truce periods in June —this was that despite their concessions there would be no settlement. The Communists could not, therefore, agree to a 10 day truce for the operations against Kalgan; as a matter of fact, the Communists could not even agree to a limited armistice for the entire country. It was the Communist view that only a lasting truce would demonstrate that the Government did not desire a total split.

General Chou then presented the following points, which, he said, represented the Communist stand on military and political issues:

Military

1. The troops of both parties should resume the positions held in China proper as of January 13 and in Manchuria as of June 7.

2. The location of the troops of both parties until the time of army reorganization should be fixed.

3. Government troops moved since January 13 should be returned to their original locations in order to facilitate demobilization.

Political

Whether discussed by the Five Man Committee or by the PCC Steering Committee, the following points should be included:

1. The Communist Party and the Democratic League should have 14 seats in the State Council in order to ensure that the Administrative Program will not be violated, the distribution of these seats between the two parties to be settled by separate discussion.

2. The organization of the State Council should be carried out in conjunction with the reorganization of the Executive Yuan.

3. The Constitution Reviewing Committee should be reconvened immediately to prepare in its final form the draft constitution for presentation to the National Assembly, all parties to pledge that this constitution will be adhered to.

4. The PCC Steering Committee should decide upon the date for the National Assembly and the final distribution of seats in the Assembly among the various parties.

5. After the reorganization of the National Government, the various parties will present their lists of delegates to the National Assembly according to the number agreed upon by the reorganized Government.

6. The question of local government will be settled according to the PCC Administrative Program—that is, the *status quo* will be maintained pending the initiation of local self-government after the reorganization of the National Government.

7. To ensure the carrying out of the four promises made by the Generalissimo at the beginning of the PCC session in January, political prisoners should be released, newspapers, magazines and civic bodies banned since January should be restored and the secret police should be abolished.

8. In accordance with the military resolutions of the PCC, the division of military and civil affairs should be strictly carried out and demobilization should be commenced anew.

General Chou explained that the above-mentioned eight points were all within the scope of the PCC resolutions and should all be carried out. He further stated that the Five Man Committee and the PCC Steering Committee would merely discuss how to implement the PCC resolutions and could determine whether certain points were contrary to these resolutions. He added that these were the matters that he was going to include in his reply to the Generalissimo's memorandum of October 2.

As a further explanation of his stand, he said that the attack on Kalgan by the Government forces should be stopped indefinitely in order that a nation-wide split might be avoided. He continued that the Committee of Three, the Five Man Committee and the PCC Steering Committee should then be convened to discuss the truce and the implementation of the PCC resolutions. This, he stated, would be his specific reply to the Generalissimo. In conclusion, General Chou said that there were two other points he would like to make: (1) The Communist Party did not agree to the aid given by the U.S. Government to the Kuomintang Government while civil war was going on and could not agree to the fact that U.S. troops in China had not yet been withdrawn as had been previously promised. (2) He had noticed that the statements issued by Dr. Stuart and me were always timed to follow a Communist rejection of Government demands and not Government rejection of Communist demands. He referred to the circumstance that we had not issued a statement at the end of the June truce period when the Communists had abandoned practically all their claims and the breakdown in negotiations came because the Government still refused to sign the agreements reached. He then enumerated the circumstances under which Dr. Stuart and I had issued a statement in August and others in which we had issued no statement, and said that, while this last joint statement issued by Dr. Stuart and me contained no accusations, the timing thereof led to public misunderstanding and did not give a true picture of the situation.

In reply, I told General Chou that I would give the Government a list of the eight points presented by him but suggested that he himself make a formal reply to the Government. I explained that I had proceeded to Shanghai in order to discuss with him personally whether the situation was as serious as it had seemed to me at the time of my conversation with Messrs. Tung and Wang.

I concluded with the following statements: I appreciated his frankness and was not going into a detailed reply, as we had already covered most of the points mentioned. I could only deplore his continued insistence that the Generalissimo had planned the truce for an evil purpose, as I had spent four or five days trying to persuade the Generalissimo to stop the fighting. The truce could not possibly be considered as an effort by the Government to gain time for this movement of troops and munitions. All I could say, after having heard General Chou's statement, was that it would seem that my efforts at mediation were futile and I could see no practical basis for any other action on my part. I could but express my regret at this ending of our discussions. I had told him some time ago that if the Communist Party felt that they could not trust to my impartiality they merely had to say so and I would withdraw. He had now said so. I was leaving immediately for Nanking. I wished to thank him for coming to General Gillem's residence and for giving me the opportunity for direct conversation with him.

General Chou replied that he would like to make two points: (1) The eight points referred merely to political matters but he had also mentioned three points related to military matters. He would further say that any halt in the Government advance against Kalgan must be permanent. His written reply to the Generalissimo would be transmitted through me. (2) Although he had made a complaint regarding the joint statement just issued by Dr. Stuart and me, he wished to make clear that he did not refer to my over-all efforts throughout the entire period of mediation.

On the same day (October 9) General Chou En-lai addressed to me a memorandum, under that day's date, as his reply to the Generalissimo's memorandum of October 2 and to the proposal for a 10 day truce for the operations against Kalgan. The gist of this memorandum is as follows:[71]

> He had made no immediate reply to the Generalissimo's memorandum of October 2 as the Generalissimo had not only failed to answer General Chou's memorandum of September 30 in his communications of October 2 but had raised two points contrary to the PCC resolutions and the military reorganization plan. General Chou had, therefore, merely instructed Mr. Wang Ping-nan to deliver a verbal reply "with a view to looking forward that you and Dr. Stuart would further exert fair and impartial efforts for the peace of China."
>
> The Communist Party rejected the Kalgan truce proposal for the following three reasons: (1) According to the principles of the previous agreements, the Chinese Communist Party and the Democratic League should have 14 of the 40 seats in the State Council to ensure that the PCC Program for Peaceful National Reconstruction would not be unilaterally revised; the Government's proposal for 13 seats

[71]See Volume Two, Appendix N, Document 12, for the full text.

307

did not provide such a safeguard. (2) The list of National Assembly delegates could be given only to a reorganized government when the draft constitution had been revised by the PCC and acknowledged as the only draft to be presented to the National Assembly and when the distribution of the seats in the Assembly had been finally agreed upon; the Government proposal in this regard was contrary to the PCC procedure. (3) For effective implementation of the military reorganization plan it was essential to determine where the troops of both parties were to be located during the process of reorganization; determination of such locations should not be confined to Communist troops while Government troops were left free to move and attack at will Communist troops and the populace in the Communist areas.

General Chou had received my memorandum of October 6 to Dr. Stuart, in which he learned that the Generalissimo agreed merely to postpone the drive against Kalgan for 10 days provided the two demands in his memorandum of October 2 "would be carried out." This was obviously an ultimatum to force the Communists to surrender and "we feel therefore compelled to reject firmly that proposal." General Chou requested that I transmit the following reply to the Generalissimo:

The attack on Kalgan must be called off immediately and the attacking Government troops must be withdrawn to their original positions. If the Government should call off this attack immediately and once and for all, the Communists were willing to participate in meetings of the Committee of Three and the Five Man Committee or the PCC Steering Committee to have simultaneous discussion of two matters: (1) cessation of hostilities and (2) implementation of the PCC resolutions.

The memorandum concluded with a list of the points set forth by General Chou to me in Shanghai on October 9, three of them relating to military matters for discussion by the Committee of Three and eight of them relating to political matters to be discussed by the PCC Steering Committee or by the Five Man Committee.

The Communist Party rejection of the truce proposal ended another period of tortuous negotiations, which had begun with General Chou En-lai's absenting himself in Shanghai until a meeting of the Committee of Three should be convened. During this period the Government had launched its drive against Kalgan and had at the end of September publicly announced its intention of capturing that city. The Communists, by their insistence on a guarantee for the cessation of hostilities and the meeting of the Committee of Three for discussion of that issue prior to participation in the Five Man Committee had maneuvered themselves into such a position that the Government was proceeding apace with its military campaign while no negotiations were taking place which might have provided a basis for forcing the Government to agree to the cessation of hostilities. The Generalissimo had during this period maintained a stubborn position, refusing to issue a statement proposed by me which, I thought, gave sufficient protection to the Government and might have led to a cessation of hostilities. This attitude involved the serious danger of practically forcing the Chinese Communists completely into the hands of Soviet Russia. As the Government publicly announced its offensive against Kalgan, the Communist Party warned that this might result in a national break between the two parties. The continued use by the Government of military force and its refusal to halt the operations against Kalgan convinced me that the integrity of my own position and that of the United States through me as its representative were open to question should American mediation continue while such a campaign proceeded to conclusion. As a result of Communist propaganda attacks on American policy toward China and on me personally, I had informed the Communist representatives that, if my impartiality were in doubt, the Communists had only to inform me accordingly and I would withdraw from the negotiations. In view of the Government's actions, I felt that I should also make my position clear to the Generalissimo. This I did when I saw that he would not abandon his intention of capturing Kalgan. At this time I recommended to the President my recall and the termination of my mission, but cancelled this recommendation when I learned that the Generalissimo was willing to agree to a truce period for the operations against Kalgan to allow for discussions in the Committee of Three and the Five Man Committee under Dr. Stuart of the questions of membership in the State Council, the submission by the Communist Party of its list of delegates to the National Assembly and the location of the Communist troops, a formal termination of hostilities to follow agreement on these issues. Although the Communists had insisted on the halting of the attack on Kalgan as a prerequisite to any negotiations and although General Chou had said that he would return to Nanking when the Committee of Three should be reconvened, the Communists refused to accept these proposals. They demanded a permanent, as opposed to a temporary, halting of the drive on Kalgan and said that negotiation of the issues mentioned in the proposal, which included also the discussion of the Kalgan issue, would be equivalent to negotiation under coercion. It was difficult to understand the Communist reaction in this regard as they had for months been insisting on the cessation of hostilities, and the restriction of issues for discussion prior to the issuance of a cease-fire order had been aimed at reducing to a minimum the number of questions to be settled before the fighting terminated. This period ended with the implication in my conversation with General Chou En-lai at Shanghai that my efforts at mediation had ended, but it was felt that, in spite of the Communist propaganda attacks on the American mediation effort and American policy toward China, the Communists did not really wish the withdrawal of the United States from the negotiations.

XXVIII.
GOVERNMENT OCCUPATION OF KALGAN AND ISSUANCE OF A MANDATE FOR THE CONVOCATION OF THE NATIONAL ASSEMBLY ON NOVEMBER 12; THIRD PARTY GROUP PARTICIPATION IN THE MEDIATION EFFORT; AND RETURN OF GENERAL CHOU EN-LAI TO NANKING

Although at the conclusion of my conversation with General Chou En-lai at Shanghai on October 9 there was the clear implication that my mediation efforts were ended, it was not believed that the Communists really desired the termination of the American effort. Support for this belief was seen in a statement issued by General Chou in a press conference at

Shanghai on the night of October 9, in which he described the misunderstanding regarding terminology in the Kalgan truce proposal and set forth the Communist proposal of three military and eight political points. (These he had described to me in our final conversation at Shanghai and they had also been outlined in his memorandum of October 9 to me.) The tenor of General Chou's statement indicated a more amenable attitude than that evidenced in his conversation with me at Shanghai. Further indication of the Communist attitude was given by the call of Mr. Wang Ping-nan of the Communist Delegation at Nanking on Dr. Stuart and me on October 10 for presentation of General Chou's above-mentioned memorandum. We informed him that General Chou's reply seemed to indicate an uncooperative attitude, as he was making demands which he knew would be unacceptable to the Government, and that to set forth such unacceptable demands would close the way to any further possible negotiations. Dr. Stuart added that if the Communists had really lost faith in the American mediators there was not the slightest use in our making further attempts to mediate.

I pointed out to Mr. Wang that once the negotiations were begun along the lines of the truce proposal it would be possible to reach certain agreements for the cessation of hostilities and that I wished to add the following comments in order to avoid the possibility of misunderstanding: I was aware of the Communist demand that the Government troops return to the positions held on January 13 and I was familiar with the provisos of the January 10 agreement for the cessation of hostilities. My impression was, although there had been no definite statement by the Government on this subject, that the Government would insist on continued military occupation of the areas recently taken over by the Government forces. It was possible that the Government might compromise on this stand, but it had not given any indication thereof. I thought that the Government would accept the retention of positions in Manchuria held as of June 7. I could give no definite statement on these matters, but since they had an important bearing on the negotiation of military phases I felt it desirable to make my impressions on the subject clear. These questions would certainly be open to debate, and I was referring to this matter because I had been concerned over this particular aspect of the problem.

On October 10, the thirty-fifth anniversary of the founding of the Chinese Republic, the Generalissimo made a speech,[72] in which he outlined the achievements of the Republic and the aims of the Government. The pertinent portions of the speech, which relate to the negotiations, are as follows:

> The Government asked the Communist Party to abandon its plot to achieve regional domination and disintegration of the country by military force and to participate along with all other parties in the National Government and the National Assembly. It was the hope of the Government that the various political parties and groups would submit their lists of candidates to the State Council and of delegates to the National Assembly. The Government desired a total and permanent cessation of hostilities, but during the past three months the Communists had rejected all the Government's proposals and had also turned down the truce proposal presented by General Marshall and Dr. Stuart.
>
> The Generalissimo now proposed simultaneous meetings of the Committee of Three and the Five Man Committee, the former to seek a solution of problems bearing on the implementation of the plan for military reorganization and integration of the Communist forces into the National Army and the Five Man Committee to consider mutually acceptable measures for reorganization of the National Government. As soon as agreement should be reached on these matters, the Government would immediately issue a cease-fire order provided the Communists called a halt to their military operations and ceased their attacks on Government troops.

During this period, as a result of discussions with Dr. Stuart, a group of representatives of the Democratic League and the China Youth Party proceeded to Shanghai for the purpose of inducing General Chou En-lai to return to Nanking. At a meeting in Shanghai on October 8, attended by Dr. Sun Fo, President of the Legislative Yuan, General Chou

[72]See Volume Two, Appendix O, Document 1, for the full text.

and leaders of the minority parties, it was decided to send a delegation of the third party group to Nanking and arrange with the Kuomintang for the sending of an invitation to General Chou asking him to return to Nanking. On October 10 the Generalissimo, through Dr. Sun Fo, extended a welcome to the delegation.

Then followed in rapid succession a series of events which aroused bitter feeling on the part of the Communists and one of which created strong opposition from all minority parties. On October 10 Government forces captured Kalgan with little or no opposition from Communist troops and on the same day entered Chihfeng, the last Communist stronghold in Jehol Province and a city which had been the subject of bitter argument at the time of the negotiations in January for the cessation of hostilities. Government troops at this time were also reported to be on the verge of occupying additional Communist-held towns in north Kiangsu. On the same day the Government announced the resumption of nation-wide conscription, which had been suspended following the Japanese surrender in August 1945. Even after these events, General Chou was said by Dr. Sun Fo to be ready to return to Nanking, but the issuance by the Government on October 11 of a mandate announcing that the National Assembly would be convened on November 12, as scheduled, caused General Chou to cancel his plans. This announcement also resulted in strong criticism from the other minority parties, as they felt that it was evidence of unilateral and dictatorial action on the part of the Government. They charged that agreement was reached on April 24 in discussion between representatives of all parties and the Generalissimo for postponement of the National Assembly, then scheduled for May 5, and that it was understood that the date for convening the Assembly would be decided by discussion between all parties. The Government explained that its action was in accordance with Kuomintang regulations, which required formal notification and confirmation of the date of the National Assembly one month prior to its convocation. The result of this series of events was to cause a cancellation of the plans for the return of General Chou and the minority party representatives to Nanking.

On October 13 Dr. Stuart and I called on the Generalissimo, who inquired whether the Communists had presented further proposals. Dr. Stuart replied that they had not done so and then described to the Generalissimo remarks made to him (Dr. Stuart) by one of the Democratic League leaders that day. The latter had stated that the Government's occupation of Kalgan and the Government's issuance of a mandate for the convocation of the National Assembly had created a condition which made the Communist Party and the other minority parties extremely apprehensive regarding the possibility of continuing the negotiations, as they felt that this was the initial step toward fascism.

The Generalissimo replied that he did not feel that the minority parties had united in a stand against participating in the National Assembly under present conditions and he thought that a different reaction would become apparent within a day or two. He explained that formal confirmation by the Government of the convening of the National Assembly was routine procedure and completely justified in his opinion. He added that he wished Dr. Stuart and me to consider the possibility of his making a statement, such as that previously suggested by me at the time of his return to Nanking from Kuling, but modified in accordance with recent changes in the situation.

When I mentioned the memorandum of October 9 to me from General Chou En-lai, the Generalissimo said that he wanted no reference to that communication and that he was not considering the statements therein. I then inquired what changes in the situation were to be considered other than the capture of Kalgan. I pointed out that the important factor was the immediate cessation of hostilities and that, even if the Communists were forced to submit to various agreements by the pressure of military action, there could be no healthy results in the political negotiations and the reorganization of the government as the bitterness engendered thereby would be too deep and the spirit of revenge and distrust too great.

The Generalissimo replied that he could not agree to an unconditional cessation of hostilities without some evidence for the people and the Government leaders that some advantage had been gained for the reorganization of the government. He mentioned the submission by the Communists of their list of delegates to the National Assembly as an example.

I reminded the Generalissimo that in early July he had said that it was first necessary to deal harshly with the Communists and later, after two or three months, to adopt a generous attitude. It seemed to me now, I said, after more than three months with the Government in possession of all the important strategic points, that the time had come for the generous attitude of which he had spoken. To this, the Generalissimo agreed but repeated his previous statement regarding the necessity of obtaining certain advantages prior to the cessation of hostilities. I then asked the Generalissimo regarding the question of the reorganization of the Executive Yuan. He replied that he would make no reference to this problem in any statement to be issued and that this was a matter for decision after the National Assembly meeting. I then inquired of the Generalissimo why the Constitution Reviewing Committee had not been reconvened. His reply indicated willingness to have that Committee resume its work, but he did not clearly state why it had not been convened. The discussion ended with the Generalissimo's saying that he wished to wait for a day or two and watch developments, following which he would make his decision regarding the issuance of a statement.

Subsequent to this conversation Dr. Stuart and I agreed that this was an appropriate time to transmit to the Generalissimo a copy of the proposed statement for release by him and on October 14 we forwarded to the Generalissimo a draft[73] of such a statement including the Generalissimo's demand for submission of the names of the Communist delegates. This draft, based on the previous draft prepared by me and presented to the Generalissimo on September 27, contained the following specific points:

> The Five Man Committee under Dr. Stuart and the Committee of Three under General Marshall to hold simultaneous meetings immediately with the following understandings:
>
> (a) Opposing troops in close contact to be separated in accordance with the procedures tentatively reached by the Committee of Three in June for Manchuria.
>
> (b) The restoration of communications to be immediately resumed in accordance with the agreement tentatively reached by the Committee of Three in June.

[73]See Volume Two, Appendix O, Document 2, for the full text.

(c) The method for settling disagreements among the team members of the Executive Headquarters and the Commissioners at the Executive Headquarters to be in accordance with the agreement tentatively reached by the Committee of Three in June.

(d) The tentative agreement reached last June by the Committee of Three for the redisposition of troops in Manchuria to be confirmed.

(e) Government troops north of the Yangtze River to continue in occupation of places now under their control until agreement is reached by the Committee of Three for the redistribution, reorganization and demobilization of both Government and Communist forces for the unification of the Chinese armed forces.

(f) The PCC Steering Committee to confirm without delay any understanding reached by the Five Man Committee.

(g) Questions of local government to be settled by the newly organized State Council.

(h) The Constitution Reviewing Committee to be reconvened immediately and the agreed draft to be submitted to the National Assembly as the basis for its action.

(i) Concurrent with the cessation of hostilities which is to be effected immediately following the agreement of the Communist Party to the foregoing procedure, the Communist Party to announce its intention of participating in the National Assembly by publishing its list of delegates thereto.

On the same day (October 14) on which we forwarded this draft to the Generalissimo, Dr. Stuart handed to me a copy of a memorandum which was said to have been given by the Generalissimo to Dr. Sun Fo and which contained the measures which the Government was prepared to initiate. This memorandum reads as follows:

"In order to expedite the peace talks, the Government is prepared to initiate the following measures:

(1) The Committee of Three to be reconvened as soon as possible to work out plans for avoiding all conflicts and the reorganization of the army;

(2) The unofficial Committee of Five to meet as soon as possible to discuss the reorganization of the Government, the conclusion reached to be referred to the PCC steering Committee for discussion and agreement;

(3) The Constitution Draft Committee to meet as soon as possible to complete work on revision of the draft constitution at the earliest possible date; and

(4) As soon as solutions of any of the above-mentioned problems are found the PCC Steering Committee to be convened immediately for deliberation and agreement."

Dr. Stuart said that this memorandum had been taken by Dr. Sun Fo to Shanghai and that the latter would reconvene the minority party group upon his arrival there for discussion of these measures. Dr. Stuart added that he had seen the Generalissimo earlier in the day and that the latter had said that he was ready to issue an order for the cessation of hostilities as soon as the Committee of Three and the Five Man Committee should meet, but that he desired a guarantee from the American mediators that the Communists would conduct themselves in good faith during the negotiations. As I told Dr. Stuart, it would be just as impossible for us to guarantee the good faith of the Communists as it would be for the Generalissimo to guarantee the activities of the reactionaries in the Kuomintang.

Following the earlier failure to persuade General Chou En-lai to return to Nanking, Mr. Lei Chen, Secretary-General of the PCC, and Mr. Mo Teh-hui, a non-party Northeastern leader who had participated in the PCC, proceeded to Shanghai for discussions with General Chou and the other minority party representatives. Messrs. Lei and Mo held an all-day conference with the third party leaders on October 15 and as a result of this discussion three delegates were sent to call on General Chou En-lai and urge him to return to Nanking. General Chou was said to have remained silent during the call and to have made no comment. The minority party representatives had then returned to Nanking and had suggested that the Government send a higher ranking official to Shanghai to induce General Chou to return.

Upon learning of these developments, I informed Dr. Stuart that, while this would probably be helpful, the Generalissimo might soon issue his statement, which would change this procedure slightly. Madame Chiang had called the evening of October 15 with a rewritten version of the draft statement which Dr. Stuart and I had sent to the Generalissimo on October 14. The rewritten statement was confusing in thought and very provocative in nature. I deleted lengthy portions of the Generalissimo's version. It seemed to me that there were three important matters in connection with the statement as it then stood:

(1) There must be a definite understanding between the two parties regarding the actual meaning. In effect, the Generalissimo's statement, if agreed to by General Chou En-lai, would permit the immediate cessation of hostilities and would also constitute a complete procedure for arriving step by step at a peaceful solution. Neither side could, after expressing its agreement, delay while awaiting developments of either the Committee of Three or the Five Man Committee.

(2) It would be necessary to decide upon the means of putting the procedure into effect after agreement on the statement was given. If the Communists expressed written agreement to the procedure and understandings, it would be necessary first to convene the Committee of Three to prepare an order for the cessation of hostilities. In this connection, there would be a very delicate situation, since the Communists would wish to retain the positions held as of January 13 and the Government would insist on holding all places now under its occupation. I would attempt to settle this issue by establishing a temporary *status quo* providing for the settlement of difficulties between troops in close contact and leaving until later the question of the redistribution of troops in accordance with a revised February 25 agreement for military reorganization.

(3) In connection with the problem of local governments, the Generalissimo in his rewritten draft of the statement had excluded Manchuria. The Communists would take exception to this exclusion, which would make it very difficult for Dr. Stuart and the Five Man Committee to solve this question.

After outlining the above-described matters to Dr. Stuart, I pointed out to him that as a result of the vicious per-

318

sonal attacks on me by the Communists it would be necessary for him to handle the negotiations until the Committee of Three should actually meet and at that time I probably would be free to step back into the picture as Chairman of that Committee. We agreed that we would exert every pressure on the Generalissimo to issue without delay the public statement as altered by me.

On the evening of October 16 the Generalissimo made a public statement[74] in which he announced the Government's views and presented an eight point proposal, upon acceptance of which by the Communist Party the Government was prepared to arrange for the immediate cessation of hostilities. The Generalissimo's eight point proposal was very similar to the proposals set forth in the draft statement given by Dr. Stuart and me to the Generalissimo on October 14, the chief differences being (1) the deletion of our first point regarding the separation of opposing troops in close contact and (2) the exclusion of Manchuria from the proposal providing for the settlement of the question of local government by the State Council. Five of the points were identical with our proposals and one contained a change in wording which would require that the tentative agreement reached for the redisposition of troops in Manchuria be carried out in accordance with a fixed schedule without delay. Our proposal provided only that this tentative agreement was to be confirmed.

On October 17 General Yu Ta-wei called and handed me a letter, dated October 17, in Chinese, together with an English translation,[75] from the Generalissimo, in which were set forth the Government's proposals for continued negotiations. This letter was almost identical with the statement made by the Generalissimo on the previous evening and constituted the formal notification to the Communist Party regarding the Government's views. General Yu said that the Generalissimo had signed the letter but wished it to be presented to me in order that it might be determined whether any changes were necessary prior to its being handed to me formally. I replied that I had no comments and General Yu thereupon made formal delivery of the letter. I then directed that the English version of the Generalissimo's proposals be prepared in the

[74]See Volume Two, Appendix O, Document 3, for the full text.
[75]See Volume Two, Appendix O, Document 4, for the full text.

form of a memorandum and that it be despatched to Dr. Stuart with the request that he turn it over immediately to the Communist representatives.

Dr. Stuart delivered the memorandum to a Communist representative on the same afternoon. At the time of his receipt of this communication, the Communist representative said that he did not like the procedure whereby the troops of both parties were to retain control of areas now under their occupation. He also said that the Government should make a gracious gesture by returning Kalgan to the Communists. Dr. Stuart told him that the Generalissimo would not consider such a proposal at that time but he felt certain that Kalgan would not be permitted to stand in the way of a final settlement by either side and that a friendly solution could be found.

On October 17 Mr. Liang Shu-ming, one of the leaders of the Democratic League, called to inform me of the activities of the minority parties in Shanghai: Dr. Carson Chang, head of the Social Democratic Party and one of the Democratic League leaders, had telephoned from Shanghai to say that members of the Third Party Group (composed of members of the Democratic League and the China Youth Party and politically active non-party individuals) had held a meeting to discuss the Generalissimo's eight point proposal. Three Government representatives, General Wu Tieh-chen, Mr. Shao Li-tze and Mr. Lei Chen, had gone to Shanghai carrying with them the Generalissimo's proposal, and their arrival, together with the Generalissimo's statement, was extremely important, as it might lead to the successful conclusion of negotiations or total failure. Following the meeting of the Third Party Group, members thereof had called on General Chou En-lai. His reaction to this visit was that the Communists might have something to add to certain stipulations in the statement but he indicated that the proposal was unacceptable to the Communist Party. The Third Party Group had then decided to invite Dr. Stuart and me to Shanghai for a conference with them, as they felt many issues regarding the military aspects were known only to me and that my presence in Shanghai along with that of the Government and the Third Party Group representatives might mean a better chance for success. He (Mr. Liang) had been asked by the Third Party Group to represent them in extending to Dr. Stuart and to me an invitation to attend a Third Party Conference. He had discussed this matter with Dr. Stuart and had gained the impression that the latter felt it too early for the American mediators to make such a trip. He (Mr. Liang) felt, however, that it was not too early for such action.

I replied as follows: I would do everything in my power to help bring about an end of hostilities and to facilitate the negotiations. I appreciated the invitation and understood the circumstances perfectly, but I shared Dr. Stuart's opinion. At the present time there should be a pause in the American effort during which the Chinese should conduct discussions themselves. Following such discussions, certain decisions would be reached and it would then be an appropriate time for the American mediators to enter the discussions. The Communists had made certain attacks on my impartiality and if I should participate in the present meetings of the minority parties, the Communists would feel that I was attempting to win over the Democratic League from the Communists.

I then explained to Mr. Liang the background of the surplus property transaction and the Communist propaganda attacks thereon and the efforts that had been made to reduce the U.S. Marine Corps strength in China and Communist propaganda attacks on American military aid to the Government. Mr. Liang said that he could believe the explanation I had given but that the surplus property deal had left a deep impression on both the Kuomintang and the Communists, having served to encourage the former and having given a spiritual set back to the latter. In reply, I said that this was actually a boomerang from Communist propaganda.

Mr. Liang then said that he wished to make two points: He understood that the Communists were faced with a dilemma—on the one hand they knew that good relations must be maintained between China and the United States and on the other hand they were rooting themselves deeply in hatred against the United States through their propaganda. The Democratic League saw this clearly and was willing to serve as a bridge between the United States and the Communists in order that such conflicting views might be eliminated. The political situation in China at that time could not exclude the Communists, and the Kuomintang was wrong if it felt that it could form a government together with the China Youth Party, the non-party group and other minority parties without Communist participation.

I replied that I was in agreement with his statement and that this had in fact served as the basis for all my efforts in the negotiations to date. The principal trouble in the negotiations, I said, was that neither side appreciated the fears of the other in judging reasons, purpose of actions or proposals, and overwhelming suspicion made it difficult for both sides to accept any proposal made by Dr. Stuart and me. I emphasized the extreme difficulty we had had in persuading the Generalissimo to issue his eight point proposal and added that it was highly important for the Communists to view it carefully without suspicion. It was my opinion, I concluded, that the Committee of Three could reach agreement on an order for the cessation of hostilities within two hours if the Communists would agree to the procedures set forth in the Generalissimo's statement.

The conversation concluded with Mr. Liang's asking whether I would go to Shanghai if the Third Party Group made progress and obtained some encouragement from General Chou En-lai. I agreed that I would do so in that event.

Further indication of the Communist Party's reaction to the Generalissimo's eight point proposal was seen in a Yenan broadcast on October 18, in which it was announced that the "first telegrams" calling for the convening of a Communist national assembly for the liberated areas under Communist occupation had been despatched by a People's District Congress to the Communist Preparatory Committee of the Liberated Areas Peoples' Representatives. The Yenan radio reported that a Communist "special committee" in a statement of policy had said that the Communist "maximum concessions" required a return to the military positions held by both sides as of January 13 and adherence to the PCC decisions regarding the reorganization of the government and the integration of the armies. The broadcast charged that the Generalissimo wished to legalize his dictatorship by passing a constitution for one-party rule through his own National Assembly and called on the American mediators and the Generalissimo to "return to your original good faith."*

Although both General Chou En-lai's attitude, as described to me by Mr. Liang Shu-ming, and the Yenan reaction, as indicated in the above-mentioned broadcast, gave little promise of success in the efforts of the Third Party Group, the latter did persuade General Chou to return to Nanking for the resumption of discussions. Dr. Wang Shih-chieh informed me on October 20 that General Chou and the members of the Third Party Group had decided to return to Nanking on the

---

*As reported by the United Press at Nanking on October 18, 1946.

following day. He explained that so far as he knew no new understanding had been reached, but that the spirit of the conferences in Shanghai appeared to have offered the possibility of continued negotiations, as a result of which General Chou and the Third Party Group had decided to return. Dr. Wang described the Generalissimo as being somewhat pessimistic due to the Yenan broadcast, which he had considered as abusive and which had angered him.

At this time I felt that it was possible that the Communists might object to my participation in the Committee of Three and that this might be the reason for their propaganda attacks against me and their idea of how to obtain in the United States a popular reaction against the American attitude in relation to the Generalissimo. I had asked the Generalissimo not to rise in my defense in this regard as it was a matter for the United States Government or for me to handle. I felt that it was probably best to have the Third Party Group come to the fore in an effort to bring the two major parties together, as this procedure would operate to establish a firmer basis for subsequent negotiations. It was also my opinion that the meetings of the Committee of Three and the Five Man Committee might have to await Communist agreement to the Government's eight point proposal. In connection with the possible convening of the Committee of Three, General Yu Ta-wei informed me at this time that due to the illness of General Hsu Yung-chang, his place on the Committee of Three would be taken by General Chen Cheng, Chief of Staff, and that he (General Yu) would assist General Chen.

In early October the Generalissimo had informed me of his plans to proceed to Formosa for a brief visit of a few days, the date set for this trip being October 20. On the evening of October 19 we learned that General Chou and the Third Party Group had decided to return to Nanking. I, therefore, expressed the hope that the Generalissimo would delay his trip until the arrival of this delegation from Shanghai because of the effect his departure, the day prior to General Chou's arrival, might have on the situation. This the Generalissimo did. He remained in Nanking until General Chou's arrival on the morning of October 21, and also made arrangements to have a brief talk with General Chou and the members of the Third Party Group prior to his departure on the same day for Formosa. Before he left Nanking the Generalissimo assured me that he would be absent for only a few days, and that he would return at any moment, upon four hours' notice from me, if I felt his presence in Nanking were desirable in connection with the negotiations.

During this period between the Communist rejection of the Kalgan truce proposal and the return of General Chou En-lai to Nanking, fighting continued in various parts of north China, although the situation remained relatively quiet in Manchuria except for small scale actions and Communist disruption of lines of communications. From early October and during this period of negotiations there was general fighting along the Peiping-Hankow Railway line in the Anyang, Shih-chiachuang and Paoting areas and Communist efforts were reported to be devoted largely to destruction of the rail lines in these areas. The Government forces were apparently centering their attention on mining areas as Government troops occupied Chiaotso (northwest Honan) on October 11 and Tsao-chuang (northeast of Hsuchou in south Shantung) on October 16. These were two important coal mining centers which had been a constant source of friction and of trouble to the Executive Headquarters teams. The Government forces captured Huailai, on the rail line between Nankou and Kalgan, on October 13 after the heaviest fighting of the Kalgan campaign. Other fighting was reported during this period along the rail line in east Jehol and on the Tientsin-Pukou Railway in the Tzuyang area, which city the Government forces occupied on October 21.

Other highlights of this period were the Communist-organized mass demonstrations in Harbin and Tsitsihar in northern Manchuria directed toward the withdrawal of American troops from China and criticism of American interference in China's internal affairs. Further indications of a deterioration in the situation were seen in the gradual evacuation of Communist Party personnel from Nanking, Shanghai and Chungking to Yenan in U.S. Army planes furnished at the request of the Communist Delegation in Nanking.

There still remained, however, some basis for hope in the situation in that General Chou En-lai had finally returned to Nanking from Shanghai and in that the Third Party Group, whose chief weapon in the discussions both with the Government and with the Communists was the question of participation or non-participation in the National Assembly, was actively engaged in the mediation effort. This enabled the American mediators to remain in the background for the time being and placed the chief responsibility for the moment on the Chinese themselves.

XXIX.

CONTINUED THIRD PARTY GROUP MEDIATION; ISSUANCE OF A CEASE-FIRE ORDER BY THE GENERALISSIMO

On the morning of October 22 a delegation of nine members of the Third Party Group called on Dr. Stuart and me for a discussion of the situation. Mr. Huang Yen-pei, one of the Democratic League leaders, first described the recent efforts of the Third Party Group:

The original plan of the Third Party Group had been to persuade General Chou En-lai to proceed to Nanking but this had failed because of the capture of Kalgan and the announcement of the convening of the National Assembly on November 12. The Group had, however, continued its efforts and the Government had sent General Wu Tieh-chen, Mr. Shao Li-tze and Mr. Lei Chen to Shanghai. At this time the Generalissimo had issued his eight point proposal, which the Communists considered as an ultimatum to force General Chou to go to Nanking. The group members had explained to General Chou that it was by no means an ultimatum, and the Government representatives had informed him that the eight points were not a prerequisite to the cessation of hostilities but merely served as a basis for discussion. At this time the Yenan radio broadcast indicated two points as essential to the Communists (the return of troops to positions held on January 13 and adherence to the PCC resolutions). The Third Party Group suggested to General Chou that matters pertaining to the cessation of hostilities first be discussed to be followed by the actual termination of fighting, after which other issues would be discussed. The Communists agreed to this point. The members of the Group felt that both sides at the present time should disregard the eight point Government proposal and the two points advanced by the Communist Party. The Third Party Group desired an immediate cessation of hostilities and felt that this must entail the retention of positions presently held. General Chou had not expressed agreement on this point but he did not indicate any objection thereto. In regard to the political issues, the Third Party Group felt that

political affairs should be dealt with in accordance with the
the PCC procedures and that the PCC Steering Committee
should, therefore, handle the problems of the reorganization
of the government and the National Assembly. If this procedure were followed, the Government's eight point proposal
would be carried out automatically and the Communist Party
would automatically submit its list of delegates to the National Assembly. This viewpoint of the Third Party Group
was shared by the Government representatives, who recognized it as the correct procedure. The atmosphere during these
conferences became very friendly and optimistic and the Government representatives had finally suggested that, since
everyone agreed, the entire group should go to Nanking. The
result was that both the Third Party Group and General Chou
had decided to proceed to Nanking.

Dr. Stuart expressed his pleasure that the matter had
been carried to a successful conclusion under Chinese leadership and, referring to the misunderstanding that had arisen regarding American aid to the Chinese Government, stressed
that all that the United States had done and planned to do was
for the whole of China, a united Chinese Republic.

At this point I said that I had gathered the impression
from Mr. Huang's statement that the Government representatives had agreed or had acquiesced to the procedure suggested
by the Third Party Group—that is, discussion of cessation of
hostilities, then actual cessation of hostilities and thereafter
discussion of the Communist points and the Generalissimo's
eight points. I then inquired specifically whether the Government members agreed to that procedure or merely acquiesced
thereto.

Dr. Lo Lung-chi (Democratic League) replied as follows:
In a sense the Government representatives had agreed and in
another sense they had not. The Government representatives
had agreed to the formula proposed by the Third Party Group
at Shanghai, but the question of whether the Generalissimo's
eight points should be accepted as a basis for discussion by the
Communists was not settled. An informal exchange of views
with the Government had been held on the evening of the delegation's arrival at Nanking, but this particular point was not
agreed upon even among the Government delegates. It appeared that the Government was, however, insisting upon
Communist acceptance of the eight points, which would form
the basis of discussion for the issuance of a cease-fire order.
The Third Party Group felt that this was equivalent to an ulti-

matum given by a dictatorial government and that the Communists would not come to terms on such a formula. The Communists had not expressed strong opposition to the conditions, some of which they approved and had proposed, but the approach to these terms was not satisfactory and the Communists could not accept the attitude of—"I give you these terms, agree or not; if so, we can proceed to discuss; otherwise, we go ahead."

I then reviewed the difficulties we had encountered since May in endeavoring to obtain a cessation of hostilities and said that the confusion now seemed to be whether the Government would agree to the cessation of hostilities to be followed by discussion of the Generalissimo's eight points and the Communists' points and of any other points, or whether the Government insisted on agreement to the eight points as a condition precedent to the cessation of hostilities. I pointed out that, from my discussions with Government representatives and the Generalissimo, I had not understood that there was to be any limitation on the matters for discussion. In this present instance there were certain of the Government's eight points on which the Communists would themselves insist. The proposal was, therefore, one tempered by compromise and agreement to Communist contentions on the one hand, along with Government contentions on the other. It included, I said, several points, such as communications, on which agreement had already been reached; in short, the eight points were part Government requirements and part Communist requirements and part matters already agreed upon. I concluded that it was a matter of great interest to me whether the Government, through its representatives at Shanghai, had agreed to the cessation of hostilities to be followed by discussion of the eight points, since that, in a sense, was the kernel of the whole issue at present.

Dr. Lo replied that all the Third Party leaders felt that the eight points were "not bad" but that the question was how to approach the matter: If the Government insisted upon taking the eight points as a prerequisite to the cessation of hostilities, the Communists would not accept, as there was the question of face involved. He also pointed to the Communist insistence on retaining all of the tentative agreements reached by the Committee of Three in June rather than only those which the Government felt were to its advantage.

The meeting with the Third Party Group ended with an appeal from Dr. Stuart for every effort to overcome the distrust, suspicion and fear of both sides. He added that there were questions of face and feelings and the Americans looked to the active assistance of the Third Party Group and would do their utmost to cooperate with them.

Later on the same day (October 22) Dr. Carson Chang, one of the most prominent of the Democratic League leaders, called on me to describe the various meetings at Shanghai between the Third Party Group, the Government representatives and General Chou En-lai. He said that the Communists now felt that they had been defeated and that to accept the Government's eight point proposal would be equivalent to surrender. He went on to point out that two of the eight points were contrary to the PCC resolutions: (1) The proposal that the Communists submit their list of delegates to the National Assembly concurrently with the cessation of hostilities was not in accordance with PCC procedures, which contemplated the submission of such a list to the reorganized government and not to any present political regime. (2) The question of excluding Manchuria from consideration of the local government problem was not in keeping with the PCC resolutions, which contemplated discussion of local government in all of China. Dr. Chang also expressed the opinion that the Communist loss of Kalgan would probably mean that they would under no circumstances give up Harbin.

I said that I was seriously concerned over this particular aspect of the situation and felt that this might result in a breakdown in the negotiations and the development of large-scale war in Manchuria. In conclusion, I assured Dr. Chang that I was sure that there would be no limitation of any sort in the matters to be discussed in the negotiations and that such restrictions were not intended by the Government in its proposals.

On October 24 General Chen Cheng, Chief of Staff and newly appointed Government member of the Committee of Three, accompanied by General Yu Ta-wei, called to inquire whether General Chou had yet replied to the Government's eight point proposal. I said that he had not, but that through Dr. Stuart I had received a copy of what were said to be eleven points or questions raised by the Communists—General Chou was said to have brought them up at a meeting with the Third Party Group, at which time he specifically stressed that these were not demands but questions which should be clearly understood. The gist of these questions is as follows:

Political

(1) The PCC resolutions require the reorganization of the government and in this connection there still remains the question of the number of State Councillors, 13 or 14, to be allotted to the Communists and the Democratic League.

(2) The PCC resolutions require the convening of the National Assembly and prior thereto the reorganization of the government. Does government reorganization include the reorganization of the Executive Yuan?

(3) After decision has been made regarding the revision of the draft constitution, will the understanding that all parties guarantee its adoption in the National Assembly continue effective and will the Executive Yuan be responsible to the Legislative Yuan?

(4) Can the National Assembly be postponed?

(5) Will the number of delegates to the National Assembly be increased?

(6) The names of the delegates to the National Assembly can be submitted only to a coalition government.

(7) The PCC resolutions mean local government in all China—does it now mean local government of the whole country or only China proper?

Military

(1) The Government will not return the localities recently taken in spite of the January 13 and June 7 provisions. How then to solve the question of the one Communist division at Kalgan? The local governments in the Communist areas are elected; after occupation of these areas by the Government, will the original local governments be allowed to continue to exist?

(2) The Government still wants to occupy Harbin, which was promised by the Communists in June.

(3) The Government allocated 2½ provinces in Manchuria to the Communists in June and wanted to occupy Antung, to which the Communists did not agree. The Government, however, now wants Antung.

(4) The Government does not want to give what it promised—such as, the January 13 and June 7 positions and the application of the local government question to all of China rather than only to areas south of the Great Wall.

I then described the temporary withdrawal of Dr. Stuart and myself from the negotiations and the efforts of the Third Party Group in seeking a solution. I said that it was my impression that the real reason for the Communist objection to the fact that only certain of the tentative agreements reached in June were brought forth in the Government's eight points was based on the fact that they did not now wish to agree to the Government's establishing a symbolic force in Harbin and at the same time permit the Government to retain Kalgan, which according to the tentative agreements was to have been retained by the Communists—in other words the adjustment of the Harbin-Kalgan problem was a real issue.

General Chen indicated doubt regarding the effectiveness of the Third Party Group's mediation and said that unless the February 25 military reorganization agreement could be carried out discussion on all other issues, political or military, would be idle talk. He felt that the Third Party Group would have a difficult task in seeking to resolve the major issues, as was evidenced by the political and military points raised by General Chou En-lai. General Chen concluded that the Generalissimo would not return from Formosa until October 31.

I replied that the Generalissimo had informed me that he would return within a few days or upon four hours notice from me and that a protracted stay in Formosa would have a direct bearing on the negotiations as it would appear to the outside world that the Generalissimo was deliberately avoiding the negotiations. Referring to the question of the reorganization of the armed forces, I said that this was a basic factor in the present negotiations but that the present Government attitude was unrealistic in attempting to locate only the Communist forces, while the February 25 agreement required the location of the troops of both sides; to do otherwise would result in Communist fears that their forces would be isolated in order to facilitate subsequent liquidation by the Government armies.

At this point General Yu said that a telegram had just been received from the Generalissimo stating that he held firmly to the third of the eight points, which dealt with the readjustment of the military situation in Manchuria in accordance with the tentative agreement reached in June. The Generalissimo, he said, also insisted that the Communists withdraw from Antung and Tunghua (approximately 130 miles east of Mukden) within fifteen days after the issuance of a cease-fire order and move north of the Sungari River within one month and that the redeployment of the Communist troops in accordance with the tentative agreement be completed by the end of the year.

I inquired whether the Government thought it logistically possible for the Communists to meet this schedule and whether the Generalissimo meant all Communist troops in Manchuria should move north of the Sungari River or only those in Antung and Tunghua. General Chen said that he thought that the Communists could meet such a schedule but was not certain just what troops were meant.

At this point Dr. Stuart entered the meeting, having just come from a talk with General Chou En-lai. The gist of this conversation, said Dr. Stuart, was that the Communists could not accept the Government's eight points. The conference with Generals Chen and Yu concluded with my pointing out to them that a protracted delay by the Generalissimo in returning to Nanking would be construed as definite action to prevent the successful culmination of the present negotiations.

In the meantime during the Generalissimo's absence military activity showed no signs of abating. On October 23 Kaomi, one of the important points on the Tsinan-Tsingtao Railway about 50 miles northwest of Tsingtao, was occupied by Government forces, thus placing in Government possession all of the main stations on this line. On the Peiping-Hankow Railway Government troops were moving north toward Hantan (in southwest Hopei about 40 miles north of Anyang) and Government forces occupied Chiyuan, the terminus of a line running west from Hsinhsiang in north Honan. Fighting continued in the Paoting area along the Peiping-Hankow Railway and large numbers of Government troops were reported to be arriving in Anyang. Most serious was the opening of a Government drive on Antung, which was revealed on October 24 by Government military leaders in Manchuria to American

331

personnel of the Executive Headquarters. There was danger that action of this kind might set off the spark which would lead to a resumption of hostilities on a large scale in Manchuria.

The military situation in Manchuria had remained relatively quiet for several months, although hostilities had spread throughout north China. The Generalissimo had seemed confident in his conversations with me that there would be no large scale fighting in Manchuria and there were rumors that some understanding had been reached between the Government and the Communist leaders in that area which would ensure against widespread fighting. The situation had been complicated by the return to north Manchuria during the early summer of Li Li-san, a former Communist leader who had left the Chinese Communist Party as a result of an intra-party struggle in the 1930s and had fled to Moscow. Li had been named Political Advisor to General Lin Piao, Commander of the Communist forces in Manchuria, and the extent of his power in that area was the subject of much speculation. In view of the former struggle between Li Li-san and Mao Tze-tung and of the possibility of a more open orientation of the Chinese Communists toward Moscow, Li was obviously a figure to be watched.

Communist propaganda attacks on the United States continued and on October 24 the Yenan radio broadcast an appeal to the United Nations General Assembly to organize a special investigation committee to conduct an on-the-spot investigation of American forces "infringing Chinese territorial integrity and security." The request was conditioned on the immediate withdrawal of all American troops and support from "Chiang Kai-shek's dictatorial government."* Earlier in the month, on October 12, the Communist news agency reported that a telegram had been sent by a mass meeting of "all Yenan circles" to the Secretary-General of the United Nations charging American armed intervention in Chinese internal affairs and bringing to the attention of the United Nations Assembly the question of United States forces in China.**

*As reported by the Associated Press correspondent at Nanking on October 24.

**As reported by the Associated Press correspondent at Nanking on October 12.

It was against this background of spreading hostilities, distrust and suspicion engendered by distorted propaganda and the complications of the international situation that efforts were being made to resolve the major issues in China.

Further indications of the deterioration in the situation were seen in the reduction of Communist personnel at the Executive Headquarters at Peiping to the point that the Communist branch was practically inoperative. It was estimated by the U.S. branch of the Executive Headquarters that during the two months preceding October 25 Communist personnel in Peiping had been reduced from approximately 200 to 70. The result was that on negotiating levels the Communist personnel consisted largely of lower ranking officers, who were frequently not available for meetings. The Communists had also withdrawn their representatives from all field teams located in Government-occupied areas in China proper except at four points. The situation had become so difficult that the U.S. branch introduced a proposal for bipartite teams, composed of Government and U.S. members in Government territory and Communist and U.S. members in Communist territory. The Government had expressed agreement but the Communists had been non-committal, although they had not made any direct challenge of the integrity of the U.S. team members. General Yeh Chien-ying, Communist Commissioner, had promised General Alvan C. Gillem, Jr., U.S. Commissioner, that he would retain a structure of key Communist personnel in the Executive Headquarters and in the event of need would promptly return his personnel, but the effectiveness of the Headquarters had suffered from the Communist reductions made in spite of this promise.

On October 25 Dr. Lo Lung-chi, one of the Democratic League leaders, informed me that the Third Party Group had obtained from the Government its reactions to the seven political points or questions recently raised by General Chou En-lai in connection with the Generalissimo's eight point proposal. These reactions were as follows:

(1) The Government would grant to the Communist Party and the Democratic League 13 seats in the State Council; (2) the reorganization of the Executive Yuan is to be included in government reorganization but not until after the meeting of the National Assembly; (3) those matters agreed to by the PCC shall stand and those matters not agreed to shall be discussed by either the PCC Steering Com-

333

mittee or the PCC Constitution Reviewing Committee; (4) the National Assembly could not be delayed, although it was possible to have a postponement after the first meeting on November 12 in order to afford more time for discussions; (5) the PCC Steering Committee could decide whether the total number of delegates to the National Assembly were to be increased by 350; (6) the names of its delegates to the National Assembly must be submitted by the Communist Party at the time that agreement was reached on the cessation of hostilities; and (7) the question of the exclusion of Manchuria from the discussions regarding local government must remain unchanged.

Dr. Lo explained that the Third Party Group had suggested that the question of the number of seats in the State Council be discussed by the PCC Steering Committee and had taken the view that since all local governments were to be regulated or controlled by the reorganized government, in accordance with the PCC resolutions, the Government attitude in this respect left open to question what agency would direct or control the local governments in Manchuria. He pointed out that the Communists desired definite assurances that the Government intended to carry out the decisions of the PCC in accordance with PCC procedures and that assurances from the Government on this point would greatly assist the negotiations. He continued that the Third Party Group had conveyed to the Communists the Government's attitude as above-described and concluded that the Third Party Group, after discussion of General Chou's four military points or questions with Dr. Sun Fo and Dr. Wang Shih-chieh, had felt it best to refer these matters to the Committee of Three.

I replied to Dr. Lo as follows: It was my desire to stay out of the detailed discussions at this particular time in order not to confuse the issue. My only comment on Dr. Lo's remarks was that the views expressed by both sides contained glaring inaccuracies. The arguments advanced by General Chou appeared in some respects skillful maneuvers which clouded the major issues. The Government's greatest interest, and I agreed in that concept, was that some sort of military reorganization plan based on the principles set forth in the February 25 agreement be developed. It appeared to be a basic issue that the armies must, in effect, be neutralized, as otherwise political negotiations and the reorganization of the government would be impossible. The Communists had continuously advocated adherence to the PCC resolutions. Military reorganization was, however, a part of the PCC program, a matter not mentioned by the Communists. This was all the more reason for the resolution of that aspect of the problem. The real basis of continued negotiations was a satisfactory solution to the question of army reorganization, regarding which there had developed a difference of opinion between the Government and the Communists. The February 25 agreement had provided for the location in various areas of the armies of both sides, but the Government during the June negotiations had assumed that only the Communist troop locations were to be determined, which would have permitted the isolation and subsequent liquidation of the Communist forces by superior Government armies. I had persuaded the Generalissimo to agree to the location of units of both sides, but he had in his memorandum of October 2 to me repeated the omission of the designation of locations for Government troops. The Third Party Group might be able to get to the root of the present difficulties by finding some sort of agreement between the Communists and the Government regarding the Kalgan-Harbin issue—the Government might be willing to give up Kalgan providing the Communists would not garrison the city and would permit the establishment of a sizeable Government garrison at Harbin. In addition to this, some political concession might be reached in regard to the exclusion of Manchuria from the reference of local government to the political settlement by making Antung Province the one exception in Manchuria.

Dr. Lo replied that the Communists felt the Government's eight points were arbitrarily and dictatorially issued and on psychological grounds they refused to accept any of the points, even though some of them were acceptable to them. He pointed out that the Generalissimo apparently expected a formal acceptance or rejection of his proposal but that the Third Party Group had encouraged General Chou not to make a formal reply. Dr. Lo concluded with a request that I dissuade the Generalissimo from requiring a formal reply since (1) it would accomplish no purpose in view of the Third Party Group's participation in the negotiations between the two major parties and (2) to require a reply would mean a great loss of face to General Chou and the Communist Party.

On the morning of October 26, General Chou En-lai called unannounced at my residence, the first time that I had seen him since his return from Shanghai. I informed him that Dr. Stuart and I had learned of various aspects of the negotiations from members of the Third Party Group and then explained to him the circumstances of the Generalissimo's trip to Formosa, saying that I had not requested the Generalissimo's return, as he had suggested that I do in case his presence was needed, because I preferred that the procedure of negotiation be direct through the Third Party Group rather than through me. In reply to General Chou's inquiry regarding the military situation, I said that I had read newspaper reports of a Government attack on Chefoo and had received reports from the Executive Headquarters of other military operations and asked whether he had any information in regard to military activity he wished to tell me.

General Chou replied as follows: He had heard of various military operations—the Government's attack on Antung, beginning October 22; the Government's drive on Chefoo by land and by sea; a Government drive in north Kiangsu; a Government advance along the Peiping-Hankow Railway both from the north and the south; and fighting in north Honan and in Shansi, the Government's aim apparently being to gain control of the rail lines. Since the occupation of Kalgan the picture was one of continued Government drives on all fronts. He had returned from Shanghai, although the prospect for negotiations seemed ended, because of the efforts of the Third Party Group and because he could overlook no opportunity for continued negotiations. From outward appearances the Generalissimo's eight points seemed to be an ultimatum because the proposal called for agreement to these points prior to the issuance of a cease-fire order and the proposal was not a fair one. While the Third Party Group was exerting every effort to solve the issues, the Government's military campaign continued, thus furnishing evidence that it would take by force what it could not obtain through negotiations. Since these matters were related to military affairs, he could not wait for Third Party Group action. Since the Committee of Three was still formally in existence, he had, therefore, the responsibility of reporting the military situation to me. He felt that should these military advances continue there would be no necessity for continued negotiations and that the Committee of Three should take certain action in this matter.

I commented as follows: With regard to the Generalissimo's trip to Formosa, I regretted very much his going at this time. On two previous occasions I had thought his absence from Nanking most unfortunate—notably his long absence in Mukden and Peiping—and I took very positive issue with the Government at the time. I had also been concerned over the delay in his return to Nanking from Kuling and his delay in coming to Nanking from Chungking at the time he visited Sian. On this occasion, however, I was absolutely certain that his trip had no connection with General Chou's return to Nanking and I did not think that his trip should be judged as a deliberate action connected with the negotiations. Had the Third Party Group reached a point in the negotiations where his presence seemed imperative, I thought that it would have been easy to have obtained his return to Nanking.

With regard to his reference to the Committee of Three, I continued, I did not quite understand whether he was proposing an immediate meeting of that Committee. But, before hearing his reply in this regard, I made several remarks. I had gained the impression from Dr. Stuart (who had talked with General Chou after the latter's return to Nanking) that there was little purpose in my arguing with General Chou in regard to the various aspects of the situation because his mind seemed closed to any view other than that he had expressed to me in Shanghai. His reactions regarding some of the matters were, however, far from the facts as known to me as one of the principals in those affairs. For example, his reaction regarding the Kalgan truce proposal was in some respects almost the opposite of the actual circumstances. The Government had not wanted the truce and it was, I thought, bitterly opposed by the Government military leaders. The Government had come to consideration of the truce only when confronted with an absolute demand on my part that it must offer some compromise. I did not like the truce and, as a matter of fact, was opposed to a truce in the form of an arrangement to meet the circumstances. The result was a compromise, but a very unwilling one on the part of the Government. The truce proposal was, however, judged by the Communists as a Government device. It would be very difficult for me to argue with General Chou regarding matters which I knew to be facts and not conjecture, and there was much more to this truce proposal than I had stated. I was not discussing whether the truce proposal was a proper one, but was merely stating what actually happened.

Next, I said, it was very difficult for me to understand his views regarding the Generalissimo's eight point proposal. I could easily understand his concern regarding the Harbin issue in relation to Kalgan but could not understand his reaction to most of the other points. The Generalissimo had been insisting for some time on the Communists' naming their delegates to the National Assembly, but in this proposal he compromised that demand with his agreement for the immediate reconvening of the Constitution Reviewing Committee and for the submission of that Committee's draft constitution as the basis for discussion in the National Assembly. These last two points were desired by the Communists and represented matters on which up until that time I had been unable to obtain a positive statement from the Government. Another point had to do with local government, which had been a stumbling block practically destroying the negotiations at the end of June, especially in relation to Kiangsu Province. In this proposal, however, the question of local government was cleared for China proper. While Manchuria was excluded, a point on which I did not agree, this did nevertheless represent a very broad Government commitment. With regard to the location of troops, the eight point proposal provided for that through negotiation in the Committee of Three. As a matter of fact, and I was now dealing with facts, the points just mentioned regarding the draft constitution and its being made the basis of discussion in the National Assembly, the local government issue except for the exclusion of Manchuria and the question of the location of troops being left open to later negotiations were not included in the original points considered by the Government, and it was only through the utmost pressure on my part that they were clearly stated in the Generalissimo's eight points so that there would be no uncertainty in regard to them. There had been very determined opposition on the part of powerful members of the Government to such statements at this time and it had been no easy task to persuade the Government to commit itself in this manner. Now, again, I was not arguing whether these were proper proposals but was merely endeavoring to make clear that the assumption that they were presented for an evil purpose was not correct. I was certain that there was no devious purpose in the proposal regarding the tentative agreement on troop dispositions in Manchuria, omitting the issue raised later in the summer by the Generalissimo regarding local government in Antung. As I understood the matter, the one issue, aside from the question of local government in Antung, on which there was no clear understanding was the location of Communist troops in Yenki rather than in Mutanchiang, a larger city to the north.

I concluded that all that I was attempting to do was to make clear that he had almost entirely misjudged, I thought, what had led to the Government's issuance of the eight point proposal and that it was for this reason that Dr. Stuart and I felt completely baffled. This failure to judge correctly had never been so evident as in the case of the Kalgan truce proposal, which was a good example of being completely defeated by overwhelming suspicion. I questioned the advisability of discussing these issues at this time, but it seemed so hopeless to make an effort and then have it completely misjudged. The misjudgment was not, however, confined entirely to one side.

General Chou replied as follows: A meeting of the Committee of Three did not seem to him to be the issue and would only lead to further argument at this time, although he did not object in any way to such a meeting. With regard to the eight point proposal, the Communists would expect the terms of the Government, in case a cease-fire order were issued, to be so written that while the present positions in north and central China would be maintained the Government would demand Communist acceptance to previous terms—that is, the Communist troops would be concentrated at three points, Yenki, Tsitsihar and Hailar, and in the region of the 2½ provinces in Manchuria. This would not be acceptable to the Communists and the result would be that the Government would merely employ force to gain its ends. He informed me at this time that it seemed an established fact that the Generalissimo had ordered a nation-wide split. He was particularly concerned over the present military situation and wanted to know whether I thought there was any chance of saving it, as only such a hope would increase the prospect of Third Party Group success.

Referring to the Kalgan truce proposal, he continued, he was aware of what had occurred. I had thought that he had misunderstood, but he had a complete understanding of the great effort I had made in this matter. The Government, however, had demanded that the truce be effected under the conditions it imposed. His oral reply and the public statement issued thereafter by Dr. Stuart and me had left no room for subsequent negotiation on the matter. While I had said that some of the Generalissimo's eight points represented concessions, they were actually not concessions but were related to PCC stipulations which had been violated by the Government. With regard to these eight points, the Government adhered to three formulae: (1) The Government would not withdraw from areas now under its control while the Communists would be withdrawn into certain positions, such as the 2½ provinces in Manchuria. (2) The Government would insist on the carrying out of the promises made by the Communists in June, such as the status of Harbin, but would not carry out promises made to the Communists, such as the positions held by troops of both sides on January 13 and June 7. (3) Demands made by the Government in June, to which the Communists did not assent, would now be insisted upon—these demands were, for example, the evacuation of troops from north Kiangsu and the withdrawal of local governments in certain places in Manchuria; demands made by the Communists in June, to which the Government did not agree, would be refused—the retention of a Communist garrison at Chengte was an example of such demands. The result would be that the Government would have the entire province under its control where it held the provincial capital and there would be little left in China proper under control of the Communists and in Manchuria they would be reduced to 2½ provinces. According to the Government formula not only would the Communist troops be separated and surrounded by Government forces but also the area of local self-government would be reduced to a minimum. Within the coalition government itself the Communists would also be reduced to a point of exercising no influence and all this was tantamount to forcing the Communists to surrender. The Government felt that it had gained a victory by occupying so many cities, but the Communists had never surrendered, not even in 1927 when they had no rifles. How could the Government then expect the Communists to surrender at this time? The Government had been on the offensive and the Communists on the defensive, but if there were a total break, the Communists would also enter into an all-out offensive and exploit the many points where the Government had only small forces.

I informed General Chou that I would not undertake to discuss the various points brought up by him, but that I merely wished to say that I accepted a part of his contentions as correct from my point of view and a part I did not accept as correct. I made further comment as follows: I found a great difference between the Government and myself and between the Communists and myself, and I deplored having small things and small delays preventing an understanding for the cessation of hostilities. The question then was, what were the small things and what were the large considerations. I agreed with his view of the probability of little likelihood of success in a meeting of the Committee of Three as there seemed to be more likelihood of ill will. There were two conflicting points of view between the Government and the Communists. Certain Government leaders were convinced that the Communists would not keep any agreements and that the only solution was the use of force. The Communists feared being placed in a position where military force could practically destroy their party or where the secret police could greatly oppress or terrorize them. The problem that Dr. Stuart and I now faced was to reach a compromise where we could obtain agreement for the cessation of hostilities and then proceed with the negotiations. I had nothing to offer at the moment except to deplore bringing into the discussions any points not vital to the fundamental requirements of the two sides. The distrust was greater than ever and there was all the more need to find some method, on which both sides could agree, for terminating the hostilities. The issue was now so confused, so many points had been brought into the discussions and exceptions had been taken to so many points of view of one or the other side, that the situation presented an almost impossible prospect for agreement—unless divested of every detail not vital to either party. Accordingly my last hope was that the Third Party Group might be able to find some basis for compromise and that was infinitely preferable to a mediation procedure by Americans, because it would then be a settlement of their own difficulties by the Chinese themselves. The Third Party Group appeared to be endeavoring to act in a strictly impartial manner and I thought that it would be a great mistake for General Chou to return to Yenan, as he had indicated was desired by Yenan because of the Generalissimo's absence in Formosa and the general military campaign under way. With the discussions already held with the Third Party Group and the Government representatives and with the expected return of the Generalissimo for further discussions, it might yet be possible to do something to terminate the fighting and then discuss the outstanding issues.

General Chou replied that he would like to make two points: (1) If, within the next few days, the Third Party Group could bring forth a compromise proposal with a sound basis, he would like to discuss it with them and that was his reason for remaining in Nanking. (2) As the military situation now stood, conditions were becoming more and more serious and the Government appeared to be attacking where it pleased; if that continued, there would be no basis for any kind of negotiations, in which event his presence in Nanking would seem useless.

I pointed out to General Chou that Dr. Stuart and I had tried every means possible to stop the fighting, without result—our proposal for the Five Man Committee to which the Government finally agreed but to which General Chou would not agree; the Kalgan truce proposal which General Chou had felt was equivalent to capitulation; and now we had reached another somewhat similar situation where we wished to end hostilities, and my hope was that the Third Party Group could be successful.

The conversation ended with another reference by General Chou to the Committee of Three and my participation therein, which, I felt, was perhaps his indirect means of placing me again in the position of a mediator.

On the following day (October 27) I described the above-outlined conversation with General Chou to General Yu Ta-wei and pointed out that there was little I could say to General Chou in the face of the open resumption of the Governemnt's military campaign in Manchuria, a campaign which had begun at the moment the Government representatives in Shanghai were asking General Chou to return to Nanking to resume negotiations. This factor, I said, in combination with the fact that the Generalissimo had not yet returned from Formosa served only to highlight the tragic situation. I concluded that the Third Party Group had asked me on several occasions to request the Generalissimo to return and that General Chou had come to see me only under pressure from the Third Party Group's leaders.

Although General Yu informed me, during the above-described conversation, that the Generalissimo had arrived in Shanghai on October 27 and would return to Nanking on the next day, I had already addressed a memorandum to him under that day's date, in which I said that I felt it highly important that he return to Nanking without delay. Dr. T.V. Soong had informed me on the previous day that the Generalissimo would arrive at Nanking on October 27 but on that day General Yu had told me that he would not return until the next day.

Later, during the same day (October 27), Dr. Lo Lung-chi and two other members of the Third Party Group called at my residence to report that this Group was facing a crisis in the negotiations because of the Government's capture of Antung, which had been occupied by Government troops on October 26. According to Dr. Lo, the Third Party Group had presented to the Communist Delegation on the previous day a three point proposal, practically all of which General Chou En-lai had unofficially accepted. When, later in the evening, news had been received of the Government occupation of Antung, however, General Chou had expressed the opinion that the Communists should break off all negotiations and that it would be useless to proceed further; in the meantime he must await instructions from Yenan.

I pointed out that I had not wished to enter the negotiations by asking the Generalisimo to return to Nanking but that his continued absence coupled with the current military campaign was now detrimental to the whole situation; I had, therefore, sent a message to the Generalissimo earlier in the afternoon urging him to return to Nanking. I then made the following comment to Dr. Lo in regard to the Government's military operations: Several days ago General Chen Cheng had told me that the Communist forces had attacked a Government Army somewhere between Fushun and Antung when it was being concentrated for return to north China and demobilization and that as a result the demobilization process was stopped and the drive on Antung was in the nature of a counter-attack on the same Communist forces disrupting the demobilization. This was a possible explanation for the attack on Antung, but the Government had offered no excuse for its offensive against Chefoo.

I urged that the Third Party Group not be too discouraged over what had happened as this kind of procedure and actions had occurred many times before and would probably occur again. I said that at the present this Group must sit squarely in the middle and remember that both sides were in a measure responsible for the seeming inability to agree.

Dr. Lo then described the three point proposal of the Third Party Group as follows:

> (1) All troops throughout the country were to remain in their present positions and the cessation of hostilities was to be effective immediately.

(2) The question of local governments throughout China, including Manchuria, would be decided by the State Council.

(3) The five PCC resolutions would be carried out in accordance with the PCC procedures specified.

He explained that the Third Party Group was giving consideration to having the formal convening of the National Assembly on November 12 but postponing all business until a month later for the purpose of awaiting the arrival of the minority and non-party delegates.

I pointed out that an indefinite delay in the business of the National Assembly might be fatal and would most likely lead to a winter campaign of total war. I said that it was an impractical proposition to reorganize the government within a few weeks and it was of paramount importance that the Third Party Group do everything possible to obtain early action in the National Assembly. They should, I said, have the State Council established, in which there would be a place for debate and discussion and time was of great importance. In all this, I pointed out, it was essential to keep in mind the present weakness of the Executive Headquarters, which had been brought about by provocative Communist propaganda against Americans. In commenting on their three point proposal, I expressed the opinion that the first point was certainly sound, that the second point was merely a question of obtaining Government agreement thereto and that the third point might possibly lay them open to several pitfalls, particularly in getting involved in detailed procedure; in this it would be necessary to make compromises and the Third Party Group must preserve the condition that the government would be reorganized some time in the near future and not three or four years later. I concluded with emphasis on the necessity of avoiding involvement in statements of too general or too detailed a nature.

On October 28 I had a further conversation with Dr. Carson Chang and Dr. Lo Lung-chi, Democratic League members of the Third Party Group. Dr. Chang said that it was most important for the Group to obtain a list of the Communist delegates to the National Assembly, which he felt was essential if the Group's three point proposal were to be acceptable to both sides. He said that the Group was, however, confronted with a situation where the Government did not wish to make any further concessions beyond those already set forth in the Generalissimo's eight points; if the Government refused to make any political concessions, the Third Party Group's proposal would be considerably less acceptable to the Communists, who felt that they must insist on the reorganization of the Executive Yuan prior to naming their delegates to the National Assembly.

I then explained the efforts during the past months of negotiations to bring about the cessation of hostilities and pointed out that the designation of Communist delegates to the National Assembly and the question of local government in Manchuria now remained as unsettled issues. I again emphasized the necessity of the Third Party Group's avoiding submerging the crux of the issues in a mass of details and allowing themselves to be sidetracked into matters of detail.

Dr. Chang referred to the desire of the Third Party Group for democratic principles and stated that it seemed that the more military power the Kuomintang acquired or the stronger the army became the less democratic was the Government. He charged that the Generalissimo was a dictator and had been one for twenty years and that he was accustomed to complete and unquestioned authority. He felt that even if the State Council were established and met once every two weeks, it would be very easy for the Generalissimo to set the Council aside and ignore it. Dr. Lo, in turn, emphasized the importance of the reorganization of the Executive Yuan if the other parties were to have a chance for effective participation in the Government, as there would be no elements in the Executive Yuan to check on the elections until the Government should have been reorganized.

When Dr. Lo referred to the Generalissimo's belief that he would always have the support of the United States Government under any circumstances, I stated that Government officials had been disillusioned and discouraged considerably in that belief. I concluded that I realized that this feeling existed but I felt that they had been disabused by virtue of the fact that the Government had not been receiving military supplies or munitions from the United States for many months.

On October 29 Dr. Stuart informed me that the Third

Party Group had forwarded a three point proposal[76] to the Generalissimo, a copy of which Dr. Stuart exhibited to me. The three points were essentially those described to me by Dr. Lo Lung-chi on October 27, with the addition of more specified provisions. The first point regarding the cessation of hostilities provided that the location of the Communist troops should be determined in advance in Tsitsihar, Peian and Chiamussu (cities in north Manchuria). The second point regarding local government provided for the sending of Government railway police to take over points along the Changchun Railway except for the *hsien* already under Government occupation. The third point was less general in calling for adherence to PCC procedures and called specifically for the convening of the PCC Steering Committee and the PCC Constitution Reviewing Committee.

Dr. Stuart explained that the Generalissimo felt unable to accept the proposal and had sent for the Third Party Group representatives to tell them that they should have adopted his own eight point proposal of October 16.

I then described to Dr. Stuart my conversation of the previous evening with the Generalissimo: I had told the Generalissimo what Dr. Stuart and I had been doing and had recited recent events, some of them encouraging and some of them discouraging. I had then expanded on the efforts of the Third Party Group and the extent of their discouragement, which had become so great that they had wished to withdraw from the negotiations and return to Shanghai. I had tried to encourage the Group and had prevailed upon them not to return to Shanghai. The present Government military campaign had, however, almost ruined any prospect for agreement. When the Generalissimo had inquired of me regarding my opinion of the position and intentions of the Communists, I had replied that the Communists would now believe practically nothing that the Government said and were convinced that the Government aim was to annihilate the Communist forces and destroy the Communist Party; the Government's military campaigns against Antung and Chefoo, together with the Generalissimo's absence in Formosa, had served to destroy in the minds of the Communists any prospects of reaching an agreement. I had also told the Generalissimo that the Communists had no intention of surrendering and that they

[76]See Volume Two, Appendix P, Document 1, for the full text.

desired a complete cessation of hostilities but did not know what steps to take to obtain it. I had pointed out that the Communists had lost cities but not armies and that it was not likely that they would lose their armies, as they had no intention of making a stand or of fighting to a finish at any place. The Generalissimo might be able to take Harbin but the Government would then be in for endless tribulation. Added to the distrust of the motives of the Generalissimo and the Kuomintang leaders was the distrust the Communists now felt toward Americans.

The Generalissimo replied that the time had come to terminate the fighting but asked that I say nothing of this to the Third Party Group. I had then explained to the Generalissimo that this Group appeared to be the only hope in the situation and had urged him to show them every consideration and build up their prestige by making concessions and encouraging them to speak frankly to him. I had then asked the Generalissimo to meet with the Third Party Group representatives on the following morning (October 29) and listen to their proposals or views. This the Generalissimo had agreed to do.

On October 30 Dr. Stuart informed me that the Generalissimo had told him that day that he was prepared to make two additional concessions:

> (1) The cease-fire order would apply to Manchuria as well as to China proper. Military redispositions would follow the June settlement. Local administration would be dealt with uniformly in all of China.

> (2) Cities and *hsien* along the Changchun Railway trunkline, except for those already under occupation by the Government, would not be taken over before the reorganization of the State Council.

As I informed some of the Third Party Group members at this time, the present stand of the Communists was not logical. They always insisted that the Government generals were determined to settle present issues by force; yet the Communists were apparently risking the continuation and expansion of the war in the hope that the Government would make concessions in order to obtain the list of Communist delegates to the National Assembly. Further, the issues of the State Council and local government were not now difficult to solve and it seemed that the principal outstanding issue was now the reorganization of the Executive Yuan. The Communists and the Democratic League seemed to attach great importance to this issue as a condition precedent to the convening of the National Assembly. If the Government would agree to appoint members of the Communist Party and of the other minority parties to head certain ministries without portfolio and to one or two other ministries under the Executive Yuan, the Communists might be persuaded to come to terms. I had concentrated my efforts on building up the Third Party Group so that a political settlement could be achieved, but some of them had become so discouraged that they were considering returning to Shanghai; the problem was to make this Group aware of the fact that the military settlement was greatly affected by political issues and that the members of the Group should stand together and remain strong under the pressure of the Government and the Communists to divide them.

On November 3 Dr. Carson Chang and Dr. Lo Lung-chi called on me for further discussion of the situation. Dr. Chang stated that he had presented to the Generalissimo on the previous day the idea of an informal meeting of Kuomintang, Communist Party and Third Party Group representatives. The Generalissimo, he said, had seemed to have accepted the idea and General Chou En-lai had also been receptive to the proposal. He continued that plans had been made for a general meeting of these representatives on the following day and that an agenda of outstanding issues to be discussed by the various committees would be drawn up.

In reply to Dr. Chang's request for my comments, I said that I saw no point in a meeting of the Committee of Three at present as this Committee could deal only with military issues. I pointed out that there could be no profitable discussion regarding military dispositions unless the fighting was first terminated and that the question now was how to achieve a cessation of hostilities through political settlement. I suggested that the Third Party Group concentrate its efforts on settling the outstanding political issue between the Kuomintang and the Communists: that was, when and to whom the Communists were to submit the names of their delegates to the National Assembly. (The Government would not agree to the cessation of hostilities until the Communists submitted a list of such delegates and the Communists were willing to submit the list only to a reorganized government.)

Dr. Chang expressed the opinion that the Government should do three things prior to the reorganization of the Executive Yuan: (1) establish a uniform civil service system so that it would provide a standard of employment for all ministries; (2) set up a budgetary system so that each ministry would confine itself within the appropriation allocated to it under this system; and (3) establish a fundamental policy for each ministry.

On November 4 Dr. Stuart informed me that he had received two messages from Mr. Wang Ping-nan of the Communist Delegation, the gist of which indicated that Mr. Wang desired Dr. Stuart's frank advice in regard to Communist action in the current negotiations. Specifically, Mr. Wang wished to know what the American reaction would be if the National Assembly convened without Communist participation. Dr. Stuart said he thought that the Generalissimo would postpone the date of the National Assembly if the Communists indicated a definite intention of participating and that he would issue a cease-fire order if the minority parties, excluding the Communists, would indicate their intention of joining the Assembly.

I said that the major issue at this time appeared to be the Communist desire for the reorganization of the Executive Yuan, which was related to the Communist refusal to submit the list of the Assembly delegates except to a reorganized government—this to them meant the reorganization of the Executive Yuan. I described Dr. Carson Chang's comments on the things he considered necessary prior to the reorganization of that Yuan and mentioned the possibility of General Chou En-lai's appointment as Minister of Communications.

Dr. Stuart replied that the Generalissimo had said that he would not reorganize the Executive Yuan until after the meeting of the National Assembly and that Dr. T.V. Soong had told him today that as far as he was concerned no Communists would be included in the Executive Yuan reorganization at this time. Dr. Soong had added that possibly after the Government had been reorganized Communists could be taken into the Executive Yuan gradually in accordance with popular elections.

On November 5 Dr. Stuart and I called by appointment on the Generalissimo and held a lengthy discussion of the situation. I referred to the scheduled meeting of representatives of the Kuomintang, the Communist Party and the Third Party Group, which had been described to me by Dr. Carson

349

Chang, and told the Generalissimo that I had been informed that the meeting had not been held because the Government had declined to participate.

The Generalissimo explained that the Government would not participate because of indications that the Communists wished to eliminate American mediation. To this, I replied that I regretted the failure to meet for this reason because it was not a matter that could be settled by pressure—the Communists either accepted us as mediators or did not accept us, they trusted us or they did not trust us and the decision in this matter could not be reached in any other way.

The Generalissimo then referred to a meeting held by the Third Party Group with General Chou En-lai on November 5, during which General Chou at the request of that Group had stated the Communists' demands:

(1) The Communists would not accept an exchange of the list of their National Assembly delegates for a cease-fire order;

(2) A settlement must include more than agreement for the reorganization of the Executive Yuan as there was also the question of local government and the Generalissimo's four promises at the PCC;

(3) Troops may stay in their present positions after the cessation of hostilities; and

(4) Political procedures: (a) reorganization of the government, including the Executive Yuan; (b) convening of the Constitution Reviewing Committee with guarantees that its draft constitution will be adopted by the National Assembly; (c) agreement upon the distribution of additional National Assembly delegates and the date of the Assembly; (d) settlement of the local government question to include Manchuria and to be carried out in accordance with the PCC resolutions; (e) fulfillment of the Generalissimo's four promises;

Military: (a) total cessation of hostilities; (b) restoration of original military positions, as 80 percent of the Government troops were now in Communist territory; (c) restoration of communications everywhere; and (d) reaching of a decision regarding the authority and function of the Executive Headquarters and its field teams.

The Generalissimo continued that General Chou's reference to the settlement of disputes in teams and in the Executive Headquarters indicated the Communist desire to eliminate American mediation. I said that I disagreed, as most of the other points were involved in these adverse implications. The Generalissimo concluded the discussion by saying that the time had come to stop the fighting and that he was prepared for the unconditional cessation of hostilities and wished us to advise him regarding an announcement to that effect and also with reference to the approaching meeting of the National Assembly.

The following morning Dr. Stuart and I discussed what form an announcement by the Generalissimo should take. I felt that he should issue a cease-fire order and capitalize on it in such a way that it would give sufficient encouragement to the Communists for them to continue negotiations toward the reorganization of the government. After general discussion we agreed that the statement should contain an announcement that the Generalissimo had issued a cease-fire order as of a certain time, that he intended to convene the National Assembly as scheduled and that he was prepared to adjourn the Assembly immediately after the first meeting in order to permit: (1) the development of a reasonable plan for the Communists to designate and assemble their delegates to the Assembly; (2) completion of the draft constitution by the Constitution Reviewing Committee in accordance with the PCC resolutions; (3) allotment of 10 seats in the State Council to the Communists, thus reducing the non-party members to 2; and (4) reorganization of the Executive Yuan. A plan worked out by the Embassy at my request set forth the general ideas contained in the above-described points and provided for a division of the present 18 ministries and commissions under the Executive Yuan as follows: Kuomintang—11; Communist Party—3; Democratic League—2; and Youth Party—2. One of the principal ministries was to be given to each of the Communist Party and Democratic League under this plan and five ministers without portfolio were to be alloted to non-party persons.

Prior to the completion of our draft statement for presentation to the Generalissimo, we reached most confidentially the draft of such a statement prepared by him. It was discouraging to read his draft, as it was provocative and confusing and its language so submerged the principal idea of the cessation of hostilities that the true significance of the statement had been lost. Our draft[77] consisted of the following principal points:

> Orders have been issued to all Government troops to cease firing except as may be necessary to defend their present positions. The Government desires to reach an immediate agreement with the Communist Party for an unconditional termination of hostilities.
>
> The Government has decided formally to convene the National Assembly on November 12 and is prepared to agree to an immediate but temporary adjournment of the Assembly until the following conditions have been fulfilled:
>
> "1. Sufficient time has been allowed to permit the selection and arrival of delegates who have not yet been selected.
>
> "2. Reorganization of the State Council has been agreed to by the PCC Steering Committee and the Council established.
>
> "3. The Draft Constitutional Committee shall have completed its work on a basis of the principles set forth in the PCC agreements.
>
> "When these conditions have been fulfilled the National Assembly shall reconvene and proceed to the adoption of the Draft Constitution in the form presented."
>
> According to the PCC resolutions the reorganization of the Executive Yuan is a function of the State Council and furthermore it involves a drastic change in the administration of the Government which must be approached with careful deliberation.

The gist of the Generalissimo's draft statement is as follows:

> The Communist Party was to blame for the failure to carry out the cease-fire agreement, the restoration of communications agreement and the military reorganization agreement.

[77]See Volume Two, Appendix P, Document 2, for the full text.

That Party had been guilty of various military activities, and it had violated all the PCC resolutions. Government military activities had been self-defense measures. Orders had been issued to Government troops to remain in their present positions and to cease attacks on the Communists.

The Government would preserve the Communist quota of delegates to the National Assembly and hoped that they would participate therein. The Communists were asked to participate in a meeting of the Committee of Three to discuss troop dispositions, the immediate implementation of measures for restoring communications and the reorganization and integration of armies on the basis of the Generalissimo's eight points. The National Assembly would convene on November 12. After adjournment of the Assembly, the Government would be ready to broaden the basis of the Government in accordance with the PCC so that all parties could participate in the National Government and the Executive Yuan. The Government would submit to the National Assembly the unfinished revised draft of the Draft Constitution Committee, but the Government would show full respect to the National Assembly in free exercising of its legal functions. Within six months after adjournment of the present National Assembly, general elections would be held and in the second National Assembly all parties would have ample opportunity to propose constitutional amendments.

On November 7 Dr. Stuart and I called on the Generalissimo and presented to him a Chinese translation of our draft statement. We pointed out to him that the draft statement would receive a very unfavorable reception abroad because of its length, its repetition of old arguments and its provocative nature. We also said that, so far as we could anticipate, it would arouse bitter feeling among the minority parties and would lose most of the valuable effect which might result from a statement that hostilities would be terminated.

The Generalissimo replied that in preparing his draft he had to take into consideration a number of important points:

(a) While previously there had been a difference of opinion regarding the proper course of action for the Government, there had very recently been unanimity in the Government regarding the course to be followed—that was one of force, the belief being that by no other method could matters be finally settled.

(b) He must give careful consideration to the National Assembly delegates legally elected in 1936, who were now in Nanking. If they were ignored by a prolonged delay of the Assembly, a very serious situation would arise which might even involve riots in Nanking. Furthermore, if he unduly accentuated the PCC influence on the procedure of the Assembly in regard to consideration of the constitution, he would seriously offend this large group in the Kuomintang.

(c) He must give very careful consideration to the Army in view of the losses sustained in carrying forward a military campaign as the announcement of cessation of hostilities amounted to virtual surrender of the Government's position. He said that the reference in our draft to an unconditional cessation of hostilities could not be supported by him before the Kuomintang military and political leaders.

(d) He stood practically alone in the belief that matters could and should be settled by peaceful negotiations and the fighting stopped.

The Generalissimo concluded by asking us to consider his statements and to advise him accordingly regarding the public statement he should make.

I replied that I would have to have an opportunity to consult with Dr. Stuart as I was seriously concerned whether I should participate as a representative of the U.S. Government in the preparation of a paper in accordance with the point of view he had indicated, which was generally antagonistic to my views and, I thought, to those of my Government. I added that I would, however, discuss the matter with Dr. Stuart.

During this conversation the Generalissimo stressed his objection to temporary adjournment of the National Assembly once it had convened, as proposed in our draft, on the grounds that this would probably be of indefinite length, would provoke the Government members assembled in Nanking to serious reactions and would be taken as a rather complete surrender of the postion which had been held up to this time by the Government.

On November 8 Dr. Stuart and I again called on the Generalissimo at his request. We had hurriedly prepared a redraft of our statement to represent the points of view expressed by the Generalissimo and to eliminate those portions which were opposed to his viewpoint. The following are the main points of this draft:

> Orders have been issued for all Government troops to cease firing except as may be necessary to defend their present positions.
>
> The Government has decided formally to open the National Assembly on November 12 and would reserve the Communist quota of delegates in the hope that they would participate in making the constitution. The Government also hoped that the Communists would authorize their representatives to participate in meetings of the committees to discuss immediate implementation of measures for the restoration of communications and the reorganization and integration of armies as proposed in the Generalissimo's statement of October 16. Agreement should be reached for the reorganization of the State Council and the Council should be formally established in order that it might immediately carry out its functions for reorganization of the Government in accordance with the PCC resolutions. The Government would submit to the National Assembly the uncompleted draft of the Constitution Reviewing Committee and whatever decision should be reached by the present National Assembly should be regarded as tentative pending further revision by a body representative of all parties to be adopted at the following Assembly.

Upon our arrival the Generalissimo said that there was to be a meeting of his political and military advisers at 1 p.m. to decide (1) whether there should be a cessation of hostilities and (2) whether the National Assembly should be postponed. This was the reason he had wished to see us.

We presented our draft with an oral statement of the various points which he had made and which had been included therein. I informed the Generalissimo that in submitting this draft I wished it understood that the statement did not have my approval as a representative of the U.S. Government since we had merely endeavored to help him as staff officers might assist him in drafting his views, but in the least provocative manner. To make doubly certain that he understood my meaning, I repeated this statement very carefully at the end of the meeting and added that I was in rather complete disagreement with his military leaders.

The Generalissimo asked us to hold ourselves in readiness to meet with him after his meeting with his leaders and expressed his thanks for our efforts and his understanding of our position.

During this meeting with the Generalissimo, Dr. Stuart described at some length a meeting of the previous evening between General Chou En-lai and representatives of the Third Party Group, during which a decision had been made by the minority parties that a reply should be submitted to the Generalissimo's formal proposal of October 16. General Chou had expressed the view that the date of the National Assembly should be postponed for a limited period of one or two weeks during which successful negotiations by the committees might be achieved.

As a result of this meeting between General Chou and the Third Party Group, the former, under date of November 8, forwarded to me a letter,[78] which, in effect, constituted a reply to the Generalissimo's eight point proposal. The letter was non-committal and referred only casually to the eight points, but it did hold open hope for continued negotiations and peace. I immediately forwarded a copy of the letter to the Government on the same day.

On the evening of November 8 a member of the Generalissimo's staff brought to Dr. Stuart and me a copy of the statement which the Generalissimo proposed to issue that evening. I stated that I appreciated the Generalissimo's permitting us to see the statement prior to publication but that I had no comment to make thereon, as I was opposed to the Government's attitude. The statement,[79] which was issued by the Generalissimo that evening, differed in some respects from the final draft we had presented to the Generalissimo.

[78]See Volume Two, Appendix P, Document 3, for the full text.

[79]See Volume Two, Appendix P, Document 4, for the full text.

The main points of the statement are as follows:

The Generalissimo's eight point proposal of October 16 would be the basis for the termination of hostilities. Orders had been issued for all Government troops in China proper and in the Northeast to cease firing except as might be necessary to defend their present positions.

The Government would formally convene the National Assembly on November 12 and would reserve the quota of delegates for the Communists as well as for other parties in the hope that they would participate in the making of the constitution. The Government also hoped that the Communists would authorize their representatives to participate in meetings of the committees to discuss the immediate implementation of measures for the cessation of hostilities, disposition of troops, restoration of communications and reorganization and integration of armies, as proposed in the Generalissimo's statement of October 16. It was hoped that early agreement for the reorganization of the State Council would be reached and the Council formally established. The reorganization of the Executive Yuan could not be effected prior to the adjournment of the present National Assembly. The Government would submit to the National Assembly the uncompleted draft of the Constitution Reviewing Committee. Within six months after the adjournment of the present National Assembly, general elections would be held in accordance with the adopted constitution in order to bring into existence the next National Assembly, and amendments, if modification were found necessary in the next Assembly, could still be introduced by all parties.

The chief differences, referred to above, were in the references to the State Council, the Executive Yuan and the draft constitution to be adopted. In the statement issued by the Generalissimo, he expressed hope that the State Council would be reorganized in order to carry out its functions for the reorganization of the government in accordance with the PCC resolutions. This would include the reorganization of the Executive

Yuan, but the Generalissimo's statement merely said that such reorganization would not take place prior to the meeting of the National Assembly and made no mention of the PCC resolutions.

During the period preceding the announcement by the Generalissimo of his issuance of a cease-fire order to Government troops, there had been no signs of improvement in the military situation. Fighting continued along the Peiping-Hankow Railway in north Honan and south Hopei and there were indications of Government preparations for an offensive north from the Hsinhsiang-Anyang area in north Honan. The Communist members of the Advance Section of the Executive Headquarters at Changchun informed the U.S. members of that Section that the June 7 truce had been broken by the Government campaign against Antung and that the Communists proposed to cease their participation in field team investigations. They suggested that the teams be withdrawn and questioned the usefulness of the Advance Section under existing circumstances. The U.S. representatives urged the retention of the teams in the hope of implementing future agreements and for the purpose of investigation of the Antung offensive as a matter of official record, as a result of which the Communists agreed to continued tentative cooperation. Shortly after agreement had been reached on this point, the Government forces occupied Tunghua, which had been one of the cities in Manchuria from which the Government had demanded the withdrawal of Communist forces at the time of the Generalissimo's absence in Formosa.

Another factor of considerable importance in the situation was the decreased effectiveness of the Executive Headquarters as a result of the vicious Communist propaganda attacks on the Americans. In response to my request, the U.S. Commissioner of the Executive Headquarters prepared a study of the extent to which the functions of the Executive Headquarters had been impaired by these attacks, the principal points of which are as follows:

> The field teams have been adversely affected by the ill will against and suspicion of U.S. officers created in the minds of the rank and file of the Communist Party. Demonstrations against Americans indicate complete lack of spontaneity and anti-American campaigns in liberated areas under Communist control have apparently been unproductive

358

insofar as the people and soldiers in the non-formal army are concerned. There is no doubt that the distrust and feeling of antagonism on the part of the regular army and the usual petty officials with whom the teams are in frequent contact have been intensified. The work of teams in the Communist areas will be retarded but the effect of the propaganda has not yet reached the point of destroying their usefulness. However, the situation would be largely overcome by successful negotiations in Nanking leading to a truce. Thereafter, a reversal of the present anti-American propaganda would greatly assist the U.S. members in achieving complete effectiveness in contacts with the Communists.

The Generalissimo's issuance of a cease-fire order set the stage for the convening of the National Assembly against a background of peace rather than civil war. The method of stopping the fighting, however, was not, in my opinion, conclusive and it still held, in effect, the evident threat of renewed fighting to force a political decision. Of more importance the Government's approach to the National Assembly was not sufficiently in accordance with the PCC agreements and meant that, if all the delegates appeared, a simple majority vote of the overwhelming Kuomintang members could determine the character of the constitution without much consideration of the fundamental guarantees agreed to in the PCC. The Government had been unwilling to agree to any temporary adjournment after the formal convocation, which had been proposed by Dr. Stuart and me, and had missed, we thought, an excellent opportunity of capitalizing in a conciliatory manner on the proposal to stop the fighting.

XXX.
INFORMAL MEETING OF THE COMMITTEE OF THREE; CONVENING OF THE NATIONAL ASSEMBLY ON NOVEMBER 15; AND THE RETURN OF GENERAL CHOU EN-LAI TO YENAN

On November 9 General Yu Ta-wei presented to me a

memorandum from General Chen Cheng, Government member of the Committee of Three, in which he stated that the President of the National Government had issued an order on November 8 to all troops in China to stop fighting and remain in their present positions and that this order would become effective at noon on November 11. General Chen asked that I notify the Communist representative on the Committee of Three and request his attendance at a meeting of that Committee to discuss measures for the cessation of hostilities.

In reply to my question regarding the Generalissimo's intentions in connection with such a meeting, General Yu said that it would first probably be necessary for the Communists to issue a cease-fire order and then for the Committee of Three to confer in order to develop various provisions that would be necessary to establish troop redispositions or readjustments, as the separation of troops was perhaps the most important thing to be done.

I replied that the separation of troops would immediately involve the Committee of Three in certain arrangements which would have to be worked out very carefully in order that there would be common understanding by all concerned.

On the following day (November 10) General Chou En-lai, to whom I had sent a copy of General Chen Cheng's memorandum, called to seek more information regarding the situation with particular reference to the Government's issuance of a cease-fire order and its request for a meeting of the Committee of Three.

I commented as follows to General Chou: I assumed that the Generalissimo's cease-fire order was intended to create a more favorable situation for the meeting of the National Assembly. My efforts had been to obtain an agreement for the formal cessation of hostilities and I had been encouraged by General Chen Cheng's request, as my assumption was that he would desire to discuss the cessation of hostilities and wanted agreement on an order for the troops of both sides. (General Yu Ta-wei confirmed to me later in the day that the Government intention was to discuss in the Committee of Three only the question of the cessation of hostilities.)

In reply, General Chou made the following remarks: He recalled that the Government order to its troops at the end of the June negotiations had been phrased somewhat like the present cease-fire order, but, in the months following, the Government had embarked on a large scale military campaign. He felt, therefore, that, except for changing the atmosphere in Nanking, the cease-fire order would bring no substantial change in the situation. The manner of convening of the National Assembly was contrary to the PCC resolutions and the Assembly would not be recognized by the Communist Party. The crux of the issue now was that the Government would either call off the National Assembly and, in accordance with the PCC resolutions, convene the PCC Steering Committee to settle all issues in accordance with those resolutions and PCC procedures—that is, reorganization of the government, completion of the revision of the draft constitution, discussion of matters regarding the Assembly and local government and the protection of the freedom and rights of the people—or else the Kuomintang Government would ignore the opinions of the Communists and the other parties and formally convene the Assembly on November 12 as a legal organ. Should that occur, there would be nothing that could be done, the PCC procedures would be completely destroyed and there would be absolutely no basis for any kind of meeting for discussion of political issues. The Communists welcomed a meeting of the Committee of Three, but prior to that meeting General Chou felt he must have a clear understanding of two points: (1) If the discussion of political matters during the two days intervening before the scheduled meeting of the National Assembly were not successful and the Assembly were not postponed, there would be, in effect, a political split, which would exert an effect on military matters—the question, therefore, was whether the discussion of a cease-fire agreement would be successful. (2) According to the Generalissimo's statement, discussion in the Committee of Three would be based on the eight point proposal, which was unacceptable to the Communists; in other words, the meeting would open with little likelihood of success.

I informed General Chou that it was my impression, judging from General Yu Ta-wei's statement, that the Generalissimo desired results from the Committee by the morning of November 11, that the question was only one of the issuance of a joint cease-fire order, as the limited time would certainly not permit of agreement on troop redispositions or related matters. As the Communists had long been insisting upon the total cessation of hostilities, I thought that General Chou should take advantage of this opportunity to terminate the fighting prior to a settlement of political issues.

General Chou made the following reply: It was true that the Communists had been struggling for a cessation of hostilities, which they wished to be a genuine and lasting peace and not a false one as occurred after the March 27 agreement and the end of the June negotiations. Yet if agreement were reached on the cessation of hostilities and at the same time the Kuomintang went ahead with its plans for the National Assembly, the effect would be a military truce on one hand and a political split on the other. In that event, the effectiveness of a military truce would be open to doubt. If there were no possibility of calling off the National Assembly and convening the Committee of Three and the PCC Steering Committee for the purpose of reaching an over-all solution, his whole mission would be placed on a questionable basis and the Communist Delegation would need to return to Yenan for the purpose of discussion and seeking new instructions under the changed situation.

I replied as follows: I had had no information which would indicate that the Government would agree to a delay in convening the National Assembly or to a temporary adjournment after the formal convocation for the purpose of certain actions, such as the completion of the draft constitution by the Constitution Reviewing Committee and the reorganization of the State Council. I had hoped for some such compromise to allow for taking such actions. I frankly felt that General Chou had, regardless of the provocation, reached the point where he believed nothing because of his overwhelming suspicions. Time after time I had exerted pressure on the Government to obtain a moderation of its stand only to find that my results, representing matters desired by the Communists and the other minority parties, were viewed with suspicion. I had welcomed the entry of the third parties into the negotiations to relieve me from the burden of misunderstandings, and I had been encouraged by the Government's request for discussion of the cessation of hostilities. Now, however, I was discouraged by General Chou's reaction. I thought that he should be on guard against such overwhelming suspicion in endeavoring to estimate logically the situation, especially in view of the tremendous factors involved for the people of China.

General Chou replied that in view of the apparent indications that the National Assembly would not be postponed, he was confused regarding the way in which he should report to Yenan, as he did not understand how a military cease-fire could work out along with a political split.

I replied that I agreed with him regarding the confusion as I was not accustomed to the peculiar ways of Chinese political maneuvering and could not always be certain of what was behind the various political moves of the two sides; but that I believed, "where there is life there is hope" and I had been going ahead on that basis for many months. I felt that the Communists, I said, had given more attention to details of procedure than to principles in their insistence on the PCC resolutions. I would certainly advise General Chou to participate in the Committee of Three meeting, by which he could determine whether it was merely a matter of a cease-fire order. This, I pointed out, could be agreed to very quickly and he would also be able to determine whether that might lead to adjustments regarding the issues of the National Assembly and the reorganization of the Government. I added that I felt for some time that we had missed an opportunity to head off much that had happened militarily since last summer by the proposal for the Five Man Committee to decide on the State Council issue. This, I said, could have been achieved if General Chou had not insisted on an unconditional cessation of hostilities. General Chen's proposal meant just that and I had been encouraged and had felt that success on this matter would improve the chances for effecting some agreement on political issues.

General Chou said that there were now different factors to be considered, as at the time of the proposal for the Five Man Committee there remained ample time for discussion of the National Assembly and the Government had since that time occupied many Communist areas. He added that he would attend an informal meeting of the PCC Steering Committee that day to make another effort on the political side and would be willing to participate in an informal meeting of the Committee of Three so that he might learn General Chen's ideas regarding military matters and their relation to political issues.

As a result of General Chou's agreement, an informal meeting of the Committee of Three was held on the morning of November 11, the first meeting of the Committee of Three since the negotiations in June. At the outset, I requested the members of the Committee to exercise as much restraint as possible in the discussion in view of the strong feeling of which we were all aware.

General Chou first stated that the cessation of hostilities was the most important of the military problems and he hoped that that subject would be discussed, leaving the related problems, such as reorganization of the armies and restoration of communications, for discussion in the very near future.

General Chou commented as follows: He recalled two different kinds of experience in the past. The first of these included the January 10 cease-fire agreement, the March 27 agreement for the entry of teams into Manchuria, and the armistice agreement for Manchuria during June. The second kind of experience was that at the end of June when the Government issued a unilateral cease-fire order. Under that order, Government troops had made great military gains and eighty-six percent of the Government troops had been massed in areas adjacent to Communist territory or in the Communists' own areas. In view of these two experiences, he was very much confused regarding the present Government cease-fire order for the following reasons: (1) He had received reports indicating Government encirclement of and movement toward Yenan and (2) the Government liaison officer at Yenan was preparing to evacuate and Government reconnaissance planes were active over Yenan. As the Government forces were also attacking in north Kiangsu and along the Peiping-Hankow Railway, all these circumstances led him to presume that the present cease-fire order might come under the second category of the experiences he had described. A more serious political factor was the meeting of the National Assembly on the next day. The Government had informed the Third Party Group that the PCC Steering Committee would not meet today and that the only way to save the situation was for the Communists, the other minority parties and non-party personnel to submit their lists of delegates to the National Assembly. There now seemed to be no basis for approaching the question of the cessation of hostilities as military matters always followed political matters; on the one hand there would be a political split and on the other a unilateral cease-fire order which retained the convenient "pretext of defense." He wished to ask the Government members (General Chen and General Yu Ta-wei) if they thought that there was still some chance to save the situation. If there were still some possibility of saving the political situation, he could also give every consideration to possibilities in the military field.

General Chen then outlined his idea of the measures for the cessation of hostilities: First, hostilities would be terminated on the spot and field teams would be sent to make the necessary adjustments; second, after the arrival of the teams, ways and means would be worked out to separate opposing forces and to arrange for the necessary movement of forces;

and third, some means would be worked out for solving disagreements in the field teams and in the Executive Headquarters. General Chen concluded that if agreement were reached on military problems he hoped that it would have an influence on the political problems leading to a better understanding on political issues.

I then made the following comments: The important step was to have this meeting of the Committee of Three. I had stated in a number of meetings that I did not agree with either side and I wished to restate that most emphatically at this time. Whatever the political complications now in view of the meeting of the National Assembly on the next day and whatever the determining effect that meeting might have, I felt that an arrangement for the termination of hostilities—not a truce—could not fail to have a beneficial effect in restoring some measure of confidence, which would enable a political compromise of some kind to be reached. The fact that the Government had issued a cease-fire order under certain conditions in a unilateral decision was incidental, in my opinion, to the important question of whether the opportunity should be seized to terminate hostilities in a definite manner. Certainly there would be no loss involved in the cessation of hostilities so far as the Chinese people were concerned. I agreed with General Chou that the situation was curious and complicated in that with very serious political differences existing at this moment, we were, I assumed, approaching a possible military agreement. When I thought, however, of all the complications which had robbed us of success during the past ten months, this particular complication which involved the cessation of hostilities was the least serious. I had resented throughout my connection with these discussions the continuation of hostilities and I had deplored the actions of retaliation which had been our greatest evil. My views might be summed up as follows—if we could find an immediate way to end hostilities, it could not fail to improve the general situation; the quicker this was done, the better for all.

General Chou said that the difficulty at present was the scheduled meeting of the National Assembly, at which time all political discussion would have to be stopped. He felt that since political discussions could not possibly be held today it was inconceivable to attempt to solve military issues. Once the National Assembly convened, he added, the party in power would say that it was a legal body and the opposing parties would deny its legality—thus the country would be split.

General Chou continued that he was not yet in a position to give a concrete reply as he was not prepared, but that he would still make every effort and would like to hear General Chen's detailed statement on his proposal, following which he would be able to report to Yenan and make his own study of the matter.

General Chen replied that the following was the Government's unilateral proposal as a basis for further discussion: (1) The commanders of forces in close contact or engaged in actual fighting would immediately cease firing and seek a local truce by establishing liaison with the opposing commanders pending the arrival of a field team; (2) field teams would, if necessary, require readjustment of troops in close contact or engaged in fighting, requiring withdrawal for specified distances of one or both according to the circumstances—the local situation believed to have existed as of noon on November 11, 1946, would be the basis for determining adjustments; (3) if disagreement occurred among members of field teams, in the Advance Section at Changchun or in the Executive Headquarters, it should be settled by following the stipulations provided for in June; and (4) reorganization and disposition of armies would be further discussed and settled by the Committee of Three at the earliest possible time.

General Chou commented as follows on these points: If there were needed some reference for discussion, he would like to point out that the Committee of Three had four draft papers during the June negotiations, which might serve now as a basis. If they were compared with General Chen's paper, certain points would be found to be similar but there was also wide disparity. This disparity could be interpreted in two ways —first, that the cease fire arrangement would be implemented on the spot, on which point there was common ground, but the second point was the question of what status would be restored in reference to troop positions. In the June documents there were two steps—within 10 days the June 7 status would be restored throughout the country and, as the next step, within 20 days the January 13 status would be restored in China proper. Of this General Chen's proposal made no mention. General Chou was not prepared to discuss the proposal at this time, but he would commit himself to transmit it to Yenan and to make his own study thereof. In this informal meeting he was assuming the attitude of trying to exercise some influence on the political negotiations and was thus making his last effort.

General Chen pointed out that the question of troop dispositions would certainly be a matter for discussion but that the first thing to do was to settle the question of the cessation of hostilities. He said that he did not recall what garrison areas were stipulated in the cessation of hostilities document for Manchuria during the June negotiations.

I interposed to say that the garrison areas in Manchuria were stipulated, to which General Chou said that during the June truce negotiations there were stipulations regarding the restoration of troop positions on the basis of the status of June 7 but that no agreement was reached on the stipulation regarding the location of divisional commands, although both parties had made proposals on this matter.

After further comment by General Chou on this subject, I suggested that the Committee adjourn to meet at a time agreed upon by the two Chinese members. No date was agreed upon during this meeting, and the discussions ended with General Yu pointing out that it was not advisable to waste too much time on debate as this would only delay the solving of the cease-fire question.

Dr. Stuart informed me at this time that General Chou had requested a postponement of the National Assembly during a meeting at Dr. Sun Fo's residence and that the PCC Steering Committee had practically agreed on the composition of the State Council and appeared to have agreed that the reorganization of the Executive Yuan should be planned for prior to the National Assembly but not announced until after the adjournment of the Assembly. The Government had apparently stopped the meetings of the PCC Steering Committee at this point, as the Third Party Group had been informed by the Government representatives that the Committee would not meet on November 11 as scheduled. They were, however, resumed on November 12, when an informal meeting was held at Dr. Sun Fo's residence. This probably had some connection with the Generalissimo's decision on the night of November 11 to delay the convening of the National Assembly for three days. He informed Dr. Stuart that at the urgent request of non-party delegates he had agreed to this postponement and that they had promised that if such a delay were granted the Third Party Group would submit their lists of delegates and possibly the Communists would also do so.

On November 12 I had another long conference with General Chou En-lai, who informed me that he had just come from the informal meeting of the PCC Steering Committee. General Chou described this meeting as follows:

Dr. Wang Shih-chieh had made a two point proposal: (1) he hoped that the other parties would recognize the National Assembly, which would meet on November 15, and that they would participate in this meeting and (2) he hoped that after the convening of the Assembly the other parties would not regard it as a split but would continue the negotiations. He had informed Dr. Wang that the Communist Party would not participate in nor did it approve of the National Assembly since it had been convened by the Kuomintang unilaterally and postponed in the same manner. He had also told Dr. Wang that it was the Government and not the Communists which had initiated a political split.

General Chou continued that the Communists had shown forbearance at the time of the capture of Kalgan and had returned to Nanking for further negotiations in spite of this act. The Communists had continued negotiations after the Government occupation of Antung and he himself had been in Nanking, at the request of the Government, for 18 days before he had had an opportunity for direct discussions with the Government. The Communists had been patient because they knew these were matters of minor importance in comparison with the National Assembly. If the Communists now returned to Yenan, such action could not be construed as indication that they wanted a national split, as that depended entirely upon the Government. With the Assembly now scheduled for November 15, the intervening period was too short to allow any prospect of successful negotiation on the various political and military issues and the Government had rejected the Third Party Group's proposal for a temporary adjournment of the Assembly to permit continuation of discussions. Some of the non-party people and the Youth Party had now promised to attend the Assembly and the Government would seize upon this to prove that the Assembly was a legal one. The Government had made a gesture of inviting negotiations with the Communists, but actually its desire was to have only a part of the non-Kuomintang delegates participate in the Assembly so that it could show that the Assembly was democratic, that the Government was determined to restore power to the people and that the constitution was a democratic one.

It was now immaterial, said General Chou, whether the fighting first ceased, to be followed by discussion, or whether discussion preceded the fighting. Either procedure would be agreeable to the Communists. The Government had clearly indicated that it had no intention of settling the issue by negotiations with the Communists and had not even discussed matters direct with the Communists until two days ago. There was now one specific matter of which he wished to speak—that was the military discussion. He would have to await instructions from Yenan or else return there to receive new instructions. Another question in this connection was whether there was any possibility of adopting the June procedure of discussing not only the cessation of hostilities but also other questions regarding demobilization and disposition of troops during the army reorganization. In June the Government had insisted on the settlement of these questions in an over-all manner prior to a settlement because the Communists forces constituted a threat to them. Now the situation was reversed, as the Government had occupied many Communist areas and was now preparing an attack on Yenan. He felt that the June procedure was entirely justified by the existing situation. He wished, therefore, to ask whether all issues could be discussed as was done during June.

I replied that I did not think there was any question regarding the Government's desire to discuss all these matters to which he had referred. I added that he probably meant that all such matters should be discussed and settled prior to the termination of hostilities as the Generalissimo had stipulated in June and asked him if my assumption were correct.

General Chou explained that there was one complication; that was the National Assembly. If the Assembly could be further postponed, he would agree to a cessation of hostilities prior to anything else. But, since the Assembly would probably meet, thus affording the Government a chance to exert pressure through the Assembly on the Communists if a cease-fire agreement broke down, he would have to require a guarantee on military matters and an over-all settlement of the military issues before the Communists would agree to a cease-fire arrangement—otherwise, under such circumstances there would be no political guarantee.

I pointed out to General Chou that the real issue in relation to General Chen Cheng's proposal was the question of the date—whether it would be January 13, June 7 or November 11, as proposed by General Chen. Returning to his general statement, I made the following comment: To an important extent we were being defeated by suspicions and misapprehensions and I knew this, in part, to be true because of incidents in which I had been the principal actor or at least the initiator. I had found the results of my efforts misjudged and the Government accused of some evil purpose. I knew of statements made

369

by various Government leaders which were not pacifying or reassuring, but I was convinced that he was laboring under misapprehensions to the great disadvantage of the Communist Party. There had been undoubtedly a very serious battle within the Government ranks and General Chou apparently failed to perceive or understand the fatal effect on liberals in the Government of abrupt and almost contemptuous refusal or suspicion by the Communists of proposals which had been wrung from the Government political and military leaders with the greatest difficulty. Along with the complete lack of faith and trust on each side was the insistence that each detail of PCC procedure, not fundamental principles of the PCC, be followed in a meticulous manner. I was just as much interested in and gave as much importance to the procedure for the draft constitution and the treatment of that constitution as he did, but the fight was not being made on that. Instead, it was being spread over a dozen details, which I thought was a great mistake. In view of this attitude, I was at a loss to know what could be done to save the situation.

General Chou replied that it was not in his opinion a matter of procedure and then cited the Communist agreement during the PCC meeting to allow Government delegates elected in 1936 to sit on the National Assembly as a concession to obtain Kuomintang agreement to other portions of the PCC resolutions. Now, he said, the Generalissimo was ignoring the PCC resolutions, but he was retaining these Kuomintang delegates and unilaterally convening the National Assembly with such delegates.

I then stated that it was my understanding that the Communists and the Third Party Group contended that the draft constitution should be agreed to by the PCC Steering Committee and that draft formally confirmed, but not amended, by the National Assembly as a formal action to make it the law of the land. I asked him whether this was correct. When General Chou confirmed my understanding on this point, I then said that I failed to see the tremendous importance of arguments about the delegates and the many complications. It seemed that the great issue was the constitution and the basis of its acceptance and even the State Council became of minor importance because that was only a temporary arrangement. It seemed to be a great mistake not to concentrate on the draft constitution and how it was to be handled, as otherwise the entire affair might collapse on procedural details to the tragedy of the Chinese people. I told him that I had been urging the Generalissimo all during the summer to reconvene the

370

PCC Constitution Reviewing Committee and to have whatever agreement was reached confirmed by the PCC Steering Committee. I pointed out that I had finally obtained his agreement to the Five Man Committee and he had agreed to the reconvening of the Constitution Reviewing Committee if the former seemed to be reaching agreement. I had done this, I said, because it seemed to be a matter of paramount importance. I concluded that it had been my hope during this great emergency that the fighting could be resolved around a few great fundamentals, notably the constitution and the cessation of hostilities.

I then made the following comment to General Chou: Stated in its simplest form, the situation was that on one side there was the belief of certain Government leaders that the Communists would not go through with any agreement and on the other there was complete suspicion of the good faith of the Government in every proposal. The problem was how to resolve that situation. There were many liberals in the Government and a more far-sighted policy on the part of the Communists might have had the effect of practically putting those liberals in control. I had similarly assumed that there were liberals in the Communist Party who were defeated by the action of radicals in the ranks of the Government, in their efforts to reach a compromise within the Communist Party. My sole object was the termination of hostilities and a two-party government in China. There must be an opposition party as this was the only procedure that made possible a democratic form of government as we understood it in the United States. I had been asked informally a long time ago to come to China as an adviser to the Government and had been approached on the same matter last summer. My reply had been that I could give the necessary advice briefly and immediately — reformation and modernization of the government depended on the creation of an opposition party. Without a genuine opposition party to compete with, to criticize or to force reforms, there could be no reform of the Government or of the Kuomintang. The Kuomintang could not be reformed from the top; there must be opposition. Therefore, I had thought that the Communist Party, with its interest in the peasantry, the largest class in China, could render a very important service to the Chinese people in the role of an organized legal opposition party. In some way the army menace would have to be removed and I hoped and we had made plans to have parallel actions on the two problems.

General Chou replied that, in principle, he had the same understanding on these matters which I had described and that the Communists would not otherwise have cooperated for a fairly long time. It was for that reason, he said, that the PCC was successfully completed. He then referred to the Communist efforts to have the Constitution Reviewing Committee convened, the Generalissimo's failure to summon that Committee and his own recent efforts to have that Committee as well as the others convened. He concluded that this had been a point of the utmost importance to the Communists but the Government even now continued to advance its conditions regarding the National Assembly and the submission of the list of delegates.

A matter of considerable importance at this time was the possible attitude of the United States in the event that the Government convened the National Assembly with minority party representation but without Communist participation. Earlier, members of the Chinese Embassy staff in Washington had endeavored to ascertain at the Department of State what attitude the United States would take toward the formation of a coalition government in China without Communist participation. A Communist representative at Nanking had approached Dr. Stuart in this regard and the Generalissimo had on November 6 asked Dr. Stuart what the United States policy toward China was going to be.

A member of the China Youth Party showed the same interest in a conversation with me on November 14, when he informed me that the postponement of the National Assembly had been accepted by the Generalissimo on the condition that the Youth Party would attend the Assembly. He explained that the Generalissimo had instructed the Legislative Yuan to examine the revised draft constitution and complete the unfinished portions. The Legislative Yuan, he said, had refused to follow the Generalissimo's suggestion and endorsed the May 5, 1936 Draft Constitution, which had the support of the conservative group in the Kuomintang. The Generalissimo, however, he stated, had informed one of the Youth Party leaders on the previous day that he would guarantee that the constitution would be adopted in spite of the opposition of the Legislative Yuan and the Youth Party was insisting that the National Assembly follow the PCC resolutions and procedures. He felt, however, that the Government really intended to form a coalition government in name only and that it would continue to be a one-party government in practice.

I had attempted to make clear to various Government officials that the United States would not support a civil war in China and on November 13, in a conference with Dr. Wong Wen-hao, Vice President of the Executive Yuan, I informed him that I intended to be brutally frank in the following statement: The United States was very interested in helping China but would not support a government not representative of the people. The United States in February had been prepared to asssist China with large amounts of money and supplies. Some of this assistance had had to be curtailed because of certain of the political group in power who had exercised a determining influence on procedures detrimental to political reformation. If there were no genuine political reformation in China, U.S. assistance could not be counted upon.

The National Assembly was formally convened on November 15 with a decidedly limited representation from non-Kuomintang groups. The names of additional delegates from non-party and Youth Party personnel were submitted on the night of November 15, but the Communist Party and the Democratic League were not represented. (I had been informed that General Chou En-lai had returned to Nanking on October 21 only after the Third Party Group members had bound themselves to stand with the Communists against naming their delegates to the National Assembly until the Government had been reorganized in strict accordance with the PCC resolutions.) Dr. Stuart attended the opening session of the Assembly as the United States Ambassador, but I had thought it best for me to be absent, as I did not wish it to appear that I concurred with the Government in its approach to the Assembly and Dr. Stuart's presence fulfilled the diplomatic requirements. The Generalissimo's address[80] at the opening of the Assembly was mild in tone and was devoted chiefly to the achievements and objectives of the National Government. Its chief points were:

> The Generalissimo outlined the efforts to achieve constitutional government in China and the role of the present Government to that end. He explained the previous postponement of the Assembly and the results of the Political Consultation Conference and pointed to the faithful adherence thereto by the Na-

[80]See Volume Two, Appendix Q, Document 1, for the full text.

tional Government. He concluded that the Government had been carrying on the struggle of national revolution and reconstruction for the country and the people for the realization of the Three People's Principles and democratic government based upon the Five Power Constitutional System—that was the ultimate objective of the revolution.

The Assembly planned to proceed on a rather tentative basis for the first two weeks, during which there would be opportunity for the various delegates to be heard, the presidium to be elected and the various committees to be formed. The postponement for three days had resulted in the promise of attendance by some of the Third Party Group, but it had had the effect of disrupting the unity of action of that Group and had seriously, if not fatally, weakened its influence for good as a balance between the two major parties.

On November 16 General Chou En-lai issued a statement[81] to the press regarding the National Assembly. The statement was strongly critical of the Kuomintang and gave notice that the Communist Party did not recognize the Assembly. The following are the principal points of this statement:

> The National Assembly is a creation of the Kuomintang one-party Government contrary to the PCC decisions and the will of the Chinese people. It is strongly and firmly opposed by the Communist Party. During the past ten months the Kuomintang has totally destroyed the *status quo* as established by the cease-fire agreement of January 10, has completely broken the four promises of the Government during the PCC sessions through the acts of the Kuomintang gestapo and has violated the PCC decision on local government. The Communists, during the negotiations at Nanking in the past month, have asked that the National Assembly be called off in order to afford an opportunity for concurrent meetings of the Committee of Three, the PCC Steering Committee and the Constitution Reviewing Committee to straighten out the various current military and political problems on the basis of the cease-fire agreement of

[81]See Volume Two, Appendix Q, Document 2, for the full text.

January 10, the military reorganization agreement and the PCC resolutions. The Government, however, has refused. The Chinese Communist Party refuses to recognize this National Assembly and the door of negotiations has now been "slammed" by the hand of the Kuomintang authorities.

On the same day (October 16) General Chou called at my residence to inform me that he was preparing to return to Yenan and wished to leave on November 18. He said that other members of the Communist Delegation were returning with him but that Mr. Tung Pi-wu (member of the Communist Party's Central Executive Committee and a Communist delegate to the PCC) would remain at Nanking because the Communists would still maintain a headquarters at that city. He inquired regarding transportation facilities for his trip. General Chou pointed out also that there were still about 40 Communist members of the Executive Headquarters at Peiping and that he had recently received an inquiry from General Yeh Chien-ying asking what they should do if the Government launched an attack on Yenan. General Chou said that, if the Government attacked Yenan, it would then be evident that the Government had blocked the last possibility for mediation in the future, in which event the Communist personnel in Peiping would have no place to go. They, therefore, wished to inquire whether prior to the Government attack on Yenan the U.S. branch of the Executive Headquarters would assist them in returning to Yenan. General Chou explained that a small number of Communists would remain at Nanking and Shanghai and that General Yeh had told General Gillem, U.S. Commissioner at the Executive Headquarters, that he would like to maintain liaison in the Executive Headquarters even though there was almost nothing to do. General Chou added that he had also told General Gillem of his desire to retain such liaison and that, while he assumed that I would approve of this measure, he was not certain of the Government's views. He said that if the Government attacked Yenan, it would indicate that it actually wished to "get rid of everything."

General Chou commented further as follows: During the past ten months he had felt very grateful for my personal efforts, despite the fact that, due to various reasons, including some change in American policy during the last part of this year, the negotiations had not been successful. He still had high respect for me personally, particularly since I had been confronted with even greater and more insurmountable difficulties since the end of the negotiations in June—for which I had his deepest sympathy. By opening the National Assembly, however, the Kuomintang had closed the door to negotiations and he, therefore, had to return to Yenan and made a study of the over-all situation. The Kuomintang, and particularly the Generalissimo, was intoxicated with the idea that force could settle everything, but the Communists would never surrender to force, and believed that only the people could settle the issue. The Communists believed that the only way out for China was peace, democracy, independence and unification and would therefore struggle for peace through democracy, which meant coalition government. The Communists would not be willing to resume negotiations until there was an opportunity for a true peace and for peaceful negotiations.

I informed General Chou that I would arrange for his transportation to Yenan but must await clearance from Yenan due to the danger of the plane's being fired upon unless properly cleared. With regard to the safety of Communist personnel in Peiping, Shanghai and Nanking in the event of an attack on Yenan, I said, I knew nothing about such an attack, but if it became desirable for such Communist personnel to evacuate I would accept the obligation to provide the necessary planes. (I felt that this was my obligation as I had been largely responsible for their presence in Government-controlled cities during the period of negotiations.) The problem was, I pointed out, whether there would be a suitable airfield in the region to which they would wish to go. I repeated that I knew nothing about an attack on Yenan and emphasized that I would deplore such action and would do my best to stop it.

General Chou replied as follows: Although the door to negotiations had now been closed, the Communist Party was retaining a few people in Peiping, Nanking and Shanghai, even though there was little to do, so that they might be there in the event of any future opening for negotiations. If, however, the Government attacked Yenan, he believed that Yenan would order their complete withdrawal. This was his personal opinion, as he had not inquired of Yenan in this regard. An attack on Yenan would force the Communists out of their present areas and they would have to penetrate Kuomintang territory, which would bring about immense chaos and block every possibility of negotiations. He believed that not only should the Kuomintang restrain itself from taking such action but also that some official within the U.S. Government, such as Dr. Stuart or myself, who wanted to see peace in China and also were thinking of world peace, must give sober thought to this matter. He concluded that this was "coming out of my heart."

I replied as follows: I appreciated his personal opinion and hoped that his fears regarding Yenan would prove groundless. I would certainly do my best to avoid such a calamity. There was one matter which I wished him to take up in Yenan. It was useless for me to endeavor to mediate if I were not trusted as being sincere in an effort to be impartial. It did not matter what the Communists might feel or think regarding American policy; the fact remained that if Yenan did not consider me in a position to be sincerely impartial it was perfectly useless for me to remain in China and, I should imagine, my remaining here would do more harm in the end than it could possibly do good. Therefore, I wished him to determine formally from the proper authorities at Yenan whether specifically they wished me personally to continue in my present position. I asked that his colleagues view the matter as a plain business proposition without regard to the Chinese consideration of "face." I was not interested in "face." My interest was solely in whether there was a possibility of my being able to render some service by way of mediation. If Yenan had lost confidence in me, I knew that I could not do so, and I certainly did not wish to continue in this painful position any longer than I had to. As I had told him previously, Dr. Stuart was here and his heart was in China. He would continue to be here and the question then was: "What is the best arrangement toward a possible peace and adjustment here in China? I am making a specific request of you and I will await your answer from Yenan." I concluded that if the Government launched an attack on Yenan the matter would be settled otherwise, because I thought that under those circumstances President Truman would recall me.

The conversation ended with General Chou's stating that he sympathized with my request and that he would put the question before Yenan without any reservations.

By November 16, of the 36 regular conflict control and communications group field teams of the Executive Headquarters only 11 were fully operative. Only three of this number were in China proper, two in Government areas and one in

Communist territory, the remaining eight teams being in Manchuria. Eleven of the teams were in Peiping and 14 of the teams were inoperative because of the absence of one or both of the Chinese members. The Communists were the worst offenders on this score as they had withdrawn their members from 13 teams located in Government areas, while the Government had withdrawn its members from one team in Communist territory and members from four teams in areas under its own control.

On November 18 General Chou En-lai had furnished me a list of Communist personnel in Nanking, Shanghai and Chungking, who, in case of emergency, would require my assistance in providing air transportation facilities either to Yenan or to some other destination to be arranged at a later date. This indicated that the Communists were retaining the following personnel at the above-named cities: Nanking—50 members of the Communist Delegation; Shanghai—10 members of the Delegation and 7 members of the Liberated Areas Relief Office; and Chungking—approximately 100 members of the Communist office and press.

Militarily, attention was centered at this time chiefly on the possibility of a Government attack on Yenan. General Chen Cheng had denied, during the Committee of Three meeting on November 11, that the Government intended to attack Yenan and Dr. Wong Wen-hao, Vice President of the Executive Yuan, had made a similar statement to me on November 18. The Generalissimo had also denied to me that the Government had such intentions. U.S. personnel of the Executive Headquarters at Yenan reported that the Communists were evacuating schools and hospitals and non-essential persons from Yenan, that the National Government liaison office there was being evacuated to Government territory and that National Government reconnaissance planes were making daily flights over that city. The Communist authorities at Yenan indicated that they did not wish American personnel to accompany them in the event of enforced evacuation at the time of an attack but might welcome American liaison personnel after a new headquarters should be established elsewhere. They urged the U.S. liaison group to remain at Yenan until an attack should become imminent and keep radio service and airfield operations in readiness for a late evacuation.

Little military activity was reported during this period except for fighting along the Peiping-Hankow Railway in south Hopei and north Honan, Communist harrassing attacks in east Jehol and in the Tatung (Shansi) area and Communist disruption of rail communications in the Ssupingchieh area between Mukden and Changchun.

General Chou En-lai departed from Nanking for Yenan on November 19 in a U.S. Army plane, calling on me socially with Madame Chou the previous afternoon. His departure brought to an end, at least temporarily and indefinitely, the long period of negotiations and discussion begun in January of this year. The door had not been closed to further negotiations by either side, but it seemed likely that a fresh start would have to be made before there would be any possibility of bringing about an understanding between the two parties. The attitude of the Communist Party and the Democratic League indicated their belief that the PCC resolutions had been totally destroyed and that it would be necessary to convene another conference of all parties similar to that held in January.[82]

Two things seemed apparent to me: One was that the Government military leaders were now in the saddle and were thoroughly convinced that the Communists would not carry out any agreement reached. The other was that the strong political clique in the Kuomintang was firmly convinced that a coalition government was not possible because the Communists would merely disrupt such a government. With these two forces working together and the Communist repulse of every overture Dr. Stuart and I had persuaded the Government to make, the present tragic situation had developed. It seemed to me that the Government had been using the negotiations largely to prove the correctness of its point of view regarding the Communist Party or to justify its actions. Since June, the Government had been waging war on a constantly increasing scale, heavily absorbing Government funds. These military expenditures served to increase inflation at the same time that the Government was asking the United States for large loans.

On the other side, the Communist Party had, in my opinion, defeated itself through its own suspicions, refusing to agree to possible procedures which might well have resulted

[82]See Volume Two, Appendix Q, Document 3, for a copy of a memorandum containing the views of the Kuomintang, the Communist Party and the Democratic League in regard to the PCC resolutions.

in a settlement of the issues. This had been particularly true of its rejection of the proposal for the Five Man Committee under Dr. Stuart, which might have led to the organization of the State Council and the carrying out of the other PCC agreements, and of its almost contemptuous rejection of the Kalgan truce proposal. It had misconstrued each overture engineered by Dr. Stuart and myself, and had apparently been convinced by its own campaign of public misrepresentation of American intentions and actions. It also chose to ignore in discussions and in criticisms of Government actions its own military and other actions that were violations of agreements.

In the background there was, of course, the international situation in connection with U.S.-Soviet relations, which was perhaps a major cause for the breakdown of the negotiations in March. It was a fact that the Kuomintang leaders feared a connection between the Chinese Communists and Soviet Russia and considered the former to be puppets of the Soviets. Accompanying this feeling was the idea that, in spite of the statement of American policy toward China announced by President Truman in December 1945 and in spite of the continued American mediation effort, the United States in the long run must support the National Government against the Chinese Communists. The Kuomintang, therefore, felt, I believe, that if it could reduce the Communist forces to a relatively weak position militarily during this period, when, according to their intelligence reports, the Soviet Union would be in no position to interfere openly by aiding the Chinese Communists, then it could afford to forego for the moment desired American military, financial and economic aid. That would come, they apparently thought, after they had succeeded in strengthening their hold on the country in opposition to the Communists and had introduced constitutional government through adoption of a constitution and participation in the government of all minority groups except the Communists.

CHAPTER XXXI
ROLE OF THE UNITED STATES MARINES IN CHINA AND FACTORS INVOLVED IN THEIR WITHDRAWAL

The Third Amphibious Corps of the United States Marine Corps landed in north China in early September 1945 following the Japanese surrender. The mission of these forces was as follows: (1) Occupy and secure certain designated ports and airfields in north China—Tientsin, Peiping, Chinhuang-tao, Tsingtao and Chefoo*—in order to facilitate the movement into this area of Chinese Government troops; (2) assist in receiving the surrender of the Japanese military forces in this area and in disarming them; (3) assume control and security of the surrendering forces and their equipment for turning over to the Chinese authorities as soon as practicable; (4) assist and advise the Chinese authorities in processing and repatriating Japanese military and civilians in the occupied areas; (5) assist in the release and repatriation of American and Allied prisoners of war and civilian internees in the occupied areas; and (6) take measures to investigate and apprehend war criminals. Specifically these responsibilities included the following functions in addition to those for the Marines' own security: (a) security for the line of communications between Tangku and Chinhuangtao; (b) security for the Kailan Mining Administration mines and installations in the Tangshan-Linhsi area (between Tientsin and Chinhuangtao); (c) provision of guards on coal trains in the Peiping-Tientsin-Chinhuangtao area; (d) security for airfields at Tsingtao, Peiping and Tientsin; and (e) security for the ports of Tientsin, Chinhuangtao, Tangku and Tsingtao.

As set forth in President Truman's statement on December 15 of American policy toward China, the United States Government, in continuation of its collaboration with the Chinese Government in the prosecution of the war and consonant with the Potsdam Declaration, was assisting and would continue to assist the Chinese Government in disarming and repatriating the Japanese in China and the United States Marine forces were in China for that purpose. Directives issued by the Joint Chiefs of Staff to the Commanding General of the United States Armed Forces in China required that points occupied by the United States Armed Forces be surrendered only to the Chinese National Government and the mission of the United States Marines was related to this directive.

The original plans for the landing of the United States Marines in China called for a force of 62,000 men, but this was subsequently reduced by the deletion of units which were never lifted from other areas in the Pacific or never landed in

*Chefoo was occupied by Chinese Communist forces at the time of the landing of the U.S. Marines in north China and the Marine forces did not, therefore, land at that port.

China. At the time of the landing, therefore, the Marine strength was approximately 55,000 men. Upon my arrival in China in December 1945, I informed the Commanding General of the United States Armed Forces in China of my decision to reduce the strength of the Marine forces in north China by 20 percent. By the beginning of February 1946 the Marine strength in north China was about 45,000 and it was further planned to reduce this number to approximately 28,000. At the same time plans were being drawn up for the active participation of the U.S. Marines in the repatriation program of the Executive Headquarters. This program envisaged the disarming of the Japanese military by the Marines at the ports of embarkation, the Japanese equipment and supplies to be properly invoiced and stored by the Marines and impounded under their supervision. The Marines were expected to guard this equipment until the final disposition thereof had been determined. The repatriation program in this connection was drawn up in consultation among representatives of the Chinese Ministry of War, Chinese Supreme Headquarters, SCAP, the U.S. Seventh Fleet and the U.S. Marine Corps. It was felt that a figure of 28,000 officers and men was sufficient to carry out the plans being developed by the Executive Headquarters for repatriation activities.

Another important function of the U.S. Marine forces in north China, which developed as a result of the establishment of the Executive Headquarters at Peiping, was that of providing logistical support for the American personnel of the Executive Headquarters and air transport for the Executive Headquarters field teams. The provision for guards on coal trains and those carrying U.S. supplies, as well as guards for the railway line between Tangku and Chinhuangtao and the coal mines in that area, was absolutely vital to the economic life of both north China and the Yellow River and Yangtze River Valleys. Without the Marine guards the lines would inevitably have been cut by guerrilla forces and the coal supply for the urban centers and railroads in north China and those in the Shanghai-Nanking-Hankow area would have been drastically reduced, if not entirely cut off; this would have made even more serious the economic difficulties confronting the country.

During February and March, in view of the probable inactivation of the China Theater on May 1, I was hopeful that I might be justified in proposing the beginning of the complete withdrawal of the Marines at an early date, except for air transport, housekeeping and small local guard units. A study of this question by the U.S. Army Forces in China resulted in recommendations that all U.S. Marine units in China, except an air transport group needed by the Executive Headquarters, a rifle battalion, the necessary housekeeping elements and repatriation teams for the ports of embarkation be withdrawn, and April 1 was suggested as the target date for the beginning of this program.

On April 17 an approved operational directive was issued by the Commanding General of the U.S. Armed Forces in China to General Keller E. Rockey, Commanding General of the U.S. Marine Third Amphibious Corps. This directive set forth the final mission of the Marines while under the operational control of the Commanding General, U.S. Armed Forces in China, and at the same time specified that operational control of the Marines would pass to the Commander of the U.S. Seventh Fleet on May 1, the target date for the inactivation of the China Theater. The directive provided:

> The U.S. Marine Forces in China will execute the following tasks under the operational control of the Commanding General, China Theater, until May 1 and thereafter under the operational control of the Commander of the 7th Fleet:
>
> a. Maintain garrison forces charged only with the protection of their own forces and U.S. Marine supplies and installations in the following areas:
>
> (1) The Peiping-Tientsin area with such detachments in both areas as are required for their own support.
>
> (2) The Tsingtao area.
>
> b. Continue to assist and provide logistical support to the Executive Headquarters until relieved by the U.S. Army Forces in China.
>
> c. Continue to assist the U.S. Army Forces in China in the repatriation of Korean and Japanese personnel until this repatriation is completed.
>
> d. Coordinate relief by the Chinese Government forces of U.S. Marine forces engaged in providing security in north China except that required by the Marines for their own

security and support. The Commanding General of the U.S. Armed Forces in China accepts the responsibility of arranging with the Chinese Government for the Chinese troops required and with General Marshall for the authority for their movement.

e. Conduct no activities which prejudice the basic U.S. principle that the United States will not support the Chinese Government in fratricidal warfare. This does not preclude U.S. commanders from taking such action as they deem necessary for the protection of U.S. property and the lives of U.S. personnel.

f. Prepare a plan for the withdrawal of the Marine forces and be prepared to execute this plan as directed by the Chief of Naval Operations.

On March 28 General A.C. Wedemeyer, Commanding, U.S. Armed Forces, China Theater, had advised the Generalissimo that the U.S. Marines would be greatly reduced in strength at an increasingly rapid rate and had asked what provisions could be made for Chinese troops to relieve the Marines which would not constitute troop movements in violation of the Cessation of Hostilities Order of January 10. It was not until April 26 that a reply was received to General Wedemeyer's above-described memorandum. On that day the Board of Military Operations addressed a memorandum to General Wedemeyer asking for water transportation for the Chinese Government's 5th and 26th Armies to Tientsin and Tsingtao, respectively, for the purpose of relieving the U.S. Marines at those points.

In view of the prohibition against troop movements contained in the January 10 agreement for the cessation of hostilities, it was necessary to obtain approval of both Chinese sides prior to such movements. Under date of April 25, therefore, having learned of the Chinese Government's request, I addressed a memorandum to General Chou En-lai on this subject. I pointed out that a plan was being developed for the relief of the U.S. Marines in China by troops of the National Government and indicated the two armies under consideration for this purpose. Explaining that I was desirous of expediting the initiation of the withdrawal of the U.S. Marines, I asked whether the movement of Government troops for this purpose met with his approval or whether he considered it essential that it be discussed by the Committee of Three.

On April 26 General Chou forwarded to me a memorandum in reply. In this memorandum he said that he saw no connection between the movement of National Government forces and the withdrawal of the U.S. Marines. He felt that Government troops in the Peiping-Tientsin area were sufficient in number to make unnecessary any reenforcement. He concluded with the request that I convey to the Government representative his objection to the contemplated movement.

In view of General Chou's reply and the lack of sufficient Government forces in north China to relieve the Marine unit, no further action could be taken at this time to proceed with the desired withdrawal of the Marines. Negotiations were continuing for a settlement of the differences between the Kuomintang and the Chinese Communists. The withdrawal of the Marines at this time would have had considerable effect on these negotiations as the withdrawal might have caused a spread of hostilities as a result of Communist efforts to occupy points to be evacuated by the Marines, such as, the port of Tsingtao in Shantung. There were insufficient Government forces to defend this city against a determined Communist attack, such as actually threatened Tsingtao in June.

Plans were made, however, during May for carrying out quietly a material reduction in the Marine strength at Tsingtao, the reduction to begin on June 10. In this move, as in other similar cases, an effort was made to avoid publicity.

Coincidental with the announcement of the truce period beginning on June 7, the Chinese Communists launched a general attack along the rail lines in Shantung seriously threatening Tsingtao, for the defense of which the National Government had less than 5,000 troops. The Communist attacks continued until June 15 despite the fact that a general truce had been agreed to on June 7. As a result, the National Government rushed reenforcements (54th Army) by sea to Tsingtao, and thus commenced the general reenforcement of its troops in north China which had been restricted by the agreement of January 10.

In July I informed the Commander of the U.S. 7th Fleet that I desired him to proceed with the reduction of the Marines in Tsingtao so that there would remain at Tsingtao only a small garrison force sufficient to guard the naval facilities ashore, an air unit to provide essential air communications and the necessary service troops to care for and dispose of the large quantity of property which could not be withdrawn with the troops. This reduction proceeded as quietly as possible and was not attended by any publicity.

During this period there began a series of incidents involving attacks on U.S. Marine personnel by the Chinese Communist forces, which were apparently motivated by a desire to arouse American public opinion to demand the withdrawal of the Marines from China. The first of these incidents was the capture of seven U.S. Marines by Communist forces in east Hopei on July 13 and their detention until July 24. They were released unharmed on that day after an Executive Headquarters team had made an effort to obtain the release of the captives and representations had been made by the American side to the Communist Party. The serious incident at Anping occurred on July 29, on the highway between Peiping and Tientsin, during which Communist forces ambushed a motor convoy of supplies for Executive Headquarters and UNRRA escorted by U.S. Marines, killing three Marines and wounding twelve others. In August there were cases of firing by unidentified persons on Marine personnel. The net effect of these incidents was not, however, that hoped for by the Communists as the American press on the whole seemed to feel that, while the Marines should be withdrawn as soon as their mission had been completed, there should be no surrender to attacks of this kind and the Marines should not be withdrawn in the face of such tactics.

The spread of hostilities in north China and the Government's movement of reenforcements into that area led me to the decision to have the Marine coal train and railway bridge guards replaced by Government troops. On August 22, therefore, I informed Admiral Cooke, Commander of the U.S. 7th Fleet, of my decision and pointed out that, as an additional Government army was then in the process of being moved to north China from Formosa, it would be extremely helpful if this army and other Government troops in north China were obligated to take over Marine functions. This would serve the double purpose of assisting in withdrawing the Marines and at the same time causing deployment of National forces southward instead of toward Jehol Province and Manchuria, where, I feared, serious fighting would soon develop.

On the following day Admiral Cooke informed General Rockey, Commanding General of the Marine Forces in north China, that he should exert pressure on the local National Government commander to have Government forces take over at the earliest possible moment responsibility for guarding all bridges, coal trains and mines then under guard by Marine units. He was instructed to inform the National Government commander that this action was to permit the concentration of the Marines at Chinhuangtao, Tangku, Tientsin and Peiping and to point out that a general civil war might result in the immediate withdrawal of Marines from these areas if not replaced with National Government forces. On August 28, fearing that the National Government commanders might delay the relief of the Marine units, I instructed General Rockey to prepare a reasonable schedule of planned withdrawals and merely present it to the appropriate Government commander as a declaration of intention in the matter.

General Rockey informed me in a radio of August 28 that the National Government commander had agreed in principle to the proposed relief of the Marines by Government forces. The Government Commander had already relieved some coal train guards and promised that the remainder would be relieved on about September 5. The National Government Commander explained to General Rockey that National Government offensive operations in this area had been ordered on a time schedule to last until about September 21 and that during this period no Government forces would be available to relieve the Marines. The Conference with the Government Commander had ended with the understanding that the Marine Headquarters would work out a plan for the progressive relief of bridge and mine guards with the Government's 94th Army.

On August 31 General Rockey informed Admiral Cooke and me that he had reached an agreement with the National Government commanders on a schedule for relief for mine and bridge guards beginning on September 23 and ending on October 15, and asked if such a schedule were satisfactory. It was my feeling, as I informed Admiral Cooke, that a delay of more than three weeks before relieving a single bridge or mine guard for reasons only of a military campaign which we deplored was unacceptable. In view of these circumstances, I discussed the matter with the Generalissimo and informed him that a delay until September 23 in providing relief for the Marine units in question could not be tolerated. The Generalissimo replied that he would issue instructions immediately to expedite the arrangements for the relief of the Marines. On September 3 I informed Admiral Cooke of this conversation and asked that he have General Rockey take similar action to expedite the arrangements despite his previous commitment to the date of September 23. On September 7 Admiral Cooke informed me that he and General Rockey had conferred with the Government commanders that day and that the latter had agreed to advance the schedule for relief of the Marine units to September 15. The Government commanders had requested that representations be made to the Generalissimo for additional forces to carry out this task, but I declined to make such representations as it would involve military dispositions and was not compatible with my position as a mediator.

As scheduled, the relief of the Marine units from the coal mines and the railway bridges between Tangku and Chinhuangtao began on September 15 and on September 30 the entire program of relief was completed, in each case the Marines having been relieved by National Government forces. At this time the Marine forces in north China were concentrated at Peiping, Tientsin-Tangku, Peitaiho-Chinhuangtao and Tsingtao. Continued and gradual reduction of the Marine forces in China had by September 24 reduced the total number of Marines in China to 14,367.

Chinese Communist Party attacks on the presence of the U.S. Marines in China were now being paralleled by Soviet criticism of the continued stationing of the Marines in China. On September 24 a representative of the Minister for Foreign Affairs called to tell me of Soviet official statements regarding the Marines in China and to ask my advice regarding the instructions which the Chinese Government should send to its representatives in Paris in this regard. When I explained that I should prefer to request the opinion of the Department of State, the Chinese representative pointed out that their instructions must be sent by radio to Paris that evening. I suggested, therefore, that a statement of the facts be made and nothing more—that the U.S. Marines were here with the sanction of the Chinese Government; that their original purpose under the armistice agreement was to facilitate the repatriation of Japanese; that this repatriation was virtually completed; that the Marines were now safeguarding the operation of the Tientsin-Chinhuangtao Railway to ensure the transport of vitally necessary coal; that they were further concerned in providing for the maintenance and security of American personnel of the Executive Headquarters at Peiping; and that the strength of the Marine forces was steadily being reduced. The Foreign Office representative indicated that the facts regarding the railway mission and possibly other details would not be used in any statement issued by the Chinese Government.

An increasing number of incidents involving the Chinese Communists and the Marines during September and October served to indicate Communist resentment at the continued presence of the Marines in north China. These incidents included firing by snipers on Marine sentries on railway bridges and on sentries guarding ammunition dumps. The evident shortage of military equipment led in one case to a concerted attack by a Communist force on an isolated Marine ammunition supply depot in the Tangku area. Other incidents including firing on Marine hunting parties; one such incident on October 20 culminated in the disarming of one group and the detention of two Marines in the group until November 7, following protracted negotiations for their release between Communist and U.S. Marine representatives and representations by me to General Chou En-lai.

The completion of the mass repatriation of Japanese on October 31 and the withdrawal of all U.S. Marine guard units from the coal mines, coal trains and railway bridges on September 30 reduced the functions of the Marine forces in north China in November to those of providing logistical support and security to the U.S. personnel of the Executive Headquarters and of maintaining the necessary guard units for the U.S. Navy training establishment at Tsingtao. Accordingly, I requested Admiral Cooke and General Gillem at this time to furnish me with their comments and suggestions regarding further possible reductions in the Marine forces in China.

The U.S. Marine Forces in north China were at this time giving the Executive Headquarters the following supply and service support, which was essential to the continued functioning of the U.S. branch of the Headquarters: food stocks for the U.S. branch and the U.S. Army Troop Carrier Squadron, which furnished the air transport facilities for all branches of the Headquarters; all petroleum supplies for the air and ground units; and the necessary service to deliver these stocks from shipside at Tangku to Peiping, this service involving lighterage, port handling, warehousing, guarding, transporting, and issuing. To maintain these services, the Marines required guard, signal, medicine and supply detachments and Marine units performing these services were stationed in Peiping, Tientsin, Tangku (the port of entry for supplies), Chinhuangtao (an alternate port), and a small detachment at Peitaiho.

Admiral Cooke informed me that it was his basic assumption that as long as the Executive Headquarters remained the Marine forces would continue to support it logistically and tactically by maintaining the Tangku-Tientsin-Peiping ground line of communications and the Tsingtao-Tientsin-Peiping air line of communications. On this assumption and in order to effect an early reduction in the Marine forces in China, he suggested that approximately 4,000 officers and enlisted men be scheduled for an early withdrawal. He pointed to the difficulties connected with such withdrawals involved in preparation of reception and housing at the points to which they might be sent, in providing for the safeguarding and movement of essential supplies and equipment and in obtaining the required shipping for such movements.

On November 16 I informed the Department of State that Admiral Cooke and I had reached agreement in a conference at Nanking on that day on the immediate reduction of the Marine forces in China by 5,000 men, leaving a strength of approximately 10,000. The troops scheduled to leave were those north of Tangku in the Chinhuangtao-Peitaiho area, an air squadron from Peiping and some troops from Tientsin. I directed that discussions be held shortly after this date in Peiping between the Marine commanders and General Gillem to determine the amount of reduction there and in Tientsin that could be carried out without detriment to the supply and security of the Executive Headquarters. Should later developments make the continuation of the Executive Headquarters impractical, a complete withdrawal of the Marine forces in China, except for a guard detachment at Tsingtao, would be in order. I concluded that shipping for most of these troops involved in the immediate withdrawal was available, but that the Navy Department and the Commander-in-chief of the U.S. Pacific Fleet had not yet had an opportunity to pass upon this evacuation plan which we had agreed upon in China.

At the same time I informed General Gillem at Peiping that the Marine commanders would discuss with him the question of minimum Marine strength required for the continued operation of the Executive Headquarters and for reasonable precautions involved in the safe evacuation of U.S. personnel of the Headquarters in the event of open civil war and the abandonment of that organization. I pointed out that the objective was still the total withdrawal of the Marine forces at the earliest possible moment without prejudice to his operations and/or evacuation.

On November 18 the Acting Secretary of State informed me that there was no pressure from Washington for the reduction, as such, in the strength of the Marine forces in China but that the question of their mission in China and the date of their withdrawal had been raised in various quarters. He stated that the Department of State supported the view that the primary reason for retaining the Marines in China was to protect the lines of supply and communication and maintain the security of the Executive Headquarters, and added that, if the Executive Headquarters were disbanded and the U.S. personnel thereof were withdrawn, a reduction in the Marine strength in China to a guard and training unit at Tsingtao would probably be appropriate.

On November 19 I informed the Acting Secretary of State of my complete agreement with the Department of State's views as set forth in his message of the preceding day. I continued that it was an inescapable requirement that the Marines provide logistical support and security to ensure the safe evacuation of U.S. personnel in the event of the disbanding of the Executive Headquarters; in order to make clear the United States position in China and to do this while there was no pressure for such action, I was endeavoring to effect the maximum reduction of Marine forces without prejudice to the Executive Headquarters and the shore guards for the U.S. Fleet while at Tsingtao. I concluded that forces beyond those requirements were too small to serve any large purpose and would be a continual source of incidents.

General Gillem informed me on November 18 that it had been agreed in his conference at Peiping with the Marine commanders that the total estimated Marine strength in north China required for the sole purpose of meeting minimum tactical and logistical requirements for the continued operation of the Executive Headquarters and the safe evacuation of the U.S. personnel thereof was 4,055 men.

On November 20 Admiral Cooke expressed his agreement, in a radio message to me, to the requirements set forth in General Gillem's message and stated that, in addition to those estimated minimum requirements for the support of the Executive Headquarters, the Marine commanders would need a service regiment of about 875 men, in progressively decreasing strength until excess Marine property had been disposed of by shipment elsewhere or by being declared surplus. He further stated that the estimated reduction in Marine strength in China, including the 5,000 reduction discussed with me on November 16, would approach 10,000 men. He added that

391

none of this reduction contemplated any change in the Marine organization and strength at Tsingtao, except for the withdrawal of one service battalion when it should have disposed of the Marine excess and surplus property. He expressed the opinion that the additional reduction set forth in this message was the maximum that could be contemplated under existing conditions, since the forces remaining would constitute the minimum strength essential for the support of the Executive Headquarters and the disposal of surplus or excess property.

On November 21 I informed the Department of State of the agreement for the additional reduction of Marine strength by approximately 5,000 men, a total reduction of about 10,000, which would bring the resultant strength down to approximately 5,000 Marines in China. I indicated that the distribution of this strength would be as follows: The bulk would be in Tientsin to ensure the movement of supplies and the protection of the line of communications between Tangku and Peiping; the remainder would be at Peiping and Tsingtao, with a detachment at the port of Tangku. I explained that the first withdrawal of 5,000 men could be undertaken almost immediately upon receipt of approval from the Navy Department, as the required shipping was then available, but that the movement of the second 5,000 men would depend upon later shipping arrangements.

On November 23, Admiral Cooke having not yet been notified by the Navy Department of its approval of the reduction plan outlined in the preceding paragraph, I instructed my representative in the Department of State to endeavor to expedite formal approval by the Navy Department of this plan.

On the following day I was informed by my representative that he had discussed the matter with the Secretary of the Navy, who had said that the Navy Department was awaiting a reply to its message to Admiral Cooke asking for his recommendations on the original proposal for an initial reduction of 5,000 Marines. The Secretary apparently had the impression that I might have misunderstood the problem and was recommending a reduction in Marine strength purely because of pressure from Washington and perhaps against my better judgment. My representative had assured him that such was not the case and had brought to his attention the exchange of messages between the Acting Secretary of State and me regarding the desirability of a reduction of Marine strength in China.

On November 25, upon receipt of this message, I further instructed my representative in Washington to "inform all parties concerned" that it was my best judgment that the immediate reduction of the Marine strength by 10,000 men, thus leaving a total Marine strength of 5,000, was highly desirable and should be undertaken before some new incidents might create the impression that the reduction was being made under hostile pressure. I pointed out that the numbers to be withdrawn did little or no good and actually complicated the situation and that I, therefore, recommended prompt action.

On November 30, the Acting Secretary of State forwarded to me the following message: He had seen Dr. Stuart's message (supporting the immediate reduction of Marine strength in China), was wholeheartedly in agreement with my views and had pressed for a prompt decision. The Secretaries of State, War and Navy had stated their agreement to the primary mission of the Marines as proposed by me. His position had consistently been that the question of the number of Marines required to perform the stated mission was a military matter to be determined by the responsible American military authorities in China and that agreement had been reached by Admiral Cooke and me that 5,000 Marines were adequate for this mission. The Secretary of the Navy had informed him that the Navy had already authorized the immediate withdrawal of approximately 3,400 Marines and had asked Admiral Cooke to confer with me a view to submission of a further report on the final reduction figure. The Navy Department felt that it had the residual responsibility for reviewing Admiral Cooke's recommendations. Any announcement regarding the withdrawal of the Marines should be made as a routine matter in China.

On December 1 the Secretary of Navy informed me that my representative had conveyed to him my views regarding the immediate reduction of Marine strength in China and that orders were being issued for the immediate withdrawal of Marine units at Peitaiho and Chinhuangtao. He continued that the officers who had the military responsibility for accomplishing the mission of the Marines in China, as then defined, should determine the strength needed for that purpose and that, accordingly, orders for further reductions would be deferred until those officers should report the additional tactical units which could be released without impairing their ability to meet military responsibilities.

393

On the same day the Chief of Naval Operations instructed the Commander-in-chief of the U.S. Pacific Fleet to issue
orders for the withdrawal of the Marine units in the Chinhuangtao-Peitaiho area and to direct Admiral Cooke, after
conference with me, to report any additional tactical units
which could be released without impairing the ability of the
Marine forces to perform their assigned mission in China.

On December 3 Admiral Cooke informed me by radio
that he had been instructed by the Commander-in-chief of the
U.S. Pacific Fleet to evacuate the Marine units in question,
utilizing shipping available to the U.S. 7th Fleet. He explained
that the shipping available to him at the moment was sufficient for the personnel involved but that, pending the receipt
of instructions regarding the disposition of heavy equipment,
no firm estimate could be made with regard to cargo lift requirements. He continued that all available shipping would
be used for the initial movement of the troops concerned to
the United States, but that this would require a two months'
round trip and his shipping would not be available for a further evacuation of Marine units before March 1. He added
that, depending upon the amount of equipment to be withdrawn, it might be practicable to include an additional artil-
lery battalion in the initial movement and he was prepared to
make a recommendation to that effect.

In reply to Admiral Cooke's inquiry regarding a statement he might make at a press conference on December 5, I
suggested that he state that the continued reduction of Marine strength in China was under way, that approximately
5,000 men were now being withdrawn largely from the Chinhuangtao-Peitaiho area and that other withdrawals would be
made when shipping became available.

Future developments regarding the reduction of Marine
strength in China will be reported as extensions of this report.

XXXII.

PROGRAMS OF MILITARY ASSISTANCE TO CHINA
AND STOPPAGES OF SUCH ASSISTANCE

Certain of the programs of military assistance to China
were commenced during the War or shortly after V-J day.
Others were not commenced until after I arrived in China. Regardless of when the programs were initiated, the authority

for the provision of military assistance to China lies in President Truman's verbal commitment to Dr. T.V. Soong on September 14, 1945, and in the President's statement of policy toward China on December 15, 1945. These programs, which are in various stages of completion, are described below.

As it became apparent during my mission in China that the continuation, at that time, of some phases of these programs was not conducive to peace and unity in China nor in the best interests of the United States, action was taken to suspend certain portions of the programs which might have a bearing on prosecution of hostilities and the internal situation in China. Accordingly, the Department of State, beginning in August 1946, withheld approval of export licenses for the export to China of combat type items of military equipment included in these programs. On September 29, 1946, I caused to be issued a directive temporarily suspending the delivery of all military type items for the Reoccupation Program (paragraph 2, below) and the Chinese Air Force Program (paragraph 6, below). In addition to this action, the Department of State adopted a policy regarding the transfer of equipment to the Chinese Government, requiring that any contract signed with the Chinese Government include a proviso stating that military end-use items being transferred are destined for "an integrated and representative national army under a coalition government," and further stating that if it appears in the best interests of the United States at the time of delivery, the contract can be terminated by the United States. All programs, with the exception of the 8⅓ Air Group Program and the Military Advisory Group, are being or have been implemented under the terms of the Lend-Lease Act.

1. *Lend-Lease:* Lend-Lease Aid to China was initiated during the war for the purpose of strengthening the Chinese armed forces. By Presidential Directive, the authority to continue military assistance to China under the Lend-Lease Act was extended to June 30, 1946 (the date of expiration of Presidential authority to provide lend-lease assistance to foreign countries) and on June 28, 1946, a contract was signed by the Department of State with the Chinese Government, under the terms of paragraph 3(c) of the Lend-Lease Act, which provided for the continuation of Lend-Lease, on a reimbursable basis, of the following programs:

(a) The Reoccupation Program and the Training and Equipment Program, together not to exceed $25,000,000 nor to extend beyond October 31, 1946.

(b) The Occupation Program, in an amount determined to be necessary by the Senior U.S. Commander in Japan, not to extend beyond June 30, 1949.

(c) The Air Force Training Program, the Ground and Service School Training Program and a Naval Training Program, not to exceed a total of $15,000,000 nor to extend beyond December 31, 1947.

2. *Reoccupation Program:* This program was designed to assist the Chinese Government in the reoccupation of, and the restoration of order in, those Chinese areas previously held by the Japanese. Authority was given to the Commanding General of the U.S. Armed Forces in China shortly after V-J day to provide whatever military assistance he considered necessary to accomplish this. Under this authority the Commanding General turned over the supplies in the pipeline originally intended for the 39 Division Program (this ceased on V-J day—see paragraph 8) and requisitioned certain additional munitions and other items which were required by the Chinese armies in order to take over from the Japanese. Records were maintained of all such supplies actually turned over to the Chinese in order that these transfers could be applied against any 39 Division Program commitment which the Chinese might consider to remain. It was originally expected that this program would be completed prior to the expiration of Lend-Lease, but when it became apparent that this could not be done, the Department of State entered into an agreement with the Chinese Government authorizing the completion of this program under reimbursable Lend-Lease, as described in 1(a) above. On October 31, 1946, it was directed that supply action in implementation of this program be terminated and that all remaining unfilled requisitions be cancelled. The FLC has, however, made a contract with the Chinese Government to provide certain supplies for the completion of this program through Surplus Sales.

3. *Training and Equipment Program:* During my discussions leading to the agreement for military reorganization and integration of the Communist armed forces into the national

army in February 1946, I came to the conclusion that the integration of the Communist forces would be facilitiated if a moderate amount of equipment could be made available to the Communist divisions which were to be integrated. Accordingly, I made arrangements to make available to the Chinese Government, for the 10 Communist divisions to be retained in the new integrated National Army, the T/E equipment for approximately 11 battalions of Infantry and 11 batteries of FA. This action was approved by the State and War Departments, and the equipment was made available under the terms of reimbursable lend-lease which extended this program, together with the Reoccupation Program, to October 31, 1946. Most of this equipment (244 long tons) was stockpiled in Peiping under control of the Peiping Headquarters Group. The equipment was not turned over to the Communists prior to October 31, 1946, nor after that date, since it did not appear at that time that either the National Government or the Communist Party intended to follow through with the agreement for the military reorganization and integration of Communist forces into a National Army which was reached in February. Nor was the equipment turned over to the National Government since that action would have been contrary to State Department policy previously described. With the inactivation of Peiping Headquarters Group, the equipment will be disposed of, I assume, according to standard supply procedures and all requisitions for the completion of the program cancelled.

4. *Occupation Program*: The Chinese Government was invited to share in the occupation of Japan by a letter of January 1, 1946, signed by Mr. Walter S. Robertson, United States Charge d'Affaires at Nanking. It was subsequently agreed that the Chinese Government would provide a force of 15,000 men to share in the occupation of Japan and SWNCC directed the Department of State to negotiate an agreement, on a governmental level, which has already been tentatively signed by General MacArthur. This agreement specifically charges the Chinese Government with the responsibility for the logistic support of its troops but recognized that some logistic assistance will be required from the United States, since the Chinese lack the organization necessary to provide such support. Under the terms of the 3(c) Lend-Lease Agreement, the Senior U.S. Commander in Japan is authorized to make available to the Occupation Forces such equipment as he feels is necessary in the execution of their mission. As no Chinese occupation troops have yet reached Japan, no action has yet been taken to transfer equipment under this program.

5. *Chinese Training in the United States:*

(a) *Air Force Training Program:* During the war the United States conducted the training of Chinese Air Force personnel as a part of the CAF program, under the provisions of the Lend-Lease Act. After the termination of hostilities, the CAF training program was scheduled to be continued only until November 30, 1945, under the provisions of the President's directive concerning the termination of lend-lease. The Generalissimo, however, in November 1945 requested that the President continue the training of Chinese Air Force personnel in the United States, plus approximately 1,280 CAF personnel still in China, so that the training program envisaged at that time could be completed. The President agreed to the completion of this training and later extended Lend-Lease aid to China until June 30, 1946. Authority to train personnel for the Chinese Air Force was included in the 3(c) Lend-Lease Agreement of June 28, 1946, in an amount not to exceed $8,750,000 in cost to the U.S. Government and not to extend beyond December 31, 1947. Completion of this program will provide a total of 5,127 CAF personnel training by the United States.

(b) *Ground and Service Training Program:* Although the Military Advisory Group had not officially been activated, the Army Advisory Group, China, has had the mission of advising and assisting the Chinese Government in the reorganization of the Armed Forces of China. As a part of this reorganization program, Nanking Headquarters Command (the nucleus for the Military Advisory Group) requested the training of 325 Chinese officers in U.S. service schools to form the faculty for Chinese service schools to be activated later in China. Additionally, the Commanding General, U.S. Forces, China, requested training in the United States for 132 Chinese medical students. This was approved by both the War and State Departments, and the program known as the "Ground and Service School Program" has been established; authority to implement this program under Lend-Lease was contained in the 3(c) Lend-Lease Agreement of June 28, 1946, in an amount not to exceed $1,250,000 in cost to the United States and not to extend beyond December 31, 1947.

6. *The Chinese Air Force Program:* This program, generally known as the 8⅓ Group Program, was initiated during the war under Lend-Lease in order to build up China's Air Force. It was originally planned to provide aircraft, equipment and trained personnel for a balanced air force of 18 groups. This

was subsequently reduced to 13 groups and, after the end of the war, was revised to 8⅓ groups, as a size more nearly within the capacities of the Chinese Government to support. The transfer of equipment under this program has been handled partially under the provisions of the Surplus Sales Act and partially under the provisions of Lend-Lease, until the time of expiration of the Lend-Lease Act (June 30, 1946), after which time all equipment was transferred under the Surplus Sales Act and handled by FLC. This method of transfer was adopted primarily because the Department of State, at the time of the expiration of Lend-Lease, considered it politically unwise to overload the 3(c) Lend-Lease Agreement with additional programs. Subsequently, the Department of State in August 1946 stopped the transfer of undemilitarized equipment for this program through FLC, which action later concurred in by me, and completion of the 8⅓ Group Program was thus temporarily deferred. On October 22, 1946, authority was given to the War Department to turn over civilian type items remaining in the program, but no release has yet been given on military type items.

7. *Military Advisory Group to China:* This group consists of Army, Navy and Air Corps personnel, assigned to give advice to the Chinese Government on the reorganization of the Chinese Armed Forces. The group provides advice only and has assiduously avoided Chinese operational activities of any kind, intelligence or otherwise. The establishment of such a group was originally requested by the Generalissimo and this request was recognized by President Truman in his verbal statement to Dr. T.V. Soong on September 14, 1945, when he said in part: "The exact size, composition and functions of an advisory mission will be dependent upon the status and character of the mission and on the size and composition of the Chinese armed forces which may be agreed between the U.S. and Chinese Governments." General Wedemeyer, Commanding General, China Theater, was directed by the War Department on October 21, 1945, "to make plans and preparations for such U.S. Military Advisory Group to China as may be established in collaboration with Commander Naval Group China." By Presidential directive the President on February 26, 1946, directed and authorized the Secretaries of War and Navy to establish jointly a U.S. Military Advisory Group to China. The strength of the group was limited to 1,000 officers and men. The mission of this group was "to assist and advise the Chinese Government in the development

of modern armed forces for the fulfillment of those objectives which may devolve upon China under her international agreements, including the United Nations Organization, for the establishment of an adequate control over liberated areas in China, including Manchuria and Formosa, and for the maintenance of internal peace and security." After discussion with the War and Navy Departments, the Department of State forwarded a draft governmental agreement regarding the establishment of this mission to the American Embassy at Nanking and discussions of this agreement have taken place with the Chinese Government, although no final action in this regard has yet been taken. The Army section of this group has been functioning under the title of the Army Advisory Group China and, operating on an informal basis, has served to assist the Chinese Government in the reorganization of its Ministry of National Defense and to perform vital staff work related to the reorganization of the National Government and Communist armies as envisaged in the military reorganization agreement of February 25, 1946. Authority for the official establishment of the Military Advisory Group exists under the war powers of the President, but no legislative authority yet exists for the Army section of this group. However, Public Law 512 authorizes the establishment of a Naval Advisory Group, and if the war powers of the President are revoked before legislative authority exists to activate the group as a whole, the Naval section may be activated formally.

8. *39 Division Program:* This program, as a program, ceased as of V-J day. (The term "program," as used here, is the mechanical means of implementing a plan or a commitment). During the war, the 39 Division Program was the mechanical means of transferring the moderate amounts of equipment (3000 tons per division for those divisions in China) with which it was intended to equip 39 Chinese divisions in order to strengthen the Chinese Army. Effective on V-J day, the President, on August 11, 1945, directed the Commanding General, U.S. Forces, China Theater, that "military assistance will be continued for the present for the purpose of supporting Chinese military operations essential in the reoccupation by Central Government forces of all areas in the China Theater now held by the Japanese. . . ." This directive automatically precluded any assistance except that required to support the Reoccupation Mission, and, therefore, did away with any program as such designed only to strengthen the Chinese Army. This did not, however, nullify any commitment which might

have been made to the Chinese Government, and in view of the President's verbal commitment to Dr. T.V. Soong on September 14, 1945, "to complete the 39 Division Program," there still existed a requirement to provide the supplies required to satisfy the commitment. Accordingly, to prevent duplication in transfer of equipment, the Commanding General, U.S. Forces, China Theater, was directed to maintain records of all equipment transferred to support the reoccupation mission (Reoccupation Program) and to apply the equipment so transferred as a credit against the 39 Division commitment. The Reoccupation Program can, therefore, be considered as satisfying both the support required for the reoccupation mission and also the supplies required for the 39 Division commitment. The total amount of equipment transferred under the Reoccupation Program has already completed, in terms of equipment required, the commitment to complete the 39 Division Program.

9. *Chinese Peace Time Army Program:* The military reorganization agreement of February 25, 1946, required the reduction of the National Government and Chinese Communist forces to 50 National Government and 10 Communist divisions at the end of 18 months, at which time they would be integrated into a national army. In March 1946 the Commanding General, U.S. Forces, China Theater, proposed a further reduction to a total of 50 divisions (10 active and 40 inactive), believing that China's economy would be more nearly able to support such an armed establishment. In order to assist in the organization and equipping of such an army, he also proposed that the United States Government supply whatever shortages existed in the 10 active divisions (using as a basis the U.S. Army divisional T/E, modified as required for China), and assist the Chinese Government in acquiring the equipment required for the 40 inactive divisions. The provision of equipment for this 50-division, integrated army has been termed the Chinese Peace Time Army Program. This program has never been officially approved, either by the United States Government or by the Generalissimo and remains in the discussion stage, no commitment having been made in this regard to the Chinese Government. Official recognition of this program has been given by the Department of State, which has concurred in the policy of continuing discussions with the Chinese and holding the equipment for 10 divisions, such equipment being held by the U.S. Army in the Pacific from surplus stocks in CINCFE.

10. *Legislation to Provide Military Assistance to China:*
As it became apparent that military assistance to China
would be required for some time subsequent to the close of
the war, the Army, the Navy and the Department of State
considered the introduction of bills to Congress which would
authorize the United States Government to extend military
assistance to the Chinese Government. Three such bills were
introduced to Congress and one has become law.

(a) A bill "to provide military advice and assistance to
the Republic of China, to aid it in modernizing its armed forces for the fulfillment of obligations which may devolve upon
it under the charter of the United Nations" was introduced by
the Department of State at the request of the War Department. The bill was considered by both the House and Senate
Military Committees of the 79th Congress, but no action was
taken on the bill. It was originally my opinion that the passage of the bill would facilitate the efforts being made toward
peace and unity in China and toward the establishment of
unified national defense forces. It was expected that the aid
to the Chinese armies envisaged in this bill would be carried
out in accordance with the program for the reorganization of
the Chinese armies and the integration of the Communist forces into a national army as agreed upon by both sides. Subsequent political and military developments in China, however,
made it inadvisable to press for consideration of this bill and
for the formal establishment of the Military Advisory Group
provided for under this bill. I, therefore, recommended that
action on this bill be deferred for the time being until the political situation in China should warrant further consideration
of such aid by the United States Government.

(b) A bill to provide for the establishment of military
missions to assist foreign governments was proposed by the
Department of State as a part of its over-all policy regarding
the establishment of such missions. Passage of such a bill
would authorize the establishment of the Military Advisory
Group to China, but would not authorize the training of Chinese personnel or the transfer of supplies and equipment to the
Chinese Government. No final action was taken on this bill by
the 79th Congress.

(c) A bill proposed by the Navy Department, providing
assistance to the Chinese Navy and authorizing the establishment of a Naval Advisory Group, the transfer of U.S Naval
equipment and the provision of naval training to Chinese students was passed as Public Law 512 on July 16, 1946. Under

402

authority of this law a Naval Advisory Group may be established separately from the joint military advisory group.

11. *Surplus Property Sales:*

(a) *West China:* On November 29, 1945, the Commanding General, China Theater, entered into an agreement with the Chinese Government whereby the Chinese purchased all United States Army property west of the 110 degree meridian. This was executed because of excessive banditry, looting and promiscuous rifle firing, which were endangering American lives.

(b) *East China:* All surplus property sales in east China have been handled through the FLC. On August 30, 1946, FLC completed a contract with the Chinese Government whereby all surpluses in China, Okinawa, Guam, Saipan, Tinian, Eniwetok, Marcus, Kwajalein, Los Negros, Ulithi, Majuro, Makin, Manus, Pelelieu, Finschafen, Iwo Jima, and Roi, with the exception of aircraft, non-demilitarized combat material, ships and other maritime equipment, and fixed installations outside of Chinese territory, were sold to the Chinese Government.

XXXIII.
THE NATIONAL ASSEMBLY AND THE NEW CONSTITUTION; PRESIDENT TRUMAN'S STATEMENT OF AMERICAN POLICY TOWARD CHINA

Following General Chou En-lai's departure for Yenan and the termination, at least for the time being, of negotiations, attention was centered chiefly on the National Assembly and the question of the type of constitution it might adopt. There were early indications that the Kuomintang reactionaries were opposed to the adoption of a constitution along the lines of the PCC resolutions and that they were endeavoring to obtain approval of the May 5, 1936 constitution in substantially unchanged form. The National Assembly gradually evolved rules for procedure and heated discussions took place in the Assembly, one of the delegates even going so far as to contest an issue with the Generalissimo on the floor. There were indications that the determined efforts of the Kuomintang reactionaries would compel the Generalissimo to take a strong stand if the constitution to be adopted were to be in general accord with the PCC resolutions.

In addition to the question of the constitution, there was also the question of the possibility, as alleged by the Communists of a National Government attack on Yenan. Any possible plans for an attack on Yenan were apparently given up during the latter part of November as there was no further publicity on the part of the Chinese Communists regarding such action. At this time, in discussion of the conditions under which the Communist branch of the Executive Headquarters would withdraw, General Yeh Chien-ying, Communist Party Commissioner, informed me that the action of the National Government in convening the National Assembly was a step toward a political split and that a Government attack on Yenan would result in a military split that would make further negotiations impossible. General Yeh then went on to describe Communist strategy. The Communists had evacuated large cities because they did not want local victories but an over-all victory. The Communists had learned during the past five months that the National Government did not have sufficient military strength to conduct simultaneous campaigns in Manchuria and north China. The Government was now conducting a vigorous campaign of recruiting and taxation, and, while Communist strength had remained more or less intact, the Government had had considerable losses. The greatest obstacles for peace were the "CC" clique, the secret police and the Kuomintang militarists. He hoped that I would study the situation carefully and endeavor to convince the Chinese Government of the necessity for a peaceful settlement.

I replied that it was utterly wrong for either side to use military force, as I felt that the situation could not be settled by force, and that I had not agreed with either side in its military operations.

General Yeh's statements gave some indication of possible Communist tactics. The Communists were so deeply distrustful of the National Government that they would not again enter into negotiations unless the Government could be convinced that the Communists could not be destroyed by force; unless the Government should have reached the point of collapse as a result of economic deterioration; or unless the Government were willing to enter into negotiations on terms acceptable to the Communist Party.

On November 30 Mr. Tung Pi-wu, ranking member of the Communist Party delegation at Nanking, informed Dr. Stuart that he knew of no promise made by General Chou in regard to obtaining Yenan's reaction to American mediation and stated frankly that he did not trust the American mediation efforts. He did, however, agree to send a message to Yenan in regard to this question. In contrast to Mr. Tung's comment on American mediation was that made to me during this same period by Chinese minority party representatives, who said that they felt that the Communist Party did desire the continuation of the American mediation effort. However, in view of the failure of the Communist Party to reply to my direct question regarding my participation in the mediation and of the attitude of the Kuomintang reactionaries, my position was becoming increasingly difficult. I felt that the Kuomintang reactionary group viewed my role as an undesirable necessity, since by keeping me continually in the picture these reactionaries could continue their undemocratic practices and military campaigns under the guise of willingness to negotiate, thus placing me in a position which could compromise American policy.

On December 1 I held a lengthy conference with the Generalissimo, which revealed the wide divergence of our respective views on what course should be followed to reach a peaceful settlement in China. The Generalissimo asked what should be done in the present situation—the Communists not having replied to my inquiry regarding American mediation and having refused to participate in the National Assembly or in further negotiations.

I replied as follows: In my opinion the complete distrust of the National Government in the good intentions of the Communist Party during the past spring had been replaced by an overwhelming distrust on the part of the Communists of the good intent of any proposal advanced by the Government toward a peaceful settlement of the differences. In the recent negotiations Dr. Stuart and I had found it impossible to convince the Communists of the good intentions of the Government or even of our own integrity of action. It was my view that even the most tolerant approaches of the National Government, notably that represented by the Generalissimo's eight point proposal of October 16, had been neutralized by military action—in this particular case an attack on Antung and Chefoo at the time of the announcement of this proposal. At this time the only hope I could see of obtaining Communist cooperation in the establishment of a representative form of government was along the following lines: adoption by the National Assembly of a constitution in accord with the PCC principles, such action to be followed by the establishment of the State Council with seats accorded the Communist Party and the Democratic League and by a bona fide reorganization of the Executive Yuan. The constitution presented to the National Assembly seemed to be in reasonable accord with the PCC. If this constitution were adopted without vitiating amendments voiding the protections insisted upon by the liberals, if definite steps were taken to put this constitution into effect, if the other above-described steps were also taken, and if the Government sent a representative to Yenan to invite Yenan participation in this procedure, I thought that the Communists would be in a weak position. It would, of course, be necessary to cease military operations except those of a defensive nature, which must be for bona fide purposes of defense and not by way of retaliation. I felt it advisable for the Government to approach the Communists privately in these matters in order to prevent the usual Communist charges of the National Government's unilateral action intended for propaganda to the world.

In regard to the economic situation, I continued, military expenditures were reported at this time to be consuming about 90 percent (this figure is disputed) of the National Government budget, thus creating a vacuum in Government assets in order to support extensive military efforts at the same time that I was being pressed to recommend various loans by the United States Government. In the event of a financial collapse the Kuomintang would be imperiled and a fertile field would be created for the spread of communism. The National Government military commanders in the field were wholly unaccustomed to any consideration of financial restrictions; national economy was not a factor with them as it was almost conclusively with the United States Army officers and as it had been my principal preoccupation for years. The Communists were aware of the approaching crisis and this entered into their calculations in forming plans. Directly opposed to this economic problem was the view of the National Government military leaders that the issues could be settled by force. I not only disagreed with this view from a military standpoint but also felt that before sufficient time could elapse to prove the accuracy of such a view there would be a complete economic collapse. The inability of the National Government to keep open the railway between Tientsin and Chinhuangtao since the withdrawal of the United States Marines was an example. Another was the fact that sections of Hopei Province presumably reoccupied by the National Government forces were still dotted throughout with Communist headquarters.

I summed up the situation with the statement that the Communists were too large a military and civil force to be ignored and that, even if one disregarded the brutality of the inevitable procedure necessary to destroy them, they probably could not be eliminated by military campaigning. Therefore, it was imperative that efforts to bring them into the Government should continue and that the greatest care should be taken to avoid having military action disrupt the procedure of negotiations.

In a statement of more than an hour, the Generalissimo made the following reply: He was firmly convinced that the Communists never intended to cooperate with the National Government. They were acting under Soviet Russian influence and their purpose was to disrupt the National Government and to influence its foreign policy. He felt it necessary to destroy the Communist military forces and believed that if this were done there would be no great difficulty in handling the Communist question. The situation was different from that existing during early campaigns against the Communist forces in that roads were available at this time to permit freedom of military movement. He felt confident, therefore, that the Communist forces could be exterminated in from 8 to 10 months.

Referring briefly to the economic situation, the Generalissimo continued that, while the situation was more serious in the cities, the Chinese economy was based largely on the agrarian population and there was no danger for about two years of the collapse which I had indicated.

The Generalissimo went on that the most valuable part of Manchuria was that south of Changchun and that he felt the National Government was able to maintain itself in this area. He would refrain from advancing on Harbin because he felt that so long as he did not take this step the Soviet Union would take no action inimical to the National Government. He discussed at length the matter of Soviet reactions; his experience and belief were that when the Chinese Government showed its strength the Soviets acquiesced to peaceful arrangements. He cited the Soviet reaction following the National Government's capture of Antung and expressed the opinion that as long as the National Government showed a strong hand the Soviets would at this time cooperate with the Chinese Government in negotiations and arrangements. It was his belief that the Soviets intended to avoid complications in the Far East as long as they were heavily involved in Germany.

The Generalissimo then referred to his age of 60 years and said that he was no longer capable of the activity and energy of former years and he must, therefore, soon terminate his role as a leader. He felt, however, that it was his duty to the Chinese people not to surrender this control until he had positively settled the Communist question. In this connection, he continued, I should not consider my mission as confined exclusively to bringing together the National Government and the Chinese Communist Party. Since the Communists had displayed unwillingness to cooperate, my role should be to facilitate the development of stability in the present government in China and in the Far East. The United States should redefine its policy regarding China in the light of the present situation. (He evidently meant, in effect, that it should no longer be thought practical to consider the Communist Party as a working part of the Government.) He concluded by saying that he would do everything he could to bring the Communists into the Government by peaceful negotiations and would consider suggestions from Dr. Stuart and me to that end.

With reference to his implication regarding American policy and the Communist Party, I briefly, but firmly, restated my view that this large Communist group could not be ignored and that the National Government was not capable of destroying it, in my opinion, before the country would be faced with a complete economic collapse. I did not discuss what to me was of vital concern—that was the possibility of a collapse of the Kuomintang and the evident growing disapproval of the people of the character of the local government, or misgovernment, that the Kuomintang was giving the country.

During this period, in conversations with the Generalissimo and with other National Government leaders, I was endeavoring to emphasize the importance and necessity of the adoption by the National Assembly of a constitution in keeping with the PCC resolutions, which would be at least an initial step in the direction of representative government in China. On December 4 I voiced these views to General Yu Ta-wei and pointed out that the only chance for the Communists to come into the National Assembly was for the Government actually to make some changes. For example, the National Government should adopt the present constitution without disrupting amendments and tricky phrases. If the State Council were then reorganized with seats left vacant for the Communists and the Democratic League, and if the reorganization of the Executive Yuan were then begun, the Communists would be placed in a rather difficult position. While these steps were being taken, the Generalissimo, I said, should send representatives privately to Yenan to discuss with the Communists ways of their coming into the National Assembly. I felt that he should avoid making a public statement for fear of arousing the usual Communist reaction of distrust and suspicion and above all such action must be accompanied by the cessation of aggressive military action on the part of the Government. One difficulty would be that the Government might resort to much abused "self-defensive" measures and it was my hope that the Government military leaders would not become involved in retaliation, as that would destroy all chances of Communist participation in the Government.

I described to General Yu the Generalissimo's comments regarding the economic situation and his statement concerning an 8 to 10 months' campaign to destroy the Communists and said that I disagreed entirely with these views. I informed General Yu that the Export-Import Bank had recently rejected my recommendations, approved by the Department of State, for the extension of loans for the Canton-Hankow Railway and for the Yellow River Bridge in north Honan and that the Bank had given as the reason for this action that there was "not sufficient prospect of amortization" to justify the loans. When General Yu said that he did not understand why the loans had been rejected since they had nothing to do with the Government's military campaign, I explained that it was the character of the Kuomintang Government and the open corruption as well as the military policy of the Government which entered into consideration of loans. I pointed out that in the past the National Advisory Council and the Export-Import Bank had agreed to grant loans only to a China that had achieved peace and evident reforms in the Government.

During this conversation with General Yu I referred to a recent dispatch of the Kuomintang Central News Agency regarding a report of conferences between General Chou En-lai and me, which I had given to General Yu as a result of the Generalissimo's request. I pointed out that I had done this only because the Generalissimo had made a request that he be permitted to see the pertinent portions of my latest meetings with General Chou and that I had not asked General Chou's permission, as I had always done in the past, because he had already departed for Yenan. Although the portions I had given to General Yu had contained only General Chou's reasons for returning to Yenan, this publicity had placed me in an unfavorable light as being a reporter to the National Government. General Yu expressed his regrets at the publicity and said that he did not know the "authoritative source" quoted in the news dispatch.

Under date of December 4 Mr. Tung Pi-wu forwarded to me a memorandum,[83] containing a message from General Chou En-lai, the substance of which was as follows:

> With the inauguration of the "one-party manipulated" National Assembly, the PCC agreements have been completely destroyed by President Chiang Kai-shek and there is "short of basis for negotiation" between the Kuomintang and the Chinese Communist Party. However, with a view to complying with the aspirations of the Chinese people for peace and democracy, the Chinese Communist Party "takes the stand" that if the Kuomintang would immediately dissolve the "illegal" National Assembly and would restore the troop positions as of January 13 in accordance with the Cessation of Hostilities Order, negotiations between the two parties may still "make a fresh start." It is requested that the foregoing be transmitted to Generalissimo Chiang Kai-shek.

A copy of this memorandum was forwarded, without comment, by my office to General Yu Ta-wei on December 5 for transmission to the Generalissimo.

General Chou's message made no reply to my request for indication by the Communist Party of its attitude toward my mediation efforts and was unrealistic in that it posed conditions which the National Government obviously could not be expected to accept.

Dr. Stuart and I discussed this message on December 5. He felt that General Chou's statement was tantamount to a Communist acceptance of the Generalissimo's challenge to settle issues by force and suggested that the Generalissimo be told outright that if he persisted in following a policy of force, American aid would be totally withdrawn. He felt that, conversely, the Generalissimo should be told that if he reformed

[83]See Volume Two, Appendix R, Document 1, for the full text.

the Kuomintang and broadened the Government on a democratic basis, he could expect American aid in military and economic matters, but that American supervision would, however, be necessary to ensure the carrying out of political reforms.

I replied that the Generalisimo had already been told emphatically that the United States would not support a campaign of force and that consideration should be given to the announcement of a new policy in the event that the Generalissimo did follow a course of reform. I doubted that hostilities could be stopped unilaterally in any case since the Government always claimed to be fighting in self-defense. The immense task confronting the Government in guarding long vital lines of communications required a large army and it would be impossible to achieve any demobilization of the Government forces as long as active hostile Communist forces were in the field and as long as the Generalissimo was bent on the military destruction of the Communist Party. The final disposition of the Communist armies would have to be determined before any appreciable demobilization of the Government forces could be accomplished.

I recounted to Dr. Stuart my many efforts to break the power of the reactionary group in the Government and pointed out that this was an important issue. The Communists by their actions were, however, playing directly into the hands of the reactionaries. When Dr. Stuart said that the Generalissimo must, once and for all, break with the reactionary group and expressed the opinion that this was a definite possibility, I replied that I doubted this possibility, particularly since the Generalissimo was convinced that a policy of force was the only practicable solution and since he completely distrusted the Communists and their purposes in entering the government. I added that whenever the Generalissimo made concessions, he did so, I thought, against his own better judgment and that in moments of crisis he was therefore influenced by reactionary associates. The Communist Party, I felt, was at this time practically beyond our reach and had in effect rejected American mediation.

Returning to consideration of a new policy, I said that no new policy could be recommended until we knew the answers to certain questions: (1) The Communist attitude toward me personally; (2) the type of constitution adopted by the National Assembly; (3) the method of implementing that constitution; (4) the reorganization of the State Council and the

411

Executive Yuan; and (5) the extent to which, or manner in which, the door was left open for Communist participation.

At this time Dr. Stuart advanced to me his idea of an American policy toward China along a three point program of military aid in the reorganization of the National Government armies, technical assistance in the economic field and technical advice in the political field. I agreed with these three points but was doubtful whether such a program could be carried out under existing conditions. Further demobilization by the National Government was not to be expected as long as the Communists retained their armies in the field. The question was whether a peaceful atmosphere could be obtained in the field to permit advancement along political and economic lines. I felt that technical assistance should be given and cited as an example the matter of the loan to China for the development and rehabilitation of the Canton-Hankow Railway, which had been disapproved by the Export-Import Bank. I hoped that some sort of acceptable constitution might be adopted before I should undertake to approach the United States Government again and urge the granting of this loan. Limited support for the Chinese Government had, however, two drawbacks in that it would give encouragement to the reactionary elements and military clique and would therefore make more difficult the reform of the Government, the breaking of the Party domination of the Government and the keeping open of a way for the Communists to re-enter the negotiations. A proper balance between these two aspects was a matter of the greatest concern to me at this time.

In early December the Generalissimo had informed Dr. Stuart of the Chinese Government's desire to obtain my services as adviser. Dr. Stuart had informed him that he did not think that I would consider such a position in view of the existence of civil war in China. In discussing this matter with Dr. Stuart on December 9, I told Dr. Stuart that the best answer at this time was a definite "no." It was unreasonable to expect that my services as adviser to the National Government could materially promote a beneficial reaction within the Government when as a mediator with full backing from the United States Government I was unable to influence the Chinese Government. In subsequent discussion of this matter with the Generalissimo I had categorically refused to accept his invitation to remain in China as an adviser to the National Government. An American could not accept such a position in the face of civil war and the position of the United States in China would be embarrassed since my services as an adviser would tend to stultify all my previous actions in the mediation effort.

In a conversation on December 9 with Mr. Wei Tao-ming, Vice President of the Legislative Yuan and former Chinese Ambassador to Washington, I repeated my view of the necessity of the adoption of a sound democratic constitution and the reorganization of the government as a possible means of arriving at a peaceful settlement. I pointed to the dangers of a policy of force to exterminate the Communist Party and stressed the need for reforms in the Kuomintang as a means of strengthening that party and attracting popular support.

Although I had counselled the Government leaders to give no publicity to their sending a peace delegation to Yenan, a report of this plan did "leak out." The Communist reaction was not favorable. I felt that the Government might have purposely disclosed such a plan in order to test the Communist reaction. It seemed that while the Communists had previously wished to stop the fighting, they felt that either their conditions (return to troop positions of January 13 and dissolution of the National Assembly) had to be met or they would prefer to fight. It was my opinion that the procedure of the Communists at this time was actually pleasing to the reactionary political and military clique in the National Government and that the latter were allowing the Communists to play into their hands.

On December 13 Dr. Stuart informed me that the Generalissimo had shown deep feeling and embarrassment the previous day in regard to the situation in China. The Generalissimo had expressed a desire for American aid in making China strong, modern and efficient and, stating that the primary problem was one of government organization, indicated that he desired advice in this field much more than loans and material aid. The Generalissimo had gone on to express the belief that I could aid greatly in leading China out of her ancient inefficiencies and in giving the country honest government and an efficient army.

I told Dr. Stuart that the basic question was where the most important service to China could be rendered. I was struggling with two problems—the power of the reactionaries in the Government and the difficulty of dealing with the Communist Party in view of its immense distrust of the Kuomintang. The best way to defend against Communism, I said, was for the existing government of China to accomplish such

413

reforms that it would gain the support of the people. I commented on the destructive influence of the reactionaries in the Government and said that the Generalissimo's own feelings were so deep and his associations of such long standing that it was most difficult to divorce him from the reactionary group. The solution, in my opinion, seemed to call for the building up of the liberals under the Generalissimo while at the same time tearing down the reactionaries. To attack the reactionaries by a statement in China would only provide tremendous encouragement to the Communists, but a statement made in the United States would be widely reported and would be reflected with less distortion all over China. Such a statement must be forceful, must explain the situation to the people of the United States, must make the reactionaries in China plainly see the handwriting on the wall and must strengthen the position of the liberals. No statement, however, should be made until the constitution should have been adopted and the National Government should have taken steps to enforce the constitution and reorganize the government.

Referring to the Generalissimo's desire for American advice, I pointed out that the machinery already existed for providing military and naval advice and the question was how to make practical use of this machinery, which at this time was being neutralized by the civil war. One of the prime needs of the Government was to place its financial procedure on a sound basis; other fields included the establishment of a firm budget and a general overhauling of the taxation system. American advisers could be helpful in these matters if they were given sufficient authority and had direct access to Government figures on decision levels. Corruption within the Government could not, however, be eliminated through advice but only through the existence of an effective opposition party.

Dr Stuart had on the previous day submitted a memorandum to the Generalissimo covering the subject of American technical assistance and advice, included in which was a scheme for the reopening of the two north-south railways in north China (Peiping-Hankow and Tientsin-Pukow Railways). Dr. Stuart informed me that the Generalissimo had accepted the idea regarding the rail lines and had expressed his willingness to approach the Communists on this subject. I told Dr. Stuart that I doubted that the Communists would agree to the railway proposal as they would, in their distrust of the Government, regard the proposal as a guise for moving troops into Communist areas. The railway issue was, however, I felt, extremely vital. I suggested that it might be more realistic to begin with the Tientsin-Pukow Railway since it did not traverse the heart of the Communist area; if the experiment proved successful, sufficient mutual faith might be developed to permit application of the procedure in other areas. Successful completion of such a program required faithful keeping of the peace and this would be extremely difficult because of the mass of misrepresentation to be encountered on both sides.

Dr. Stuart said that the Generalissimo wished to discuss with us the questions of American advice and supervision of modernization of the Chinese governmental system to permit the establishment of a progressive and democratic government.

In furtherance of this idea of endeavoring to build up the liberal group in China to a position of influence, I took every opportunity in conversation with minority and non-party Chinese to emphasize the necessity of the unification of the minority parties and the organization of a liberal group in China to serve as a balance between the Kuomintang and the Communist Party. As I told Dr. Lo Lung-chi during a conversation on December 18, the liberal Chinese must band together into a single liberal patriotic organization devoted to the welfare of the people and not to the selfish interests of minor party group leaders. They would then, I said, be able to exert influence in the political situation, an influence which would increase as the party gained positions and patronage. Such a party could stand between the two major parties and neither of the major parties could normally take a decisive step without the support of the liberal party. At this time, I continued, the minority parties had allowed themselves to be divided and were consequently unable to influence the situation or prevent the use of military force by the Government or promotion of economic collapse by the Communists. In the midst of this deplorable situation stood the Chinese people alone bearing the full weight of this tragedy.

I referred to the vicious campaign of misrepresentation by the Communists and explained that I had remained in China in the hope that my presence would facilitate the adoption of a genuine democratic constitution, although I could not be expected to sit silently forever under this malicious deluge of misrepresentation. I said that I had often felt in the past that the National Government desired American mediation as a shield for its military campaigns and I felt at this time that the Communists had no desire for further American mediation but feared being placed in an unfavorable position if they were to reject formally such mediation. I had, therefore, I said, become a convenience to the Communists just as I had once been used for the convenience of the Kuomintang. I had asked the Communist Party a simple direct question and I did not consider that my question had yet been answered. I would, however, not allow myself to be used as a convenience by either party and definitely would not allow the United States Government to be maneuvered into a position where its integrity could be questioned. When Dr. Lo said that there were indications that the Communists intended to recapture certain areas to strengthen their position in the peace negotiations, I said that I did not intend to serve as an umpire on the battlefield. My usefulness as a negotiator, I pointed out, had practically been wrecked by the recent Communist actions of rejection of all Government overtures, actions which played directly into the hands of the reactionaries in the Government from whom my chief opposition had always come.

Dr. Lo then commented as follows on Communist intentions: The possibilities of peaceful negotiations would be lessened if the reorganization of the government were accomplished without Communist participation therein, as the latter would consider unilateral reorganization of the government as positive indication that the Communists were not wanted in the Government. He did not believe that the Communists' two conditions were rigid. The first, dissolution of the National Assembly, would soon be overtaken by events, and the second, return to troop positions of January 13, referred not so much to restoration of military positions as to retention of the local governments. Dr. Lo then described three conditions recently laid down by General Chou En-lai for the resumption of negotiations. These required a new inter-party conference, the establishment of a coalition government and the convening of a new National Assembly. Dr. Lo recognized that a compromise would be necessary in connection with the third point as the Government could not be expected to accept the constitution adopted by this Assembly. The important question, therefore, in his opinion, concerned the inter-party conference. He felt that such a conference should follow the spirit but not the form of earlier PCC meetings and said that it was possible, although very difficult, for the minority parties to reconcile all differences. He concluded that the Democratic League had refrained from participation in the National Assembly in order to show the Communist

Party that it was not alone and that it still had friends who would stand by it in the event of new negotiations.

In connection with the question of American mediation, Mr. Wang Ping-nan, member of the Communist delegation at Nanking, on December 18 informed Dr. Stuart that he did not think it "profitable" for the Communist delegation to send another message to Yenan asking for a direct reply to my query regarding American mediation. Mr. Wang said that General Chou's message of December 4, although vague, implied that the Communist Party did desire American mediation and added that the Communists probably wanted a formal reply to that message from the Chinese Government. Dr. Stuart and I agreed that we should not press the Government for a reply since the Communists had not answered my direct question and since, if this document was to be considered as the Communist reply to my question, it did not require acknowledgment by the National Government. We felt that it was also very likely that the Communists desired a reply in the realization that it would be vitriolic, thus providing a convenient face-saving way for the Communists to reject the Government's peace delegation to Yenan.

In discussion of this and other matters with Dr. Stuart on December 18 I made the following comments: I had noted in recent conversations with the Generalissimo definite inconsistencies with reference to Dr. Stuart's proposal regarding the reopening of the two main railways in north China. The Generalissimo had emphasized his desire to make every effort to bring the Communists into the Government but at the same time had said that it was useless to attempt to negotiate with the Communists over the railways, which would have to be cleared by force. The Generalissimo had also said that if the railways were taken by force, the Communists would then be compelled to come to terms. A similar attitude had been taken by the Generalissimo last June, when he said that "given time, the ripe apple will fall in our laps," and again in August, when he said that "if hostilities are stopped, there would be no way to force the Communists to attend the National Assembly." I felt that both the National Government and the Communist Party found it convenient to have continued American mediation—on the Government side for the purpose of covering an active military campaign and on the Communist side to avoid the possibility of being charged with breaking off the negotiations. Even the Generalissimo's request that I serve as an adviser to the Chinese Government was possibly an indication of the Government's desire to use my influence to obtain future American loans. It seemed to me that all these circumstances left me with the necessity of deciding on the best course of action at this time. About the only thing that could be done immediately was to exert all effort toward the adoption of a genuine democratic constitution in keeping with the PCC and toward the reorganization of the government.

Dr. Stuart and I agreed that the question of reopening the two major railways in north China should not be made a major issue in any discussion which might take place in Yenan, since it appeared quite obvious that if this question were made the main issue, the Communists would immediately resist any attempts toward subsequent negotiations. We felt that a definite agenda should be prepared and that the Government delegates should go to Yenan prepared to offer sufficient concessions to the Communists to encourage their re-entry into the political picture—such as the establishment of the State Council with seats for the Communists, the reorganization of the Executive Yuan with definite indications and promises for Communist participation and a definite and fair proposal for the operation of the two north China railways. We decided that when specific and liberal proposals along these lines were developed by the Government, not before that time, Dr. Stuart should then urge that the delegation go to Yenan and clear the matter through the Communist delegation at Nanking.

I felt, however, that the prospect for the renewal of negotiations at this time was slight. As I informed Dr. Stuart, it was my opinion that I should return to the United States for consultation and that, after President Truman had issued his statement reaffirming American policy toward China, I should issue a statement of my own. This statement would be designed to tear down the military leaders and the reactionary political clique in the Chinese Government as well as the devastating obstructionist attitude on the part of the Communist Party. By this means I would hope to assist in building up the liberals in both parties and at large and to appeal to the Generalissimo to rely upon these liberals for the reform of the governmental establishment in China.

The Department of State had earlier felt that the issuance by the President of a statement regarding American policy toward China was desirable in order to provide clarification of the situation with respect to American aid to China. The Department prepared such a statement and forwarded it to me for study and approval, which I gave after making some minor changes therein. On December 18 President Truman issued this statement[84] at Washington. It was in general a reaffirmation of existing American policy toward China and a review of that policy as it had developed during the past year.

Interpretation of the President's statement and its significance varied according to the political slant of the Chinese newspapers concerned. The Chinese Government and party press generally interpreted the statement as being an endorsement of the National Government's policy and position. Left-wing and liberal comment pointed with approval to the hope expressed in the statement for the broadening of the Government. The Communist Party spokesman stated that, while the President had not frankly admitted that an erroneous American policy had caused the failure of the peace talks and the aggravation of civil war, he had indicated understanding that the various agreements reached between the two parties had been disregarded and that a coalition government must include the Communist Party. In general the statement was taken as an endorsement of the views held by the newspaper concerned.

General Chou En-lai, however, made a strong attack at Yenan on the President's statement, describing it as "mainly an apology for the United States Government's reactionary policy toward China since March of this year." He said that it contained nothing new and was intended to "blindfold public opinion at home and abroad and block embarrassing criticisms from all quarters" so that the American "reactionary policy toward China" could continue without change.

On December 24 an incident occurred at Peiping involving the alleged rape of a Chinese girl by an American Marine. This incident served to bring to a focus the anti-American feeling in China, and university and middle school students throughout the country organized demonstrations demanding the punishment of the Marine involved in this incident and the withdrawal of American troops from China. While there was undoubtedly Communist participation in and encouragement for these demonstrations, there were indications that the demonstrations were aimed indirectly against the National Government and were a sign of general feeling against the

[84]See Volume Two, Appendix R, Document 2, for the full text.

Kuomintang. They served as an outlet for the feeling against the Kuomintang and were probably as anti-Government as they were anti-American in character. These demonstrations served to indicate the general feeling of unrest in the country and the danger of the use of other incidents to arouse widespread feeling against the United States. Shortly before this incident, I had told the Kuomintang Minister of Information that there appeared to be a growing solidarity of feeling within China against the National Government and that, while much of this feeling was directed against the United States at this time because of the strong anti-American Communist propaganda, the National Government should expect this feeling to shift directly against the Government in the near future.

On December 25 the National Assembly adjourned after having adopted a new constitution[85] in substantially the same form as that originally presented to the Assembly. The new constitution seemed to be in general agreement with the PCC resolutions and of a reasonably democratic character. Early meetings of the Assembly had been spirited and there were sharp discussion and argument, the Kuomintang reactionary group giving evidence of definite intent to change the constitution to conform to the May 5, 1936 Draft Constitution, which was generally felt to be an illiberal document. In the end it had been necessary for the Generalissimo to exercise a determined personal leadership in order to overcome the opposition of the Kuomintang reactionaries. In this he had been assisted by almost all other groups and individuals in the Assembly in opposing the extreme right-wing "CC" clique. The Assembly had ended with the Generalissimo in full and confident control of the situation, thus demonstrating his ability to override the Kuomintang reactionaries and restoring his prestige through his action in securing the adoption of a constitution in reasonable accord with the PCC resolutions.

Prior to its adjournment, the Assembly passed resolutions providing that the new constitution would be enforced on December 25, 1947, that the Government would during the next three months draw up election laws and abrogate all laws now on the statute books which were in violation of the constitution and that the elections themselves would be completed within nine months. The existing Assembly would continue in power until a new Assembly should have been elected.

[85]See Volume Two, Appendix R, Document 3, for the full text.

After the adoption of the new constitution, the Kuomintang Minister of Information told the press that the Kuomintang Ministries of Information, Organization and Overseas Chinese Affairs would continue as Party agencies and would not become official Government Ministries with the adoption of the new constitution. He indicated, however, that the expenses of these three Ministries would in the future be paid from Kuomintang funds entirely and not from the Government Treasury. Mr. Chen Li-fu, Kuomintang Minister of Organization and leader of the reactionary "CC" clique, stated just before the adjournment of the Assembly, however, that the National Government and the Kuomintang would retain their present status during the transitional period between the promulgation of the new constitution and its enforcement. Later reports from apparently reliable sources indicated that the title to various properties was being quietly transferred from the Chinese Government to the Kuomintang, apparently against that time when the Party would be divorced from its position of access to governmental revenues.

Even prior to the adoption of the new constitution, the Communist Party had denounced the National Assembly as a "one-party controlled, illegal splitting" organization and had said that "any alleged constitution passed by this National Assembly is, therefore, a phony constitution." General Chou En-lai stated at Yenan on December 28 that the Communist Party would not recognize the National Assembly and the new constitution as legal and valid and that the Communists advocated the "nullification" of the Assembly and the convening of a new National Assembly.

Chinese reaction in Kuomintang-controlled areas ranged from eulogistic comment on the new constitution by the Government press to pleas from the opposition press that the Government make this constitution more than "just another paper constitution and put it into force despite its imperfections." An influential independent newspaper characterized the constitution as "comparatively progressive in nature" and said that the greatest weakness of the new constitution was not in the document itself, but in the fact that the Assembly was not held in an atmosphere of peace and unity since one of the major political parties did not participate in the Assembly and civil war was going on in half of the country.

While the new constitution was a reasonably democratic document, my chief concern was the degree and manner of its enforcement. The passage of the constitution was only the beginning and the only guarantee of an honest reorganization of the government and a genuine enforcement of the constitution lay in the development of a truly liberal group in China. I feared that if the minority and non-party liberal groups continued to operate individually, the reorganization of the government might be a synthetic one. I continued, therefore, to emphasize the importance of the organization of the liberals in China into an effective force, which would have as its objective the support of whatever appeared to be good government.

The adoption of the new constitution brought to an end another phase of my mission to China. I had endeavored during this period to use my influence toward the adoption of a democratic consitution in accord with the PCC principles, toward the organization of a truly liberal group for the support of good government in China and toward the carrying out of governmental reorganization in such a way that it would favor a resumption of negotiations and the reentry of the Communist Party into the political picture. The prospects seemed slight for renewal of the negotiations as the Communist Party was apparently adamant in its stand on refusal to recognize the National Assembly and the new constitution and on demanding the acceptance of its two conditions as prerequisite to further negotiation. Communist propaganda attacks on the United States grew stronger during this period and Communist spokesmen indicated the probable Communist strategy—the use of constant harassing tactics on Kuomintang weak points to prevent the reopening of lines of communications and the refusal of further negotiation until the Government had become weakened by economic deterioration. The Communists had made no reply to my inquiry regarding my mediation role and General Chou En-lai had stated at Yenan on December 23, in reply to a question whether the Communist Party had reached a decision in this matter, that it was "up to the United States to determine that."

During this period orders had been issued for the withdrawal of 4,000 United States Marines from the Chinhuangtao-Pietaiho area and plans were agreed upon for the withdrawal of an additional 1,200 Marines from north China as soon as shipping should become available.

There had been completed at the end of this period the mass repatriation of Japanese nationals from China proper, Formosa and Manchuria, with the exception of those held in connection with war crimes, stragglers and technicians retained by the Chinese Government. The final total* of the Japanese repatriated, at the completion of mass repatriation on December 31, was as follows:

Area	Military	Civilian	Total
China (excluding Formosa and Manchuria)	1,036,922	462,475	1,499,397
Formosa	154,634	318,682	473,316
Manchuria	41,688	969,149	1,010,837
TOTALS	1,233,244	1,750,306	2,983,550

The question of the Executive Headquarters was of some importance at this time, since the Communists apparently desired to retain that agency, I believed, largely because of its usefulness for radio and transport purposes. The Communists had utilized the Executive Headquarters as a communications center and had utilized American communications equipment to make propaganda attacks against the United States. The National Government wished to continue the Executive Headquarters because it did not desire the United States to withdraw from the negotiations. It was apparent that some action would have to be taken in the near future to clarify this situation.

*As compiled by CINCFE, Tokyo.

XXXIV.

TERMINATION OF MY MISSION AND OF AMERICAN PARTICIPATION IN THE EXECUTIVE HEADQUARTERS

Following the adjournment of the National Assembly, the Generalissimo expressed a desire to discuss with me the steps that might be taken in an effort to reopen the negotiations with the Communist Party. Dr. Stuart and I had previously suggested a course of action: If a sound constitution were adopted—this had now been done—and if the Government proceeded with the establishment of the State Council and began a genuine reorganization of the Executive Yuan, the Generalissimo might well send two or three representatives, men of importance and liberal standing, to Yenan to discuss the question of reopening negotiations for the cessation of hostilities and Communist participation in the reorganization of the government. We had stressed that these moves be done quietly without publicity. However, before the good faith of the National Government had been at least partially established by the adoption of a sound constitution in accord with the PCC resolutions, news of the Government's purpose had leaked out, intentionally or otherwise. The Communist reaction had been unfavorable. There were indications that the Communists would resent the reorganization of the State Council and the Executive Yuan prior to any consultation with them. They presumably felt that this would close the door on any possibility of responsible participation on their part.

In discussion of these matters with the Generalissimo on December 27, I suggested, therefore, that the visit of a Government delegation to Yenan be carried out prior to the above-mentioned reorganization procedures. The Generalissimo agreed with my point of view regarding the inadvisability of any publicity in the matter but wondered if it might not be desirable to consult the minority parties. I said that such a move would be desirable but that I did not think it advisable for the Government to declare its position since this would inevitably result in a public leak and precipitate a propaganda war with the Communists. It was my opinion, I explained, that if the Government took this action, it should make a genuine effort to avoid any complications by military actions or public statements of a provocative nature, such as those that had wrecked our previous efforts time after time. The Generalissimo appeared to accept my suggestions and said that as the Executive Councils of the minority parties were to convene at Shanghai shortly he thought it best to wait until these meetings had taken place.

In reply to the Generalissimo's request for my comments on the situation, I made the following remarks: In my opinion it was unlikely that the Communists would commit themselves to an agreement at this time due to their overwhelming suspicion that it was the Government's intention to destroy them by military force. The Government military commanders had erred considerably, I thought, in the optimistic estimates of what they could achieve toward suppression of the Communists. They had stated last June that Kiangsu Province could be cleared of Communist forces within two months and the Province had not yet been cleared. At the same time they had said that the Communists could be brought to terms from a military standpoint within three months. That had not occurred after six months. The Government's refusal to terminate hostilities in order to force the Communists to participate in the National Assembly had failed of its purpose. I felt it important, therefore, that the Government military leaders not be permitted to destroy by statement or action the possibility of successful negotiations, to which I believed them inalterably opposed.

I continued that if the Communists would not reenter the negotiations, it was most important that the Government go ahead with the reorganization, leaving the door open for Communist and Democratic League entry. The Generalissimo, by his leadership in the National Assembly in opposing the reactionaries and securing the adoption of a reasonably sound constitution, had, in my opinion, gained a great moral victory which had rehabilitated, if not added to, his prestige. It was most important, therefore, that he demonstrate at this time that the new constitution was not a mere collection of words and that he was determined to institute a democratic form of government. Therefore, he should proceed without de-

lay with the reorganization of the State Council with conspic-
uous representation by liberals from the Kuomintang and va-
cancies left for the Communist Party and the Democratic
League. He should also start at once on the reorganization of
the Executive Yuan. I emphasized that, in my opinion, he
must by his own indirect leadership father a coalition of the
minority groups into a liberal party, since, unless such a sizeable minority group existed, his efforts in the National Assembly to secure a sound constitution would be regarded as
mere camouflage for an intention to proceed with one-party
government. The various minority groups could not of themselves manage an amalgamation and such action would require his active assistance. He should also call on the minority party leaders to nominate men for various posts rather
than follow previous practices of neutralizing the opposition
leaders by bribing them with attractive appointments. If he
did not take such action, I emphasized, there could be no genuine two-party government and his integrity and position
would, therefore, be open to serious attack. It was my opinion that the organization of the minority parties into a large
liberal group would assist him greatly and he could place himself in the position of the father of his country rather than to
continue merely as the leader of the Kuomintang one-party
government. (I emphasized this point in every way possible
because I was convinced that this was the key to the immediate future in China.)

I went on to say that I felt that, if the Communists declined to reopen negotiations—in other words repulsed the
National Government's overtures—and if the Government
were not guilty of provocative statements or actions, the time
had come to begin dismantling the Executive Headquarters. I
was already of the opinion that the Communists no longer
had any intention of accepting American mediation along former lines and that I was definitely *persona non grata* to them.
Under those circumstances I felt that their recently expressed
desire for the continued operation of the Executive Headquarters had for its probable purpose the maintenance of American
air facilities for communication with the scattered Communist
forces throughout north China, their representatives at Shanghai, Nanking and Chungking and their people at Harbin. I
had recently directed the withdrawal of the American representative of the Executive Headquarters at Harbin because
he was being allowed little liberty of action or movement and
since I felt that his continued presence at Harbin was merely

a convenience to the Communists which provided them with air passage to and from Harbin on the weekly plane.

The Generalissimo expressed complete agreement with my ideas regarding a liberal party. While he gave no indication of his reaction regarding the Executive Headquarters, I felt that he recognized the situation as much as I did. As matters stood at this time, I foresaw the following developments: The Communists would refuse to reopen the negotiations and the National Government would probably resort to aggressive military action to reopen the railways. Under those circumstances I thought that the Executive Headquarters should be reduced to a mere cadre and American participation in its mediation functions should be terminated. This would immediately facilitate the withdrawal of the United States Marine units from Tientsin and Peiping.

As I informed President Truman at this time, I thought that I should be recalled. I gave the President an explanation of my reactions as follows: I was of the opinion that I might be able to do something to weaken seriously if not to destroy the power of the reactionaries in the Government and bring liberal elements into control by a frank statement on the occasion of my arrival in the United States. At the same time I would be in a position to paint a true picture of Chinese Communist misrepresentations and vicious propaganda against the United States in a manner that would weaken their position and give some guidance to misinformed people in both China and the United States. It was rather paradoxical to find at present a large number of Chinese university and business groups so naive in their acceptance of Communist propaganda that they were honestly convinced that the United States was responsible for the civil war in China and that I had personally contributed to that situation. The surplus property and Lend-Lease transactions had played a large part in this belief. Fortunately Dr. Stuart had been built into a position where his services in the negotiations would automatically continue to be sought by all sides and would increase in importance as time went on. While even his integrity had been questioned by the Communits, I felt that he could triumph over that phase of the situation.

It was quite clear to me that my usefulness would soon be at an end for a number of reasons. I had continued on in Nanking since the breakdown of the negotiations in order to make certain the adoption of a respectable constitution. The initial outlook had been very depressing at the opening of the

National Assembly and I had made it clear that anything less than a fair approximation of the fundamental principles agreed upon by the PCC would be fatal to the National Government so far as the United States was concerned. The new constitution had been adopted and there was no real place for me in the coming maneuvers to reopen negotiations. My continued presence would constitute embarrassment to future adjustments, especially if I spoke out, as I felt I must. This would arouse bitter feeling among Chinese officials on both sides. The time had come when it was going to be necessary for the Chinese themselves to do the things I had endeavored to lead them into, but I believed that I could strengthen the position and influence of the better elements by the procedure I had indicated.

As a result of my suggestion that I be recalled at this time, the Secretary of State on January 3 informed me that the President would appreciate my returning to Washington at my earliest convenience for consultation on China. The President said that no decision would be made regarding mediation activities by Dr. Stuart until my return or until we should have an opportunity to discuss the matter. On January 6 the White House announced that "the President has directed General Marshall to return to Washington to report in person on the situation in China."

On the afternoon of January 6, prior to the release of the White House announcement regarding my return to the United States, Dr. Stuart and I called on the Generalissimo, at which time I informed him that the President had recalled me to Washington for consultation and that I was leaving Nanking on the morning of January 8. The Generalissimo expressed regret at my departure and inquired of me in regard to various things he hoped I would do for China, such as the reorganization of the army, educational matters, et cetera. I replied that I could make no statement in this regard prior to seeing President Truman.

I then mentioned, merely as an example of minority thinking in the United States without any prospect of adoption by the United States Government, a recent proposal by two United States Senators for an American-British-Russian group to endeavor to provide a stabilizing influence for affairs in China.

The Generalissimo took up this particular point and made it the subject of the entire ensuing discussion, making the following statement: Would I please say to President Truman that the Yalta decision in regard to Manchuria—the railways, Dairen and Port Arthur—without reference to the Chinese Government had come as a great shock, a matter not at all understood by the Chinese people. The Generalissimo himself, realizing something of the circumstances at the time, had accepted the decision but had felt that the action was not in accordance with the traditional stand of the United States Government and that it was an act that would continue to arouse deep feeling in China. Further, he regarded the action with regard to China taken by the Foreign Ministers Conference at Moscow in December 1945 as offensive to the dignity and sovereignty of the Chinese nation. The day following this announcement the Soviet Ambassador had called on him and had said that, while the Soviet Government had acquiesced in the action taken, it had thought it unwise, such action having been proposed by the United States. The Generalissimo asked me to tell the President that under no circumstances while he was head of the Chinese Government would he accept any action regarding the internal affairs of China which would involve the Soviet Government or the British Government. If such action were taken and forced on China, he said, he would step aside as President because such a procedure would be intolerable and an insult to the Chinese Government and people.

The Generalissimo repeated these views in varying forms of expression, continuing to emphasize the fact that he would deeply resent interference in the internal affairs of China by the Powers. I told him that I would repeat this information to President Truman and to the Secretary of State.

On January 7 Dr. Wang Shih-chieh, Minister for Foreign Affairs, informed me that the Generalissimo wished him to explain that he (the Generalissimo) was giving me a letter for President Truman but that this letter did not cover the following points which he desired me to convey orally to the President: The National Government intended to reorganize immediately, taking into the Government representatives of the non-party group, the Youth Party and the Democratic Socialist Party, as well as the Democratic League and the Communist Party if the latter were willing to participate. If the Communists and Democratic League would not participate, it was essential that the National Government proceed without further delay in the reorganization of the government and the restoration of communications. The situation would be difficult and the Generalissimo trusted that his problem would be viewed sympathetically by the United States Government. Should the United States Government decide to evacuate its troops from China, it was hoped that this would not be initiated during the present anti-foreign demonstrations as this might encourage further efforts of the same violent nature. It was also hoped that the troops would not be withdrawn until the establishment of the Military Advisory Group should have been formally confirmed by Congress. The Generalissimo also wished the United States Government to consider very carefully the plight of China with regard to the economic situation. He understood that the United States Government could not lend financial assistance until there should be definite evidence of the reorganization of the government on a more democratic basis. However, he wished me to make clear to the United States Government the critical necessity to China of materiel and means to overcome the present difficulties in communications and of material resources to assist in reducing the present inflationary conditions.

Prior to my departure from China I had spoken to Dr. Wong Wen-hao, Vice President of the Executive Yuan, and stressed to him the necessity of removing the dominant military clique and the reactionaries from the government structure. I had also discussed this matter with Dr. T.V. Soong, President of the Executive Yuan, and had informed him that I would soon make a statement on the situation in China, since I was being recalled and could no longer remain silent. I explained that although it was a disagreeable business, which I did not relish, I would have to speak frankly. It was certain, I said, that my frank statement would arouse bitterness and anger, particularly among the radicals, the reactionaries and the irreconcilables. I pointed out that I had exerted every effort in my statement to create an opportunity for the better elements in China to rise to the top and I hoped that the statement would make possible the organization of a patriotic liberal group under the indirect sponsorship of the Generalissimo. I felt that such action was imperative from the standpoint of the Generalissimo since he needed a respectable opposition party in order to prove to the world his sincerity in establishing a democratic form of government in China. I said that such an opposition party would be a strong force for good, which the Generalissimo could use to wipe out graft, corruption and incompetence in the Government and in the Kuomintang and which would provide an effective check on the existing dictatorial control of the military leaders. I concluded that without a respectable opposition party China would not

430

be given credit by the world for having established a democratic government.

Conversations with minority party leaders and prominent non-party Chinese at this time indicated their belief in the inadvisability of reorganization of the government in the near future, although there was equally strong belief that the Government would have to institute reforms. These Chinese apparently felt that to effect a reorganization of the government without Communist Party participation might do more harm than good and that there must be peace prior to such reorganization.

On January 6 I informed Dr. Stuart that I proposed to issue a strong statement on the China situation during the past year and that I had already submitted a draft of such a statement to the Department of State for approval prior to its release. After reading the statement, Dr. Stuart concurred in the desirability of its release.

On the morning of January 8 (Nanking time) I left China by plane en route to the United States. On January 7 (Washington time) the Department of State released to the press my personal statement[86] on the situation in China. It was explained at the beginning of the statement that the President had recently given a summary of the developments in China during the past year and the position of the American Government toward China and that "circumstances now dictate that I should supplement this with impressions gained at first hand." The chief points of the statement were as follows:

> "In the first place the greatest obstacle to peace had been the complete, almost overwhelming suspicion with which the Chinese Communist Party and the Kuomintang regard each other.

> "On the one hand, the leaders of the Government are strongly opposed to a communistic form of government. On the other, the Communists frankly state that they are Marxists and intend to work toward establishing a communistic form of government in China, though first advancing through the medium of a democratic form of government of the American or British type."

[86]See Volume Two, Appendix S, Document 1, for the full text.

"I think the most important factors involved in the recent breakdown of negotiations are these: On the side of the National Government, which is in effect the Kuomintang, there is a dominant group of reactionaries who have been opposed, in my opinion, to almost every effort I have made to influence the formation of a genuine coalition government."

"The dyed-in-the-wool Communists do not hesitate at the most drastic measures to gain their end as, for instance, the destruction of communications in order to wreck the economy of China and produce a situation that would facilitate the overthrow or collapse of the Government without any regard to the immediate suffering of the people involved."

"I wish to state to the American people that in the deliberate misrepresentation and abuse of the action, policies and purposes of our Government this (Chinese Communist Party) propaganda has been without regard for the truth, without any regard whatsoever for the facts, and has given plain evidence of a determined purpose to mislead the Chinese people and the world and to arouse a bitter hatred of Americans. It has been difficult to remain silent in the midst of such public abuse and wholesale disregard of facts, but a denial would merely lead to the necessity of daily denials; an intolerable course of action for an American official."

"Sincere efforts to achieve settlement have been frustrated time and again by extremist elements of both sides. The agreements reached by the Political Consultative Conference a year ago were a liberal and forward-looking charter which then offered China a basis for peace and reconstruction. However, irreconcilable groups within the Kuomintang, interested in the preservation of their own feudal control of China, evidently had no real intention of implementing them. Though I speak as a soldier, I must here also deplore the dominating influence of the military. Their dominance accentuates the weakness of civil government in China."

"Between this dominant reactionary group in the Government and the irreconcilable Communists who, I must state, did not so appear last February, lies the problem of how peace and well-being are to be brought to the long-suffering and presently inarticulate mass of the people in China. The reactionaries in the Government have evidently counted on substantial American support regardless of their actions. The Communists by their unwillingness to compromise in the national interest are evidently counting on an economic collapse to bring about the fall of the Government."

"The salvation of the situation, as I see it, would be the assumption of leadership by the liberals in the Government and in the minority parties, a splendid group of men, but who as yet lack the political power to exercise a controlling influence. Successful action on their part under the leadership of Generalissimo Chiang Kai-shek would, I believe, lead to unity through good government."

"In fact, the National Assembly has adopted a democratic constitution which in all major respects is in accordance with the principles laid down by the all-party Political Consultative Conference of last January."

"Now that the form for a democratic China has been laid down by the newly adopted constitution, practical measures will be the test. It remains to be seen to what extent the Government will give substance to the form by a genuine welcome of all groups actively to share in the responsibility of government."

In conclusion, it was stated that I had spoken very frankly because in no other way could I hope to bring the American people to even a partial understanding of the complex problem and that I was expressing my views publicly, as it was my duty, to present my estimate of the situation and its possibilities to the American people, who had a deep interest in the development of conditions in the Far East promising an enduring peace in the Pacific.

On the night of January 7 (Washington time) President Truman announced my nomination as the Secretary of State.

The simultaneous announcement of my personal statement and my nomination as the Secretary of State caused a silence to a certain extent among Chinese leaders pending a study of these developments and their possible consequence to the groups concerned.

The Kuomintang press published my statement in full except for the omission of the word "reactionary" as applied to the dominant group in the Kuomintang. The Communist press in Communist-controlled areas was said to have published only a summary of the statement, apparently stressing those portions of which the Communist Party approved.

Information reaching the American Embassy at Nanking indicated that the Communists, hardened by criticism of the Communist Party, considered my criticism of their party more than compensated for by the attack on the Kuomintang reactionaries, which they looked upon as the first open American Government criticism of the National Government.

The Generalissimo in an interview with American correspondents said that my statement should be read in conjunction with President Truman's statement to ensure a comprehensive view of the situation in China. He subsequently stated at a weekly Government Memorial Meeting that "my views cannot be said to be completely identical with those of General Marshall" and that "in view of his mission and his own position in making such a report to the American people, he may be said to be frank, impartial, sincere and friendly and the statement is a very constructive one."*

On January 10 General Chou En-lai broadcast from Yenan a speech which contained the "official" Communist reaction to my statement. He charged that I did not state that the Generalissimo was the leader of the dominant Kuomintang reactionary group and that I was relying on "the enforcement of Chiang's constitution and the reorganization of the government for prolonging Chiang's dictatorship." His speech reflected his deep suspicion and bitterness and an almost psycho-neurotic state of mind.

The Kuomintang Minister of Information announced on January 9 that the Government was willing to discuss with the Communists a "complete plan for the cessation of hostilities and government reorganization." The reaction of the Communist delegation at Nanking indicated little enthusiam, a Com-

*As Reported by the Kuomintang Central News Agency.

munist spokesman stating that unless the National Government accepted the Communists' two-point demand (dissolution of the National Assembly and the constitution, and the return to troop positions of January 13, 1946), there was "nothing to talk about at Yenan."

At the same time Dr. Sun Fo, President of the Legislative Yuan, issued a statement calling for a round table conference of all parties to solve the differences. This was also received with skepticism by the Communists, who were apparently inclined to consider the suggestion as just another Government peace offensive. A Communist spokesman said that the Communist Party had announced its two-point demand and that it was up to the Government to announce its counter-proposal as a basis for the resumption of peace negotiations.

On January 15, Dr. Stuart called on the Generalissimo, who said that he had been discussing with Government leaders during the past few days a means of reopening negotiations. The Generalissimo gave Dr. Stuart a list of four points on which agreement had been reached as a result of these discussions:

> 1. The Government desired to send a delegation to Yenan or to invite the Communist Party to send a delegation to Nanking to continue discussions, or it proposed a round-table conference of all parties.

> 2. The Government and the Communist Party should each immediately issue a cease-fire order and confer together regarding the effective implementation of such an order.

> 3. The Government desired to resume discussion of practical plans for the reorganization of the army and the restoration of communications, the plans to be based on the principles of the "former Committee of Three."

> 4. The Government desired to come to an agreement at once with the Communist Party for a just and reasonable solution in regard to the political control of the disputed areas.

The Generalissimo asked Dr. Stuart to approach the Communist delegation at Nanking to determine on behalf of the Generalissimo whether the Communists would invite a National Government delegation to Yenan to discuss matters related to peace and unity, but requested that the above-described four points not be mentioned. He also told Dr. Stuart that if the Communists made inquiry on specific points, he should tell them that General Chang Chih-chung had been tentatively selected to represent the National Government, that the latter demanded no conditions and that its delegation would be completely free to discuss all aspects of outstanding issues. The Generalissimo concluded that he hoped that through a general discussion, unfettered by terms or conditions, a settlement of issues could be reached in the spirit of the PCC agreements.

Dr. Stuart transmitted the Generalissimo's inquiry to the Communist delegation at Nanking on January 16, pointing out that he was merely acting as a transmitting medium and not as a direct participant. Dr. Stuart also replied to Communist inquiries in accordance with the Generalissimo's request.

On the same day the Kuomintang Minister of Information, at his weekly press conference, announced the Government's plan for sending a peace delegation to Yenan and its desire to reopen negotiations.

On January 18 a member of the Communist delegation called on Dr. Stuart to deliver the following reply from Yenan to the Government's peace proposal for the sending of a delegation to Yenan:

> "If the two original conditions are complied with, the peace conference can be resumed in Nanking; otherwise there is no use in a delegation visiting Yenan.
>
> "The two conditions are:
>
> 1. Military dispositions as of January 13, 1946;
>
> 2. Nullification of National Assembly and the constitution."

As a result of the Communist refusal to accept a National Government peace delegation, the Kuomintang Minister of Information issued a further statement on January 21, the first half of which was a review of past difficulties placing the blame on the Communist Party for the failure to carry out the PCC resolutions. The second half, quite unprovocative in nature, was largely nullified by the recriminations in the first half of the statement. Possibility of any reopening of negotiations in the near future thus seemed to be completely blocked.

Matters were not improved by the opening of a propaganda war between the Yenan Department of Information and the Kuomintang Minister of Information regarding the responsibility for the breakdown of the negotiations and the rejection of the Government's peace proposal.

In the light of these developments and the almost complete stalemate in the activities of the Executive Headquarters, I felt that the time had come to terminate American participation in that organization. An incident involving the confiscation of the Communist radio transmitter and receiver at Changchun by the National Government Garrison Headquarters at that city had been settled by the return of the radio equipment and an apology from the National Government, this action resulting from a protest by the United States branch of the Headquarters that the National Government had violated the directives of the Executive Headquarters.

I arrived in Washington on January 21 and took the oath of office as the Secretary of State on that day. Within a few days thereafter I discussed the question of the Executive Headquarters with President Truman and recommended to him the withdrawal of the United States branch. The President approved my recommendation and on January 29 the Department of State released to the press at Washington an announcement[87] of the decision of the United States Government to terminate its connection with the Committee of Three and with the Executive Headquarters, it being indicated that the American personnel of the Headquarters would be withdrawn as soon as possible.

The agreement for the establishment of the Executive Headquarters provided that it should remain in existence and operate until that agreement should be rescinded by the President of the Republic of China or the Chairman of the Central Committee of the Chinese Communist Party after due notification to the other. It was necessary, therefore, in terminating the American connection with that organization that the Chinese Government and the Communist Party be given prior notification of the United States Goverment's decision in this regard. This was done by Dr. Stuart at Nanking shortly before the announcement at Washington. Similar notification was given by General Gillem, United States Commissioner of the Executive Headquarters, to the two Chinese Commissioners.

Both the Generalissimo and the Communist delegation were informed that the United States would assist in return-

[87]See Volume Two, Appendix S, Document 2, for the full text.

ing authorized Communist Party personnel to reasonably accessible Communist areas and a deadline of March 5 was established for the completion of such movements. To prevent any misunderstanding in this regard an announcement was made by the American Embassy at Nanking that the United States would assist both Communist personnel in returning to Communist areas and National Government field personnel in returning to their stations of origin until March 5 and that those who remained in their present locations after that date would do so on their own responsibility so far as the United States was concerned. The Communist delegation was informed that "authorized personnel" would consist of personnel directly assigned to the Communist branch of the Executive Headquarters and personnel listed in General Chou Enlai's memorandum of November 18, 1946, to me, which had been confirmed by the Communist delegation at Nanking in December.

The Department of State's announcement of this action made no mention of the United States Marine units in China but the Department spokesman informed the press at this time that instructions regarding the relief of the Marines would be given later in conformity with approved plans for the termination of American participation in the Executive Headquarters. Plans drawn up by the United States branch of the Executive Headquarters provided for the inactivation of the United States branch and the complete withdrawal of American personnel within a period of 120 days, beginning February 5. The United States Marine units could not, of course, be withdrawn until after the withdrawal of the American personnel of the Executive Headquarters but the United States Navy authorities issued a directive to Admiral Cooke at this time to complete the preparation of a plan for the withdrawal of the Marines from north China except for those at Tsingtao.

The Generalissimo, in discussion with Dr. Stuart of this move, appeared to be pleased to hear of the American withdrawal from the Executive Headquarters. The National Government issued an announcement on January 31 in regard to the Executive Headquarters, which placed the responsibility on the Communists for the failure of the peace negotiations, expressed regret that the Government was unable "to make a mediation instrument, in which a third party had participated, continue to function" and expressed appreciation of the American efforts to achieve peace and unity in China. The reaction of National Government military leaders was favorable, since they interpreted the American withdrawal from the Executive Headquarters and the Government's announcement as the end of negotiations and an indication that the National Government was now free to seek a solution by force.

Communist reaction was non-committal, the Yenan radio emphasizing the necessity of the withdrawal of all American forces from China as the demand of "widespread Chinese patriotic sentiment."

The general reaction to the termination of American participation in the Executive Headquarters was one of regret in almost all sections of the Chinese press, including even the left-wing press which had consistently and vociferously demanded the withdrawal of American troops from China. The Kuomintang press expressed regret at the dissolution of the Executive Headquarters on the ground that it meant final American admission of failure of mediation, for which the Communists were held responsible. Some left-wing papers charged that the withdrawal of American troops was only a "trick to give an appearance of withdrawing from the internal affairs of China though actually using this move to increase American control," without, however, indicating how this could be done. Only a few independent papers openly approved the American action and they expressed regret that circumstances had made it necessary. Some of the Kuomintang newspapers indicated a fear that this might result in international intervention in China, which they felt must at all costs be avoided. There was also comment in some independent and left-wing newspapers that the United States action may have been motivated by a desire to strengthen the American position in China prior to the opening of the Moscow Conference in March.

As I informed Dr. Stuart at this time, the decision to withdraw American participation from the Committee of Three and from the Executive Headquarters should not operate to interfere with assistance by him if either side should initiate an appeal to him in his normal functioning as the American Ambassador for assistance in various problems peculiar to the Chinese situation. I stated that this action did, however, mean the conclusion of the negotiations which had been initiated by me in December 1945.

The termination of the American mediation effort did not mean that the United States intended to withdraw from China. That effort had failed to bring peace and unity to China, for reasons which were set forth in my personal statement of January 7. There was a point beyond which the American mediation effort could not go. Peace and stability in China must, in the final analysis, be achieved by the efforts of the Chinese themselves. We had endeavored to aid in attaining those goals and in the process had been subjected to bitter attack by many groups, both in China and abroad, attacks which had, deliberately or otherwise, misrepresented the intentions and purposes of the United States Government. The issue was now squarely up to the Chinese themselves. It was my opinion that only through the existence of a liberal opposition group in China could there be guarantee of good government and of progress toward stability. The future efforts of the Chinese themselves would determine whether it was possible to give peace and stability to the people of China. The United States, I felt, should continue to view sympathetically the problem facing the Chinese, and should take any action, without intervening in China's internal affairs, that would assist China in realizing those aims which represented the hopes and aspirations of the Chinese people as well as of the United States.

ATTITUDE OF THE CHINESE COMMUNIST PARTY TOWARD THE UNITED STATES

In view of the violent propaganda attacks made by the Chinese Communist Party against the United States during my mission to China, it is believed that a review of the Chinese Communists' attitude toward the United States and the American mediation effort throughout my mission will prove of interest because of its connection with the problem of Sino-American relations.

During the first two or three months the Chinese Communist Party was cooperative and gave no indication of other than a friendly and sincere attitude toward the United States and American mediation. The first indication of any change in the Communist attitude of cooperation developed toward the end of March, at a time when the situation in Manchuria had seriously deteriorated. General Chou En-lai then endeavored to halt the movement of National Government armies into Manchuria by American shipping, although such movements were permitted by the Cessation of Hostilities Order and he had previously been informed of the American commitment in this regard. The next instance of Communist reaction toward American activities related to China was that represented by Communist press criticism of the granting of a loan to the Chinese Government by the United States, this criticism being directed against the Kuomintang.

On April 21 came the first indication of serious Communist hostility toward the United States, one which also showed Communist disregard of facts in its propaganda. On that day the Yenan radio broadcast charged that American planes had openly participated in military action against "popular forces and local residents" in Manchuria and that an American officer had been found in one Kuomintang plane shot down by the "local popular forces" in the Ssupingchieh area. As a result of my representations to General Chou against such a report, the Yenan radio subsequently broadcasted a denial of the charges, explaining that the Kuomintang pilot of the plane shot down had been wearing an American uniform and that the planes making the attacks had American markings which had been exposed due to the wearing off of Kuomintang "water-paint" markings placed over the former American insignia at the time the planes were turned over to the National Government.

The incident was thus settled by this explanation, but the widespread reports of American participation in Kuomintang air activities over Communist-held territory were probably not completely offset by the later correction of such reports. At this time the Yenan radio made a particular point in its broadcasts of victories gained by the Communist forces in Manchuria over "American-equipped and -trained" National Government troops, thus tending further to emphasize the United States in the role of supporting the Kuomintang. Further instances of this Communist technique of attack against the United States by implication came shortly after the above-described correction. On May 3 the Yenan radio referred to the Kuomintang's use of American-made planes and on May 5 referred to the National Government's 60th Army as having been "entirely transported to Manchuria by American war vessels." "American-trained" or "American-equipped" Kuomintang armies and "American-made" Kuomintang planes or tanks became stock phrases in the Communist press and radio broadcasts in subsequent months.

The propaganda campaign from Yenan then halted for the time being, but the fall of Ssupingchieh on May 19 and the National Government occupation of Changchun on May 23 seemed to unleash, and be the signal for, a renewal of Communist propaganda attacks on the United States, which went far beyond the previous efforts to imply American assistance to the Kuomintang. These daily attacks lasted for almost one week and ranged from charges that American aid to the Kuomintang had been one of the important factors in "enlarging the civil war in Manchuria" to questioning the impartiality of American mediation in China. Just prior to the National Government occupation of Ssupingchieh and Changchun, I had proposed a Communist withdrawal from Changchun and the reopening of negotiations regarding Manchuria and other issues and had also communicated to General Chou certain conditions advanced by the Generalissimo. The Generalissimo's prolonged absence from Nanking during the continued northward advance of the National Government troops after the capture of Changchun, together with my own connection with the Changchun proposal, served to engender in the minds of the Communists strong suspicion of the United States and of my own position in the mediation effort and negotiations. Indication of this suspicion was evident in the antagonism displayed by the Communists toward American personnel on the field teams in Communist areas.

Another flurry of Communist attacks on the United States by the Yenan radio began in early June, but these attacks ceased at the time of the announcement of the 15-day truce in Manchuria. This brief "honeymoon" of good feeling toward the United States was disrupted, however, by another propaganda campaign at the time publicity was given to the bill for aid to China prepared for submission to Congress. The Yenan radio reported the holding of mass meetings in Communist areas attacking this bill. This was the first instance of such meetings, which subsequently were utilized by the Chinese Communist Party in areas under its control as a means of arousing feeling against the United States. Indicative of the importance attached by the Communist Party to this bill for aid to China was the issuance of a statement by Chairman Mao Tze-tung on June 23 opposing the passage of the bill. (This was one of the two official public statements issued by Mao Tze-tung during my mission in China and is all the more noteworthy as, while Communist spokesmen frequently made pronouncements of policy, Mao himself rarely made public statements.) Mao charged that the American military aid to the "Kuomintang Government" and the stationing of large American forces in China had been the "fundamental cause for the outbreak and aggravation of a large-scale civil war in China." He said that the "so-called United States military aid to China is, therefore, actually armed intervention in Chinese internal affairs" and concluded with the demand that the

United States "promptly cease and withdraw her so-called military aid to China and immediately evacuate her forces from China."

On this occasion, as was true on other occasions, the Chinese Communist Party seemed to become a prey to Communist suspicion and distrust and to tend to believe its own propaganda partially because of constant repetition of the same theme. The effect of this propaganda, however, on Chinese public opinion, both in Communist and National Government areas, should not be underestimated.

A study of Soviet newspaper and radio comment on the situation in China during this period, as reported by the American Embassy at Moscow, gives no indication that the impetus for the Chinese Communist criticism of the United States came from Moscow. In late April the Soviet press reported Chinese demands for the cessation of American intervention in China and the withdrawal of American forces. During May the Soviet press carried an occasional article quoting Chinese and American press criticism of United States policy in China and of American military aid to the Kuomintang, but there were no direct attacks made by the Soviet press against the American role in China. On June 1, however, a Soviet newspaper carried an article containing the first direct attack on the United States, charging that there were indications that American soldiers were participating in the civil war in China and that, while Soviet troops had been withdrawn from China, "American forces still remain and are taking an active part in civil war which reactionaries have unleashed." Although the beginnings of the Chinese Communist criticism seemed to be purely Chinese in origin and were repeated by the independent Chinese press, in subsequent months Chinese Communist and Soviet press attacks on the American policy toward China were more or less parallel and served to increase Kuomintang suspicion of a close connection between the Chinese Communist Party and the Soviet Union. It thus made more difficult the task of the American mediators.

Following these attacks at the end of June and in early July against the bill for military aid to China and against a statement by the Under Secretary of State explaining the aims of American aid to China—attacks which gave little consideration to facts and were full of inaccurate statements—the Chinese Communist Party issued a manifesto at Yenan on July 7. This manifesto was a strong and bitter attack on American policy toward China and, again, a protest against what the

443

Communists termed American military and financial aid to the National Government, which was said to encourage the civil war policy of the Kuomintang. These attacks occurred after the breakdown of the negotiations during the truce period in June and were parallelled by similar propaganda from Moscow.

I had a lengthy and frank discussion with General Chou on July 11 regarding Communist propaganda attacks on the United States. Following this discussion the Yenan radio toned down such attacks and, at the time of the assassination of two Democratic League members at Kunming in July, even broadcast an appeal to the "American friends of China" to take action to stop the outbreak of the "widespread liquidation of those opposing Kuomintang tyranny." Toward the end of July, however, the Yenan radio returned to the attack, charging that United States Marine units were making frequent raids into Communist-held areas.

On July 13 had occurred the first of a series of incidents involving United States Marines in China and the Chinese Communist forces, when seven Marines were captured in east Hopei by the Communists and detained until July 24.

On July 29 Communist forces ambushed a motor convoy of Executive Headquarters and UNRRA supplies at Anping on the highway between Tientsin and Peiping, which was being escorted by United States Marines, and killed three Marines and wounded 12 others. This incident, the Communist responsibility for which was privately admitted, was the signal for a renewal of the Communist anti-American campaign. It was a repetition of the familiar Communist pattern of seizing upon some incident, justifiably or otherwise, and embroidering thereon without regard to truth and accuracy to form the basis for an almost hysterical campaign of vituperation against the United States. In this particular case, the ambush was said to have been carried out by local Communist commanders without the prior knowledge of the Yenan authorities, but the latter apparently felt that they must cover up Communist responsibility and utilize the incident for their own ends.

On August 1 General Chou En-lai handed to me a copy of the Yenan radio broadcast of the Anping incident and said that this was the eighth of a series of incidents along the Peiping-Mukden Railway involving the United States Marines and the Chinese Communist forces. He said that this last incident had also involved Chinese Government troops and that this might indicate that elements of the National Government were trying to embroil the Marines in Chinese affairs by staging an incident along the railway.

I replied to General Chou as follows: I had postponed forming any conclusion regarding the Anping incident pending the receipt of a formal report from the investigating officers sent by the Commanding General of the United States Marines at the direction of Admiral Cooke and until I should have an opportunity of hearing General Chou's version. Admiral Cooke had today informed me personally of the results of an official Marine investigation group. In my opinion, in order to understand the matter, one must go back to various occurrences in Jehol Province, particularly in relation to the statement of General Lee Hsueh-jui, Communist Commander in that region, and also to the propaganda from Yenan relating to the same situation and the recent abduction of the seven Marines in east Hopei. The Yenan radio account of the Anping incident was totally different from the report by the Marine investigating officers. The latter gave the following account of the incident: One Marine lieutenant and 41 enlisted Marines were escorting a convoy of 21 small trucks (carrying the 41 men), six supply trucks carrying food and supplies for the Marine units at Peiping—most of which was for the American personnel of the Executive Headquarters, one UNRRA truck with a Chinese driver and one staff car with three United States Army officers reporting to the American branch of the Executive Headquarters. The column convoying these vehicles encountered a road block and, when the lieutenant advanced on foot to inquire what this meant, he was fired upon and killed. The attacking force of Communists instantly opened fire with rifles, machine guns and trench mortars, which fire was returned by the Marines. There was no accurate data on the number of Communists involved but it was estimated to be about 300 men. Fighting continued for about four hours and ceased when a Communist officer displayed a white flag. The column then proceeded to Peiping without all the trucks and later a relief party of Marines from Tientsin arrived at the scene of the incident, took possession of the trucks and drove them to Peiping. The town of Anping was not raided, the Communist forces were not compelled to defend themselves and no National Government troops were involved or present. These facts, I thought, were correct and, in my opinion, the Yenan broadcast had but two accurate statements—that is, there was fighting with casualties on

445

both sides and later in the afternoon Marine reenforcements arrived from Tientsin. All the rest was complete and, in my opinion, deliberate misrepresentation.

I continued that this whole matter was very important in relation to the peace efforts being made by Dr. Stuart and me, as I was always met by National Government statements that the Communists instigated all fighting. I had ignored entirely the vicious Communist propaganda, which was virtually directed against me. This had been parallelled, to my further embarrassment, by similar Soviet propaganda—embarrassment because of the effect on my relations and influence with the Chinese Government. Although the assassinations of the Democratic League members at Kunming had been tragic, they had exerted an influence on the National Government because of the effect they had had on official, political and public opinion in the United States. But, we now had this action at Anping on the part of the Communists led by the same commander who had been responsible for the previous intimidation of the American member of the field team at Chengte and who had been guilty of misrepresentations to Yenan, which were almost complete fabrication. All this was very unfortunate from the viewpoint of Communist desires as put forward by General Chou and placed me in a still more difficult position with the Government because it would have an effect on American public opinion opposite to that intended. The American people did not accept this sort of thing calmly.

General Chou then said that he had not received an official report of the Anping incident but that he was much concerned and felt that an investigation should be made. He said that he favored the sending by Executive Headquarters of its most able staff members in the form of a team to investigate this and related matters in order to determine the responsibility.

The National Government branch of the Executive Headquarters had also expressed a desire to have a special team appointed for the investigation. Although I was reluctant to permit the handling of this incident and the related investigation by the Executive Headquarters, it was difficult to ignore the wishes of both Chinese branches of the Headquarters for such an investigation. I, therefore, forwarded a message to the United States Commissioner stating that since both the National Government and Communist Party wished to have a fact finding investigation, it appeared advisable to send a carefully selected special team for that purpose.

On August 3 General Chou informed me of his receipt of a report from the local Communist commanders in the Anping area which was essentially the same as that broadcast by Yenan. In this report it was claimed that National Government troops were involved in the incident and that, as Anping lay in Communist-held territory, notification should have been given by the Marines prior to their passing through that area.

On August 6, in discussing the Anping incident with Dr. Stuart, General Chou made the following remarks: Communist reports indicated that the incident was precipitated by the entry of Kuomintang and United States troops into the Communist areas. The U.S. Marines had on several previous occasions created disturbances without, however, precipitating incidents. The likelihood of incidents along the Peiping-Mukden Railway line arose from the following circumstances: The U.S. Marines protecting the line had a tendency to move away from that line and the Communist forces, while trying to avoid conflict, could not avoid resisting when coming into direct contact with American troops. The Kuomintang utilized the railway line between Peiping and Chinhuangtao and the highway from Peiping to Tientsin to transport arms and ammunition and troops. National Government troops used this line, guarded by U.S. Marines, as a base to expand their areas and when attacked by the Communists retreated to the railway. If the Communists attacked further, they came into conflict with the U.S. Marines. The Communists did not purposely create the Anping incident with a view to forcing the withdrawal of U.S. troops from China, as was so often said, since, by so doing, the Communists would lose American friendship. The Communists had no intention of clashing with the United States.

Reports forwarded to me by Mr. Walter S. Robertson, United States Commissioner of the Executive Headquarters, of the progress being made toward an investigation of the Anping incident indicated that the Yenan authorities and the Communist branch of the Executive Headquarters were apparently making every effort to color and confuse the issue by charging that the Communists were pressing for a prompt investigation while the National Government and American branches were employing dilatory tactics. Mr. Robertson reported that the truth was exactly the reverse, as the Communists had been employing every conceivable tactic to delay

447

and obstruct the investigation.

On August 9 I informed General Chou of the gist of the foregoing and gave him an outline of the status of the investigation as reported to me by Mr. Robertson as follows: The three Commissioners signed an order on August 2 directing a special team to make an investigation. At the same time the Communist Commissioner was asked to obtain safe conduct, naming the place, date and hour, but not later than noon on August 5, for the team to get in touch with the local Communist commanders. On the morning of August 6 a message guaranteeing safe conduct was delivered by the Communist commander but no reply was made to the request for the place, date and hour for the team to get in touch with the Communist field commanders. From August 2 to August 8 the American member of the team endeavored to proceed with the examination of those eye witnesses to the incident who were still in Peiping. This procedure was blocked by the Communist member. On August 4 the Communist member did not appear at the team meeting but instead sent a subordinate without credentials, thus making impossible any action. On August 5 the Communist member did appear at the team meeting but spent the entire day in arguing points of procedure. He demanded that the team interview the Marine Commander at Peiping and then proceed to the field to interview the unnamed commander of an unidentified Communist unit. The Communist member would not agree to examine the eye witnesses until these interviews should have been completed. He further said that he would not officially accept as credible evidence the testimony of any American eye witnesses who were in the convoy. In a long speech at the team meeting, he was often almost insulting to the American member and appeared to be trying to arouse his anger. On August 6 the American member called two American eye witnesses, who were members of the Executive Headquarters, to testify. The Communist member thereupon took the floor and for two hours insisted on his suggested procedure. When reminded that the witnesses had been waiting for a long time and when requested for permission to examine them, the Communist member flatly refused and the meeting was adjourned. On August 7 at a meeting of the team, the Communist member argued for two and one-half hours, repeating his previous demands that prior to an investigation trip the team must proceed to the places suggested by him and that witnesses must be unanimously agreed upon prior to being heard, thus making it impossible to examine the witnesses brought from Tientsin to Peiping.

I reminded General Chou that I had originally declined to authorize the United States branch to proceed with a team investigation and that I had agreed only when pressed for such action by General Chou and the two Chinese Commissioners. What was happening, I said, was worse than I had anticipated and would seem to indicate that once the investigation began it would be still worse. I said that I could not, as a representative of the United States Government, accept such a situation in silence and that I was, therefore, considering the withdrawal of the American member of the team and making a public statement of what I considered to be the facts. I explained that I would not hesitate at all were it not for the tremendous and almost determining effects such action might have on the possibility of reaching a successful conclusion of the negotiations. My action would tend to confirm the contention of National Government officials who have insisted that negotiation with the Communists was not practical as they would inevitably employ obstructionist tactics to defeat the purpose of negotiation. In this instance they would be able to say that I agreed with them by virtue of my own statement. I emphasized that I regarded the matter as extremely serious and that I was unwilling to commit the United States any further in such futile procedure. After discussion of the matter with Dr. Stuart and with full realization of the serious consequences, I was willing to wait for 24 hours to receive Communist assurances—not a discussion—that this matter would be handled in an ordinary every day straight forward manner. I added that I regretted having to make such remarks even in the privacy of our meeting but that I would not be a party to procedures such as those being employed by the Communist representative in Peiping. I did not see what the Communists had to gain in the first place and they hazarded a great disadvantage at the present time.

General Chou replied as follows: From the information available to him the circumstances were almost completely the reverse of my report. The Chinese press had reported that an investigation team had been sent on the previous day or, at the very latest, would be sent on this day. He felt that the Communists were eager for an investigation and that the National Government was delaying the sending of a team in an effort to sow dissension between the Americans and the Communists.

449

I informed General Chou that we would wait and see whether the team had been sent on the previous day or was leaving on this day as the press indicated. In regard to the delay in sending the team, I said, only one argument listed by the Communist representative had a sound basis—that was the matter of rotating the chairmanship—and the Communists should be able to call in any and all witnesses. The delay seemed to me to arise from failure of the Communists to agree on calling witnesses until this or that technicality had been discussed.

The Executive Headquarters team left Peiping on August 8 on an investigation mission but returned without any results because of the failure to agree upon procedure. On August 12 I again discussed the matter with General Chou as follows: The Communist news agency had referred to repeated provocative acts of the United States Marines and had stated that the American branch of the Executive Headquarters had taken sides with the National Government, had become the initiator of military conflicts and had done its utmost to delay the special investigating team, although the Communist branch had demanded an immediate investigation. I had this day received a lengthy message from Mr. Robertson, the gist of which was as follows:

> A tentative verbal agreement was reached between Mr. Robertson and General Yeh Chien-ying, Communist Commissioner, following which it was reduced to writing in Chinese and agreed to by the National Government Commissioner. At that point General Yeh refused to sign the document, and instead later submitted a new proposal for translation, in which he had made more specific the agreement previously reached. The Commissioners met to discuss this new proposal. It contained a new factor not previously discussed and upon which no agreement could be reached—General Yeh insisting that the testimony of National Government forces which took part in the Anping incident should be heard. General Yeh was thus including in the hearings as facts matters which should be determined by the investigation. Mr. Robertson had suggested that this point be covered by saying "hear the testimony of the National Government commander of the unit alleged

by the Communists to have taken part in the conflict." The Communists also identified in this new proposal two members of the American branch of the Executive Headquarters as persons who took part in the Marine patrol activities with the suggestion that these men were in the unit of "armed Marine patrol" rather than an "escorted motor convoy." None of these proposals was accepted. Mr. Robertson felt that General Yeh was under orders from higher authority and after eight days the team had not yet been allowed by the Communists to hear the testimony of a single witness.

The Marine authorities, I continued, had reported additional incidents involving attacks by unidentified Chinese on Marine sentries at Marine ammunition dumps and on coal trains and firing on Marine personnel in the vicinity of Tientsin with resultant ambush of a relief Marine unit. I agreed with Dr. Stuart's feeling that an immediate statement should be made by me of the facts known to me regarding the Anping incident and of the delaying tactics of the Communists affecting the investigation. I was reluctant to do so only because it would almost completely destroy my influence on the National Government toward a settlement of political disputes by ordinary process of negotiations. Such a statement would virtually end the usefulness of the Executive Headquarters and would be taken by the Generalissimo and certain military and political leaders in the Chinese Government as positive proof of their claims that the Communists could not be dealt with on a basis of ordinary negotiation procedures. I was at a complete loss in my efforts to understand the Communist Party tactics in this matter. Perhaps they were victims of reaction to conventional procedure or perhaps their local leaders in Hopei and Jehol Provinces were so anti-American that they could not be controlled. It seemed clear that their action in this matter was definitely destructive of any possibility of a peaceful settlement in China and would confirm the National Government military and certain political leaders in a policy of force.

General Chou replied that he had never expected this delay and that he wanted a prompt investigation, having sent instructions to General Yeh incorporating a proposal for procedure. The Kuomintang Central News Agency had blamed the Communists for the delay but had said that the United

451

States and Chinese Government branches intended to hear only reports from the American side and local civilians, which would mean that no Communists would be heard as witnesses. The Communists feared that without an agreed upon procedure the Communist side might not be heard and a conclusion might be reached without Communist testimony, a possibility indicated both by General Yeh's report and the Kuomintang press. General Chou explained that due to communications difficulties the Communists had had difficulty in getting in touch with the local Communist leaders in the area of the Anping incident.

I pointed out to General Chou that the United States Commissioner had informed me that the American proposal included a visit to the area of conflict to interview the Communist field commanders and any other witnesses each branch considered necessary and that this certainly included a full opportunity for the Communist side to be heard. Any other procedure would be entirely repugnant to American conceptions of justice. The proposal also included the testimony of the Marine Commander, the National Government Commander and the senior Communist Commander in the area concerned. The Communist desire to insert in the record testimony of the National Government forces which took part in the conflict, thus accepting as fact points to be investigated, represented to me definite Communist obstructionist tactics. I could only assume that the responsibility for such tactics was not that of General Yeh, who was greatly liked and respected by the Americans, and that the higher authorities were to blame. General Chou, I said, was too wise to have matters develop in this manner. I emphasized that it was literally impossible for United States Army, Navy or Marine Corps personnel to involve themselves in deliberate misrepresentation in such an investigation. Although individuals might do so, a group would never do so, as our standards were too high and our judgments too severe to encourage or permit such collusion. The American side had made no attempt and did not intend to conceal facts or bend them to their advantage and I wished to emphasize the importance of straightforward action without delay.

As the investigation team finally proceeded with the task of investigating the Anping incident at this time, I decided not to make a statement of the facts of the case in order to permit the team to have a full opportunity to proceed to discharge its functions. The investigation included questioning

452

of the senior United States, Chinese Government and Chinese Communist commanders in the areas involved and such witnesses as were introduced by each side. As might be expected, the testimony of the Chinese sides was conflicting and the hearings again encountered Communist obstructionist tactics when the Communists endeavored to prevent the hearing of the testimony of two witnesses introduced by the National Government. At that time I had instructed the United States branch of the Executive Headquarters to withdraw from the team and complete its report on the investigation. The detailed report submitted by the United States branch to me was in accord with the facts of the incident as originally communicated by me to General Chou: namely, that a Communist force had ambushed the motor convoy of Executive Headquarters and UNRRA supplies escorted by a United States Marine unit, had killed three Marines and wounded 12 others and that no National Government troops were present or involved in the incident.

During August the Yenan radio continued its critical comment on the United States, placing chief emphasis on the United States Marines in China and the Anping incident. The issuance by Dr. Stuart and me of a joint statement on August 10 in regard to the breakdown of the negotiations was the occasion for the strongest anti-American attack up to that time, our "failure" being described as the outcome of the "erroneous policy of the United States in backing Chiang Kai-shek." The attacks subsided thereafter, but broke out with renewed violence at the time of the announcement of the Surplus Property Agreement on August 30 covering the sale by the United States Government to China of surplus property in China and in the Pacific area. In spite of my explanation to General Chou of the character and background of this transaction prior to the signing of the agreement and despite further explanations to him and other Communist representatives of the nature of the agreement, Communist criticism of the surplus property transaction continued and General Chou addressed to me a formal protest, from the Communist Party to the United States Government, against this transaction.

In mid- and late September the Yenan radio embarked upon a campaign directed both against the United States and against me personally. Yenan charged that I had not opposed the aggravation of the civil war and that my greatest concern was my inability to cover up the American policy of creating civil war, which had resulted in the failure of American mediation. My prestige was described as being at its lowest ebb; I

453

was accused of "side-stepping" the cease-fire discussions and the reconvening of the PCC; and I was charged with promoting the Five Man Committee as "window dressing" for Washington. American imperialism was said to be taking the place of Japanese imperialism.

In late September as the Communist attacks against me grew more violent following General Chou's departure for Shanghai, I discussed this matter with Communist representatives at Nanking and pointed out that if the Communists had lost faith in my impartiality they had only to notify me accordingly and I would withdraw from the negotiations. As on many other occasions the Communists privately expressed confidence in my mediation efforts while the public attacks from Yenan continued.

Perhaps as a result of my statements in this regard, the Communist propaganda attacks diminished for the time being and the Yenan radio devoted its chief attention to the "misconduct" of American troops in China culminating during late October in a "quit China" campaign directed toward the withdrawal of American troops from China.

More significant during October were statements made by Chairman Mao Tze-tung in reply to an American newspaper correspondent's questions and a statement by the Central Executive Committee of the Chinese Communist Party, both of which were critical of the United States and American policy toward China. In reply to the correspondent's question regarding American mediation in China, Mao Tze-tung made the following statement: He doubted that the United States could be said to have mediated in China, judging from the large scale aid given to the National Government to enable the Generalissimo to launch a civil war; American policy had strengthened the Generalissimo under cover of mediation to suppress Chinese democratic forces and to make China an American colony through the Generalissimo's policy of "slaughter." The Central Executive Committee statement charged the United States Government with bad faith in extending military aid to the Generalissimo after the Japanese surrender and during the civil war. It went on to say that the Generalissimo and the United States wanted to subdue and exterminate the Chinese democratic movement, that the military activities of the Generalissimo and the United States were designed for this purpose and that mediation and a political settlement covered up military activities to this end. The statement concluded that the United States had no desire for peace and democracy in China and that the Generalissimo and I should value our good faith and character and should honor the "sacred agreements" signed by us.

During November and the first part of December the Yenan radio concentrated on the theme of American imperialism and was particularly bitter in its comment on the Sino-American Commercial Treaty signed at Nanking on November 4, 1946, charging that this Treaty marked the "road to colonization" and was comparable to the infamous Japanese Twenty-one Demands.

A comparison of statments made privately by the Communist representatives to me and to Dr. Stuart regarding the American mediation effort and the Yenan radio broadcasts, which voiced violent criticism of the American policy toward China, reveals a wide difference in tone. The first specific instance of the Communist Party's attitude toward my mediation efforts was that contained in a statement made to me by General Chou En-lai on June 10, shortly after his return from a visit to Yenan. He said that the Yenan leaders felt that only through my efforts could the existing situation be saved and that my services as mediator would be required for a long time. During the months following this statement General Chou and other Communist representatives continued to express privately a desire for American mediation, although the Communist radio and press were at the same time criticizing American policy toward China and were frequently questioning the American mediation effort. During October and November General Chou made no reference to my role as a mediator and in a conversation with me on October 26 referred several times to our both being members of the Committee of Three, which was apparently an oblique means of restoring me to the role of negotiator. At this time I had remained more or less withdrawn from the negotiations, which were being carried on chiefly by the Third Party Group.

On November 16, however, when General Chou called at my residence to inform me of his plans to return to Yenan, I asked that he determine specifically from the Yenan authorities whether they wished me personally to continue in my present role as mediator and told him that I would await his reply from Yenan. No direct reply was ever received from the Communist Party to this question.

On December 28 the Yenan radio broadcast General

Chou's comments on President Truman's statement of December 18, attacking this statement as an "apology for the reactionary American policy toward China" and as an excuse which would enable "the American mediator to remain in China." Commenting on the question of the impartiality of the American mediators, General Chou referred to the negotiations during June, Dr. Stuart's efforts at mediation during August, the Kalgan truce proposal and the Third Party Group mediation during October and said: "The answer to the question about the attitude of the United States mediators can be found in these talks" and "collaboration between Chiang Kai-shek and the United States to destroy the cease-fire agreement and the PCC line became clearer and clearer with passing days."

The only other direct public reference to the American mediation effort by the Communists was that made by General Chou at Yenan* on January 10 in a speech on the anniversary of the signing of the truce agreement. He said that all Chinese had welcomed the Truman statement of December 1945 and my mediation effort but that the true nature of the China policy of the American imperialists was later exposed; that while the Kuomintang reactionaries had started the civil war and had destroyed the PCC the "American witness who affixed his signature" to the cease-fire agreement "has never again mentioned the January cease-fire order."

It had become clear that the Chinese Communist Party did not desire American mediation in China. In a New Year's message by Chairman Mao Tze-tung on December 31, broadcast by the Yenan radio, he stated that the "front against the aggressor policy of American imperialists" would develop rapidly in 1947 and that the Kuomintang "under direction of the American Government" was busy "adorning themselves with a National Assembly of division and a dictatorial constitution in order to legalize their war and the American aid." An editorial in the Yenan newspaper at this time indicated the complete abandonment of any last vestiges of caution in anti-American attacks. Charges were made of American imperialism and its "running dogs" in China and American imperialists were said to have replaced the fascists of Germany, Italy and Japan as world aggressors and the public enemy of all humanity. Seven demands listed in the editorial included

*General Chou had gone to Yenan on November 19 and from that time until my departure from China on January 8, 1947, he did not return to Nanking.

456

the withdrawal of American troops from China and the abrogation of the Sino-American Commercial Treaty. Similar statements by the head of the Communist Party's Information Department at Yenan indicated the new Communist line of identification of the United States as the new imperialist power taking the place of Germany and Japan with the object of dominating the world. Democracy, on the other hand, was described as being synonymous with the Soviet Union and with the masses of all countries who desired to free man from oppression and imperialism.

A full cycle during my mission in China could be seen in the study of the Chinese Communist Party and its attitude toward the United States. There was no reason to doubt the sincerity of the Communist Party during January, February and early March when agreements were being reached for the cessation of hostilities, the establishment of a coalition government and the reorganization of the Chinese armies. Successive events showed the extent of their suspicion and distrust, as they engaged in violent attacks on the United States for action which they opposed. It is difficult to draw a clear line of distinction between the purely Chinese aspects of Chinese Communist behavior and the pattern common to Communist techniques the world over, but there are undoubtedly elements of both in the actions of the Chinese Communists as they related to the United States during my mission. One of the most likely explanations for what may be described as a Chinese aspect of their behavior was that the Communists, as a means of arousing support among the Chinese people for the Communist Party, found it useful and convenient to substitute the United States for the Japanese enemy. An appeal for support against an external enemy was likely to rally followers to the Communist cause, procedure psychologically sound from a Chinese standpoint and representing a pattern familiar to the Chinese scene. At the end, however, the Chinese aspects of their behavior seemed to have been more or less submerged in the utilization of techniques common to Communist movements elsewhere in the world and their reactions and attitudes to be of a pattern with other such movements, particularly in relation to the United States.

Index

Anping, 386, 444, 446-454

Antung, 154, 163, 169-170, 172, 188, 205, 220, 231, 331, 336, 338, 339, 346, 358, 405

Anyang, 324, 331, 358

Byrnes, James F., 2, 5

Byroade, Henry A., 21, 32, 70, 95-97, 113, 134, 143

Cairo Declaration, 3

Canton, 58-60, 103, 412

Caughey, J. Hart, 60, 89

Chahar, 16, 78, 152-153, 155, 163, 165, 260

Chang, Dr. Carson, 320, 328, 344-345, 348, 349

Chang Chih-chung, named to Military Sub-Committee, 37; and title of Agreement, 42; and the gendarmerie, 43; signing of integration directive, 46; and discussion of draft agreement, 55, 61; and Manchurian field teams, 95; as National Government representative, 436

Chang Chun, formation of Committee of Three, 11-12; and Manchuria, 15; and Chihfeng-Tolun, 16-17; and establishment of Executive Headquarters, 19; and restoration of communications, 33; suggests formation of Military Sub-Committee, 36; outlines Government integration plan, 44; and Manchuria discussions, 61

Chang Fa-kuei, 103

Chang Li-sheng, 222, 229

Changchih, 165

Changchun, 6, 14, 92, 96-100, 105, 106, 110-126, 128, 134, 146-148, 160, 174, 186, 241, 272, 285, 347, 358, 366, 437

Changtien, 170

Chefoo, 59, 78, 152-153, 336, 343, 346, 381, 405

Chen Cheng, 49, 173, 177, 201, 238, 323, 328, 343, 363-367, 378

Chen Li-fu, 174, 421

Cheng Kai-min, 22, 70, 76

Chengte, 78, 160, 162-165, 167-172, 177-178, 191, 201, 218-219, 224, 260, 276, 288, 340

Chiang Kai-shek, 1; meets with Marshall, 6, 10, 11; and cessation order, 11-12; position on Manchuria, 14; position on Chihfeng-Tolun, 16-17; formation of Executive Headquarters, 21-22; opening address to PCC, 24; pledges to carry out resolutions, 24-25; and restoration of communications, 35; and reorganization of Chinese armies, 36; opposes sending field teams to Manchuria, 51; makes concessions, 53; reasserts Nationalist sovereignty in Manchuria, 67-68; and reports from Executive Headquarters, 71; meets with Marshall following attack, 101; proposes settlement of Manchurian situation, 105-106; and Marshall's proposals, 110-113; messages sent during absence, 122-131; and truce announcement, 132-136; negotiations during truce, 146, 149-158; extends truce period, 159-176; and Five Man Conference, 178; prestige lowers in American press, 187-188; during residence in Kuling, 190, 195-197; responds to Truman's message, 207; and August negotiations, 211-225; sends message to Truman, 227; stresses importance of Kalgan, 281-282; offers brief Kalgan truce, 290; and eight point proposal, 319; prepares cessation of hostilities order, 352-353, 356-358; delays convening Assembly, 367; address to National Assembly, 373-374; offers Marshall advisory post, 412-413; meets with Marshall about reorganization, 424-247; reaction to Marshall's statement, 434

Chiang Kai-shek, Madame, 6, 119, 121-127, 318

Chihfeng, 16-17, 22, 51, 103, 155, 280, 313

China Youth Party, 7, 23, 30, 234, 312, 320-322, 368, 372, 429

Chinchou, 95-96

Chinese Communist Party, 6, 7, 8, 10; presents counter-proposal, 11; position on Manchuria, 14-15; and PCC, 23; concession on National Assembly, 30; and restoration of communications, 34; and military reorganization, 34-40; fears of rapid integration, 44; refuses to submit lists, 49; position on Manchuria, 49-63; and PCC agreements, 65-66; extends control in Manchuria, 66; and the field teams, 74-80; and entry into Manchuria, 95; attack of Changchun, 98-100; and Marshall's proposals, 108-113; attitude following truce, 139; military reorganization plan, 149-151; negotiations during truce, 158-176; military situation deteriorates, 181-187; August negotiations, 206-207; economic situation deteriorates, 226-227; positions on military and political issues, 304-305; propaganda attacks on U.S., 332; refusal to sub-

mit lists of delegates, 347-357; attacks presence of Marines in China, 388; attacks National Assembly, 421; reaction to Marshall's statement, 434-435; attitude towards U.S., 440-457

Chining, 22, 78, 277, 280

Chou En-lai, meets with Marshall, 8; and cessation order, 12; position on Manchuria, 14-15; and Chihfeng-Tolun, 16-17; and restoration of communications agreement, 33; approves Military Sub-Committee, 36-37; named to Committee, 37; and title of Agreement, 42; and the gendarmerie, 43; feelings on reorganization, 44-46; signing of integration directive, 46; expresses desire to send field teams; meets with Mao, 52; and discussion of draft agreement, 54-55, 58-59; returns to Yenan, 60; and attack of Changchun, 100; meets with Marshall after attack, 104-108; makes counter proposal, 113; describes Communist attitude, 116-117; and Chiang's proposals, 124-130; and truce announcement, 133-136; truce negotiations, 136-158; following extension of truce, 158-176; and Five Man Conference, 178-180; condemns American policy in China, 181; situation deteriorates, 181-191; expresses hope Marshall will continue, 193-195; gives view of situation, 197-201; reaction to Marshall's press statement, 206; attacks surplus property agreement, 218-219; and Chiang's conditions, 224-226; proposals for cease fire order, 231; and calling of Five Man Committee, 237-245; drafts paper for Yenan, 246-247; leaves for Shanghai, 257-258; insists on cessation of hostilities, 266; replies to truce proposal, 294-295; meets with Marshall in Shanghai, 299-307; returns to Nanking, 323-324; meets with Marshall in Nanking, 336-342; and Committee of Three, 363-367;

issues statement on National Assembly, 374-375; attacks Truman's statement, 419; reaction to Marshall's statement, 434; and Anping incident, 448-452

Chungking, 1, 2, 7, 10, 11, 33, 48, 52, 63, 69, 73, 96, 98, 101, 103, 197, 208, 278

Chu Teh, 175

Committee of Three, established, 11; cessation of hostilities order, 11-13; and Manchuria, 14-15; and Chihfeng-Tolun dispute, 17; removal of communications obstructions, 17-18; agreement on Japanese troops reached, 19; discusses draft, 53-56; 58-59; compromise reached, 60; establishment of truce in Manchuria, 132-136; truce negotiations, 140-156; informal meeting, 363-367

Control Yuan, 28

Cooke, Admiral, 386-394, 445

Dairen, 6, 14, 61, 89-91, 429

Democratic League, 7, 23, 31, 65, 68, 105, 110, 114, 182, 185, 197, 208, 219, 283, 291, 302-304, 312, 320-322, 328, 345, 348, 406, 416, 425, 444

Enivetok, 403

Examination Yuan, 29

Executive Headquarters, establishment provided for, 13; organization of, 20; functions of, 20; initial difficulties of, 22-23; and directive on integration, 46-48; entry of field teams into Manchuria, 51-58; and Canton and Hankow, 59-60; offices established, 69; functions set forth, 69; divisions of, 71; functions of divisions, 71-73; functions of field teams, 73-74; disputes over teams, 74-78; and Japanese repatriation, 83; assumes responsibility for repatriation program, 86; situation in Manchuria, 95; establishment of advance section in Manchuria, 136; negotiations during truce, 143-158; decreased Communist parti-

cipation, 333; and Marine support 389-390; Marshall suggests dismantling, 426; termination of U.S. participation, 437-439; and Anping incident, 446-454

Executive Yuan, 26-27, 29, 212-213, 243, 249-250, 274, 315, 329, 345, 348-357, 409, 424, 430

Faku, 137, 153

Five Man Committee, attempts to convene, 192-196, 208, 220; agreed to by Chiang, 222; opposed by Chou, 226; agreement on composition, 230; attempts to persuade Chou to join, 237-245

Five Man Conference, formation of, 177; meetings discontinued, 181; 193

Formosa, 81, 83, 84, 87, 323, 330, 358, 386

Fugh, Philip, 227

Gillem, A. C., Jr., 46, 56-57, 62, 89, 95-97, 299, 333, 375, 389-391, 437

Guam, 403

Hainan Island, 87

Hankow, 59-60, 78, 103, 142-143, 166, 182, 331, 336, 358, 382, 412

Harbin, 98, 105, 107, 109, 116, 144, 153, 163-164, 166, 170, 188, 199, 203, 241, 303, 324, 328-330, 338, 340

Heilungkiang Province, 124

Hill, Donald C., 131, 138-141, 159

Honan Province, 78, 204, 324, 358, 379

Hopei Province, 76, 165, 197, 280, 288, 331, 358, 379, 386, 406

Hotse, 165

Ho Ying-chin, 103, 174

Hsin Heilung-chiang, 163, 192, 193

Hsingan, 163, 192, 202

Hsingtai, 167

Hsinhsinang, 78, 331, 358

Hsiung Shih-hui, 16-17, 95, 112

Hsu Yung-chang, 103, 106, 134-135, 138, 144, 151, 154, 323

Hsuchow, 78, 142, 162, 165, 190, 204, 219, 324

Huaiyin, 165, 169, 173

Huang Yen-pei, 325-326

Hulutao, 6, 14, 88, 89, 91, 109

Hupeh Province, 78, 175, 189

Hu Tsung-nan, 184

Jehol Province, 16, 50, 75, 78, 103, 152-153, 155, 164, 166, 172, 175, 192, 195, 202-203, 205, 220, 224, 260, 276, 288, 313, 324, 379, 386

Judicial Yuan, 28

Kalgan, 78, 156, 166-167, 260, 265; attack of, 274-282; and truce proposal, 290-310; 324

Kiangsu Province, 78, 160, 163-173, 175, 178-179, 182, 184, 192-193, 199, 202-204, 206, 220-221, 224, 241, 252, 260, 313, 336-338, 425

Kuling, 182-183, 190, 195, 218, 233, 236, 245-246, 264, 314, 337-338

Kuomintang, 7, 8, 10, 23; opposition to PCC, 24; and government organization, 25-26; concessions on government organizations, 30; on the Draft Constitution's revisions, 31-32; and PCC resolutions, 63-65, 67-68; attack of Changchun 100-102; military situation deteriorates, 180-183; secret police, 185; condemned by Chou, 196-200; and attack of Kalgan, 276-282; Marshall hints at collapse, 408; reactionary wing of, 412-414; reaction to Marshall's statement, 434

Kwajalein, 403

Kwangtung, 59, 78, 90, 92

Lafa, 135, 153

Laoyao, 84

Lee Hsueh-jui, 445

Legislative Yuan, 28, 64, 372, 413, 435

Lei Chen, 317, 320, 325

Liang Shu-ming, 320-322

Li Li-san, 332

Lin Piao, 332

Lo Lung-chi, 326, 333, 343-345, 348, 415-416

Los Negros, 403

Lunghai Railway, 140, 142, 143, 170, 173, 192, 202, 204, 207, 213

MacArthur, Douglas, 5, 87, 397

Manchouli, 109

Manchukuo, 16

Manchuria, 2, 3, 5, 6, 12; dispute over control, 14-15; cease fire agreement: applicability of, 49-63; Communists extend control, 66-68; and repatriation of Japanese, 85-94; entry of field teams, 95-101; situation deteriorates, 101-109; and Marshall's proposals, 109-113; negotiations over, 113-132; truce announcement, 133-136; negotiations during truce, 136-158, 160-176

Mao Tze-tung, 10, 11; and cessation order, 11-12; and formation of Executive Headquarters, 21; accepts Marshall's integration proposal, 44; conclusions on Manchuria, 52; and reports from Executive Headquarters, 71; delays fighting, 176; attacks U.S., 442-443, 454, 456

Marcus, 403

Marshall, George C., basis of mission established, 1; arrives in China, 6; meets with Chiang Kai-shek, 6-7; summarizes China situation, 7; meets with Communist representatives, 8; and formation of Committee of Three, 10-11; and discussions over Manchuria, 14-15; and Chihfeng-Tolun, 16-17; formation of Executive Headquarters, 21; instructs Colonel Byroade, 21; emphasizes the need for CCP-Kuomintang cooperation, 23; and restorations of communications, 33; participation in Military Sub-Committee, 36-37; effects compromise on title of Agreement, 42; feelings on demobilization and reduction, 44; offers to provide training prior to integration, 45; stresses need to establish Headquarters authority in Manchuria, 50; questions Chiang Kai-shek's motives for re-

462

fusal, 51; meets with Mao over Manchuria, 53; feels agreement has been reached, 56; criticizes compromise document, 63; and reports from Executive Headquarters, 71; praises performance of Executive Headquarters, 80; addresses Soviet Ambassador, 88-89; attack of Changchun, 99; meets with Chiang Kai-shek following attack, 101; and deterioration of situation, 102-108; withdraws from mediation, 108; advances idea for solution, 108-113; states views on Manchurian situation, 115; condemns propaganda attacks, 121-122; messages to Chou and Chiang, 123-131; negotiations during truce, 144-158, 159-176; and Five Man Conference, 178-180; military situation deteriorates, 181-191; meets with Chiang at Kuling, 195; talks with Chou, 197-201; statement to press, 205; and August negotiations, 205-227; attempts to persuade Chou, 237-245; sends memo to Chou, 246; meets with Tung and Wang, 269-276; considers withdrawal from negotiations, 277-279; recommends Truman terminate mission, 289-290; delays sending message, 290; insists on longer truce, 292; meets with Chou in Shanghai, 299-307; meets with Chou in Nanking, 336-342; urges Chiang to return, 343; meets with Lo and Chang, 343-345; drafts cessation of hostilities order, 351-355; and Committee of Three, 363-367; meets with General Yu, 407-409; refuses Chiang's offer, 412-413; condemns Kuomintang reactionaries, 413-414; meets with Dr. Stuart, 417-418; meets with Chiang about reorganization, 424-427; suggests his recall to Truman, 427-428; statement on the situation in China, 431-433; nominated as Secretary of State, 434; sworn in, 437; and Anping incident, 448-453; propaganda attacks against, 453-454

McCabe, Thomas B., 214, 215

Military Sub-Committee, 33; formation of, 36-37; military reorganization agreement, 37-39; fundamental issues before, 41-45; adopts title for agreement, 42; reaches agreements on the gendarmerie, 43; directive on integration, 46-49; implementation of plan postponed, 49; agreement on reorganization and integration, 63-64

Mo Teh-hui, 317

Mukden, 57, 61, 89-91, 95-100, 109, 119-129, 140, 174, 337

Mutanchiang, 154, 339

Nanking, 6, 86, 121, 127-130, 146, 171, 182, 187, 199, 217, 236, 245, 264, 291, 295, 323-324, 372, 376, 382, 398, 427, 435

Nankou, 276

National Assembly, 27-28, 30, 209, 217, 233, 261, 291, 302, 312-316, 329, 333, 343-345, 348, 420-422

National Government of China, 3, 4, 6, 7; proposes cessation of hostilities, 11; position on Manchuria, 14; organization of, 25-26, 28-29; and military reorganization agreement, 39-40; plan for employment of deactivated military personnel, 47; suspicion of Soviet aims in Manchuria, 48; and Manchuria discussions, 49-63; and field teams, 74-80; entry into Manchuria, 95; attack of Changchun, 99-101; and deterioration of the situation, 102-104; and Marshall's proposals, 108-113; enters Changchun, 121; military reorganization proposals, 149-151; negotiations during truce, 158-176; military situation deteriorates, 181-187; and August negotiations, 206; economic situation deteriorates, 228-229; attack of Kalgan, 274-280; capture of Kalgan, 313; programs of assistance from U.S., 394-403

Nenchiang, 163, 192, 202

Okinawa, 403

463

Paichen, 154

Peiping, 13, 33, 48, 50, 68, 73, 76, 85, 86, 96, 101, 103, 129, 135, 142-143, 146-148, 165, 174, 183, 199, 204, 275, 288, 303, 331, 336, 376, 358, 381, 339, 397, 419, 444-445

Political Consultation Conference (Political Consultative Council) (PCC) 1, 8; background of, 9; Committee of Three established, 11; consultative nature of, 24; chief topics of discussion, 25; resolutions of, 25-29; on Government organization, 25-26; on national reconstruction, 26-27; on military problems, 27; on the National Assembly, 27-28; and the 1936 Draft Constitution, 28-29, 31-32; public reaction to agreements, 63; attempted implementation of agreements, 64; failures to implement, 198, 206; and Executive Yuan, 249-250; informal meeting of Steering Committee, 367-368

Port Arthur, 90-91, 429

Potsdam Declaration, 3, 381

Robertson, Walter S., 21, 70, 397, 447-451

Rockey, Keller E., 383, 386-388

Saipan, 403

Shanghai, 6, 84, 171, 188, 214, 217, 236, 257-258, 260, 293, 336, 346, 376, 382, 425

Shansi, 61, 78, 84, 85, 165, 175, 184-185, 188, 192-193, 197-198, 204, 260, 276, 280, 336

Shantung Province, 59, 61, 78, 136-137, 152-153, 155, 161, 165, 171-172, 184, 188, 190, 192-193, 198, 204, 219, 260, 272, 324

Shao Li-tze, 173, 177-178, 320, 325

Shihchiachuang, 324

Sino-Soviet Treaty and Agreements of August 1945, 3, 50, 54-55, 132

Soong, Dr. T.V., 126, 128, 209, 212, 218, 261, 273, 279, 342, 395, 399, 401, 430

Spruance, Admiral, 5

Ssupingchieh, 118, 120, 441

Stuart, Dr. J. Leighton, confirmed as U.S. Ambassador to China, 186; and attempts to convene Five Man Committee, 192-196; makes proposal to Chou, 202; statement to press, 205; and August negotiations, 211-221; meets with Chou, 237-252; discussions in Nanking, 254; discusses possible withdrawal with Marshall, 278; meets with Chiang, 298; gets concessions from Chiang, 347; drafts cessation of hostilities order, 351-355; attends opening of National Assembly, 373; meets with Marshall, 417-418; continues negotiations, 435

Suchien, 165

Suiyuan Province, 78, 142-143, 166, 276, 280

Sun Fo, 64-65, 312-313, 316-317, 334, 367, 435

Sun Yat Sen, 4, 67, 180

Tai li, 43, 76

Taiyuan, 78, 197, 204

Taming, 165

Tangku, 83, 86, 382, 389

Ta Shih Chiao, 90

Tehsien, 182

Tenghsien, 165

Third Party Group, mediation efforts, 325-333, 343-355

Tientsin-Pukou Railway, 140, 142-143, 165, 171, 175, 182, 198, 324

Timberman, Thomas S., 134

Tinian, 403

Tolun, 16-17, 79, 288

Truman, Harry S., 1; sets U.S. policy toward China, 3, 6, 80, 200; sends message to Chiang, 206; 289, 381, 395, 399; reaffirms American China policy, 418-419; nominates Marshall as Secretary of State, 434; and Executive Headquarters, 437

Tsanghsien, 182

Tsinan, 78, 137, 139, 143, 158, 161-164, 171-173; 178, 192, 202, 206, 220, 224, 260, 331

Tsingtao, 83, 86, 137, 139, 143-144, 152, 158, 162-165, 171-173, 178, 182, 192, 202, 206, 220, 224, 260, 331, 383, 389

Tsitsihar, 105, 144, 167, 324, 339, 346

Tu Li-ming, 66-67, 136, 271

Tung Pi-wu, 8, 177, 229, 265, 269-276, 279-280, 285-287, 296-299, 375

Tunghwa, 154, 331, 358

Ulithi, 403

United States, policy toward China of, 3-6; interest in disarmament of Japanese troops in China, 18-19; interest in repatriation of Japanese, 80-81; policy condemned by Chou, 181; propaganda attacks on, 332; programs of assistance to China, 394-403; Communist attitude towards, 440-457

United States Marine Corps, mission of, 380-381; role in China, 381-389; reduction of, 389-394

U.S.S.R., 3, 6, 7; and Manchuria, 14-15, 53-58, 66-67; and Japanese repatriation, 89-91; troop presence in Manchuria, 96-98

Vincent, John Carter, 177

Wang Ping-nan, 262-264, 269-275, 279-280, 285-287, 293-299, 417

Wang Shih-chieh, 64, 173, 177, 193, 273, 322-323, 334, 368, 429

Wedemeyer, A. C., 2, 5, 384, 399

Wei Tao-ming, 413

Weihsien, 165

Wenhsi, 165

Wong Wen-hao, 373, 378, 430

Wu Tien-chen, 64, 222, 230, 235, 320

Yangtze River, 59, 104, 184, 201, 316, 382

Yeh Chien-ying, 8, 22, 70, 333, 375, 404, 450

Yen Hsi-shan, 184, 205

Yenan, 52, 57, 60, 68, 104, 106, 116, 122, 131-132, 153, 156, 172, 183, 198, 244-245, 276, 285, 294, 303, 366, 376-379, 404, 419, 421, 424, 453-457

Yenki, 339

Yingkou, 6, 14, 50

Yu Ta-wei, 108, 111, 119, 131, 138-143, 147-148, 154-155, 158, 179, 183, 188, 197, 203-204, 211, 243, 252, 261, 264, 268, 319, 342-343, 408-409